# Original Intent and the Framers of the Constitution

## A DISPUTED QUESTION

### Harry V. Jaffa

WITH BRUCE LEDEWITZ, ROBERT L. STONE,
GEORGE ANASTAPLO

*Foreword by Lewis E. Lehrman*

REGNERY PUBLISHING
*Washington, D.C.*

Library of Congress Cataloging-in-Publication Data

Jaffa, Harry V.
Original intent & the framers of the Constitution : a disputed
question / Harry V. Jaffa, with Bruce Ledewitz, Robert L. Stone,
George Anastaplo ; foreword by Lewis E. Lehrman.
p.     cm.
Includes bibliographical references and index.
ISBN 0-89526-496-X (acid-free paper)
1. United States—Constitutional law—Interpretation and
construction.   2. United States—Constitutional history.   I. Title.
II. Title: Original intent and the framers of the Constitution.
KF4550.J35   1993
342.73′029—dc20
[347.30229]                    93-5881
                              CIP

Published in the United States by
Regnery Publishing, Inc.
An Eagle Publishing Company
422 First Street, S.E.
Suite 300
Washington, D.C. 20003

Distributed to the trade by
National Book Network
4720-A Boston Way
Lanham, MD 20706

Printed on acid-free paper.

Manufactured in the United States of America.

10 9 8 7 6 5 4 3 2

TO HENRY SALVATORI
*Patriot and Lover of Liberty*

"He loved his country partly because it was his own country, but mostly
because it was a free country; and he burned with a zeal for its advancement, prosperity, and glory, because he saw in such, the advancement,
prosperity and glory, of human liberty, human right and human nature."
A. Lincoln.

# About the Contributors

**Harry V. Jaffa** is the Henry Salvatori Research Professor of Political Philosophy Emeritus at Claremont McKenna College and Claremont Graduate School. He is widely known for his writings on Aristotle, Shakespeare, the American Founding Fathers, Abraham Lincoln, Mark Twain, and Winston Churchill. He was the author of Barry Goldwater's acceptance speech at the 1964 Republican National Convention.

**Lewis E. Lehrman** received his B.A. from Yale in 1960 (where he was a Carnegie Teaching Fellow in 1961), and his M.A. from Harvard in 1962. He is a former president of Rite Aid Corporation, the chairman of the board of trustees and president of the Lehrman Institute, New York City, and senior adviser and managing director, Morgan Stanley and Company, New York City. He was chairman of Citizens for America, 1983–1986, and is a trustee of the Heritage Foundation. He is also chairman of Lehrman Bell Mueller Cannon, Inc., a financial forecasting firm. In 1982 he was the Republican-Conservative candidate for governor of New York.

**Bruce Ledewitz** is a professor of law at Duquesne University School of Law. He is the founder and director of the Allegheny County Death Penalty Project, a volunteer clinic that provides assistance to defense attorneys in death penalty cases. From 1985–1990, Professor Ledewitz served as secretary of the National Coalition to Abolish the Death Penalty.

**Robert L. Stone** is an assistant professor of law at Oklahoma City University School of Law. He is the author of *Civic Education, Holidays, and the United States' Regime* (Chicago: 1986), author and editor of *Essays on the Closing of the American Mind* (Chicago: 1989), and co-author and co-editor, with John A. Murley and William T. Braithwaite, of *Law and Philosophy: The Practice of Theory*, 2 vols. (Athens: Ohio Univ., 1992).

**George Anastaplo** is a professor of law at Loyola University of Chicago, lecturer in the liberal arts at The University of Chicago, and professor emeritus of political science and of philosophy at Rosary College. Among his many books are: *The Constitutionalist: Notes on the First Amendment*, *Human Being and Citizen*, *The Artist as Thinker*, *The American Moralist*, and *The Constitution of 1787: A Commentary*. He has been nominated annually since 1980 for the Nobel Peace Prize.

# Acknowledgments

I wish first of all to express my gratitude to Professor Ronald K. L. Collins, of the George Washington University School of Law. Professor Collins was a visiting professor at the University of Puget Sound School of Law when I circulated the first drafts of the title essay of this book. It was he who arranged for its publication in the *UPS Law Review* and who, in addition, conceived and organized the contributions of my interlocutors, Professors Ledewitz, Stone, and Anastaplo.

I would also like to express my appreciation to these same dialectical partners—for I so regard them—first of all for their contributions, but also for consenting to the reprinting of their essays.

I am more than thankful to Lewis E. Lehrman for his Foreword. I can only hope there are future Supreme Court justices in our audience who will take seriously, not what he says about me, but about Abraham Lincoln as a constitutionalist.

This book, as the readers will soon discover, is uncompromising in its exposure of the legal positivism, moral relativism, and philosophical nihilism that is at the core of mainstream contemporary conservatism, no less than of contemporary liberalism. It certainly is not designed to be popular, but it would not even have seen the light of day, had it not been for the unremitting favor of William F. Buckley Jr. Having permitted me to be the gadfly of the paleocon stable in the pages of *National Review* for more than a quarter of a century, he apparently saw no reason why (let us hope) an even larger audience should not experience this exhilarating annoyance! His generosity is seemingly boundless, and I can do no more here than express my gratitude.

—Harry Jaffa

xi

# Contents

# PART III
# Three Critiques
## 107

# PART IV
# Jaffa Replies to His Critics
## 235

PART V
# Afterword
387

# PART I

# Foreword

# On Jaffa, Lincoln, Marshall, and Original Intent*

## LEWIS E. LEHRMAN

If it should be said that Abraham Lincoln was one of the framers of the post-Civil War Constitution, then it may also be said that Professor Harry V. Jaffa is Lincoln's John Marshall. For in Jaffa's evangelization of Lincoln one discovers not the temperament of a lawyer but of a lawgiver, not the profession of a judge, but of a prophet of first principles of jurisprudence. One need not agree with Jaffa, the philosopher and apologist of Lincoln, to declare him indispensable to the American republic. Indeed, if Harry Jaffa did not exist, I would want to invent him, if only to recover for conservatives the first principles of the American Founding—the true meaning of the Declaration of Independence. This I would do because the future of the world depends in no small measure upon the future of America—and, therefore, upon American constitutional principles.

In the ongoing debate over the authentic Constitution, consider only several unresolved but fundamental issues: Are the legal positivists and legal realists, heirs of Justice Oliver Wendell Holmes, Jr., and Charles Evans Hughes, right when they declare constitutional law to be whatever the highest legislators or Supreme Court justices say it to be? And is it then unappealable, even if such "law" plainly violates the fundamental law by which the nation was founded? Moreover, is the original intent, the meaning of the Framers, undiscoverable in the four corners of the Constitution itself, or in its history? And further, are these considerations irrelevant, as the "noninterpretists" imply, when finding and applying the fundamental law of the land?

On the other hand, and above all, are Jefferson, Madison, Washington, Adams, and Lincoln right when, according to "the laws of nature and of

* As it appeared in *University of Puget Sound Law Review*, Spring 1987, Vol 10, No. 3, p.343.

nature's God," they "hold these truths to be self-evident, that all men are created equal, that they are endowed by their Creator" with the unalienable rights to life, to liberty, and to the pursuit of happiness? And do the Framers thus not correctly hold that any legislation or judgment of a court fundamentally in violation of *these unalienable rights* is by its nature obnoxious to the Constitution? Is it not obnoxious because according to the very words of the Declaration of Independence, "to secure *these rights*,[1] governments are instituted among men," so "that whenever any form of government becomes destructive of these ends [namely, securing the unalienable rights to life, liberty, and the pursuit of happiness] it is the right of the people to alter or abolish it and to institute new government"? Is it true that in the Constitution of 1787 a number of guarantees were provided to the institution of chattel slavery, as it had grown up and become deeply rooted before independence, when the Crown forbade the colonists to interfere with the importation of slaves from Africa. And chattel slavery, considered in itself, was assuredly a complete violation of the right to liberty of each person. But the Framers of the Constitution acted, in Lincoln's words, on the maxim that it is better to "consent to any great evil, to avoid a greater one."[2] The more perfect union of 1787 could not have been formed without the concessions to slavery: but the union thus formed was committed more strongly than heretofore to the ultimate extinction of slavery. Only the stronger union, created by the Constitution of 1787, was strong enough to oppose the expansion of slavery and meet the crisis of the union in 1861. Thus, by Lincoln's statesmanship—by his unswerving commitment to the principles of the Declaration of Independence, as the principles of the Constitution—was the prudential wisdom of the Framers vindicated, and slavery itself destroyed. The "just powers of government" are thus, in the long run, derived not only from the consent of the governed, but from that consent which is consciously directed to securing the natural rights with which all men are endowed by their Creator.

The principles laid down at the birth of the republic on July 4, 1776, are manifestly what the Framers meant to implement, since Madison himself, the Father of the Constitution, held that the Declaration was "the fundamental act of union"[3] of the States. That is to say, it was the first lawful instrument by which to illuminate the constitutional principles of the American union. The implications of the fundamental law of the union are too often ignored by constitutional scholars who, nevertheless, cannot deny that the Declaration is placed at the head of the statutes-at-large of the United States Code, and is described herein as one of the "organic" laws of the United States. Therefore, I would argue that, just as the Fourteenth Amendment may have incorporated certain of the first ten amendments into the state constitutions, so too has the original intent of the Founders and the United States Code incorporated the Declaration of Independence into the Constitution of the United States.

The durable issue of our age, with great consequences for future generations, is the current debate over how to interpret the American Constitution. The issue is now joined within the conservative movement. Shall the meaning of the Constitution itself—the original intent of the Framers of the Constitution—as revealed in the document and in its history, prevail in the Supreme Court? Or, is this intent, the meaning of the Framers, too imprecise and thus unknowable, leading inevitably to the conclusion of the legal positivists that the law can only be what the judges and legislators say it is; or more plausibly yet, what the "sovereign" people vote it to be—no matter if judges, legislators, and even the people decide and vote, say, for slavery or legislated murder? From such an outcome, is there no appeal under the Constitution? In this struggle between the natural law (the Declaration of Independence) and legal positivism (judge-made law), Americans will soon have to choose—in presidential and congressional elections. There is no more important choice before us as a people.

Professor Jaffa makes his case in his following essay well enough without help from me. He is one of the most persuasive advocates of what Professor Edward S. Corwin called the "higher law" doctrine of the Constitution; namely, that the first principles of the American regime, according to which the positive law of the Constitution must be interpreted in ambiguous cases, are codified in the natural law doctrine of the Declaration of Independence, the Magna Carta of the Founding. Jaffa's view, however, is a minority view, confronting as it does a prevailing and contrary consensus in the Supreme Court and among legislators and law schools. The consensus may best be summed up in the words of my friend Professor Benno Schmidt, former dean of Columbia Law School and now president of Yale, who in discussing this issue with me said, "American constitutional law is positive law, and the Declaration of Independence has no standing in constitutional interpretation whatsoever."

There are two main schools of constitutional theories. But, ironically, both legal philosophies are ways by which to decide constitutional intent by referring to authorities *outside* the four corners of the Constitution. Attorney General Edwin Meese, in his Dickinson College speech, Sept. 17, 1985 (quoted at length in Appendix A. herein) agrees with Jaffa (not to mention Jefferson, Madison, Marshall, and Lincoln!) that "there exists in the nature of things a natural standard for judging whether governments are legitimate or not."[4] That extrinsic authority—the standard of the Constitution—one finds in the Declaration of Independence. In the other case, as with Professor Schmidt or Justice Harry Blackmun,[5] the extrinsic authority one can find in the supervening extraconstitutional opinion of the Supreme Court justice.

But while Jaffa does not explicitly consider it, and the Supreme Court today all but ignores it, there is another authoritative way to discover original intent, as Professor Christopher Wolfe shows in his book *The Rise of Modern Judicial Review.*[6] That way was the work of Chief Justice John Marshall, whose authority has been claimed not only by traditionalists, who hold that the Supreme Court justice must always find the meaning of the law in the original intent of the Framers, but also by judicial suprema-cists, who hold that the judge must and should legislate himself. But let us hear Chief Justice Marshall himself on the issue: "[J]udicial power is never exercised for the purpose of giving effect to the will of the judge; always for the purpose of giving effect to the will of the law"[7] made by the legislator. And further, "we [judges] must never forget that it is a Constitution we are expounding,"[8] not the legislative opinions of judges. And in *Marbury v. Madison* he declares, "[I]t is emphatically the province and duty of the judicial department to say what the law is."[9] But (from *McCullogh v. Maryland*) he emphasizes that "where the law is not prohibitive," for judges "to undertake here to inquire into the degree of [the law's] neces-sity would be to pass the line which circumscribes the judicial department and to tread on legislative ground."[10] Moreover, Marshall's legal reason-ing and opinion show that the original intent of the Framers and of the Constitution can generally be discovered intrinsically, that is, by analysis of the *full* text of the document itself—by carefully applying rational rules of legal construction that depend primarily upon the plain meaning of the words themselves, the full context of the words, the subject matter with which the words of the law deal, and the obvious spirit or cause that gave rise to the law. That the law itself must do justice in all cases, whatever the rule of construction, is Marshall's first principle of jurisprudence. This he makes clear in *Marbury v. Madison* by asking the simple question: "[C]an it be imagined that the law furnishes to the injured party no remedy?"[11] To this Marshall rejoins, "[I]t is not believed that any person whatever would attempt to maintain such a proposition."[12] Moreover, these principles of natural justice, argued Marshall in *Ogden v. Saunders*, were the very princi-ples of "the [F]ramers of our Constitution" who "were intimately ac-quainted with the writings of those wise and learned men, whose treatises on the laws of nature and nations have guided public opinion. . . ."[13] The meaning of the phrase "obligation of contracts" in the Constitution, Marshall declared, was that of "an original intrinsic obligation."[14] In this case Marshall plainly affirms that the meaning of the Constitution is to be found in its incorporation of the natural law into the positive law. "We must suppose that the [F]ramers of our Constitution took the same view of the subject [viz., as the "wise and learned men" who wrote the "treatises on the laws of nature"]," Marshall concluded, "and the language they have used confirms this opinion. . . ."[15] In short, the judge cannot know in such a case what the positive law of the Constitution is unless he knows what the natural law is.

Thus Marshall found it simple, if painstaking, to decide whether a law, or act, or judicial decision was unconstitutional; and he enshrined his reasoning in the *Marbury* decision, one of the most important judicial opinions of Supreme Court history. In this opinion, often cited by both judicial supremacists and legal positivists who reject natural law, Marshall considers "the question, whether an act, repugnant to the Constitution, can become the law of the land. It seems only necessary to recognize certain principles, supposed to have been long and well established to decide it."[16] And by what *principle* shall it be decided? To which Marshall had an unequivocal answer: "That the people have an original right to establish, for their future government, such principles as, in their opinion, shall most conduce to their own happiness, is *the basis* on which the whole American fabric is erected." "The principles, therefore, so established, are deemed fundamental [emphasis added]."[17] But why or how is Marshall so absolutely sure of "the basis" and "the principles" deemed fundamental to the Constitution—to the "whole American fabric?" Because, in fact, Marshall draws the very words of this part of his opinion almost exactly from the Declaration of Independence itself—from the second paragraph, which reads, "it is the right of the people . . . to institute new government laying its foundation on such principles . . . as to them shall seem most likely to effect their safety and happiness."[18]

Thus the basis of the American Republic is found by Marshall in the Declaration of Independence. But, echoing Marshall, one must then ask: can it be supposed that the Declaration, the fundamental act of union, which provides the basis, the original right of the people to establish fundamental principles of government—can it truly be supposed that this great charter of American liberties is to be ignored by Supreme Court justices, members of Congress, presidents, attorneys general, and law school professors, to be set aside in favor of judicial supremacy, narrow positivist doctrine, and "result-oriented" jurisprudence, whether of the Right or of the Left? Shall it truly be supposed that both legal positivists and judicial supremacists, even advocates of original and strict construction, all of whom cite Marshall, may properly abandon the Declaration of Independence as the source of these fundamental rights and principles by which the inevitable ambiguities of constitutional interpretation should be decided—when Chief Justice Marshall himself finds that "the[se] principles . . . are deemed fundamental,"[19] because they stem from the Declaration?

Surely, "[i]t is not believed that any person whatever would attempt to maintain such a proposition."[20]

And so, for his love of truth, for his luminous intellect, for the light of the world he shines on the philosophy of law, we read and honor Harry Jaffa.

# On Jaffa, Lincoln, Marshall, and Original Intent

1. Emphasis added.
2. R. Basler, *Abraham Lincoln: His Speeches and Writings*, 308-09 (1946).
3. *The Writing of James Madison*, 219-221 (G. Hunt ed. 1010).
4. E. Meese, Speech at Dickinson College (Sept. 17, 1985).
5. *See e.g.Roe v. Wade* 410 U.S. 119 (1973).
6. C. Wolfe, *The Rise of Modern Judicial Review* (1985).
7. *Osborne v. Bank of the United States* 22 U.S. (9 Wheat.) 738 (1824).
8. *McCullough v. Maryland*, 17 U.S. (4 Wheat.) 159, 207 (1819).
9. *Marbury v. Madison*, 5 U.S. (1 Cranch.) 137, 177 (1802).
10. *McCullogh*, 17 U.S. at 200.
11. *Marbury*, 5 U.S. at 165.
12. *Id.*
13. *Ogden v. Saunders*, 25 U.S. (12 Wheat.) 212, 213 (1827).
14. *Id.*
15. *Id.*
16. *Marbury*, 5 U.S. at 176.
17. *Id.* (emphasis added).
18. The Declaration of Independence ¶2 (U.S. 1776).
19. *Marbury*, 5 U.S. at 176.
20. *Id.* at 165.

# PART II

# What Were the "Original Intentions" of the Framers of the Constitution of the United States?

HARRY V. JAFFA

$T$HE FOLLOWING LETTER to the editor of *Policy Review* was published in the Spring 1986 issue of that journal.

Attorney General Meese, writing in the Winter 1986 *Policy Review*, defends a constitutional jurisprudence of "original intent." It is one that, he says, seeks fidelity to the Constitution, and not one that seeks political results from the decisions of the Supreme Court. The judges, he says, should uphold the law, and not seek to enact their own personal or political preferences.

As the leading exhibit of the evils that result from a departure from these principles, Mr. Meese offers us the following:

> In the 1850s, the Supreme Court under Chief Justice Roger B. Taney read blacks out of the Constitution in order to invalidate Congress' attempt to limit the spread of slavery. The Dred Scott decision, famously described as a judicial "self-infliction wound [sic]," helped bring on the Civil War. There is a lesson in such history. There is danger in seeing the Constitution as an empty vessel into which each generation may pour its passion and prejudice.

Unfortunately for Mr. Meese's argument, no one, on or off the Court, has ever expounded the theory of original intent with greater eloquence or conviction than Chief Justice Taney in the case of *Dred Scott*. In considering whether Negroes might have standing to sue in United States courts, or whether slave property might be afforded less protection than any other kind of property, the chief justice wrote:

> No one, we presume, supposes that any change in public opinion or feeling, in relation to this unfortunate race, in the civilized nations of Europe or in this country, should induce the Court to give to the words of the Constitution a more liberal construction in their favor than they were intended to bear when the instrument was framed and adopted. Such an argument would be altogether inadmissible in any tribunal called on to interpret it. If any of its provisions are deemed unjust, there is a mode prescribed in the instrument itself by which it may be amended; but while it remains unaltered, it must be construed now as it was understood at the time of its adoption. It is not only in the same words, but the same in meaning, and delegates the same powers to the government, and reserves and secures the same rights and privileges to the citizen; and so long as it continues in its present form, it speaks not only in the same words, but with the same meaning and intent with which it spoke when it came from the hands of its framers, and was voted on and adopted by the

people of the United States. Any other rule of construction would abrogate the judicial character of this court, and make it the mere reflex of the popular opinion or passion of the day. This court was not created by the Constitution for such purposes.[1]

Never has the judicial doctrine of original intent been stated with greater perspicuity. Never has a judge, in giving judgment, been more clearly committed in his own mind to repudiating the "passion and prejudice" of his own "generation" than chief justice Taney in *Dred Scott*.

Taney decided that Dred Scott, as a member of an inferior and degraded race (inferior and degraded, that is, by the law of the Constitution) was not and could not become a citizen of the United States. But he also decided that under the Constitution, there was no ground upon which Congress could discriminate between slave property and other forms of property. Here is the chief justice, speaking again.

It seems, however, to be supposed, that there is a difference between property in a slave and other property ... But if the Constitution recognizes the right of property in a slave, and makes no distinction between that description of property and other property owned by a citizen, no tribunal acting under the authority of the United States ... has a right to draw such a distinction ... Now ... the right of property in a slave is distinctly and expressly affirmed in the Constitution. The right to traffic in it, like every other ordinary article of merchandise and property, was guaranteed ... in every State that might desire it for twenty years ... and no word can be found in the Constitution which gives Congress a greater power over slave property, or which entitles property of that kind to less protection than property of any other description.[2]

The chief justice was then very far, in his own mind, from attempting to "read blacks out of the Constitution in order to invalidate Congress' attempt to limit the spread of slavery." It was the attempt of others to read blacks *into* the Constitution to which Taney objected. Opinion, he said (quite erroneously), had become more "liberal" in the intervening years since the adoption of the Constitution. But he denied that such "liberal" opinion ought to govern him as a judge, so long as the words of the Constitution remained unamended. (What sentiment could be more gratifying to Mr. Meese than that!) And looking at the words of the Constitution what he saw was that the slave was regarded as "an ordinary article of merchandise."[3] Because of this, the only constitutional power of Congress over slavery in the Territories was "the power, coupled with the duty, of guarding and protecting the owner in his rights."[4]

Whatever is wrong with this opinion, it is not because the chief justice did not hold to the doctrine of original intent. It was not because he thought for a moment that the Constitution was an empty vessel "into which [his own] generation [might] pour its passion and prejudice." What he said was exactly the opposite. The attorney general has a long way to go to make the doctrine of original intent intellectually defensible.

Since the publication of the foregoing letter there has been no response from the attorney general, or from any one of his staff, explaining how the doctrine of original intent might be defended as the basis for interpreting the Constitution. I am well aware of how little time these busy men have to answer mere pedants. My intention in writing the letter, however, was not to rebuff the adherents of the doctrine of original intent but to demonstrate that, however necessary or desirable, it was very far from being sufficient as a basis for interpreting the Constitution. Clearly, subscribing to the doctrine of original intent does not tell us *what that original intent was*. The Civil War was fought by two sides, both of which believed (as did Chief Justice Taney in *Dred Scott*) that they were defending the Constitution of the United States, understood as it had been originally intended to be understood.

The deepest political differences in American history have always been differences concerning the meaning of the Constitution, whether as originally intended, or as amended. Since the Civil War, the debate has often taken the form of a dispute as to whether or not the Civil War amendments, notably the Fourteenth, have changed the way in which the whole Constitution—and not only the amended parts—is to be read or interpreted. Does not the abolition of slavery, and the extension of United States' citizenship to "all persons" born and residing in the United States—of whatever race or color—change the substantive understanding of all the rights which it is the function or purpose of the federal Constitution to secure? How could this be otherwise, if in the original Constitution, some of those referred to as "persons" were elsewhere considered to be chattels, and some of these same persons were also counted as three-fifths of a person? If legally a person can be three-fifths of a person, does not this mean that "personality," and all constitutional rights to life, liberty, and property, have their origin solely in positive law? For surely in nature there cannot be three-fifths of a person, any more than there could have been half a child to settle the claims of each of the two women who came before King Solomon.[5]

Mr. Meese has attacked the "incorporation" doctrine recently—that is to say, the doctrine according to which certain of the first ten amendments have become applicable to the states, no less than to the United States. Whether right or wrong he took his position on the basis of the alleged intention of the original Constitution, without addressing the question of how, or even whether, that Constitution had been transformed by the Civil War amendments. It is, however, either naive or disingenuous to think that one can appeal to the "original intentions" of those who framed and those who ratified the Constitution without facing forthrightly the question of what those intentions actually were. It is not possible even to discuss how or whether the Civil War amendments transformed the original Constitution, without saying first of all what that original Constitution was.

Although the attorney general appears to be wholly unaware of the fact, the greater part of those who aggressively invoke the doctrine of original intent today are self-styled conservatives whose chief intellectual progenitor would appear to be—from all the available evidence—not the Father of the Constitution, James Madison, or any of his coadjutors, but John C. Calhoun. That is to say, these conservatives largely follow the man who, more prominently than any other, rejected the proposition that all men are created equal, and who affirmed on the contrary that slavery was a "positive good." I believe, however, that it is undeniably true that it was the paramount intention of the Framers of the Constitution—and of the people for whom they framed it—"to institute new government" in the sense in which the Declaration of Independence speaks of instituting new government. Indeed, Madison is explicit in the 43rd *Federalist* that the Convention was justified by the right of revolution in transcending its instructions from the Congress of the Confederation. It was to be the purpose of the new government better "to secure these rights." And these rights were the unalienable rights with which all men had been equally "endowed by their Creator" under "the laws of nature and of nature's God." We are confronted, therefore, with the paradox that those who today most aggressively appeal to the doctrine of original intent are among its most resolute antagonists. As we shall prove in Appendix C, this is especially true of the new chief justice of the United States, Mr. Justice Rehnquist.

In the present controversy we find that Mr. Justice Brennan's Constitution is one of "overarching principles" whose application seems to be virtually uncontrolled by the specific provisions of the text, or by anything that those who drafted, and those who ratified such provisions, might have meant by them. For example, Justice Brennan brushes aside the references to capital punishment in the Fifth Amendment, and holds nonetheless that capital punishment is unconstitutional by reason of the provision against "cruel and unusual punishments" in the Eighth Amendment. And he does so notwithstanding the fact that the Fifth and Eighth Amendments were passed and ratified at the same time. Mr. Justice Brennan's "overarching principles" enable him to reject the provisions of the Constitution that he does not like, and give the ones he does like whatever meaning he chooses them to have. Clearly, this is the negation of constitutionalism. Perhaps, however, he thinks that because the same Constitution that sanctioned capital punishment also sanctioned slavery, that therefore the abolition of slavery implied the abolition of the equally barbarous (according to his opinion) practice of capital punishment. This argument would be more persuasive were it not for the fact that the Fourteenth Amendment repeats the language of the Fifth in declaring that no state shall "deprive any person of life, liberty, or property, without due process of law," signifying thereby that persons *may* under certain circumstances be deprived lawfully of their lives, as well as of their liberty and property. Mr. Justice Brennan's "overarching principles" appear, therefore, to be part of an evolutionary process, in which a progressively more exalted meaning is to be discovered in the various provisions of the Constitution (most particularly the equal protection and due process clauses of the Fourteenth Amendment), a meaning which is revealed by the historical afflatus to his progressive judicial conscience. Consider these remarks about Mr. Justice Brennan's supreme constitutional principle, "human dignity."

> We are still striving toward that goal, and doubtless it will be an eternal quest. For if the interaction of this Justice [viz., himself] and the constitutional text over the years confirms any single proposition, it is that the demands of human dignity will never cease to evolve.[6]

It is then an evolutionary process that enables Justice Brennan to discover the true meaning of the Constitution even in a flat contradiction of the text itself. And this same process enables him to contradict, not only the actual Constitution, but whatever it is that anyone else may think the Constitution ought to be held to mean. For Justice Brennan is explicit that he alone may truly represent the community, even when no one else in the community shares his opinion!

> On this issue [but why not any other?], the death penalty, I hope to embody a community striving for human dignity, although perhaps not yet arrived.[7]

Thus Mr. Justice Brennan finds the true meaning of the Constitution, not in the text, and not in any interpretation of the text by others, including the entire political community acting through the political process, but in some kind of "striving," albeit "not yet arrived." This "striving" may have the character of a revelation vouchsafed to the justice, but not to anyone else. Yet such "striving" appears to him to be sufficient ground for the authentic meaning of human dignity, and therefore of the Constitution. Such visitations by the evolutionary *zeitgeist*[8] parallel those of the proletarian consciousness which, as Lenin discovered, were not vouchsafed to the proletariat itself, but to the Central Committee of the Bolshevik party, and more particularly to its chairman, namely, himself.[9]

One can therefore fully sympathize with Attorney General Meese's (and indeed Mr. Justice Rehnquist's) repudiation of this idea of "a living Constitution." And one can sympathize as well with the desire to see constitutional jurisprudence anchored in what the Constitution actually says, and not what the justices might wish it to say. But if it can be said that Mr. Justice Brennan's Constitution is one of "overarching principles" uncontrolled by the actual text, so it might be ventured that Mr. Meese's Constitution is a text without overarching principles.

In a speech delivered at Dickinson College, September 17, 1985,[10] the attorney general asserted that the principles of the Declaration of Independence were the principles of the Constitution. And that is indeed the truth of the matter, according to the greatest of all interpreters of the American Constitution, Abraham Lincoln. But Mr. Meese's Constitution Day speech seems to have had no precedent and no consequence either within the Justice Department, or among the cognoscenti of his judicial nominees. I do not know of a single judicial nominee—and least of all the new chief justice—who gives the least credence to the proposition that there are "laws of nature and of nature's God." Nor are there any, so far as I can tell, who recognize, with James Madison, that it is in the character or nature of the social compact or contract, made in pursuance of these laws, that the authority of the people may itself be discovered. As far as its theoretical recognition or its practical consequences are concerned, Mr. Meese's Constitution Day speech at Dickinson College in 1985, however praiseworthy, is a quixotic irrelevance. I have, however, given it a sympathetic notice in Appendix A.

Mr. Meese—and the new chief justice—have waged a war against judicial activism, and against legislation disguised as adjudication. With this, one can certainly agree. But their argument comes, again and again, to rest upon the proposition (with which we are also in full agreement) that legislation is properly the function of the people, or their elected representatives. Courts exist to enforce the laws—and to interpret them only as this becomes necessary as an incidence of their enforcement. But interpretation must not be a disguise by which judges invent the law—as Justice Brennan clearly does when he repudiates the actual words of the Constitution. In interpreting the laws, the judges are to ask themselves, What is the law? Not, What ought the law to be? For it is the will of the people that the courts are entrusted to carry out, not the will of the judges. The will of the people is the ground of all constitutional authority. What, however, is the ground of the authority of the will of the people? This question too must be answered.

For the Justice Department and the epigones of "original intent," the supremacy of "the people" is a brute fact, an axiomatic premise from which everything follows, but which cannot—and therefore need not—have any justification. But this was not the understanding of the Founding Fathers, nor can it be reconciled with their "original intentions." James Madison, the Father of the Constitution, declared over and over again that "all power in just and free government is derived from compact."[11] By this he meant that the will of a people is not the will of any chance aggregate of discrete individuals, but rather that of a body incorporated under "the laws of nature and of nature's God." It is a civil society deliberately and rationally formed for the purposes of civil government, which purposes are not themselves the invention of the people, but are rather given to them with their nature, and flow from that nature, as rationally apprehended. The people as understood by the Founding Fathers were characterized not by will merely, but by a rational will. Said the author of the Declaration of Independence in his inaugural address:

All too will bear in mind this sacred principle, that though the will of the majority is in all cases to prevail, that will to be rightful must be reasonable; that the minority possess their equal rights, which equal law must protect, and to violate would be oppression.[12]

We are reminded as well that in the first number of the *Federalist* Alexander Hamilton defined the enterprise embodied in the Constitution as an attempt

to decide the important question, whether societies of men are really capable or not of establishing good government from reflection and choice [viz., by reason], or whether they are forever destined to depend for their political constitutions on accident and force.[13]

It cannot be too greatly emphasized that the people's will, properly so called, is a rational will, whose inherent right to be obeyed is attenuated to the extent that it becomes merely arbitrary or despotic. "An elective despotism was not the government we fought for," wrote Jefferson in the *Notes on Virginia.*[14] Certainly the courts should not usurp the powers of legislation. But neither should majorities usurp the rights of minorities, nor should legislatures exercise powers that the people have not by the Constitution delegated to them. For the doctrine of the Framers of the Constitution was a doctrine of *limited* government. And the idea of limited government must be understood, not only in relationship to what the people collectively have reserved to themselves, and have not delegated to their government. It must be understood as well in relationship to what the individuals, in forming a people, have reserved to themselves. What individuals have thus reserved, even the people collectively have no rightful power to delegate to government. Such reservations imply therefore that even the collective sovereignty of the people—such as that which ordained and established the Constitution—is limited. The sovereignty of the people does not authorize the establishment of any government whatever, with any powers whatever. The people have no rightful power to do whatever "is not naturally impossible" (as the textbook account of the legal sovereignty of the "Queen in Parliament" asserts). The question of judicial usurpation in a free government is part of a much larger problem, a problem wholly invisible to the legal positivists of contemporary conservatism, who see only the will, but not the reason of the people, informing their sovereign authority.

The elements of rationality implicit in the choice of a free government obligate one not to impose despotism upon others, except insofar as it may become necessary as an incidence of the natural right to self-defense. These same elements of rationality inform the ordering of a free, as distinct from a despotic, government. Separation of powers, for example, was generally understood to be an indispensable feature of free government. The idea of the rule of law—flowing from the proposition of natural human equality—is embodied in the reciprocal requirement that those who live under the law should share in making the law they live under; and that those who make the law should live under the law that they make.

The attorney general, apart from his one spasmodic effort in the Dickinson College speech of 1985, seems to regard the question of the Constitution's principles as something that one discovers merely by looking at the Constitution. The Constitution, however, as nearly everyone agrees, is a bundle of compromises. And there is nothing in the Constitution itself by which one can discover the "prudence" of the Constitution—that is to say, by which one can distinguish the compromises of the Constitution from the principles of the Constitution. Eleven states attempted in 1861 to "secede" from the Union and establish an independent government, the Confederate States of America. They did so because Abraham Lincoln had been elected president of the United States on a platform that called for an end to the extension of slavery into United States Territories. They declared this intention to end the extension of slavery—or, as Lincoln himself put it, to place slavery "in the course of ultimate extinction"[15]—to be a fundamental breach of the faith upon which the constitutional compact rested. It constituted such an invidious discrimination between the property and social institutions of the states as to make the continuation of the political union between them a moral and political impossibility. Nothing in the text of the Constitution, they declared, warranted such a distinction between the forms of property recognized to be such by the laws of the different states of the Union. And for this they had what they claimed to be the highest of all constitutional authorities—the Supreme Court of the United States speaking through its chief justice in *Dred Scott*. The Constitution, they insisted, had recognized the institution of chattel slavery in various ways, above all in the requirement that the government of the United States return fugitive slaves to their masters.

For a president, and a party, to hold in moral abhorrence an institution sanctioned by the laws of fifteen states and by the Constitution made political friendship among the states impossible. It was common ground to Lincoln and his antagonists that common citizenship implied and required agreement on the morality of such a fundamental institution as slavery. (The first platform of the Republican party, in 1856, condemned both "polygamy and slavery" as "twin relics of barbarism.") Lincoln's House Divided speech had declared that a point had been reached in which a decision in principle had to be made between slavery and freedom.

In *Dred Scott* the Court had declared that there was no lawful way to exclude slavery from any United States Territory. Once public opinion had accepted this as a premise, there would, Lincoln said, be another decision, for which *Dred Scott* was merely the prologue, declaring that there was no lawful way to exclude slavery from any state of the Union. At that point, said Lincoln, slavery would become lawful in all the states, old as well as new, North as well as South. This, according to Lincoln, was the crisis of the house divided: either slavery was wrong and ought to be restricted, or it was right and ought to be extended. The question about Dred Scott was not, as the attorney general (and Chief Justice Rehnquist) suppose, whether or not the Court had usurped powers belonging to Congress, the question was whether Negroes (free or slave) had any natural rights which the Constitution was bound to recognize.

Mr. Meese and his coadjutors come to the question of original intention through the medium of a conservative movement which, at its heart, is in agreement with the argument of the South, when it attempted to break up the Union in 1861. It comes to the question of original intent having rejected the ground of the Constitution in natural justice, having rejected the distinction between despotism and freedom, as that distinction was asserted in the Declaration of Independence.

In 1825 James Madison and Thomas Jefferson considered what books and documents the Board of Visitors ought to recommend as *norma docendi*, as authoritative principles of instruction, for the faculty of law of the new University of Virginia. The question uppermost in their minds was how best to educate the lawyers—those most likely to be the legislators, executives, and judges of the future—those whose vocation would make them in a peculiar sense the future guardians of the Constitution and of republican freedom. Madison and Jefferson were aware of the delicacy of proposing to tell the professors what to teach. They would not think of doing so, Jefferson said, in most of the branches of science in which the university would offer instruction. And yet he wrote—and surely not without reason—"there is one branch in which we are the best judges . . . It is that of government."[16]

So these two ex-presidents and Founding Fathers concluded—and recommended to the Board of Visitors of which both were members and Jefferson was president—that, of the "best guides" to the principles of the Constitutions, of Virginia, and of the United States, the first was "the Declaration of Independence as the fundamental act of Union of these States."[17] Let it be noted that Jefferson and Madison here refer to the Declaration, not only as the instrument by which the thirteen colonies separated themselves from Great Britain, but as the instrument by which they combined with each other to become one Union—thirteen states indeed, but thirteen states *united*. As the "fundamental *act* of Union" the

Declaration was and remains the fundamental legal instrument attesting to the existence of the United States. From it all subsequent acts of the people of the United States, including the Constitution, are dated and authorized. It defines at once the legal and the moral personality of that "one People" (who are also said to be a "good people") who separated themselves from Great Britain and became free and independent. It thereby also defines the source and nature of that authority which is invoked when "We the people of the United States" ordained and established the Constitution. For the same principle of authority—that of the people—that made the independence of the states lawful, made lawful all the acts and things done subsequently in their name. This tells us why the Constitution ought to be obeyed, why we have a duty to obey it, why and in what sense it may be truly said that the voice of the people is the voice of God. For these reasons the Declaration remains the most fundamental dimension of the law of the Constitution. It is the Declaration that tells us why and in what sense the government of the people is a government of right and not merely of force. It is by virtue of the principles of the Declaration that the Constitution must be said to reject the thesis that justice is nothing but the interest of the stronger. It is by virtue of the principles of the Declaration that, in the words of Leo Strauss, "The United States of America may be said to be the only country in the world which was founded in explicit opposition to Machiavellian principles."[18]

To repeat, the Declaration of Independence, as seen by Jefferson and Madison, tells us why the political authority of the United States is also a moral authority, and why the physical force by which the United States may protect and defend itself is a moral force, and not merely the expression of collective self-interest. Finally, it tells us why slavery must be regarded as an anomaly, a necessary evil entailed upon the Constitution, but not flowing from—or consistent with—its genuine principles.

One would have thought that the fact that the author of the Declaration and the Father of the Constitution—who were also the third and fourth presidents of the United States—had agreed upon the Declaration of Independence, both as the fundamental act of Union, and as guide to the principles of the Constitution, would have made this opinion canonical. Yet in all the discussion of "original intent" it has apparently not occurred to any of the luminaries of present-day conservative (or of course liberal) jurisprudence even to consider it. Even in the attorney general's Constitution Day speech of 1985, in which he declared the principles of the Declaration to be those of the Constitution, this assertion of Madison and

Jefferson, which could have greatly strengthened his argument, is ignored. In truth, however, the denial of what Jefferson and Madison affirmed has been at the very core of constitutional theorizing in contemporary American conservatism. The source of this denial is not difficult to discover. It is to be found in the slavery controversy that began not long after Jefferson and Madison had passed from the scene. It is to be found in the fact that, far more prominent in shaping American conservatism—and indeed American legal thought generally—than Jefferson or Madison, has been John C. Calhoun.[19]

At the center of Calhoun's constitutionalism was his doctrine of state sovereignty and state's rights. The essence of the doctrine of state sovereignty was not more an affirmation of the legal rights and powers of the states, vis-à-vis the federal government, than a denial of "the fundamental principles of the Revolution"—as Madison called them in the thirty-ninth *Federalist*—the doctrine of the natural rights of individuals, as the source of the authority of the state, and of civil society as such. Calhoun's conception of sovereignty as set forth in his *Disquisition on Government*[20] was of a right that belonged to the collective entity called the state (technically, government representing society). State sovereignty was *sui generis*, not derived from any antecedent principle or right. Sovereignty, however, as understood in the Declaration of Independence—and in all the great documents of the Revolution—was originally, and by nature, the equal and unalienable possession of individual human beings. The original equality of all human beings was an equality of sovereignty—no man had more right to rule another than the other had to rule him. The exercise of the natural right to rule one's self is transferred voluntarily to civil society, by virtue of that social contract by which civil society is originally constituted. In the words of the Massachusetts Bill of Rights,

> The body politic is formed by a voluntary association of individuals; it is a social compact by which the whole people covenants with each citizen and each citizen with the whole people that all shall be governed by certain laws for the common good.[21]

As noted above, James Madison repeated over and over again, that "compact is the basis of all free government," implying that the ground of all legitimate authority is a social contract based upon natural equality. The ground of all positive legal rights in civil society—above all the right to property—is the antecedent natural right, grounded in natural equality, which every human person possesses in himself. And this right is *a fortiori* a right of each human person to possess the fruit of his labor. The aforesaid natural right or rights—to life, liberty, and property—are the ground of all authority, all sovereignty, in civil society.

Calhoun's doctrine of state sovereignty—on the contrary—rests upon the denial of any such antecedent natural rights. No rights, to life, liberty or property, have any existence independently of society. In this respect—in their assigning an absolute priority of the social to the individual—Calhoun and Marx stand upon identical theoretical ground. Here is one of the deepest causes for the stultification of the present-day conservative critique of communism. Conservatives most often attack communism on the grounds of its rejection of Christian revelation. But they do so in part because the "rationalism" of communism so closely resembles their own. To disguise this fact, they declare that "there is a better guide than reason."[22] This better guide, however, turns out to be not revelation, but the collective prejudices of their communities on such subjects as race, religion, and ethnicity, prejudices which they are at once unwilling to abandon and unable to defend. They are also—it needs to be said—prejudices utterly inconsistent with Christianity.

A corollary of Calhoun's doctrine of state sovereignty was what Abraham Lincoln called that "ingenious sophism"[23] by which

> any State of the Union may consistently with the national Constitution, and therefore lawfully and peacefully, withdraw from the Union without the consent of the Union or of any other State.

Calhoun's constitutionalism is frequently represented as a defense of minority rights against "the numerical majority."[24] Secession—like nullification—has been represented as a constitutional device to prevent the tyranny of the majority. But having denied individual rights as the basis of majority rule—how could Calhoun defend minority rights as such? The minority with whose defense he was particularly concerned was the particular minority which had a vested interest in that "peculiar institution," the institution of human slavery. To say the least, it is paradoxical to identify a defense of slavery as a defense of minority rights.[25]

A major feature of the antebellum debate was the attack by Calhoun and his followers on the teaching of human equality in the Declaration of Independence. While the Declaration continued to be appealed to in public debate for its pronouncement that the just powers of government are derived from the consent of the governed (secession was justified as a legitimate withdrawal of consent) the proposition that all men are created equal was scorned and rejected. It was scorned and rejected notwithstanding the fact that the equality of man is the ground or reason for the requirement of consent. For if there were an inequality among men, such as there is among the other species, there would be no reason for consent to give legitimacy to government. No one asks his cattle (viz., chattels)— his dog or his horse or his cow or his pig—for its (or their) consent. On the other hand, every human being has the indefeasible right to ask anyone proposing to exercise authority over him, "Why should I obey?" And every human being has the identical right to reply with deleted expletives to such answers as "Because I am better than you are," or "Because it is in my interest that you should obey." The divorce of consent from equality, which was at the heart of antebellum Southern constitutionalism, remains at the heart of conservative constitutionalism to this very day.[26]

By denying the principle of equality, Southern defenders of slavery (e.g., Taney) denied that any constitutional distinction could be drawn between slave property and any other species of property. And they insisted, notwithstanding the antislavery views of the Founding Fathers, that those antislavery views had no constitutional standing. What mattered was not the personal views of the Founding Fathers on slavery, but the constitutional commitment to slavery that had been "nominated in the bond" of the Constitution. Constitutional morality constituted fidelity to that bond. From the Southern point of view in the antebellum debate, the "original intentions" of the Founding Fathers consisted in their commitment to constitutional morality, something entirely independent of whatever private views they (or others) may have entertained. For the Southerners took their stand on the Constitution as the moral and political embodiment of Union. Whatever denied the authority of that bond—as the equality principle of the Declaration seemed to do—must be of no power or effect in interpreting the Constitution. And so on the Southern side of the antebellum debate—inherited by contemporary conservatism—the Declaration of Independence was read out of the authoritative role it had had in the American political tradition for the entire revolutionary generation, and most certainly for those who framed and those who ratified the Constitution of 1787.

Equally important to Calhoun's constitutionalism was the denial of Jefferson's and Madison's assertion that the Declaration of Independence was "the fundamental act of Union" of the states. The idea that secession was a legal and constitutional right required that it be believed that the Union was formed, not in 1776, but in 1787 and 1788, and solely by the acts by which the states ratified the Constitution. From this—the official constitutional theory underlying the formation of the Confederacy—acts of secession would be acts of deratification. The Declaration, from Calhoun's point of view, created not one Union, but a league of thirteen separate and independent states. All Confederate apologists, from Jefferson Davis and Alexander Stephens to the late Willmoore Kendall, would repeat this. Kendall would refer to "the baker's dozen" of independent states resulting from the Declaration, an expression repeated without question by Gary Wills (once a Kendall disciple) in his recent book on the Declaration, *Inventing America*.

Taney's opinion in *Dred Scott* is a sport of the parent Calhounian stock. To give slavery the unequivocal moral sanction of the Constitution, Taney did not deny the authority of the Declaration, as did Calhoun. Instead, Taney denied that Negroes had been included in the proposition that all men are created equal. He simply ignored the reference in the Declaration to "the laws of nature and of nature's God," and treated the principles set forth by the Declaration as if they were merely human or positive rights or law. This is all the more astonishing since, as a Roman Catholic, he should have had some acquaintance with the Thomistic distinction between natural law and human law, as well as the Aristotelian-Thomistic conception of the role of prudence in mediating between ends and means. He treated as irrelevant the fact that, whatever the status accorded Negroes by custom or positive law, by nature they were certainly human. And he simply ignored such statements concerning slavery as Jefferson's in the *Notes on Virginia* by which it was certain beyond any possible doubt that according to its author, Negroes were included in the Declaration. He admitted that the meaning of the words of the Declaration in and of themselves included all members of the human race, of whatever color. But he denied that the signers of the Declaration could have meant what they said, because had they done so they would—as moral men, he thought—have immediately set about abolishing slavery.

Taney's utterly absurd and mistaken belief that the rights set forth in the Declaration of Independence were understood to apply to whites only is today perhaps the most commonly held view of the Founding. For example, the 1968 Report of the President's Commission on Crime and Civil Disorder held "white racism" to be the chief cause of the evils the commission had been charged to investigate. As evidence of the endemic character of this racism was the alleged fact that Negroes had not been included in the proposition of equality in the Declaration of Independence! The staff director of the commission had relied, he said, on "expert" opinion. This proved to mean certain "New Left" (or "Black Power") historians. Facts meant no more to these "scholars" than to their unsung hero, Roger B.

Taney. The agreement today between the radical Left and the radical Right (e.g., between the advocates of Black Power and the KKK or White Citizens Councils) is striking. On neither side is there the least awareness of or concern with such a statement as Lincoln's on the prudential character of the relationship between the theory of the Declaration and the practice of the Founding generation. Here is how Lincoln in 1857 met the objection that Negroes could not have been included in the Declaration because the Founding Fathers had not abolished slavery.

> Chief Justice Taney, in his opinion in the *Dred Scott* case, admits that the language of the Declaration is broad enough to include the whole human family, but he and Judge Douglas argue that the authors of that instrument did not intend to include Negroes, by the fact that they did not at once, actually place them on an equality with the whites. Now this grave argument comes to just nothing at all, by the other fact, that they did not at once, *or ever afterwards*, actually place all white people on an equality with one another . . . They did not mean to assert the obvious untruth, that all were then actually enjoying that equality, nor yet, that they were about to confer it immediately upon them. In fact they had no power to confer such a boon. They meant simply to declare the *right*, so that the *enforcement* of it might follow as fast as circumstances should permit. They meant to set up a standard maxim for free society, which could be familiar to all, and revered by all, constantly looked to, constantly labored for, and even though never perfectly attained, constantly approximated, and thereby constantly spreading and deepening its influence and augmenting the happiness and value of life to all people of all colors everywhere.[27]

A writer espousing the Justice Department's polemic against "judicial activism" has recently denounced this passage from Lincoln's speech on the *Dred Scott* decision as if it were a justification of Justice Brennan's evolving judicial conscience as a mode of constitutional interpretation. But this is nonsense. Lincoln is speaking of the meaning of the Declaration of Independence apart from the Constitution and before there was a Constitution. He is addressing the meaning of the Declaration of Independence, as the act of the Continental Congress, which was a legislative, not a judicial body. He is discussing the meaning of the Declaration as the authoritative statement by the American people of the purposes to be served by whatever government they might choose to institute. But that same Declaration of Independence itself speaks of the dictates of prudence, as the means by which the Declaration's principles are to be implemented. The "standard maxim of free society" was, as the words assert, a maxim for *society*, for the political community, as a guide for the direction of public policy, the shaping of which is, of course, primarily a function of legislative prudence.

Lincolnian morality—the morality of the Founding Fathers—was prudential. Principles are the necessary, but not the sufficient, condition for deciding cases. We cannot decide upon an intelligent policy to deal with slavery, unless we know that slavery, in principle, is morally wrong. But knowing that it is wrong does not, of itself, tell us what to do about it. Prudential morality means doing the most good, or the least evil, in any given situation. As Lincoln once said, "I would consent to any great evil, to avoid a greater one."[28] The guarantees given to slavery in the Constitution were necessary if the slave states were to acquiesce in the far stronger central government proposed in the Constitution of 1787. Yet it was better, so Lincoln thought, even from the most antislavery point of view, that there be such a stronger Union. For only such a Union could—its guarantees to slavery notwithstanding—place the institution as a whole "in the course of ultimate extinction." Purists might have formed a smaller Union without slavery. But slavery itself would have grown far greater. We cannot forbear noticing that the purpose Lincoln attributed to the Founding Fathers— long before he became president—of containing slavery and placing it in the course of ultimate extinction, was fulfilled in his presidency.

The idea of prudential morality—the morality celebrated by Aristotle, Thomas Aquinas, Burke, and the Declaration of Independence—found no favor with Taney, and has little favor today. Taney adopted the essentially Kantian view of supposing that the Founding Fathers could not have meant what they said about human equality, had they not acted upon it categorically. That meant acting upon their alleged perception of the rightness or wrongness of each particular action, without regard to the consequences. Taney moreover deduced the meaning of the Fathers' words from what he believed to be the purport of their actions. He paid no attention to what *they* said about what they meant. He insisted upon *his* understanding of their actions as the sole guide to the meaning of *their* words. This is the same procedure used today by behavioral scientists and Marxist historians (or social scientists), and accounts at least in part for the popularity of Taney's, rather than Lincoln's interpretation of the Declaration of Independence. But let us not forget either that the reconciliation of slavery and the Founding was first and foremost the work of Calhoun, and it is Calhoun's interpretation of the Founding that to this day dominates American conservatism.

In his speech on the Oregon Bill, June 27, 1848, Calhoun, addressing the proposition "That all men are created equal," made these remarks:

All men are not created. According to the Bible, only two, a man and a
woman, ever were, and of these one was pronounced subordinate to the
other. All others have come into the world by being born, and in no sense . . .
either free or equal . . . [This proposition] was inserted in our Declaration of
Independence without any necessity. It made no part of our justification in
separating from the parent country . . . Breach of our chartered privileges,
and lawless encroachment on our acknowledged and well-established rights
by the parent country, were the real causes, and of themselves sufficient
without resorting to any other, to justify the step. Nor had they any weight in
constructing the governments which were substituted in the place of the
colonial. They were formed of the old materials and on practical and well-
established principles, borrowed for the most part from our own experience
and that of the country from which we sprang.[29]

The doctrine that the American Revolution was fought to defend "our
chartered principles" has become canonical in American conservatism,
replacing the principles of the Declaration of Independence, recognized by
Jefferson and Madison (and indeed by all the Founding Fathers). "Chartered principles" represent prescriptive right, right sanctioned by usage—
by custom or the mere lapse of time—but not by reason or nature. It is a
right in which the "ought" has been assimilated by the "is," in which all
right is positive right—which is of course another way of saying that
whatever is, is right, or that "justice is nothing but the interest of the
stronger." The idea of prescription as the ground of right was of course
wholly favorable to the idea of the legitimacy and indefinite perpetuation
of slavery. After all, slavery, next to the family, is the oldest (and hence most
prescriptively right) social institution known in human history.

Thus Irving Kristol, inaugurating the American Enterprise Institute's
Distinguished Lecture Series on the Bicentennial of the United States,
referred only obliquely to the great proposition which Calhoun had denounced openly, when he said that "To perceive the true purposes of the
American Revolution it is wise to ignore some of the more grandiloquent
declamations of the moment."[30] According to Kristol one should instead
"look at the kinds of political activity the Revolution unleashed," above all
at the state constitutions. (Notice the resemblance to Taney's "Look at
what they did, not at what they said" interpretation of the Founding.)
These constitutions, said Kristol, "were for the most part merely revisions
of the pre-existing charters." The purpose of the American Revolution,
according to Kristol—speaking in the spirit and very nearly in the words of
Calhoun—"was to bring our political institutions into a more perfect
correspondence with an actual 'American way of life' which no one even

dreamed of challenging." The late Martin Diamond, agreeing with the late Willmoore Kendall, also insisted (in the lecture that followed Kristol's in the AEI series mentioned above) that the Declaration of Independence offers "no guidance whatsoever" for the construction of the constitutions, state or federal, that were adopted after 1776.[31]

Recently Judge Robert Bork has written that "Our constitutional liberties arose out of historical experience . . . *They do not rest upon any general theory.*" Compare this with Abraham Lincoln:

> Public opinion on any subject always has a "central idea" from which all its minor thoughts radiate . . . the "central idea" in our political public opinion at the beginning was and until recently has continued to be "the equality of men."[32]

That central idea—central not only to political public opinion but to a Constitution based upon such opinion (since "Our government rests in public opinion")—Lincoln also characterized as *"an abstract truth, applicable to all men and all times."*[33] Judge Bork, however, denounces all

> attempts to frame a theory that removes from democratic control areas of life the Framers intended to leave there . . . [which attempts] can only succeed if abstractions are regarded as overriding the constitutional text and structure.[34]

But it was precisely attention to "constitutional text and structure" divorced from the "abstractions of moral philosophy" that led Taney to his conclusions in *Dred Scott.* Yet Bork goes on to contrast the American and French Revolutions, declaring that

> the outcome for liberty was much less happy under the regime of "the rights of man."[35]

Since the doctrine of the rights of man (embracing as it did "the abstractions of moral philosophy") was at least as prominent a feature of the American as of the French Revolution, one wonders whether Judge Bork has ever read a single document of our Founding. Not only does the Declaration of Independence proclaim the rights of man, but eight of the thirteen revolutionary state constitutions do so. Massachusetts, for example, proclaims that

> All men are born free and equal, and have certain natural, essential, and unalienable rights . . .[36]

These assertions of abstract truths, "applicable to all men and all times," were—Kristol and Bork to the contrary notwithstanding—the very heart of the revolutionary activity, at the state no less than at the national level. And no one questioned that it was so before the slavery controversy made such abstractions so very inconvenient, and "history" began to replace natural rights as the ground of political and of constitutional theory. But our genuine history—and not the factitious history invented by the neo-Calhounites—places the doctrine of the rights of man at the very center of our historical experience.

Consider further the following from our recent and very distinguished ambassador to the United Nations, Jeane Kirkpatrick. Mrs. Kirkpatrick, celebrating Independence Day 1982, in the pages of *National Review*, declares that

> the freedom of the American people is based not on the marvelous and inspiring slogans of Thomas Paine but, in fact, on the careful web of restraints, of permission, of interests, of tradition woven by the Founding Fathers into the Constitution and explained in *The Federalist Papers*. And rooted, of course, in our concrete rights as Englishmen.[37]

Irving Kristol, in the bicentennial lecture referred to above, had called Tom Paine "an English radical who never really understood America [and who] is especially worth ignoring." Here is the neoconservative dictum on Tom Paine, whose *Common Sense* was credited by no one less than George Washington for having given the greatest impulse to the movement for independence, and who carried a musket in the Battle of Trenton. Mrs. Kirkpatrick is less slighting of him than Kristol, although it is worth recalling how "marvelous and inspiring" some of Paine's words actually were. Think of what Churchill's "We will fight on the beaches. . ." speech meant to Great Britain in 1940. Think of what it must have meant to the freezing soldiers—and their beleaguered Chief—at Valley Forge to be told that

> These are the times that try men's souls. The summer soldier and the sunshine patriot will, in this crisis, shrink from the service of their country; but he that stands it *now*, deserves the love and thanks of man and woman. Tyranny like hell is not easily conquered; yet we have this consolation with us, that the harder the conflict, the more glorious the triumph.[38]

This is the St. Crispin's Day speech of American history, worthy of Shakespeare himself, and it ill beseems any American—any lover of human freedom—to slight its author. The truth, however, is that it is Jefferson who is being depreciated in the slighting of Paine.[39] But he is too large a figure to be attacked directly. And it is not the *Rights of Man*, but the Declaration of Independence, which by indirection is the object of their patronizing condescension. While we are anxious to share with Mrs. Kirkpatrick her admiration for the Constitution's "careful web of restraints, of permission, of interests, of tradition," we would like to know her explanation of the very prominent place of human slavery in that web. Certainly Article IV, section 2, paragraph 3, weaves a very careful "web of restraints" around those unfortunate human beings who were attempting to escape from bondage, and it gave careful recognition (as did other sections of the Constitution) to the interests of slaveholders (but not of the slaves). If, as Kristol says, it was true that there was an actual American way of life which no one then thought of challenging, then no one thought of challenging American slavery, certainly a most conspicuous feature of that way of life in 1776 and 1787. To believe what Kristol believes about this unquestioned American way of life one would have to read the documents of the period—including the Constitution—the same way Chief Justice Taney did in Dred Scott.

One must ask Mrs. Kirkpatrick, however, how she thinks that her black fellow-citizens can discover their rights as Americans "rooted" in their "concrete rights as Englishmen." Is she thinking of the concrete rights of slaves and free Negroes in colonial America, or of the rights embodied in the African slave trade before Independence, a trade protected by the British Crown over the protests of colonial Americans? The Declaration of Independence speaks of the rights with which we are "endowed by our Creator." Does Mrs. Kirkpatrick believe that God is an Englishman? We yield to no one in praise of "the Constitution . . . explained in the Federalist Papers." But we would like to know how Mrs. Kirkpatrick explains the provisions of the Constitution cited by Taney to justify his view that the original Constitution permits no distinction between slave property and any other form of property. We would like to know how she distinguishes between the protection of slave property as an end of the Constitution from any of the other ends or purposes of the Constitution. Are not those "slogans" of which Mrs. Kirkpatrick speaks so lightly (or the "grandiloquent declamations" dismissed by Irving Kristol) precisely the reason why Madison and Jefferson turned first to the Declaration of Independence— and not to the Constitution itself (or the *Federalist*)—to instruct the young law students at the University of Virginia in the principles of the Constitution?

"A word fitly spoken is like apples of gold in pictures of silver." According to Abraham Lincoln,

> The assertion of that *principle* ["that all men are created equal"] . . . was *the* word, "*fitly spoken*" which has proved an "apple of gold" to us. The *Union*, and the *Constitution*, are the *picture* of *silver*, subsequently framed around it. The picture was made, not to *conceal*, or *destroy* the apple; but to *adorn* and *preserve* it. The *picture* was made for the apple—*not* the apple for the picture.[40]

That "abstract truth applicable to all men and all times," so scorned by John C. Calhoun and his legion of present-day conservative epigones, was, according to Lincoln, what gave life and meaning to the Constitution. It is what enables us to distinguish, in the Constitution of 1787, the principles of that Constitution from its compromises. It is what enables us to say that the securities given to slavery in the Constitution represent concessions for the sake of the stronger Union, and are ultimately in the interest of the antislavery cause itself. But Lincoln is saying—albeit in poetic language— nothing that was not implied in Madison's own judgment that the first place to look for the principles of the Constitution was the Declaration of Independence. How is it that Mrs. Kirkpatrick, so eloquent in her praise of the *Federalist*, disregards the judgment of one of its major authors in this most crucial of all respects?

In all the great documents of the American Revolution the equality of the natural rights of mankind is the fundamental doctrine to which appeal is made. Historical experience was consulted by our revolutionary Fathers. But it did not, indeed it could not, provide more than partial instruction in an enterprise in the most important respects so novel. Madison on at least one occasion called the Constitution—rather infelicitously—"nonde-script."[41] He did so, he said, because there was no name yet for a form of government so unprecedented. What was unprecedented, however, was not only the system of dual federalism, of a government "partly national, partly federal."[42] What was above all unprecedented was the attempt—as stated in the first number of the *Federalist*—to establish "good govern-ment from reflection and choice."[43] This, of course, required that prudence—and hence experience—should be consulted. Experience may instruct us in what is possible in given circumstances. But of itself it does not tell us what is desirable. And what is prudent is what is the more desirable among those alternatives that are possible. Prudence and history must be in the service of philosophic truth concerning the just and the unjust, the right and the wrong, the good and the bad. It must be in the service of "words fitly spoken."

The past, merely as past, was no prologue to the future for our revolutionary forebears. The past, merely as past, showed men by and large "depending for their political constitutions on accident and force." The decisive and salutary historical fact governing the formation of American republicanism, according to George Washington in 1783, was that its foundations "were not laid in the gloomy ages of ignorance and superstition, but at an epoch when the rights of mankind were better understood and more clearly defined than at any other period."[44] The Burkeans among us are constantly praising, as indeed they ought, the "funded wisdom of the past." But for George Washington it was equally important to distinguish the ignorance and superstition of the past from its wisdom. History furnishes no lessons to those who do not have the criteria, supplied by right reason, to distinguish the good things from the bad things that have happened. During the Revolution, Alexander Hamilton had declared:

> The sacred rights of mankind are not to be rummaged for among old parchments or musty records. They are written, as with a sunbeam, in the whole volume of human nature, by the hand of divinity itself, and can never be erased or obscured by mortal power.[45]

Without exception the Fathers held—as the Declaration of Independence asserts—that the only legitimate purpose of government was to secure rights whose origin is antecedent to all charters or human or positive laws. These rights are grounded in "the laws of nature and of nature's God," and as such belong equally to all members of the human race. These rights may have been recognized in good traditions. But it is not in tradition as such that the ground of such rights is to be found. Thus Lincoln:

> Slavery is founded in the selfishness of man's nature—opposition to it in his love of justice. These principles are an eternal antagonism. Repeal the Missouri Compromise—repeal all compromises—repeal the Declaration of Independence—repeal all past history, you still cannot repeal human nature.[46]

It cannot be emphasized too often that mere tradition carried no authority, either to the Founding Fathers or to Abraham Lincoln. The past, merely as past, encompassed "the gloomy ages of ignorance and superstition." It was in reason and nature that the purposes or ends of government were to be discovered. The ultimate ground of rights is first and foremost a matter of cognition ("We hold these truths to be self-evident. . ."). As such they are not a matter of volition. What belongs to man as man is therefore "unalienable" and therefore not subject to deliberation. What makes legitimate civil society a voluntary association is itself rooted in an unchanging human nature. We do not reason together to decide whether we wish ourselves or others to be, or to become slaves. To be governed by reason rather than will is to be governed by law rather than force. For law in its essence is, as Aristotle said, "mind unaffected by desire."[47]

Let us submit facts to our candid countrymen. In the "Letters of the Massachusetts General Court" (viz., the Massachusetts Colonial Legislature) to the British Ministry, it is said over and over again, as it was on January 29, 1768,

> That it is an essential, unalterable right, in nature, ingrafted into the British Constitution, as a fundamental law, and ever held sacred and irrevocable by the subjects within the realm . . . that what is a man's own is absolutely his own; and that no man hath a right to take it from him without his consent; [and] may not the subjects of this province, with a decent firmness . . . plead and maintain this natural constitutional right?[48]

The substance of these Letters was incorporated into the Massachusetts Circular Letter of February 11, 1768, drafted by Sam Adams. Repeating much of the foregoing, it adds

> That the American Subjects may therefore, *exclusive of any consideration of charter rights*, with a decent firmness adapted to the character of free men and subjects, assert this natural and constitutional right.[49]

In these assertions by Massachusetts in 1768 we may see encapsulated the whole political theory of the American Revolution—and of the Constitution of 1787 as a fruit of that Revolution. "No taxation without representation." The product of a man's labor is his own property. This right of property is understood—as it is in Locke's *Second Treatise of Civil Government*—to be an extension of his right to life and to liberty. In this there is a categorical condemnation in principle of all slavery as a violation of the laws of nature. For slavery is nothing but the most extreme form of taxation without representation. Property as the fruit of one's labor is an "unalterable right in nature," and therefore belongs to all human beings as human beings. With respect to it, therefore, all men must be understood to be created equal. It belongs to subjects of the British Crown, not because they are British but because they are human. This natural right is said to have been "grafted into the British Constitution." The right in question is not deserving of respect because it is British. Rather does the British Constitution deserve respect because it recognizes the right. But the origin of the right is not the British Constitution. Its origin is in nature.

What these pristine documents of the Revolution assert is in direct contradiction of Calhoun, as it is of Kristol, Bork, Kirkpatrick, and the whole tribe of present-day publicists. What these documents assert also contradicts that greatest of all gurus of contemporary American conservatism, Russell Kirk. For more than thirty years he has, with notable success, been pursuing the path of John C. Calhoun in reading the Declaration of Independence—and its reasoned teaching of equal and universal natural and human rights—out of the American political tradition. A summary of what one finds in his many books is the following from the Introduction to a recent reprinting of Albert Jay Nock's *Mr. Jefferson*:

> Nock's book has very little to say about the Declaration of Independence. That is as it should be, for the Declaration really is not conspicuously American in its ideas or its phrases, and not even characteristically Jeffersonian. As Carl Becker sufficiently explains, the Declaration was meant to persuade the court of France, and the *philosophes* of Paris, that the Americans were sufficiently un-English to deserve military assistance. Jefferson's Declaration is a successful instrument of diplomacy; it is not a work of political philosophy or an instrument of government, and Jefferson himself said little about it after 1776.[50]

Think of it, the Declaration of Independence "not conspicuously American"! But if not the Declaration, what? Not Yankee Doodle, not General Washington, not the Continental army, not the Minute Men, not Paul Revere, or the Old North Church! For the conservative *illuminati* who rapturously acclaim such doctrine it would seem that the only things "conspicuously American" are "our rights as Englishmen"! One may wonder whether any greater foolishness has ever been condensed into fewer words anywhere in the world's records of writing on politics. As to Kirk's attribution to Carl Becker the opinion that in the Declaration

Jefferson was diplomatically fawning upon the French to persuade them that the Americans were un-English, here is what Becker actually wrote:

> Democratic impudence could not well go farther than to ask the descendant of Louis XIV to approve a rebellion based upon the theory that "governments derive their just powers from the consent of the governed." If the French government received the Declaration, it did so in spite of its political philosophy because it could not forego the opportunity to take a hand in disrupting the British empire.[51]

To this, one might add that some of the worst excesses of the king of England denounced in the Declaration were among the most ordinary practices of the French monarchy. That the Declaration was welcomed by the *philosophes* for very different reasons than by the French court is certainly true. But neither the court nor the French patrons of the Enlightenment needed to be taught that the Americans were "sufficiently un-English" now that they had expressed their determination to reduce the British empire by the separation from it of its most valuable portion—the thirteen colonies.

Russell Kirk would have us think that the doctrine of the equal natural rights of mankind was introduced into the rhetoric of the American Revolution by the Declaration, and then only to please Frenchmen! Recently he has written that

> The Declaration of Independence, calculated to please Paris and Versailles, had broken with the constitutional argument of the Americans that had been advanced ever since the passage of the Stamp Act. Until 1776, protesting Americans had pleaded that they were entitled to the rights of Englishmen, as expressed in the British constitution, and particularly in the Bill of Rights of 1689. But Jefferson's Declaration of Independence had abandoned this tack—what did Frenchmen care for the real or pretended rights of Englishmen?—and had carried the American cause into the misty debatable land of an abstract liberty, equality, fraternity.[52]

One would think, from the foregoing, that when Paul Revere called out "The British are coming" he meant that they were coming to rescue us from French philosophy. But whatever it was that Paul Revere meant, it is clear that Russell Kirk—like John C. Calhoun before him—means to deliver us from the pernicious and un-American abstractions of the Declaration of Independence! And so we are again reminded of Mrs. Kirkpatrick's belief that, not the rights of nature and of nature's God, but the rights of Englishmen, are the "roots" of the American Revolution. Such is the "conservative" vision of American history today.

What Russell Kirk asserts about the Declaration of Independence "breaking" with the constitutional arguments that the Americans had hitherto advanced in the quarrel with Great Britain is sheer nonsense. Jefferson and the Congress did not "abandon" any "tack" in abandoning the argument from the rights of Englishmen. There was nothing in the least "diplomatic" in their statement of principles, as Becker notes, and what they said had nothing whatever to do with conciliating Frenchmen. They said what they believed in the most unequivocal and uncompromising language the world has ever witnessed. We Americans have as much right to be proud today of the fearlessness with which they asserted their convictions as of the courage with which they fought to uphold them. They had indeed hitherto used arguments drawn from the real or alleged principles of the British or English Constitution—but always as reflections or embodiments of the more fundamental laws of nature. Now, however, they were no longer Englishmen! Hence there could not any longer be any legal or political reason for grounding their actions—certainly not the action by which they separated themselves from England—in the laws of England. How in the world could Russell Kirk have expected them to appeal to their rights under the laws of England at the precise moment that they were telling the world that they were no longer Englishmen?

That the second paragraph of the Declaration embodies a concise but complete epitome of political philosophy has not, so far as I know, been denied by anyone except Russell Kirk. This is not to say that many—most notably the disciples of Calhoun and of Marx—have not regarded it as false. Carl Becker, as we have seen, refers to the Declaration as a work of political philosophy as a matter of course. And we know that both Madison and Jefferson regarded it as an instrument of government when they called it "the fundamental act of union of these states." That Jefferson, according to Kirk, "said little about" the Declaration after 1776 is contradicted by the fact that he, together with Madison, agreed to require the faculty and students at the law school of the University of Virginia to look to it as the primary source of guidance in the principles of the constitutions both of Virginia and the United States. Nor is it consistent with the inscription Jefferson composed for his tombstone, an inscription naming the three things by which he wished most to be remembered. The first of these three things was his authorship of the Declaration of Independence.

As we have seen, and shall see again, the abstract truths of the Declaration, in one form of expression or another, were present from the very beginning of American resistance. What Massachusetts called a "natural and constitutional right" can hardly be considered primarily or inherently British. It is by definition a right of all who share in mankind's common humanity. With respect to it, therefore, it must be true "that all men are created equal." The doctrine of the Declaration long antedates the decision for independence and in itself has nothing whatever to do with the exigencies of diplomacy. In the Declaration and Resolves of the First Continental Congress, October 14, 1774, we are told

> That the inhabitants of the English colonies in North America, by the immutable laws of nature, the principles of the English Constitution, and the several charters or compacts, have the following Rights:[53]

The ground for the authority of the ensuing rights is seen in their order. First is nature, next the English constitution, and then the colonial charters. Constitution and charter reinforce the rights grounded in nature, but only because they themselves incorporate and reflect that ground. Of course, the Americans will appeal to rights grounded in English law as long as they regard themselves as English. Once they cease to be English, however, the ground of their authority, the right to be bound by laws of their own making, is solely in virtue of those rights with which they have been "endowed by their Creator," their rights under "the laws of nature and of nature's God."

Long before the decision for independence it was clear that the ground of the American argument was not the English Constitution but "the immutable laws of nature." As long as the argument was addressed to the Crown, or to fellow subjects of the Crown, the appeal to English law strengthened their side of the political argument. But intrinsically—as distinct from politically—in the order of importance, natural law always took precedence. The primacy of rights and of right, understood in the light of the laws of nature, was the argument of the American Revolution from the beginning. And this argument must be understood to constitute the "original intent" governing American constitutionalism, as it took shape in the Convention and in the ratification process—and in the adoption of the Bill of Rights that followed.


Irving Kristol, as we have noted, asks us to pay especial attention to the kinds of activity unleashed by the Revolution, and in particular the kind found in the state constitutions. But characteristically he shows little familiarity with the documents to which he invites our attention. In saying that the constitutions were for the most part "revisions of pre-existing charters," he speaks truly. Like Calhoun (and Kirk, Kirkpatrick, and Bork), however, he ignores the relationship asserted by the colonial Americans between those charters and "the immutable laws of nature." Even more conspicuous is the fact, to which we have already adverted, that when the newly independent states drew up their constitutions they—or at least eight of the thirteen—prefaced those constitutions with elaborate and ringing statements of the natural law doctrine upon which their positive law was founded. We have already quoted from the Massachusetts Bill of Rights of 1780, but we give here the parallel beginning by Virginia, which actually preceded the Declaration of Independence by three weeks. It is

> A Declaration of rights made by the representatives of the good people of Virginia, assembled in full and free convention; which rights do pertain to them and their posterity, as the basis and foundation of government.

And the first paragraph in this declaration is as follows:

> That all men are by nature equally free and independent, and have certain inherent rights, of which, when they enter into a state of society, they cannot by any compact deprive or divest their posterity; namely, the enjoyment of life and liberty, with the means of acquiring and possessing property, and pursuing and obtaining happiness and safety.[54]

What is distinctive—and indeed unprecedented, but also characteristic—in Virginia's revolutionary state constitution is the unwillingness to mistake or confound the ground of authority in reason and nature with that of prescription, custom, or tradition. For what is here called the "basis and foundation of government" for themselves and their posterity is, *ex vi termini*, the permanent or unchanging "basis and foundation" in nature. It is not such a basis or foundation as is revealed in Justice Brennan's emergent ( or "arrived") evolutionary conscience, nor is it one discovered in colonial charters, or any authoritative written record as such. Historical experience means experience in time, but what is permanent is recognized as an intelligible necessity—or as grounded in an intelligible necessity—outside of time. It is this understanding of what is due to man as man, in and by human government, because of what man is, that is the basis for the "original intentions" properly so-called of the Founding Fathers, whether in Virginia, Massachusetts, or anywhere else in revolutionary America. In asking what were the original intentions of the Founding Fathers, we are asking what principles of moral and political philosophy guided them. We are not asking their personal judgments upon contingent matters. We are asking what were those principles—those truths "applicable to all men and all times"—to which they subscribed. The crisis of American constitutionalism—the crisis of the West—lies precisely in the denial that there are any such principles or truths. It is no less a crisis in the heart of American conservatism than of American liberalism.

We return again to Irving Kristol's assertion that the aim of the American Revolution was to harmonize our political institutions with an "actual 'American way of life' which no one even dreamed of challenging."[55] Yet the American Revolution unleashed a movement of reform perhaps unprecedented in human history. This movement proceeded on a broad front. Once the connection with the British Crown was dissolved there was no motive for Americans to pretend that their institutions were not—or ought not to be—as republican as possible. Here again, conservative writers have misled us. The late Martin Diamond, in the lecture that followed Kristol's in the American Enterprise Institute's Bicentennial Series, wrote that "the Declaration holds George III 'unfit to be the ruler of a free people,' not because he was a king, but because he was a tyrannical king." Diamond would have us believe the Declaration is "neutral" as between the different forms of government, and implies no brief against monarchy or oligarchy or any other form of government, as such. But this is to ignore the Whig theory by which Jefferson and the Congress had interpreted the English constitution and its monarchy. Here is how Jefferson addressed the British monarch in *A Summary View of the Rights of British America*, a year before independence.

> . . . and this his Majesty will think we have reason to expect when he reflects that he is no more than chief officer of the people, appointed by the laws, and circumscribed with definite powers, to assist in working the great machine of government, erected for their use, and, consequently, subject to their superintendence.[56]

Clearly, Jefferson's characterization of the British monarchy is that of a republican chief executive. The eighteenth-century Whig theory of the British constitution—the theory formed under the influence of John Locke by those who made the Glorious Revolution—was that it was a republic under the forms of a monarchy (just as today we would say that it is a democracy under the form of a monarchy). The American Whigs were willing to pretend that the monarchical and aristocratic or oligarchical features of the British constitution were compatible with their natural rights, as a concession that any people might prudently make "while evils are sufferable," rather than "abolishing the forms to which they are accustomed." But when evils were no longer sufferable and revolution became necessary, prudence no longer dictated restraint to Americans in making their institutions wholly republican. Once Americans saw their liberties as no longer connected in any way with their "rights as Englishmen," but dependent solely upon their rights as men under the laws of nature, an enormous energy for change and reform was released. The direction that that change was to take was toward far greater civil and religious liberty—and far greater popular or democratic republicanism—than the world had ever seen before. Let us remember that by Article IV of the Constitution, "The United States shall guarantee to every State in this Union a republican form of government . . ."

Given the many anomalies of the Constitution—and none greater of course than slavery—it is good to have Madison's and Jefferson's word that the principles of the Constitution, the principles of republicanism, nowhere defined in the Constitution itself, are those of the Declaration of Independence. From this we are enabled to say that the principles of the Constitution condemn chattel slavery, even as its compromises offer it a temporary security.

To repeat, after the American people had made good their independence, there was no reason for them to continue any of the aristocratic (or oligarchic) or monarchic features of the constitution of the mother country. They proceeded to lay the ax to both, as well as to the connection between church and state that had arisen in English history because the king had been head of the church. The constitutional freedom of Englishmen in England—and in America so long as Americans were English—was seen to subsist in that connection between crown and church that was formed by Henry VIII's separation from Rome. Henry's assumption of the headship of the Church of England in the sixteenth century was, among other things, a means of preventing the pope from placing a Spanish (or Habsburg or other Catholic and foreign) prince on the English throne. Henry's confiscation and redistribution of the lands of the monasteries (and other church lands) following the break with Rome, formed a new propertied class in England, whose title to their property was no better than the king's title as head of the English church. The union of church and state in England was therefore an instrument of national independence and national freedom.

Once America had separated from England the accidents of Reformation history no longer carried the practical meaning in America in regard to civil and religious liberty that they still possessed in England. When Hamilton in the first number of the *Federalist* speaks of the desirability of "establishing good government from reflection and choice," rather than "forever depending for our political constitutions on accident and force," he is undoubtedly thinking of some of the accidental features of the British constitution which, although happy in their effects in Great Britain, would have been utterly irrational in an independent America. The separation of church and state, the election of both houses of bicameral legislatures and of chief magistrates, state or federal, the steady broadening of the franchise, the ending of primogeniture and entail—the legal foundation of hereditary aristocracy—all were consequences of emancipating the principles of republican government from any deference to or dependence upon the constitution of England. All these are among the reasons Jefferson and Madison believed that the principles of the Declaration of Independence ought to be the *norma docendi* of the faculty and as such taught to the law students at the University of Virginia, as the principles of the constitutions of Virginia and of the United States.

The assertion that the American Revolution was intended to bring our institutions into a more perfect correspondence with an actual American way of life "which no one even dreamed of challenging" may be regarded as true—if somewhat hyperbolic—but in a sense of which Irving Kristol himself never dreamed. There was an American way of life that was actually in the minds of the American people. That way of life was expressed in the Declaration of Independence—which Jefferson himself in 1825 declared to be "an expression of the American mind."[57] It embodied that "standard maxim of a free people" which should, as Lincoln said, steadily and continuously augment "the happiness and value of life to all people of all colors everywhere."[58] That the Great Seal of the United States should proclaim the *novus ordo seclorum* would be sufficient evidence to everyone except the pseudo-Burkeans of American conservatism (who list Burke and Calhoun but not Lincoln among the "Defenders of the Constitution") that the Founding of the United States looked forward, not backwards.

We find ourselves [Lincoln wrote in 1838] under the government of a system of political institutions conducing more essentially to the ends of civil and religious liberty, than any of which the history of former times tells us.[59]

Since nothing in "the history of former times" can serve as a model for our own "system of political institutions," ours is not a way of life defined by tradition or prescription. Tradition and prescription might be incorporated into the new regime: experience was to be consulted, but there was to be no identification of the old with the good, except as the old might justify itself at the bar of reason and nature. One cannot too often repeat Washington's words, that the foundations of American government were "not laid in the gloomy ages of ignorance and superstition . . ." The American Revolution retained the old Puritan dream of a City on a Hill. But this City—now emphatically republican or democratic—was no longer defined by the exclusive revealed theology of the Puritans, but by the inclusive, philanthropic, tolerant, but not less moral theology of

> a benign religion, professed indeed and practiced in various forms, yet all of them inculcating honesty, truth, temperance, gratitude, and the love of man; acknowledging and adoring an overruling Providence, which by all its dispensations proves that it delights in the happiness of man here and his greater happiness hereafter.[60]

In one respect, the reforming impulse of the Revolution fell short—and that was with respect to Negro slavery. As to the American way of life that no one dreamed of challenging—surely one of the most unfortunate historical characterizations ever ventured—consider the following from *The Revolutionary Records of the State of Georgia*. At Darien, on the southern border of settled Georgia, a group of citizens met in January of 1775 to align themselves with the rebellion against Great Britain. These Georgians, including slave owners, promulgated a set of resolutions specifying both British evils and American goals. This was the fifth resolution.

> To show the world that we are not influenced by any contracted or interested motives, but a general philanthropy for all mankind of whatever climate, language, or complexion, we hereby declare our disapprobation and abhorrence of the unnatural practice of slavery in America (however the uncultivated state of our country or other specious argument may plead for it), a practice founded in injustice and cruelty and highly dangerous to our liberties (as well as lives), debasing part of our fellow creatures below men, and

corrupting the virtues and morals of the rest, and which is laying the basis of the liberty we contend for (and which we pray the Almighty to continue to the latest posterity) upon a very wrong foundation. We, therefore, resolve at all times to use our utmost endeavors for the manumission of our slaves in this Colony, for the most safe and equitable footing for the masters and themselves.[61]

This resolution is remarkable for saying nearly everything that Jefferson's famous diatribe against slavery in the *Notes on Virginia* says. But it is all the more remarkable for saying it nearly eight years before the *Notes on Virginia*. Indeed, it is some three months before Lexington and Concord, and eighteen months before independence. Moreover, it was made by anonymous citizens, not by leaders of the Revolution or (as Russell Kirk would have us think) by Francophile intellectuals. And the southern border of Georgia was very far from the Quakers of Philadelphia or the radicals of Boston. Here is conclusive evidence of the popular roots of the belief in human equality, conclusive proof that Taney could not have been more wrong than when he said that, in the revolutionary period, it was a

fixed and universal opinion . . . which no one thought of disputing or supposed open to dispute [that black men were] beings of an inferior order . . . and so far inferior that they had no rights which the white man was bound to respect . . . and that the negro might justly and lawfully be reduced to slavery for his benefit.

I do not recollect a single piece of documentary evidence to support Taney's contention, and all the evidence I have seen from this period is fully consistent with the Georgia resolution. The "prevailing" (not "fixed and universal") opinion of the revolutionary and Founding generation was expressed by Alexander Stephens, vice president of the Confederacy, in his famous "Cornerstone Speech," delivered in Savannah, Georgia, in April of 1861, before the firing on Fort Sumpter.

The prevailing ideas entertained by [Jefferson] and most of the leading statesmen at the time of the formation of the old Constitution, were that the enslavement of the African was in violation of the laws of nature: that it was wrong in principle, socially, morally, and politically. It was an evil they knew not well how to deal with, but the general opinion of that day was, that somehow or other, in the order of Providence, the institution would be evanescent and pass away.[62]

Here we have powerful witness against Taney (and against Kirk, Kirkpatrick, Bork, et al.) and in favor of Lincoln's account of political public opinion at the time of the Founding. It is also of decisive importance with respect to the "original intentions" of those who framed and those who ratified "the old Constitution." It is authoritative, in part, because Stephens speaks as a disciple of Calhoun's doctrine of state sovereignty. But Stephens is more reliable than Calhoun himself on the intention of the Framers of the Constitution of 1787, because he no longer speaks as a citizen of the Union engaged in controversy over the interpretation of the "old Constitution." Calhoun had perversely denied the authority of the Founding generation's conviction concerning the natural rights of mankind for the interpretation of the Constitution, because he meant to have his own opinions (against natural equality, and in favor of the "positive good" theory of slavery) substituted as the genuine "original intent."

In his *Discourse on the Constitution and Government of the United States,* Calhoun had systematically argued for the superiority of his own understanding. He meant to have it replace that of the Founding Fathers—as it has largely succeeded in doing in the minds of American conservatives. His followers (after his death in 1850) believed that effort had come to naught with the election of Abraham Lincoln. But Calhoun's constitutionalism had triumphed nevertheless in the framing of a new Constitution—that of the Confederate States of America. But the Union victory in the Civil War canceled that triumph. Calhoun's heirs have, ever since, returned to the original Calhounian project, of restoring his anti-antislavery view of the Founding, and of the "original intent" of the Framers. Let us remember that Stephens in the "Cornerstone Speech" is speaking as vice president of the Confederate States of America at the high tide of Confederate optimism—before the firing on Fort Sumpter—when it was not only hoped but believed that the separation of the states would be both peaceful and permanent. That is to say, he spoke before the American people—and the world—had come to know what difference it made whether it was James Buchanan or Abraham Lincoln who as president of the United States declared secession to be unlawful, and the Union unbroken.

After the Civil War was over and Stephens came to write his classic *Constitutional View of the Late War Between the States,* he pretended that slavery was not the real cause of the conflict. The cause of the South, he then held, was its defense of state rights against the tyranny of the majority. However, it cannot be too often repeated that the defense of state rights and the defense of slavery became one and the same when Calhoun divorced the idea of sovereignty from any connection with the natural rights of individual human beings. In his "Cornerstone Speech" Stephens was, as we have seen, entirely correct in his characterization of the thought of those who framed and those who ratified "the old Constitution." And in 1861 he was candid in contrasting that thought with the thought of the founders of the new Confederacy. In the decisive respect, said Stephens, the ideas of the "old" Fathers

> were fundamentally wrong. They rested upon the assumption of the equality of the races. This was an error . . . Our new government is founded upon exactly the opposite idea; its foundations are laid, its cornerstone rests upon the great truth that the negro is not the equal of the white man. That slavery—the subordination to the superior race—is his natural and normal condition. This our new government is the first in the history of the world based upon this great physical and moral truth. This truth has been slow in the process of development, like all other truths in the various departments of science.[63]

Stephens was not a pure legal positivist (like Chief Justice Rehnquist). He did not reject the idea of nature—or the Creator—as the origin and source of political rights. But he thought that the progress of science placed both nature and the Creator in a newer and better light. In so thinking he also showed that the Confederacy—certainly in his mind— was the very antithesis of a traditional society: on the contrary, in breaking with "the old Constitution" in the name of science it was more radically modern than any other. It is no accident that this speech was delivered two years after the publication of Darwin's *Origin of Species.*

> The architect, in the construction of buildings, lays the foundation with proper materials . . . The substratum of our society is made of the material fitted by nature for it, and by experience we know that it is best, not only for the superior, but for the inferior race that it should be so. It is indeed in conformity with the ordinance of the Creator . . . The great objects of humanity are best attained when conformed to His laws and decrees, in the formation of government, as well as in all things else. Our Confederacy is founded upon principles in strict conformity with these laws. This stone which was first rejected by the first builders "is become the chief stone of the corner" in our new edifice.[64]

Let us be clear about what Stephens has just said. The "stone . . . rejected by the first builders" is the "great truth that the negro is not the equal of the white man." "Scientific racism" may be said to have been in its infancy in 1861, but we now know well what it is when it is fully grown.

The idea of evolution as a feature of political—and not only of biological—thought, in one manifestation or another, had been looming ever more prominently in the "climate of opinion" of the nineteenth century. It undoubtedly received its greatest impulse from Rousseau's 1754 *Discourse on the Origin and the Foundations of Inequality Among Men*. But it was in the course of the nineteenth century that it was transformed from "philosophic" to "scientific" status. That is to say, it was thus transformed at a time when science was achieving status as the highest authority in human affairs, while philosophy was being relegated into a minor academic discipline. Stephens compares the discovery of the inequality of the races to Harvey's discovery of the circulation of the blood, as well as to the discoveries of Galileo and Adam Smith. Here we see, as noted, the early version of that "scientific racism" that came to its fullest flower in Houston Stewart Chamberlain—and Adolph Hitler. But we must not fail to notice as well the parallel of Stephens' thought—no less than that of Calhoun—to that of Karl Marx. Marx also rejected eighteenth-century natural rights teaching on the ground that it too had been superseded by later scientific discoveries, most notably his own. For Marx, the primacy of classes paralleled that of races. Whether as the struggle of races (or nations) or as the struggle of classes, neo-evolutionary social Darwinism became the predominant form of late nineteenth-century political thought. The crucial fact about Calhoun, Marx, and the neo-Darwinian racists is their denial of individual rights according to nature, and their assertion of the primacy of society, whether as race, class, nation, or as "concurrent" social grouping.


In our remarks above on Justice Brennan, we observed that it was "evolution" operating through the judge's conscience that defined the genuine Constitution, even if that Constitution differed from the explicit and unambiguous words of the unamended written document. Contemporary liberalism—as represented by Mr. Justice Brennan—rejects the natural rights teaching of the Founding for the same underlying reason that it was rejected by Calhoun and Stephens, viz., because it has been superseded by the progress of "science." Jefferson and Madison, the authors of the Declaration of Independence and of the tenth *Federalist*, subscribed to a conception of nature which modern liberals believe to have been superseded by the great discoveries of Marx, Darwin, and Freud. The modern

liberal believes with his conservative brother that society is in every fundamental respect antecedent to the individual. He believes, therefore, that
there can be no individual "rights" which limit the scope or action of
government, because the "individual" whose rights are to be vindicated
only exists in the future as a potentiality of the society that is to be
reformed. Modern liberalism and modern conservatism thus viewed stand
upon common ground. They are mirror images of each other. They differ
only as to where Right and Left are located on the images.

# What Were the "Original Intentions" of the Framers of the Constitution of the United States?

1. *Dred Scott* v. *Sanford*, 60 U.S. (19 Howard) 393 (1857).
2. Ibid., pp. 451, 452.
3. 60 U.S. at 451.
4. Ibid., p. 451.
5. 1 Kings 3:16.
6. W. Brennan, to the Text and Teaching Symposium, speech at Georgetown University (Oct. 12, 1985), reprinted in *The Great Debate: Interpreting Our Written Constitution*, published by the Federalist Society, 1986.
7. Ibid., p. 24.
8. "Zeitgeist" (German) refers to the spirit of the age, the feeling or thought of a particular period.
9. Lenin, "What Is To Be Done?" (1902).
10. Major Policy Statements of the Attorney General: Edwin Meese III, 1985–1988. U. S. Government Printing Office: 1989, pp. 14–21.
11. E.g., "Of all free government compact is the basis and the essence," *The Writings of James Madison*, Gaillard Hunt, ed. Putnam, 1910, Vol. IX, pp. 569, 573.
12. Jefferson, First Inaugural Address. Reprinted in Commager, Documents of American History (7th edition, 1963), pp. 186, 187. (Hereafter, Commager.)
13. Cooke edition, p. 3.
14. *The Complete Jefferson*, Saul Padover, ed., Tudor Publishing Company, New York, 1943. p. 648. This passage is quoted by Madison in the 48th Federalist.
15. *The Collected Works of Abraham Lincoln* (Hereafter, CW), Roy P. Basler, ed., Rutgers, 1953, Vol. II, p. 461.
16. *The Writings of Thomas Jefferson*, H. A. Washington, ed., Vol. VII, p. 483.
17. *Writings of James Madison*, Hunt, ed., Vol. IX. p. 221. Jefferson's resolutions,

incorporating Madison's suggestions, are in *The Complete Jefferson*, Padover, ed., p. 1112.

18. Leo Strauss, *Thoughts on Machiavelli* (1958), Midway Reprint, University of Chicago Press (1984), p. 13.

19. The Center for Judicial Studies, Cumberland, Virginia (a major conservative "think tank" in the Washington area), recently publicized as "Defenders of the Constitution" James Madison, John Marshall, Joseph Story, Daniel Webster, John C. Calhoun, and Edmund Burke. Madison, Story, and Webster violently opposed Calhoun in the Nullification Crisis of 1828–1833 (on grounds that Marshall certainly agreed with). Madison's last years were largely preoccupied with refuting the theory of nullification (and its attendant "sophism": the right of secession). The Madison of this conservative think tank (like Marshall, Story, and Webster) has been sanitized of his opposition to Calhoun and his association with the natural rights theory of the Declaration. Why Burke—who died in 1791—is called a defender of the American Constitution is, I suspect, because he is identified erroneously as an enemy of the doctrine of natural rights in the Declaration of Independence. What is most striking about this gallery of honor, however, is the inclusion of that great enemy of the Declaration—John C. Calhoun—and the exclusion of its greatest defender, Abraham Lincoln.

20. *In Union and Liberty: The Political Philosophy of John C. Calhoun*, Liberty Classics edition, Ross M. Lence, ed., 1992 (Hereafter, Union and Liberty), pp. 5–72.

21. Commager, p. 107.

22. Cf. M. E. Bradford, *A Better Guide Than Reason: Studies in the American Revolution*, Sugden, 1979.

23. CW, IV, p. 433.

24. Calhoun makes this the center of his argument in the "Disquisition on Government," and it has been repeated countless times since then. But note the endorsement of Calhoun by Lord Acton in his 1861 essay, "Political Causes of the American Revolution," in *Essays in the Liberal Interpretation of History*.

25. This, however, is what Calhounites, then and now, have always done. See Meyer, "Lincoln Without Rhetoric," *National Review*, August 24, 1965, p. 725. In rebuttal of Meyer, see Jaffa, "Lincoln and the Cause of Freedom," *National Review*, September 21, 1965, p. 827. (Reprinted in Jaffa, *The Conditions of Freedom*, The Johns Hopkins University Press, 1975.)

26. See, e.g., Bradford, "The Heresy of Equality: Bradford Replies to Jaffa," *Modern Age*, Winter 1976, p. 62. "Equality as a moral or political imperative . . . is the antonym of every legitimate conservative principle."

27. CW, II, pp. 405, 406.

28. CW, II, p. 270.

29. *Union and Liberty*, p. 566.

30. "The American Revolution as a Successful Revolution," in *America's Continuing Revolution*, Anchor/Doubleday, 1976.

31. In "The Revolution of Sober Expectations," in *America's Continuing Revolution*. Diamond's lecture followed Kristol's inaugural lecture in the American Enterprise Institute's Distinguished Lecture Series on the Bicentennial of the United States.

32. CW, II, p. 385.

33. CW, III, p. 376. Emphasis added.

34. "Tradition and Morality in Constitutional Law," a lecture at the American Enterprise Institute, reprinted in *Views from the Bench: The Judiciary and Constitutional Politics* (M. Cannon and D. O'Brien, ed., 1985) Emphasis added.

35. Bork, "Tradition and Morality . . ."

36. Commager, p. 107.

37. "Why Not Abolish Ignorance (While We're At It)?" July 9, 1982. p. 829.

38. *The Complete Writings of Thomas Paine*, Collected and Edited by Philip S. Foner. The Citadel Press. New York. 1945. Vol. I, p. 50.

39. More recently, however, Kristol has become less shy in expressing his real opinion of Jefferson. Consider the following:

> . . . the authors of the Constitution . . . were for the most part not particularly interested in religion. I am not aware that any of them ever wrote anything worth reading on religion, especially Jefferson, who wrote nothing worth reading on religion or almost anything else.

In *The Spirit of the Constitution*, Robert A. Goldwin and Robert A. Licht, eds., The AEI Press, Washington, D.C. 1990. So much for the author of the Declaration of Independence and the Virginia Statute of Religious Liberty!

40. *Abraham Lincoln: His Speeches and Writings*, Roy P. Basler, ed. (one-volume edition), World Publishing Company, 1946, p. 513. Lincoln's punctuation and emphasis.

41. *The Writings of James Madison* (Hunt, ed.), Vol. IX, p. 511.

42. Federalist # 39 (Cooke ed.), pp. 250–257.

43. Federalist #1.

44. *George Washington, A Collection*, W. B. Allen, ed., Liberty Classics, 1988, pp. 240, 241.

45. *The Papers of Alexander Hamilton*, Vol. 1, p. 12.

46. CW, II, p. 271.

47. Politics, 1287 a 30.

48. Commager, p. 65.

49. Ibid., p. 66. Emphasis added.

50. Hallberg, Delavan, Wisconsin, 1983.

51. *The Declaration of Independence*, Knopf, 1942, p. 230.

52. Intercollegiate Review, Winter 1985–1986, p. 6.

53. Commager, p. 83.
54. Commager, p. 103.
55. *America's Continuing Revolution*, p. 13.
56. *The Complete Jefferson*, Padover, ed., p. 18.
57. Letter to Henry Lee, Ford, ed., vol. x, p. 343.
58. CW, II, p. 406.
59. CW, I, p. 108.
60. Jefferson's inaugural address, Commager, p. 187.
61. Revolutionary Records of the State of Georgia, 1906.
62. *The Political History of the Great Rebellion*, E. Mcpherson ed., 1865, p. 103.
63. *Political History of the Great Rebellion*, p. 103.
64. Ibid., p. 103.

# Attorney General Meese, the Declaration, and the Constitution

## HARRY V. JAFFA

Attorney General Meese's speech at Dickinson College, Carlisle, Pennsylvania, on September 17, 1985—Constitution Day—was his "first address relating to the Bicentennial of our Constitution." In this speech the attorney general asserted unequivocally that the principles of the Declaration of Independence are the principles of the Constitution. Since this is, as we have seen, what Jefferson and Madison said, and what Lincoln believed, and what we are convinced is the truth of the matter, we wish this speech had been the occasion for greater rejoicing. Unfortunately, the attorney general's great and true assertion about the relationship of the Declaration of Independence to the Constitution was made in a desultory and confused manner. It was made without any apparent awareness of the fact that it was controversial: indeed, that it is as controversial today as at any time in our past, including that of the generation of the Civil War. He seemed oblivious of that rejection of the Declaration so characteristic of conservative jurisprudence, which we have so amply documented above. Indeed, although Mr. Meese is often referred to these days as the keeper of the conservative flame in the flickering Reagan "revolution," I am not aware of a single instance in which Mr. Meese has persuaded anyone, in or out of the Department of Justice, of the truth of his contention concerning the relationship between the Declaration and the Constitution. I do not know of a single one of Mr. Meese's judicial nominees who supports this view. Most conspicuous is its absolute rejection—in the name of radical positivism and relativism—by the new chief justice, Mr. Rehnquist. Mr. Rehnquist's opinions on this matter we have subjected to critical examination in Appendix C.

Mr. Meese writes that

> The Civil War . . . was nothing less than a war between brothers for the very soul of the American Constitution—the principle of human equality . . . and we have endured precisely because through that bitter conflict our politics were forced to conform to our most ennobling principles.

The "very soul of the American Constitution" and "our most ennobling principles" are contained—according to Mr. Meese—in that paragraph of the Declaration of Independence beginning "We hold these truths to be self-evident . . ." Commenting on it, he observes that the rights with which men are said to be endowed by their Creator are

> rights that existed *in nature* before governments and laws were ever formed. As the physical world is governed by natural laws such as gravity so the political world is governed by other natural laws in the form of natural rights.[1]

But we have here a radical confusion between the concept of natural law, as governing the physical, and as governing the political (or moral) world. Gravity, as a law of the physical world, merely states an invariant relationship between matter and motion. Matter "obeys" the law of gravity because it cannot do otherwise. Indeed, we have here two different—and in certain respects opposite—conceptions both of nature and of reason, although Mr. Meese appears to be unconscious of that difference.

In an article entitled "The Moral Foundations of Republican Government"—an article, we observe, that repeats textually much of the speech at Dickinson College—Mr. Meese injects this added gloss on his view of the Founding Fathers:

> . . . we first need to remember that our Founders lived in a time of nearly unparalleled intellectual excitement. They were the true children of the Enlightenment. They sought to bring the new found faith in human reason to bear on practical politics. Hobbes and Locke, Harrington and Machiavelli, Smith and Montesquieu—these were the teachers of our Founders. These were the authors of celebrated works that had called into question long-prevailing views of human nature and thus of politics. Our nation was created in the light cast by these towering figures.[2]

This seemingly academic assertion raises disturbing questions. Leaving aside the other authors for the moment, in what sense can it be said that Machiavelli was one of the teachers of the Founders? Leo Strauss has written that "The United States of America may be said to be the only country in the world which was founded in explicit opposition to Machiavellian principles."[3] To which he has added that "contemporary tyranny has its roots in Machiavelli's thought, in the Machiavellian principle that the good end justifies any means." When Mr. Meese speaks of a "new found faith in human reason," what is implied—whether he knows it or not—is the faith in what reason can accomplish when it is divorced from moral restraint. It is curious that Mr. Meese mentions the names only of modern philosophers as "the teachers of our Founders." Surely he must have known that Jefferson, when writing of the sources of the Declaration of Independence (letter to Henry Lee, May 8, 1825), mentioned "the elementary books of public right, as Aristotle, Cicero, Locke, Sidney, etc." By writing as he does of a "new found faith in human reason" Mr. Meese implies the rejection of that old faith in human reason, represented transcendently by Aristotle and Cicero, a faith in human reason in which reason's concern for means is never divorced from reason's concern with ends. The typically modern view, on the other hand, implies that reason has nothing whatever to do with ends, because ends—in the sense of good and bad, just and unjust, right and wrong—are themselves essentially unknowable.

In the case of Hobbes, for example, the only ends recognized as having any authority over reason are those that are the objects of the strongest passions. It was Hobbes, after all, who declared that tyranny was merely "kingship misliked." One can hardly imagine language that more directly contradicts the central thesis of the Declaration of Independence, a document which itself continues a very old tradition of tyrannicide.

In Aristotle and Cicero, however, reason is inherent in nature itself, and nature is understood to be a source of norms of human conduct. The specifically modern view of nature is one of mindless matter and energy, with no end or purpose discernible by reason. Mr. Meese, by silently dropping Aristotle and Cicero from Jefferson's enumeration, unknowingly gives credit to the view that "the laws of nature and of nature's God" referred to in the Declaration have no moral content whatever. This would justify Chief Justice Taney (and Senator Stephen A. Douglas), in maintaining that the proposition of equality meant only that the British in America were equal to the British in Great Britain, and had nothing to do with black men or any other human beings! This agrees also with Mr. Justice Rehnquist, when he writes that there is no way to "logically demonstrate" that the judgments of any one "conscience" are superior to those of any other.[4] Above all, a commitment to unalloyed modernity and to Machiavellianism means a commitment to atheism. Walter Berns, for example—who finds Hobbesianism at the core of the Founding—has declared that there is a "parade of evidence . . . that Washington, Jefferson, and Madison were opposed to revealed religion and understood it to be incompatible with an attachment to 'Nature's God.' "[5] But if revealed religion—most especially Christianity—is incompatible with "the rights of the laws of nature" then it is incompatible with a government devoted to securing such rights. Such a government must pursue a policy designed to lessen, if not eliminate, the influence of Christianity (and other revealed religions) in the minds of the citizens of such government. That, according to Berns, was the hidden agenda of "Washington, Jefferson, and Madison." Does Mr. Meese—who spends his spare time drafting constitutional amendments authorizing school prayer, prayer, we had supposed, directed for the most part to the God of revealed religion, the God of the Bible—really believe such nonsense? Why then does he place Machiavelli—but not Aristotle or Cicero—among the teachers of the Founding Fathers?

The laws of the political world, unlike the laws of gravity, or of "scientific" laws generally—are laws only because they can be disobeyed. But it is not only the case that political laws can be disobeyed; it is also the case that there is a variety of political laws on the human scene. Not only are there different laws in different places at the same time, and different laws in the same place at different times, but sometimes even what may be called the same law—e.g., the law of the Constitution of the United States—may be said to differ at different times. For example, it has both permitted and forbidden human slavery and intoxicating liquors. In the case of intoxicating liquors, it has permitted, forbidden, and then permitted them again. It is an interesting question whether "We the people . . ." have the same inherent authority to repeal the Thirteenth, as to repeal the Eighteenth Amendment. If the sovereignty of the American people means supreme power, without any qualification, then the American people have the same constitutional right to institute or adopt slavery as to abolish it. If however the sovereignty of the American people—or of any people—can be rightfully exercised only in the service of the inherent and unalienable rights with which all human beings have been equally endowed, by the laws of a moral and rational nature, then there can be no rightful and lawful exercise of sovereignty ultimately inconsistent with such ends.

Human reason investigates—but does not deliberate upon—the physical laws of nature. And although there may be differences of opinion as to what the "laws" governing matter are, it is supposed on all sides that there can be only one such law governing any given phenomenon. But all moral and political questions are—characteristically—matters of dispute. And human beings deliberate in the face of moral and political alternatives. For there is nothing in the moral or political universe but is, as Aristotle says, "capable of being otherwise." Men can be free, and men can be slaves. Men can enslave their fellow men or emancipate them. Men can choose death rather than slavery, or slavery rather than death. Which is the better—red than dead, or dead than red? Which laws—or moral injunctions—should be obeyed? Does calling laws or rights natural laws or natural rights make them decisively authoritative? Is not calling them authoritative because natural merely a rhetorical trick? Certainly the natural rights doctrine of the Declaration has had few adherents among the main-line conservatives who list John C. Calhoun—but not Abraham Lincoln—among the "Defenders of the Constitution."

Mr. Meese asserts however—with Jefferson, Madison, and Lincoln—that there exists

> a natural standard for judging whether governments are legitimate or not. That standard is whether or not the government rests upon the consent of the governed. Any political powers not derived from the consent of the governed are, by the laws of nature, illegitimate and hence unjust.[6]

Unfortunately, however, Mr. Meese has not been consistent in his commitment to the ideas of natural rights and natural law expressed in the Declaration of Independence. In a speech delivered to the St. Louis University School of Law, September 12, 1986, Mr. Meese went out of his way to denounce the idea of natural law as a standard for constitutional jurisprudence. The speech as a whole was designed as a eulogy of the late Mr. Justice Hugo Black, on the occasion of Black's hundredth birthday. In it the attorney general singled out for praise Black's dissent in the *Griswold* case (1965), in which the Court ruled unconstitutional a Connecticut statute that "proscribed the use of birth control devices and made it a criminal offense for anyone to give information or instruction on their use." It was in this case that the Court, speaking through the late Mr. Justice Douglas, discovered a constitutional "right of privacy" among the "emanations" and "penumbras" of the First, Third, Fourth, Fifth, and Ninth Amendments. And it was this discovery of a right to privacy in the *Griswold* case that enabled the Court, in *Roe v. Wade*,[7] to make the further discovery that a woman's right to an abortion was within the compass of the right to privacy. One can understand the attorney general's desire to enlist the authority of Black in his campaign against the legal foundations of *Roe v Wade*. But how can one account for this:

> ... Douglas's opinion in *Griswold* allowed the Court to return to a most constitutionally pernicious doctrine, that of resting constitutional interpretation on the "mysterious and uncertain" ground of natural law.[8]

In the Dickinson College speech, as we have seen, the attorney general is unequivocal in asserting that the principles of the Declaration of Independence as principles of natural law are the principles of the Constitution. And according to the Declaration, the right to life is the first of the rights to be secured by government, under "the laws of nature and of nature's God."[9] We have just seen Mr. Meese in the Dickinson College speech asserting that there is "a natural standard for judging whether governments are legitimate or not." How can there be such a standard for declaring the legitimacy of governments but not one for declaring whether the acts of government—in certain fundamental respects—are legitimate? If it is true, moreover, that the principles of the Declaration are the principles of the Constitution, then we do not look outside the Constitution but rather within it for the natural law basis of constitutional interpretation. Justice Black's attack on alleged appeals to the natural law, as a pretext for judicial usurpation, is based upon his positivist prejudices against the idea of natural justice—the central idea of the American Founding and hence of the American Constitution.

The St. Louis speech demonstrates that Mr. Meese's constitutionalism sometimes becomes self-contradictory, if not incoherent, in the presence of his passion against judicial activism. For example, he quotes with full approval the following from Black's dissent in *Griswold*:

> There is no provision of the Constitution which either expressly or impliedly vests power in this Court to sit as a supervisory agency over acts of duly constituted legislative bodies and set aside their laws because of the Court's belief that the legislative policies adopted are unreasonable, unwise, arbitrary, capricious, or irrational.[10]

Certainly the Court has no right to set aside statutes as unconstitutional merely because it regards them as unwise, or even as arbitrary. But surely Mr. Meese (and Justice Black after he left the Ku Klux Klan) would regard the Jim Crow laws of many States, from the end of Reconstruction until the 1960s, to be not only unreasonable and arbitrary, but utterly inconsistent with the ends of free government and hence of the Constitution. Mr. Meese himself in his Dickinson College speech argues against racially based quotas or preferences, as follows.

Counting by race is a form of racism. And racism is never benign, never benevolent. It elevates a perverted notion of equality and denies the original understanding of equality that has guided our political thinking since we began as a nation.

When Mr. Meese speaks here of "the original understanding of equality" he must refer to the Declaration of Independence, since the words "equal" or "equality" do not occur in the Constitution of 1787. The word "equal" enters the text of the Constitution only with the Fourteenth Amendment. The aforesaid "original understanding of equality" must then be that of "the laws of nature and of nature's God." What then, according to Mr. Meese, is the constitutional status of this "original understanding?" Here is Mr. Meese at Dickinson College again:

In practice this principle means that there must be a regard for *individual* rights; for by being created equal . . . each person has dignity as an individual . . . This original understanding of liberty and equality is undermined by those who seek to claim group rights and to secure group remedies. There are constitutional and legal obligations in the United States to enforce the principle of nondiscrimination. The equal protection clause of the 14th Amendment and the various pieces of Civil Rights legislation demand it. This principle is offended by policies that seek to bestow special rewards on the basis of race or gender or any other immutable and morally irrelevant characteristic, just as it is offended by policies that purposely deny opportunities on the basis of race.

Here Mr. Meese is categorical in asserting that the right not to be discriminated against is an *individual* constitutional right (the emphasis above is by Mr. Meese), arising from the fact of being "created equal." Here the attorney general regards it as a constitutional right—at least since the adoption of the Fourteenth Amendment—*because it is a natural right*. And the Fourteenth Amendment is here seen as a measure bringing the Constitution as a whole more in conformity with its original foundation in the natural law. This foundation was flawed by the concessions to slavery arising from "necessity" but not from "principle." If such is the case, however, would not a legislative enactment discriminating on the basis of race, by a State or by the United States, be an unconstitutional violation of that right? Would not individuals have the right to claim remedies for such discrimination in the courts, and finally in the Supreme Court? Does not Mr. Meese here assert that the right of individuals not to be discriminated against by race—or any other "morally irrelevant characteristic"—flows from the original natural law intent of the Constitution, embodied finally in the positive law of the Constitution by the Fourteenth Amendment? Is not Mr. Meese right in asserting the Declaration's understanding of equality as the basis for interpreting the Fourteenth Amendment, over against Mr. Justice Brennan's wholly subjective "evolutionary" conception of "human dignity?" But is it not also the responsibility of the courts to protect such rights against infringement by legislatures as well as by the action of the executive branch of government? Hence *in such cases* must not the Supreme Court necessarily "sit as a supervisory agency over the acts of duly constituted legislative bodies and [in certain cases] set aside their laws"? Of course, it cannot do this if the justices—as for example Mr. Justice Brennan and Mr. Justice Rehnquist—do not accept what Mr. Meese says here about the natural law conception of equality as the ground of constitutional jurisprudence.[11]

Mr. Meese is aware of the fact that in 1860 and 1861 eleven states of the Union "deratified" the Constitution by acts of "secession." In so doing they declared themselves to have withdrawn their consent from the government of the Constitution of the Union. The subsequent exercise of the authority of the Union over them was the result, they said, not of consent but of conquest. But "consent of the governed," Mr. Meese says,

> is a political concept that is the reciprocal of the idea of equality. Because all men are created equal, nature does not single out who is to govern and who is to be governed . . . Consent is the means whereby equality is made politically operable.

The foregoing statement goes to the root of the meaning of both the Declaration and the Constitution. Mr. Meese here asserts that consent gives rise to the "just powers of government" only as the logical correlate—the "reciprocal"—of natural human equality. In doing so he is indeed expressing his agreement with Jefferson, Madison, and Lincoln. In doing so he is also affirming that conception of abstract truth, of reasoning about man and nature, as the very ground and basis of all political right, that we have seen so categorically rejected by the main line of conservative thought. For if consent is the reciprocal of equality, then the consent of the Declaration of Independence is *enlightened* consent, and consent properly so called cannot be granted to anything not inherently consistent with the equality of rights of the consenting individuals. If consent is the reciprocal of equality, then genuine consent implies a fundamental limitation— discernible by reason, and ultimately enforceable by the right of revolution—upon the lawful powers of governments, whether acting by majorities or otherwise. Consent properly so called does not then arise merely from agreement, from consensus, from "chartered rights" however ancient, or from community sentiment divorced from the reasoned ground of natural law and natural rights. Not long tradition nor even the free vote of a free people can make slavery an institution that can be said to be justified by the "consent of the governed." By this Mr. Meese rejects Calhoun's argument of the right of any state, at its pleasure, to secede from the Union. For Calhoun completely divorced the conception of the legal and political equality of the states from any connection with the natural equality of human beings as such. In so doing he grounded consent entirely in will as distinct from reason. In denying natural equality he denied that concept of consent as the "reciprocal" of equality affirmed by Mr. Meese. Hence, Mr. Meese places himself squarely on the side of Abraham Lincoln—as opposed to that of John C. Calhoun (and Jefferson Davis)—with regard to secession as a constitutional right. For there cannot be a constitutional right to carry out a purpose inconsistent with the ends of constitutional government—which is what eleven Southern States attempted to do in 1861.

Hence, Mr. Meese continues,

This theory of government, this philosophy of natural rights, is what made the institution of slavery intolerable. For there is nothing that one can imagine that denies the idea of natural equality as severely, as completely as slavery.

But if the institution of slavery was "intolerable," how does Mr. Meese account for its presence within the Constitution whose bicentennial we celebrate this year? Here is what he says:

> It is a common view that the Framers of the Constitution made concessions to slavery . . . But that rather common view is, in fact, a common mistake. The Constitution did *not* make fundamental concessions to slavery at the level of principle.

Mr. Meese sustains this opinion by quoting Frederick Douglass, writing in 1863, as follows:

> I hold that the federal government was never, in its essence, anything but an anti-slavery government. Abolish slavery tomorrow, and not a sentence or syllable of the Constitution need be altered. It was purposely so framed as to give no claim, no sanction to the claim of property in man . . .

With all due respect, however, this is mere hyperbole, and is not sustained by the text of the Constitution itself. One can speak of the "essence" of the antebellum federal government being "anti-slavery" only if one is thinking of the doctrine of universal human equality in the Declaration of Independence as that essence. But the Constitution of 1787 does not expressly repeat that doctrine, and the text is filled with "accidents" that are very difficult to reconcile with such an "essence." Or, to speak more precisely, the doctrine of the Declaration is present in the Constitution only if one links the opening words of the Preamble, "We the people . . ." with the "one people" (who are also "the good people of these colonies") of the Declaration. This, however, the attorney general fails to do. Failing to do so he leaves unexplained the actual provisions of the Constitution relating to slavery, above all those provisions cited by Chief Justice Taney in *Dred Scott* (as we have shown in our letter to *Policy Review*).

We have already noted the clause which counted three-fifths of a slave as a man for purposes of representation (Article I, Section 2, para. 3).[12] We must again ask, however, how can three-fifths of a person be counted, when there is no such thing in nature? Is personality a creation of positive law, or does positive law rest upon distinctions existing in nature? We cannot fail to notice that the representation to which the slaves contributed augmented the political power of their masters, and was in fact opposite to the interest of the slaves themselves. Yet it is "representatives and direct taxes" that are apportioned in Article I, section 3. This clause actually augments the representatives of the slave-owning districts at the same time that it augments their liability for direct taxes. We must take note of this fact, even if it is true that direct taxes were not levied before the Civil War. The "three-fifths" clause initiates that treatment of the "personality" of the slaves that is followed in the rest of the Constitution: which is that they are treated simultaneously as subhuman chattels and as human persons. This is notwithstanding that the definition of a chattel—as lacking a rational will—and that of a person—as possessing a rational will—are mutually exclusive.

The most powerful evidence of slavery within the Constitution—the most powerful evidence cited by Taney in *Dred Scott*—is, however, Article IV, section 2, paragraph 3.

> No person held to service or labor in one State, under the laws thereof, escaping into another, shall, in consequence of any law or regulation therein, be discharged from such service or labor, but shall be delivered up on claim of the party to whom such service or labor may be due.

The passage is preceded, in Article IV, by the "full faith and credit," the "privileges and immunities," and the criminal extradition clauses. All three are modelled with only minor variations upon parallel passages in Article IV of the Articles of Confederation. But there is no precedent in the Articles for the fugitive slave clause. This massive addition of both power and responsibility to the new government constitutes *prima facie* evidence of what was meant by a "more perfect Union." On its face, it represents a change in the fundamental law of the United States wholly favorable to slavery. Not to recognize it as such, whether by Mr. Meese or by ourselves, would be, as John Locke would say, "foolish as well as dishonest." For not only does it give federal constitutional recognition to the law of chattel slavery within the slave states, but it requires the government of the United States to assist in the enforcement of that law. This made the federal government a partner in the maintenance of the institution of slavery which it would be disingenuous to deny. But there is worse to come! The final section of Article IV of the Constitution is as follows:

> The United States shall guarantee to every State in this Union a republican form of government, and shall protect each of them against invasion; and on application of the legislature, or of the executive (when the legislature cannot be convened) against domestic violence.

Here we have the greatest single stumbling block to the proposition to which Jefferson, Madison, Lincoln, the attorney general, and I subscribe: that the principles of the Declaration of Independence are the principles of the Constitution. What is that "republican form of government" guaranteed to each state by the United States? To say that a republican form of government is sufficiently defined as one in which "No title of nobility shall be granted" would be silly and trivial. No people were ever more alive to the difference between mere names and the substance of reality than the Founding Fathers. The forbidding of titles of nobility was a necessary but far from a sufficient condition for republicanism. Jefferson once declared that

> The republican is the only form of government which is not eternally at open or secret war with the rights of mankind.[13]

"To secure these rights," e.g., to life and to liberty, is clearly the function which the form of republican government is to serve. In the light of this function, as Mr. Meese has declared, "the institution of slavery [is] intolerable." However, by declaring that the United States "shall guarantee" the republican form to every state, the Constitution implies that every state then existing was already republican. It implies thereby not only that there was no "intolerable" conflict between slavery and republicanism, but that there was no conflict at all! And still worse follows. For the same sentence enjoining the guarantee, also enjoins upon the United States the responsibility of protecting each of the states against invasion and "domestic violence." As a general proposition, one might say that this surely was a leading purpose of any "more perfect Union." But protection against "domestic violence" was also understood in 1787 to apply to any efforts by the slaves towards their own freedom. Taken in conjunction with the fugitive slave clause, it meant that the new government would use all its force to return escaped slaves to captivity, and with that same force suppress any efforts they might make towards freedom in the places of their captivity. And it would be committed to doing these things in the very Article in which it is committed also to guarantee "a republican form of government" to every state! This is the hardest of all nuts to crack, if one is successfully to oppose the Calhoun-Taney interpretation. Far more is required of us than the attorney general's simple denial that the Constitution of 1787 made any compromises on the level of principle.

Before fulfilling that requirement, however, we need to complete the case against ourselves. In the words of Lord Charnwood, the true obligation of impartiality is that one conceal no fact that tells against one's own view. Article I, Section 9 reads in part:

The migration or importation of such persons as any of the States now existing shall think proper to admit, shall not be prohibited by the Congress prior to the year one thousand eight hundred and eight . . .

Mr. Meese, in defending the antislavery character of the Constitution of 1787, says that it

made explicit provision for a time in the not-so-distant future when Congress could seek to restrict not only the slave trade but the institution itself.

But Article I, section 9 does not prohibit the foreign slave trade. On the contrary, it prohibits the prohibition of that trade by Congress for twenty years. Moreover, it permits, but does not require, the prohibition of that trade after twenty years. But what ground does Mr. Meese have for saying that it seeks to restrict, not only the foreign slave trade, but slavery itself? Some years ago, Walter Berns argued very persuasively that the word "migration" in the foregoing section of the Constitution, in addition to "importation," was intended to give Congress power over the interstate, no less than over the foreign slave trade, after twenty years.[14] Yet James Madison scotched that interpretation in the first Congress, and not even Abraham Lincoln ever claimed that the power of Congress to regulate commerce among the several states (whether on the basis of Article I, section 8 or of Article I, section 9) might be used to interfere with the interstate commerce in slaves. Lincoln implicitly accepting Madison's interpretation—took the guarantee embodied in the fugitive slave clause as a pledge not to use the commerce power as the basis of an attack upon the existing institution of slavery. There is then no justification for the attorney general's belief that the text of Article I, section 9 of the Constitution, taken by itself, is evidence of an intention to abolish slavery.[15]

How then shall we defend the antislavery character of the Constitution? We return to the attorney general's misreading of *Dred Scott*, in which he abandons the principal ground upon which the honor of the Constitution may truly be defended. "The issue in Dred Scott," Mr. Meese writes in the Dickinson speech,

was not whether slavery was right or wrong but only whether Congress had the legitimate power to keep it out of the new territories. Congress and Lincoln and Dred Scott said Congress did have that power. The Supreme

Court said it did not. By declaring the Missouri Compromise unconstitutional, the Court, in the view of some, made war inevitable.

The truth is, however, that whether slavery was right or wrong was the *only* important question in *Dred Scott*. In a letter dated December 22, 1860, Lincoln wrote to his old friend Alexander Stephens—soon to become vice president of the Confederacy—as follows:

> You think slavery is *right*, and ought to be extended; while we think it is *wrong*, and ought to be restricted. That I suppose is the rub. It certainly is the only substantial difference between us.[16]

What was "the only substantial difference" in the secession crisis was *a fortiori* "the only substantial difference" in *Dred Scott*. Taney's opinion in *Dred Scott* turned upon the judgment that those human persons denominated as chattels by the laws of the slave states remained in the legal condition of chattels after entering the Territories. They did so notwithstanding the fact that the Territories, prior to statehood, remained under the jurisdiction of the Congress, and hence under the authority of the Fifth Amendment to the Constitution, which provides that "No person shall be . . . deprived of life, liberty, or property, without due process of law . . ." The central question in *Dred Scott* was this: which took precedence when a slaveowner entered a Territory with his slave, the Negro slave's human personality, under "the laws of nature and of nature's God," or his chatteldom, under the laws of the slave state whence he came? Taney decided upon the latter, and hence decided that under the Fifth Amendment the Negro not only remained a slave in a Territory but that his owner was entitled to the full protection of the government of the United States to assure the enjoyment of his right of property in that slave. "The only power conferred," viz., on Congress by the Constitution, Taney had written, "is the power coupled with the duty of guarding and protecting the owner in his rights."[17] From the moment Taney issued this dictum, the deep South regarded any failure of the government of the United States in providing less protection to slave property than to any other kind of property in the Territories, to be an invidious discrimination between the different forms of property within the several states, a discrimination not sanctioned by the Constitution, and inconsistent with the legal and political equality of the states within the Union. Taney's opinion led directly to secession and civil war when the deep South insisted (and the upper South later followed its lead) that the government of the United States had a constitutional duty not only to permit the ingress of slavery into the Territories, but that it also had the duty to provide federal police protection of slavery there, if the Territorial government failed to supply that protection.

The first—and in some respects the greatest—of the secession crises provoked by *Dred Scott* was the withdrawal of the delegates from the deep South from the Democratic National Convention in Charleston, in May of 1860. They withdrew in protest against the refusal of the majority of the convention to adopt a plank calling for a federal slave code for the Territories. The convention, under the leadership of Senator Stephen A. Douglas (who would shortly become the convention's nominee for president) refused, clinging to Douglas's popular sovereignty doctrine, under which the protection of property of all kinds in the Territories remained the responsibility of the legislatures of the Territories—not of Congress. But Taney's opinion in *Dred Scott* had undercut Douglas's doctrine of popular sovereignty no less than the Republican doctrine of congressional exclusion. Yet Lincoln, in his debates with Douglas—and elsewhere—repeated endlessly that if Taney was right (as Douglas said that he was) in holding that the Negro slave remained a chattel in the Territories, then his owner was entitled to the protection he demanded.[18] There was only one way to resist the consequences that the delegates from the deep South drew from Taney's opinion in *Dred Scott*, and that was to deny the truth of the opinion. That opinion was in itself fatal to the idea of constitutional freedom, not because it was held by the chief justice of the United States, and a majority of the Court, but because the opinion was in itself destructive of constitutional government. In fact, the opinion would have been equally, if not more, pernicious had it been adopted by majorities in both houses of Congress as a result of the ordinary operation of the political process. We must remember that Hitler came to power by constitutional processes. In short, we must hold that the word "person" in the Fifth Amendment refers to a human person, a member of the species *homo sapiens*, without any further qualification. In the law of the Constitution the meaning of personality which must be given precedence is that of nature. Personality as such must not be looked upon as a creature of positive law. Positive law must reflect the truths of nature. If not, there is no person who might not become an "unperson" by the same positive law that regarded him as a person. And an "unperson" has no right to life, liberty, or property. In the antebellum Constitution, the positive law of the slave States, in making a person by nature into a chattel by law, reversed the presumption that governed the Constitution as a whole. Under their police power, the states might depart from the normal (because natural) understanding of the rights of Negroes, because of circumstances in which it was judged that freedom for the slaves would jeopardize what was believed to be a compelling and overriding interest in personal security of whites. Slavery, in short, was justified as a necessary evil, a temporary departure from a natural norm. Nothing in such a departure could, however, justify the extension of slavery, the bringing of this evil into places where it did not already exist. The extension of slavery could be justified only on the assumption that it was either a "positive good," or that it was morally neither a good nor evil. In short, one could justify the extension of slavery only by the explicit rejection of the doctrine of natural human equality.

The judgment in *Dred Scott* declaring the Missouri law of 1820 unconstitutional was, however, perfectly reasonable once one conceded that the question of the Negro's personality was purely a matter of positive law. It was reasonable also in the light of the legislation of 1850 providing Territorial government for Utah and New Mexico. Congress declared that the States, to be formed from these Territories, "shall be received into the Union, with or without slavery, as their constitution(s) may prescribe at the time of their admission."[19] This was in itself compromise language of utmost vacuity. The crucial question was the status of slavery in the Territories *before* the framing of the constitution with which the Territory would seek admission. And the answer to this question was one upon which the Congress could not agree. What they agreed upon was language which declared that in any cases involving titles to slaves in Utah or New Mexico, an appeal could be made directly from the Supreme Court of the Territory to the Supreme Court of the United States.[20] Although *Dred Scott* as a case did not arise in either Utah or New Mexico, Congress had by this provision of the 1850 law effectively made the Territorial question a judicial question, to be resolved by the Supreme Court of the United States.

The meaning of the "republican form of government" guaranteed to every state of the Union by the Constitution can be understood only in the light of the answer to the question of who or what are the "persons" of whom the Constitution speaks. "Persons" are represented by the electoral process, and "persons" have rights which are protected by law. There is hardly space for a comprehensive consideration of this question here.[21] Before the Civil War, however, the most acute form of this question arose in *Dred Scott*. In judging that slavery was unconstitutional in the Territories because it was morally wrong, because it violated the principles of natural justice in the Declaration of Independence, Abraham Lincoln judged that slavery in the states where it existed lawfully was an evil tolerated by necessity, not something either morally indifferent or positively good. A state might then be republican, even with slavery, so long as it was assumed that slavery as such was an evil, and that public policy was premised upon its eventual extinction. Only on such a premise could the Constitution as a whole be regarded as antislavery. I think there is ample evidence to document this understanding of the Framer's intent in the Constitution of 1787.[22] Perhaps no evidence is stronger than that provided by Calhoun—in his tendentious rejection of the Declaration—and by the testimony of Alexander Stephens, in his "cornerstone speech" quoted above. This evidence comes into view, however, only when one understands that the central question in *Dred Scott* had nothing to do with the jurisdiction of Court and Congress, but only with the question of whether slavery was right or wrong, under "the laws of nature and of nature's God."

# Attorney General Meese, the Declaration, and the Constitution

1. *Major Policy Statements of the Attorney General: Edwin Meese III 1985–1988*, U.S. Government Printing Office, 1989, pp. 14–21.
2. *Imprimis*, Hillsdale College, Hillsdale, Michigan, September 1986.
3. *Thoughts on Machiavelli*, Midway Reprint, University of Chicago Press 1984, pp 13–14.
4. See below, p. 82.
5. *This World*, Spring/Summer 1984, p. 7. See also Berns "Judicial Review and the Rights of the Laws of Nature," *Supreme Court Review* 1982, pp. 49–82, for the thesis that the rights and laws of nature, in the American Founding, are to be understood as derivative solely from Hobbes.
6. Speech at Dickinson College.
7. 410 U.S. 113 (1973).
8. *Major Statements of the Attorney General*, op. cit., pp. 31, 37.
9. On the question of the relationship of the right to life, in the Declaration of Independence, and the right to life, with respect to *Roe v Wade*, see Lewis E. Lehrman, "The Right to Life and the Restoration of the American Republic," *National Review*, Aug. 29, 1986, p. 25.
10. *Griswold v Connecticut*, 381 U.S. 479 (1965).
11. See Appendix C, pp. 77–98.
12. According to William W. Freehling (*The Road to Disunion*, Vol. 1, Oxford University Press, 1990, p. 147), in the election of 1800 "the three-fifths clause probably turned what might otherwise have been the Age of Adams into the Age of Jefferson . . . Jefferson swept the South's extra electors 12–2. If no three-fifths clause had existed and house apportionment had been based strictly on white numbers, Adams would have likely squeaked by, 63–61.
13. *The Writings of Thomas Jefferson* (Ford ed.), Vol. V, p. 147.

14. "The Constitution and the Migration of Slaves," 78 *Yale Law Journal*, p. 198 (1968).
15. In his Peoria speech (October 1854) Lincoln did take note of the fact that in 1803 the Congress "passed a law in aid of one or two State laws, in restraint of the internal slave trade." *CW* II, p. 275. Since the laws in question were "in aid of State Laws" this does not affect the general point made above.
16. CW, IV, p. 160.
17. 60 U.S. at 401. Also *Commager*, p. 345.
18. See especially the joint debate at Alton, Illinois, October 15, 1858 (the last of the seven). Lincoln:

> I defy any man to make an argument that will justify unfriendly legislation to deprive a slaveholder of his right to hold his slaves in a Territory, that will not equally, in all its length, breadth and thickness furnish an argument for nullifying the fugitive slave law. Why there is not such an abolitionist in the nation as Douglas, after all. CW, III, p. 318.

19. *Commager*, p. 321.
20. *U.S. Statutes at Large*, Vol. 9, pp. 455, 456 (for Utah).
21. On whether the principles of the Declaration of Independence are republican, see my *How to Think About the American Revolution* (Carolina Academic Press, 1978), especially, pp. 118–140.
22. No better evidence can be offered than the testimony of James Madison, in *Federalist* # 54.

> . . . it is only under the pretext that the laws have transformed the negroes into subjects of property that a place is disputed them in the computation of numbers; and it is admitted that if the laws were to restore the rights which have been taken away, the negroes could no longer be refused an equal share of representation with the other inhabitants.

Clearly the "rights which have been taken away" are the rights of the laws of nature. And clearly, the restoration of these rights by positive law must be the intention of any government properly called republican.

# Are These Truths Now, Or Have They Ever Been, Self-Evident?: The Declaration of Independence and the United States of America on Their 211th Anniversary

## HARRY V. JAFFA

Leszek Kolakowski, professor at the University of Chicago and fellow of All Souls College, Oxford, began the fifteenth annual Jefferson lecture, in Washington, D.C., in April of 1986, as follows:

> Consider what is probably the most famous single sentence ever written in the Western hemisphere. "We hold these truth to be self-evident, that all men are created equal, that they are endowed by their Creator with certain unalienable rights, that among these are Life, Liberty, and the Pursuit of Happiness". . . .
> Immediately, we notice that what seemed self-evident to Thomas Jefferson would appear either patently false or meaningless and superstitious to most great men who keep shaping our political imagination: to Aristotle, Machiavelli, Hobbes, Marx and all his followers, Nietzsche, Weber, and for that matter, to most contemporary political theorists.

I would not speak as confidently as Professor Kolakowski does of how those "great men" would have viewed the central proposition of the Declaration (or, for that matter, of the Gettysburg Address), but Thomas Jefferson, in his unsophisticated innocence, said that in the Declaration, he was placing "before mankind the common sense of the subject," and that what he wrote was an "expression of the American mind." He did not, he said, aim at originality of any kind, but sought to give expression to the

75

"harmonizing sentiments of the day, whether expressed in conversations, in letters, in printed essays or in the elementary books of public right, as Aristotle, Cicero, Locke, Sidney, etc."[1] Aristotle, I might observe, although long known as "*The* Philosopher," was not a professional philosopher like Professor Kolakowski. And professional philosophers are notoriously incapable of understanding the language of ordinary human beings, above all the language of ordinary citizens, in the way that these human beings and citizens themselves understand it. But Jefferson expressed the convictions of his fellow citizens in language which, although extraordinary in its eloquence, was recognized instantly by them as representing their deepest convictions. These convictions were at once peculiarly and profoundly American, while peculiarly and profoundly representative of a natural law tradition—a belief in objective norms of conduct for both men and nations that lies at the root of everything making our human existence civilized. But this was in the days before professional philosophers, or "contemporary political theorists," had mined and sapped the vitality of ordinary language and the common sense moral judgments upon which they, like Aristotle, had once relied.

Just before he died, Jefferson wrote that

All eyes are opened, or opening, to the rights of man . . . [and to] the palpable truth, that the mass of mankind has not been born with saddles on their backs, nor a favored few, booted and spurred, ready to ride them. . .[2]

A professional philosopher would, of course, set to work immediately to point out that horses are not born with saddles on their backs either. But Jefferson knew, and his fellow-citizens knew, that the aristocrats of Paris on the eve of the French Revolution regarded their peasants in much the same light as human beings in general looked upon horses—as an inferior order in nature whose highest purpose in this world was to serve as beasts of burden to their masters. Jefferson's fellow-citizens understood him to say, as we might still understand him once we shake off the miasma of the professional philosophers, that there is no such thing as a natural or divine right of any man or class of human beings to rule others. Legitimate government arises solely from a voluntary agreement embodied in laws binding rulers and ruled by which it is understood that all government exists to secure equally the natural rights of every citizen and the safety and happiness of all. Government is not for the private advantage of any self-anointed individual or class. Republican government, the only form of government intrinsically compatible with the rights of man, is government in which those who live under the law share equally in making the law they live under, and in which those who make the law are equally subject to the laws that they make.

Let me elaborate upon the meaning of "all men are created equal," the proposition that Abraham Lincoln called the "father of all moral principle among us," and the "central idea" from which all the minor thoughts of our political tradition radiate. This proposition, although in terms no intelligent human being in 1776 failed to understand, is indeed elliptical. "Man equals man" would be true only because tautological. Much is owing to the word "created," which implies a "Creator," who is mentioned almost immediately. (No doubt this is what leads Professor Kolakowski to think that the sentence would be looked upon as "superstitious" by the cognoscenti.) "Created equal" implies a relationship between man and man as arises from a contemplation, not of man only, but of the whole Creation. In looking at man in the light of the whole Creation, we see him in comparison with what is lower than humankind and with what is higher.

Although the existence of God is certainly implied by the proposition that all men are created equal, it is not necessarily implied. What is necessarily implied is not the Creator, but Creation. In 1776 America, the language of the Bible was the language of the ordinary man. There were sophisticates, as Jefferson knew, who had considered that evolution, or the doctrine of the eternity of the universe, might offer alternative explanations to that of the Bible. To everyone, however, Creation meant the world whose existence is known to us by sense perception, and hence by such common nouns, or universals, as light and darkness, heaven and earth, land and water, the birds of the air, the fish of the sea, and the moving things, the animals, upon the land. Indeed, the world become an object of knowledge, the world accessible to the senses, and from the senses to the mind, was once familiar to most Americans as the world of which they had read in the first chapter of Genesis. To believe that this world actually exists is to believe nothing more than the evidence of our senses. (Professional philosophers, or most of them, at least since Hume, have systematically denied that our senses tell us anything reliable about the external world.) To believe that this same world is the work of the living God may be an act of faith. But for Jefferson and his fellow-countrymen there was at least no disagreement that such a world existed. Nor was there any disagreement that the facts of this world, "these truths," held the key to the right ordering of man's moral and political life. In the 26th verse of the first chapter of Genesis, God said

Let us make man in our image, after our likeness, and let them have dominion over the fish of the sea, and over the birds of the air, and over the cattle, and over all the earth, and over every creeping thing that creeps upon the earth.

For Jefferson and his contemporaries, there was no question but that the differences in natures, differences inherent in the distinctions the Bible itself draws between man and beast, had implications (as in the Bible) that were no less moral than metaphysical. Man had both power and right to exercise the dominion that the Bible said had been given to him by God. With that power and right went, of course, responsibility. Man might not gratuitously destroy the resources of the lower nature (John Locke said that it would be foolish as well as dishonest to do so): but he might use them prudently for his own ends. There were no ends of the lower nature higher than the ends that they might serve in serving man. But the rule of a man over his horse or dog is by nature. Nature itself marks out which is to be master, and which is to be servant. This, believe it or not, is self-evident!

I recall a debate once with a prominent conservative who denied that the proposition that all men are created equal (or any other nonmathematical proposition) was in truth self-evident. Finally, I asked him, was it not self-evident to him that he was not a dog? His answer was no. To this I responded that, since he did not know that he was not a dog, he might not know that I was not a fire hydrant, and I warned him to keep his distance. I might have added that even if he did not know that he was not a dog, there was no dog living that was so ignorant! In truth, however, we have here an example of someone saying what he could not possibly have believed, unless of course he had become insane. But professional philosophers, and this man suffering from this delusion, make a point of pretending to forget what they actually know in order to maintain their credentials as professional skeptics. By this they disprove the possibility of philosophy itself as it was before the amateurs of wisdom were replaced by professionals. But such peculiarities should have no weight with normal human beings who can see instantly and without argument that men are really not dogs, or gods.

The equality of man proclaimed by the Declaration of Independence is to be understood first of all by comparison with the inequality that characterizes man's relationship with the lower orders of living beings. In comparison with this inequality there is nothing more evident, in the familiar words of John Locke, than that no human being is marked out by nature to rule, while others are marked out for subjection. This does not mean that human beings are not distinguished by such important marks as age, beauty, strength, intelligence, or virtue. Nor does it mean that these differences, or some of them, are not important in determining who should rule. But the question who shall rule becomes relevant only after the recognition that it is the rights of the whole community, and of every member of that community for whose sake the government is instituted. Who has courage, moderation, justice, and wisdom to best serve the community becomes a question only after the community is formed, and the rule of law enshrined within it. It becomes a question only after there is an agreement, voluntarily entered into, that the right each man has by nature to govern himself will become valuable to him only as he has transferred the exercise of that right to a government. And a legitimate government is essentially the by-product of an understanding that henceforth the power of all will defend the right of each. Under the legitimate government of a civil society, every man obeys the law for the reason that in doing so he understands that he is enabling it to defend him, to secure his rights. This so-called "social contract" is the greatest of all practical applications of the golden rule: "Do unto others as you would have others do unto you."[3] Human virtue or excellence does indeed give some human beings, men or women, the right to hold office, the right to rule. But it is a right that can become valuable only as it is recognized as a right, not to privileges, but to service. It is a right which comes to light by virtue of the prior recognition of the equality of mankind and of the rule of law constructed upon its premises.

That the political process by which such recognition is made may be an extremely defective one was recognized by Winston Churchill when he said that "Democracy is the very worst form of government, except all those other forms that have been tried . . ."[4] Its defects reflect the fact that if man is higher than the beasts, he is very far from being God (or a god). The idea of God belongs to natural, no less than to revealed theology. This idea is formed by reflecting upon the resemblances, as well as the differences, of man and beast. Man is a compound of reason and passion. In beasts, instinct controls the mechanism of the passions. Beasts are controlled by reason only when they are controlled by human beings. But man, although possessed by the appetites of the instincts, knows that he has, by reason of his reason, the ability to control and direct instinct and passion alike. And he (that is, except professional philosophers) knows that with his reason he has been given the ability to know good and bad, just and unjust. That his reason is fallible is true: indeed, in nothing so much does man show that he is a rational animal than in recognizing such fallibility. This fallibility is moreover twofold: first, in the difficulty in knowing amidst the complexity of human affairs what is just or right; second, in doing what is just or right. Knowing what is just or right also is exposed to a twofold difficulty: the one arising from the obscurity that sometimes lies in the subject; the other (and most common) arising not from the subject, but from the influence of the passions upon reason. King David did not see his sin when he seized the wife of Uriah the Hittite and compassed Uriah's death.[5] But when the prophet Nathan presented his own story to him disguised in a parable, he was exceedingly wrathful against the offender. Only then did the prophet tell him who the offender was. Then the king judged his own offense even as God judged it, showing that the faculty of judgment was in him, when his passion did not obscure the truth. It is precisely because the human soul is a compound of reason and passion that human wisdom prescribes the rule of law as fitting the human condition. For the glory of the rule of law is that it enables human reason to take into account the defects of human nature and to transcend those very defects by taking them into account. While human government needs human wisdom in the highest degree, even the wisest men may be subject to that partiality that endangers justice. And even assuming perfect impartiality, just judgments will be questioned by those against whom the judgments are given. It is essential to the stability of government that those judgments be given not as the personal wisdom of the wise, but of the law. Only thus can governments command the confidence of the governed.

The vote of the wise is then always for the rule, not of the wise, but of the law. It is in the making of laws that the highest wisdom of the race is manifested. The meaning of law is to be found, above all, in the understanding of the difference between man and God. It is this difference, the reciprocal so to speak of the difference between man and beast, which completes the meaning of what it is that we hold to be self-evident. For further evidence of its self-evidence to our ancestors, evidence that is as compelling today as it was in 1776, we turn to the good citizens of Malden, Massachusetts, who on May 27, 1776, instructing their representatives in the Continental Congress on a Declaration of Independence, wrote that an American republic

> is the only form of government which we wish to see established; for we can never be willingly subject to any other King than he who, being possessed of infinite wisdom, goodness, and rectitude, is alone fit to possess unlimited power.[6]

The equality of mankind is then to be understood in the light of this twofold inequality: the inequality of man and the lower order of Creation, on the one hand, and the inequality of man and God, on the other. The contemplation of the very differences between man and beast instructs us in what it is that makes man by nature the master of beast. But the contemplation of these same differences instructs us in man's imperfections. Man's wisdom, goodness, and rectitude are forever limited by the fact that his passions are often at war with his reason, and his self-interest with his goodness and rectitude. Hence it is that no man is good enough, in Lincoln's words, to govern another without his consent. For consent is the reciprocal of equality. And in the reciprocity of equality and consent we find that ground of morality that Lincoln found in the great proposition. The consent arising from equality assures, as we said at the outset, that those who live under the law will share in making the law they live under, and that those who make the law must live under the law that they make. Constitutions are devices—inventions of prudence—to carry into practice these principles. But except in the light of these principles, a constitution is an empty vessel that can be a means to any ends whatever. The utopianism that lies at the root of all modern totalitarianism always presupposes the denial or abandonment of human nature and that "great chain of being" within which such nature is discovered. Unfortunately, such abandonment is equally characteristic of present-day conservatism and of present-day liberalism. A wise constitution—such as ours—ceases to be wise the moment it is separated from the principles that give it life. Man is by nature the master of what is below him in the order of Creation. But his ability to govern himself rests upon his recognition of what God is, and hence of what he is not. That "all men are created equal" means then that man is neither beast nor God. This is indeed a self-evident truth. It is the ground of our Constitution, as it is the ground of all constitutionalism. It is the supreme justification for the rule of law and, as Abraham Lincoln said, the greatest barrier against despotism ever conceived by the human mind.[7]

# Are These Truths Now, or Have They Ever Been, Self-Evident?

1. Letter to Henry Lee (1825), *The Writings of Thomas Jefferson*, Ford, ed., Vol. 10, p. 343.
2. Letter to Roger Weightman, June 24, 1826, Ford, ed., Vol. X, p. 390.
3. Matthew 7:12.
4. *The Oxford Book of Quotations* (3rd ed., 1979), p. 150.
5. 2 Samuel 12: i–13.
6. Commager, pp. 97, 98.
7. CW, III, p. 376.

# Original Intent and Justice Rehnquist

## HARRY V. JAFFA

The *Wall Street Journal* (August 7, 1986) carried an editorial page article by Professor Bruce C. Ledewitz of Duquesne University Law School entitled "The Questions Rehnquist Hasn't Had to Answer." Professor Ledewitz's theme is expressed in the following excerpts.

> We are about to elevate to Chief Justice . . . the greatest judicial skeptic since Oliver Wendell Holmes. How truly ironic it is that Ronald Reagan, Jerry Falwell, and Pat Robertson so strongly support . . . a man who does not believe there is such a thing as right and wrong . . . Justice Rehnquist's jurisprudence may be characterized as legal positivism founded upon moral skepticism. He is unable to affirm any substantive value as true or good, and so his constitutional interpretation retreats to the search for an unobtainable, objective analysis of the "original intention" of the Framers of the Constitution. Justice Rehnquist represents not a triumph of conservatism, but a triumph of modernism. As such, he is merely the most extreme and intellectually honest representative of twentieth-century American law.

I think Professor Ledewitz goes beyond his evidence in saying that Justice Rehnquist "does not believe there is such a thing as right and wrong." A man may think that there is no foundation in reason for the distinction between right and wrong—and this does, in fact, seem to be the Rehnquist view—while still believing in the distinction itself. Carl Becker declared that

> To ask whether the natural rights philosophy of the Declaration of Independence is true or false is essentially a meaningless question.[1]

Yet notwithstanding Becker's belief that reason was impotent to answer the question of whether the philosophy of the Declaration was true or false, he was himself passionately committed to it. To Becker, the Declaration expressed a "fundamental reality"[2] for which he, no less than George Washington, was willing to fight. However, in saying that the philosophy of the Declaration was grounded in a "fundamental reality," Becker exposed himself to the objection that he was calling something a fundamental reality that he also asserted to be inaccessible to reason. If reality is inaccessible to reason, how can we say it is reality? Becker was well aware, when he came to write the Introduction to the 1942 edition of his book (originally published twenty years earlier), that the followers of Adolf Hitler looked upon the doctrines of their leader with the same passionate commitment that Becker looked to those of the signers of the Declaration. What then made the reality of Thomas Jefferson more fundamental than that of Adolf Hitler? Becker could not say, even as he declared his unqualified opposition to National Socialism.

This same difficulty must be faced by Justice Rehnquist. It is, moreover, discouraging to learn that the new chief justice—in opposition to Attorney General Meese who, however, appears to be completely unaware of this opposition—does not, in the least, believe in the principles of the Declaration of Independence either as myth or as reality. He does not believe that we can say that despotism is intrinsically evil. Nor does he believe that we can say that free government and the rule of law are intrinsically good. All he can say about the former, e.g., is that Hitler's regime is in accordance with Nazi value judgments, just as Bolshevik government is in accordance with Bolshevik value judgments. In saying that Justice Rehnquist "retreats to the search for an unobtainable, objective analysis of the 'original intention' of the Framers of the Constitution," Professor Ledewitz is imputing to Justice Rehnquist an impossibility. No one can at one and the same time be a legal positivist and an adherent of the original intentions of the Framers. For the Framers were very far from being either moral skeptics or legal positivists. Their commitment to the natural rights and natural law doctrine of the Declaration of Independence represented the most profound of their original intentions. It is simply a self-contradiction to assert that Justice Rehnquist is committed to the original intentions of the Framers and to his version of moral skepticism and legal positivism, although this self-contradiction may indeed be Rehnquist's, not Ledewitz's. But Professor Ledewitz is himself profoundly mistaken, if he means to say that a genuinely "objective analysis of the 'original intentions' of the Framers of the Constitution" is "unobtainable." It would be unobtainable only if their understanding of the laws of nature, and of the rights of man under these laws, was merely subjective. But suppose that the Framers' understanding of the difference between despotic and nondespotic government—recorded for all time in the Declaration of Independence—is the true understanding. Suppose that their views of tyranny and despotism were not merely subjectively held ("We hold these truths . . .) but objectively valid. Would not an analysis of these views constitute an objective account of their most profound and guiding intention in establishing a Constitution to secure the blessings of liberty to themselves and their posterity?

In his celebrated essay on "The Notion of a Living Constitution," Justice Rehnquist takes to task those who

> ignore . . . the nature of political value judgments in a democratic society. If such a society adopts a constitution and incorporates in that constitution safeguards for individual liberty, these safeguards do indeed take on a generalized moral rightness or goodness. They assume a general social acceptance neither because of any intrinsic worth nor because of any unique origins in someone's idea of natural justice but instead simply because they have been incorporated in a constitution by the people.[3]

Here is the heart of that jurisprudence that Professor Ledewitz rightly calls into question. A constitution—and law generally—is something "a society adopts," but which prior to adoption has no "intrinsic worth." Among those things that prior to adoption have no intrinsic worth are "safeguards for individual liberty." But Rehnquist does not say that even after adoption these safeguards, and what they protect or secure, *are* morally right or are possessed of intrinsic worth. He says they "take on" a kind of moral rightness. This means no more than that they acquire a kind of veneer of opinion in their favor. I am sure that Justice Rehnquist abhors as much as I do the midnight visits of a Gestapo or of a KGB and the removal of citizens from their homes to prisons merely because they are *personae non grata* to the government. But Rehnquist will not say that such arbitrariness is unreasonable, and wrong because unreasonable. All he will say is that it is not in accordance with our value judgments, although thoroughly in accordance with Nazi or Bolshevik value judgments. But Nazi and Bolshevik value judgments are incorporated in Nazi and Bolshevik constitutions just as "our" value judgments are incorporated in our Constitution. And all value judgments qua value judgments are created equal! Rehnquist may perhaps object that Nazi and Bolshevik constitutions are not acts of "the people." But they *are* acts of the people, according to the Nazi and Bolshevik definitions of what constitutes a people.

The American definition of what constitutes a people is to be found in the Declaration of Independence and asserts that by the laws of nature and of nature's God all men are equally endowed by their Creator with certain unalienable rights, and that to secure these rights a people institute a government. By the principles of the Declaration a people that ignores these rights in instituting its government are not, properly speaking, a people. The Declaration preserves Plato's, Cicero's, and Augustine's distinction between a people, properly so called, and gang of robbers. But for Justice Rehnquist, this distinction is itself just another "value judgment." By the principles of the Declaration—by the principles that constitute the "original intentions" of the Framers of the Constitution—the moral rightness of "the safeguards of individual liberty"—is prior to and independent of its incorporation in a constitution by the people. That moral rightness was found by the signers of the Declaration *a priori* in "the laws of nature and of nature's God." If that moral rightness was not antecedent to the Constitution, it could not exist in the Constitution. One cannot repeat too often that the Founding Fathers were neither moral skeptics nor legal positivists.

As I have noted, Justice Rehnquist has given no hint how something that has no intrinsic worth becomes endowed with "generalized moral rightness" merely because it has been "incorporated in a constitution by a people." The only intelligible meaning one can assign to such an assertion is that a powerful government can compel behavior consistent with its laws. This means no more than that in obeying the laws we are yielding to a superior force or that justice is the interest of the stronger. But to most of us—and most certainly to the Founding Fathers of this nation—"moral rightness" implies something very different. Morality implies voluntary action, not compulsion. Constitutional morality implies that the individual rights safeguarded by the Constitution deserve a conscientious respect and not merely a recognition that their disregard will be punished. Rehnquist's assertion that adoption by a people, or incorporation into a constitution, transforms "value judgments" into "a form of moral goodness" is a non sequitur. Someone who says that constitutional morality has no other foundation than "value judgments" has nothing to say to the man who does not share such "value judgments." If such a man is strong enough to disobey the law of the Constitution with impunity, and can do so, whether by corruption, craft, or force, why should he not do so? To say that constitutional morality has no other foundation than "value judgments" is to say that the very idea of constitutional morality is an illusion.

Bear in mind, moreover, that when we speak of safeguarding individual rights or liberty, what we mean, first and foremost, is preventing offenses against persons, property, and society such as assault, murder, theft, rape, and perjury. According to Rehnquist's logic, to call these things evil expresses "only personal moral judgments until in some way [they are] given the sanction of law." In saying this, however, Rehnquist defies the common sense of the human race, and incidentally of the common law, that denies that these things are offensive merely as "personal moral judgments." They are believed to be prohibited because they are wrong and not wrong because prohibited. Nor can it be said that these prohibitions merely represent rules that have been useful: useful to whom? Or that these prohibitions contribute to the greatest good of the greatest number. The argument from utility does not say why anyone should obey these prohibitions who finds it useful or pleasant to disobey them, and who prefers what he regards as his own good to that of any number greater than one. The argument of American constitutionalism, the argument of Jefferson and Lincoln and the Declaration of Independence, is not merely a utilitarian argument. It is not only an argument as to why the people have an interest in preventing tyranny. It is ultimately an argument as to why potential tyrants have an interest (a self-interest rightly understood, in Tocqueville's phrase) in preferring morality to tyranny. It is an argument as to why potential tyrants ought not to become actual tyrants no matter what opportunities for despotism may arise. Lincoln's argument against American Negro slavery was a demonstration that the principles of the Declaration condemned any and every form of despotism. That argument held that government under the rule of law is in the interest of every man, because it is in accordance with the nature of man, a nature that defines the limits within which every human being must seek his good if he is to enjoy that good. It is an argument that tyranny is bad for human beings and hence is as bad for the tyrant as for anyone else. Jefferson's diatribe against slavery is his *Notes on Virginia* held that slavery corrupted the morals—and hence the well-being—of the masters.[4] In this he only made explicit what was implicit in the argument of the Declaration.

It is, of course, the common sense of mankind that morality, or at least that part of morality that consists in respecting the rights of others, is for the most part ineffectual without law. But morality without law is no more ineffectual than law without morality. It is utterly absurd to suppose that "value judgments" become morality by being adopted into law. If law, or what is called law, became the authority for morality, as Rehnquist seems to think, then Nazi or Bolshevik (or cannibal) law would result in the same "generalized moral rightness or goodness" as the law of a constitutional democracy.

Perhaps Rehnquist would say that he was speaking only of "the nature of political value judgments *in a democratic society.*" However, the sequel to the foregoing passage in "The Notion of a Living Constitution" is as follows:

> Beyond the Constitution and the laws in our society, there is simply no basis other than the individual conscience of the citizen that may serve as a platform for the launching of moral judgments. There is no conceivable way in which I can logically demonstrate to you that the judgments of my conscience are superior to the judgments of your conscience, and vice versa.

The key assertion here is that "there is no conceivable way in which I can logically demonstrate to you that the judgments of my conscience are superior to the judgments of your conscience . . ." This is not a characterization of "political value judgments" only, or merely "in a democratic society." It is an assertion concerning all such judgments by the human mind, everywhere and always. Rehnquist implies by this that he knows no way in which any moral judgment, which is bound to be a "value judgment," can be "logically" shown to be superior to any other moral judgment. Since all choices among regimes, choices between Nazi or Bolshevik or cannibal or constitutionally democratic regimes, are value judgments, no such choice can be founded upon reason. This would mean, for example, that there is no way in which the principle of a system of laws guaranteeing religious liberty could be "logically" shown to be superior to a system of religious bigotry. Yet Jefferson and Madison, whose argument is an extension of the argument of the Declaration of Independence, thought that the Virginia Statute of Religious Liberty did precisely what Rehnquist thinks impossible. Rehnquist utterly disregards the reasoned convictions of Jefferson and Madison (and of the Founding Fathers generally), which formed the guarantees of the First Amendment, but quotes with reverent admiration the words of Justice Holmes "in his famous essay on natural law":

> Certitude is not a test of certainty. We have been cocksure of many things that were not so . . . One cannot be wrenched from the rocky crevices into which one is thrown for many years without feeling that one is attacked in one's life.

What we most love and revere generally is determined by early associations. I love granite rocks and barberry bushes, no doubt because with them were my earliest joys that reach back through the past eternity of my life. But while one's experience thus makes certain preferences dogmatic for oneself, recognition of how they came to be so leaves one able to see that others, poor souls, may be equally dogmatic about something else. And again this means skepticism.[5]

This notable and notorious passage from Holmes's writing extolling as it does the virtues of skepticism is swallowed by Justice Rehnquist without the slightest trace of skepticism. Can any reasonable human being put moral choice on the same level as the preference for granite rocks and barberry bushes? The preference for granite rocks and barberry bushes, however passionate, is not a moral preference. Such preferences, Holmes says, are "generally . . . determined by early association." If that is so, it is largely because they are matters of indifference to everyone except the person holding them. But to say that one's opinions on matters of right and wrong, e.g., the choice in 1940 between the cause if Adolf Hitler and the cause of Winston Churchill, are arrived at (not *determined*) simply by one's "early associations" is to deny any role whatever to human reason or human freedom in shaping human destiny. In fact, Holmes contradicts himself in the foregoing. He says that "recognition of how they came to be," namely, "our preferences," enables us to be tolerant of the opinions of others. But learning to be tolerant of others would not be possible if our opinions are simply determined by early associations, an Oedipus complex, or anything else. If we can learn to be tolerant of some opinions that are different from our own, why cannot we learn to be tolerant of other opinions? Does not tolerance, by its very nature, engender an opposition to intolerance, especially for racial and religious bigotry?

Holmes tells us that reason can emancipate us from simple preference for our own opinions by showing us that different opinions have the same cause. However, once someone recognizes that opinions on moral questions differ, is he not bound to wonder which of the contrary opinions is right, or whether there is not a noncontradictory truth underlying the many contrary and sometimes contradictory opinions? That is the thesis of Aristotle's *Nicomachean Ethics*. This thesis is reflected in the Declaration of Independence when it speaks of "a decent respect to the opinions of mankind." It is what Abraham Lincoln had in mind when he referred to the proposition of human equality in the Declaration as "an abstract truth, applicable to all men and all times." That there is a nonsubjective morality of man as man, is the necessary presupposition of what we call Western civilization; it is the essential constitutive element of that civilization, a civilization that, despite its name, is not understood as related to a particular place any more than to a particular time. That there is such a morality is also an absolutely necessary presupposition of the Constitution of the United States of America, Holmes and his disciple Rehnquist to the contrary notwithstanding. Any discussion of "original intent" apart from this morality is ultimately vain.

Holmes (and Rehnquist) cannot grant to human reason the first step in the emancipation of the self from a crude self-preference and then declare that at that point all reasoning must stop. (This, however, is what they do!) If we were simply or merely "determined" in our moral preferences or "value judgments" we would not be capable of that "recognition" of what is common to ourselves and others of which Holmes himself speaks. Indeed, that recognition leads us away from mere self-preference. Emancipation from mere self-preference is then an essential element of our humanity. It is evidence that we are not determined in our moral choices and that human freedom is a reality. Political freedom would be meaningless if there were not moral freedom, and moral freedom would be meaningless if we were moved to action merely by sense perception, memory, and imagination, which is what is implied in Holmes's passage about barberry bushes and early associations.

Moral freedom must be based upon a metaphysical freedom of the mind that moves from mere sense perception to reason and from reason to moral choice. The comparison of alternative courses of action that constitutes moral freedom must follow from a fundamental comparison of ideas. In this comparison, the human mind makes a judgment as to the correspondence of abstract ideas with concrete phenomena. One decides whether this is a plant or an animal, and whether this animal belongs to this species or that one. (E.g., whether a Negro or a Jew is properly placed in the species *homo sapiens* with a white man or a gentile.) Only by this comparison of ideas can one say that despotism, which fits the relationship of man to beast, does not fit the relationship of man to man. This is the reasoning process that underlies and is embedded in the condemnation of despotism in the Declaration of Independence. Without it, all our ideas of constitutional development are vain and profitless. To repeat, the ability of the human mind to recognize truth ("We hold these truths to be self-evident . . .") is the metaphysical ground of the morality of the Declaration of Independence. The universality of the rights of humankind is the ground of all our constitutional morality because it rests upon the recognition that reason is the defining characteristic of the human species. But we cannot assert man's humanity as the ground of his rights, while denying the reality of human freedom grounded upon abstract reasoning in making human choices.

"Certitude is not the test of certainty" is one of those sounding truisms that often does more to obscure than to reveal the thought that it attempts to express. Leo Strauss expressed the same thought with much greater clarity when he declared that there is no difference between the subjective certainty of the philosopher and that of the madman.[6] Put somewhat differently, we might say that Napoleon himself was never more certain that he was Napoleon than the poor inmate in the lunatic asylum who thinks he is Napoleon. But notwithstanding the affectations of Holmesian skepticism, most of us will continue to believe in the objective difference between being the historical Napoleon and imagining one is Napoleon. More generally, we must attend to the objective difference between what is subjectively persuasive to the sane man, and what is subjectively persuasive to the lunatic. This difference turns upon the quality of the evidence and reasoning that supports the opinions of the one as opposed to the other. It implies that the sane man's assertions can be confirmed by his peers and that in the process of intersubjective communication the grounds of objective certainty can be discovered.

Someone familiar with the processes by which merely subjective opinions may be replaced with objective truth knows the difficulties and uncertainties that attend the exercise of human reason. For this reason the sane man is apt to be moderate in his moral judgments. Moderation, moreover, is itself a moral virtue. All the moral virtues are, moreover, in the service of human reason, including, most certainly, courage. Holmes served honorably in the Union army in the Civil War and was wounded three times. It would be a travesty of his sacrifices, as of the sacrifices of countless others, among them those who came to their final rest upon the battlefield of Gettysburg, to say that they were "determined" in what they did by their early associations or to imply that their or Holmes's "preference" for the Union cause—for the cause of human freedom in comparison with the cause of human slavery—was not qualitatively different from a childhood preference for granite rocks and barberry bushes.

The passage from Holmes's essay in natural law ends as a eulogy to the virtues of skepticism. But neither Holmes nor his disciple Rehnquist seems aware of the genuine meaning of that word. A skeptic is one who inquires. Inquiry, however, presupposes doubt or awareness of ignorance. Skepticism implies *a priori* both doubt (or an awareness of ignorance) of what one knows and faith or hope that by inquiring one can remedy that defect.

One is not a genuine skeptic, if one is certain *a priori* that one's doubt or ignorance cannot be remedied by any process of thinking. If one is perfectly convinced, as Rehnquist appears to be, that no one can employ reason ("logically demonstrate") to discover that any one moral judgment is superior to any other (e.g., that one is justified in calling Hitler's or Stalin's regimes "evil empires"), then he is "logically" free to adopt whatever moral judgment appeals to him, secure in the conviction that reason can never testify against him. This radical skepticism, which is a false skepticism, leads directly to radical dogmatism. If reason cannot rule against the most insane moral preferences, then there is no reason not to adopt whatever opinions are most agreeable to one's passions.

I am reminded of a story in one of Hitler's biographies of Himmler informing the Fuehrer that the boxcar floors in which thousands of Jews were transported could be covered with lime and burn the Jews to death before they reached their destination. Their deaths, moreover, would occur in circumstances of utmost pain and suffering as they would be steadily and continuously seared by the corrosive chemicals while packed and pressed together in unimaginable stench and filth. As the story was told, both Hitler and Himmler began to laugh and laugh ever more uproariously as they contemplated the agonies of the Jews in the boxcars. Torturing and killing Jews were the "granite rocks and barberry bushes" that they loved and from which they derived great enjoyment. According to Justice Rehnquist, however, "there is no conceivable way . . . [to] logically demonstrate" that the judgments of our consciences on this matter are superior to the judgments of Hitler and Himmler. I conclude that radical skepticism as patronized by Holmes and Rehnquist is something whereby any reasoned conviction concerning morality is abolished. Such skepticism is equally compatible with moral indifference or moral fanaticism. But it has no connection with moderation or tolerance—that "decent respect to the opinions of mankind" that forms the core of the constitutional morality of the American Founding.

Rehnquist also denounces the idea of a "living constitution." By this he acknowledges a living constitution to be one in which "the federal judiciary may address themselves to a social problem simply because other branches of government have failed or refused to do so." Rehnquist turns most appropriately to John Marshall for his understanding of judicial review under the Constitution.

All who have studied law, and many who have not, are familiar with John Marshall's classic defense of judicial review, in his opinion for the Court in *Marbury v. Madison* . . .

The ultimate source of authority in this nation, Marshall said, is not Congress, not the states, nor for that matter the Supreme Court of the United States. The people are the ultimate source of authority; they have parcelled out the authority that originally resided entirely with them by adopting the original Constitution and by later amending it.

It is worthwhile, at this point, to quote the key sentence by the great chief justice in *Marbury*.[7]

> That the people have an original right to establish, for their future government, such principles as, in their opinion, shall most conduce to their own happiness is the basis on which the whole American fabric has been erected.

Now there is not the slightest room for doubt that when Marshall penned those words, he had in mind, and everyone to whom he addressed those words had in mind, the following:

> That . . . it is the right of the people . . . to institute new government, laying its foundation on such principles and organizing its powers in such form as to them shall seem most likely to effect their safety and happiness.

The resemblance of the language of the Declaration and that of *Marbury* can no more be coincidental than the resemblance of the language of the Declaration to certain passages in Locke's *Second Treatise*. But according to the Declaration, and Locke, the original right of the people as a collectivity is not original right simply. Original right simply is grasped from the proposition that every human being is endowed by his Creator with certain unalienable rights. A people, properly so called, arises from a social contract or compact by which individual human beings agree to form a civil society, a civil society in which citizens consent to be governed for the better securing of their original rights. The Massachusetts Bill of Rights of 1780 makes explicit the doctrine of the Declaration of Independence when it says that

> The body politic is formed by a voluntary association of individuals; it is a social compact by which the whole people covenants with each citizen and each citizen with the whole people that all shall be governed by certain laws for the common good.[8]

The underlying premise of this compact or contract is, as with every valid contract, the equality of the contracting parties. And so Massachusetts declares, as the United States had already declared, that

all men are born free and equal, and have certain natural, essential, and
unalienable rights . . .

To repeat, individual human beings could not form a body politic, nor have
a government whose "just powers" are derived from their consent, had
there not been such an equality in the original endowment of rights. It is
that equal endowment of natural rights under "the laws of nature and of
nature's God," which makes "the people of the United States" (like the
people of the state of Massachusetts, or of any other state) something other
than a mere numerical aggregate. Within the framework of the laws of the
United States and of the several states, corporations may be chartered, but
only for lawful purposes. And so, men may incorporate themselves into
civil societies, but again only for purposes which are lawful by "the laws of
nature and of nature's God." The Framers of our Constitution clearly and
wisely believed that there must be a lawfulness antecedent to positive law
for positive law itself to be lawful. When Justice Rehnquist says that
constitutions do not have any ground in any "idea of natural justice," he is
repudiating the Framers, and John Marshall who followed them.
    Here we are bound to say, although mortified to say it, that the new
Chief Justice of the United States accuses himself of not understanding the
very first premise of the Constitution of the United States. By this we do
not imply that he does not understand many things about the Constitution. But viewed either ordinally or cardinally, the very first premise of the
Constitution is found in the words "We the people of the United
States . . ." with which is joined "do ordain and establish this Constitution
for the United States of America." By Justice Rehnquist's own testimony,
given on the authority of Chief Justice Marshall, the first constitutional
premise is that "the people are the ultimate source of authority . . ." But
Justice Rehnquist does not understand, indeed he denies, the only ground
upon which the people may be possessed of this authority. For "the
people," that is to say, "the good people," who became independent, are
not a collection of predators, a gang of thieves. They are not the "people"
of the Preamble merely because they have called themselves by that name.
They are a people because they have incorporated into their association
with each other the morality of "the laws of nature."[9] These laws determine their purpose "to secure these rights" and imply duties corresponding to these rights. The government they may establish, however much in
accordance with what they may think conducive to "their safety and
happiness," is not a government which may trample upon the equal rights
of others at their pleasure. A people ignorant of their rights under the laws

of nature are ignorant of the means by which they may enjoy their freedom. This is what Jefferson had in mind when he declared that for a nation to expect "to be ignorant and free" is to expect "what never was and never will be."[10] Majority rule is a rule for free government only to the extent to which the majority understands itself as the trustee of the rights of the minority or minorities. "An elective despotism was not the government we fought for"[11] is one of the axiomatic maxims of the authors of the Declaration of Independence. To understand why this is so is vital to understanding the Constitution.

To repeat, what is first about the Constitution is the fact and source of its authority. Before the Constitution, before the Articles of Confederation, it had become necessary for "one People" who were the "good people of these colonies" "to assume . . . the separate and equal station to which the laws of nature and of nature's God entitle them." By their own understanding, they had every right to which those laws entitled them, but no right to anything to which those self-same laws did *not* entitle them. Nor could they have consented to any government inconsistent with their remaining a "good people." The "consent of the governed" from which "the just powers" of government are derived is intelligent or enlightened consent; it is not anything whatever to which men may agree. There is no such thing as a right of the people under the laws of nature to form Nazi or Bolshevik constitutions. Nor was there a right simply to the institution of chattel slavery, albeit that institution did receive certain guarantees under the 1787 Constitution.

But these guarantees rested upon the premise that slavery was an inherited evil so deeply rooted that it would require some generations to overcome. The Father of the Constitution declared that the words "slave" and "slavery" were carefully kept out of the text of the Constitution (by elaborate euphemisms) so that when the institution had finally disappeared, no trace of its former existence would remain upon the Constitution's face. It was hardly remarkable that a nation of slaveholders, upon becoming independent, did not instantly abolish slavery. The true miracle of the Founding is to be found in the fact that a nation of slaveholders, upon becoming independent, declared that all men are created equal, and thereby made the abolition of slavery a moral and logical necessity. In so doing, the nation of slaveholders emancipated itself from the barberry bush and granite rocks of its upbringing and declared that what was right in itself would henceforth be the "standard maxim" for the free society the people were founding. That it took fourscore and seven years to abolish the great anomaly of the Founding is hardly surprising in itself. But it could never have happened had not the original intent of the Constitution—in the laws of nature—prevailed. Thus Abraham Lincoln in his debates with Stephen A. Douglas:

> [Judge Douglas] contends that whatever community wants slaves has a right to have them. So they have, if it is not a wrong. But if it is a wrong, he cannot say people have a right to do wrong.[12]

Lincoln, like Marshal, interpreting the Declaration as the source of the principles of the Constitution, finds the authority of the people to be subject to the moral law and not prior to or independent of that law. Neither Marshall, nor Lincoln, nor any of the Founding Fathers ever imagined that morality was a function of "social acceptance" in the wake of the adoption of a constitution. On the contrary, a constitution was adopted because of the prior acceptance of a morality whose foundation was in the reason that recognized certain truths as self-evident. The will of the people was a rational and moral will, not a mere will. Here we leave aside the matter of morality as the revealed will of God (as in the Bible), although certainly the great majority of the American people at the Founding believed that morality was known both by unassisted human reason and by divine revelation. We leave it aside, not because it is unimportant, but because the American people at the Founding believed that the laws of nature instructed by unassisted human reason and the revealed laws of God as they bore on human conduct were largely in agreement with each other, if not altogether identical. They did not deem it wise to have this moral consensus undermined by sectarian theological differences. But the moral consensus itself, understood by the light of nature and reason and supported in society by the teachings of the different churches, was an absolutely necessary condition of the idea of self-government.

We would challenge Mr. Rehnquist—or anyone else—to find a single document from the period of the framing and ratifying of the Constitution that supports the moral skepticism and legal positivism that he shares with the late Justice Holmes. Indeed, it was the rise of this skepticism and positivism in the generation before the Civil War that repudiated the Founders' view of slavery. It was the repudiation of the moral foundation of constitutionalism that led to the view that either slavery or freedom are wholly matters of positive right, because natural right does not exist. This was the deepest reason for the Civil War, and it is appalling that the underlying view of the defenders of slavery should now predominate in the Union preserved only by the destruction of slavery.

Justice Rehnquist continues "The Notion of a Living Constitution" as follows:

In addition, Marshall said that if the popular branches of government—state legislatures, the Congress, and the Presidency—are operating within the authority granted to them by the Constitution, their judgment and not that of the Court must obviously prevail. When these branches overstep the authority given them by the Constitution, *or invade protected individual rights*, and a constitutional challenge to their action is raised in a lawsuit brought in federal court, the Court must prefer the Constitution to the government acts [emphasis added].[13]

Rehnquist then goes on to declare that the

apogee of the living Constitution doctrine during the nineteenth century was the Supreme Court's decision in *Dred Scott v. Sanford* . . . The Court, speaking through Chief Justice Taney, held that Congress was without power to legislate upon the issue of slavery even in a territory governed by it . . . Congress, the Court held, was virtually powerless to check or limit the spread of the institution of slavery . . .

The Court in *Dred Scott* decided that all of the agitation and debate in Congress over the Missouri Compromise in 1820, over the Wilmot Proviso a generation later, and over the Kansas-Nebraska Act in 1854, had amounted to absolutely nothing . . . The decision had never been one that Congress was entitled to make; it was one that the Court alone, in construing the Constitution, was empowered to make.

Rehnquist has misunderstood the case of *Dred Scott* in ways so closely resembling those of the attorney general[14] that we strongly suspect that he is the source of Mr. Meese's errors. Since *Dred Scott* turns altogether upon the meaning of "We the people . . ." it is a case that Rehnquist is unable to understand.

First notice that Rehnquist's historical survey jumps from the Wilmot Proviso of 1847 to the Kansas-Nebraska Act of 1854, omitting mention of the Compromise of 1850 and the territorial legislation of that year. As noted above, in the Acts for Utah and New Mexico of that year, Congress was unable to resolve the question of the legal status of slavery in those Territories. There were at least three major differing opinions on the question, the description and explanation of which would require a separate monograph. The acts provided that when states formed from these Territories were admitted into the Union, they would be so admitted "with or without slavery, as their constitution may prescribe at the time of admission." This is what Stephen A. Douglas in 1854 claimed as the justification of his doctrine of popular sovereignty, which he incorporated into the Kansas-Nebraska Act of that year. As we have shown above, however, Congress in 1850[15] left entirely unsettled the crucial question of what the legal status of slavery in the Territory would be *before* the adoption of a state constitution. It was generally understood that the status of slavery *during* the Territorial period would determine whether the state constitution, drawn up preparatory to entry into the Union, would allow slavery or prohibit it. That the "game" would be won or lost during the Territorial period was something Lincoln never tired of repeating during his speeches after 1854. It also bears repetition that Congress in the 1850 Territorial legislation provided that any question involving title to a slave in a territory might be appealed from the Supreme Court of the Territory directly to the Supreme Court of the United States. In doing this, Congress, it might be said, laid the baby on the doorstep of the Supreme Court, rang the bell, and then disappeared. For Justice Rehnquist to speak of *Dred Scott* as if it were a case purely and simply of judicial usurpation is sheer misreading of history.

The Court's decision, and Taney's opinion in *Dred Scott*, were not merely gratuitous interventions in the political process. *Dred Scott* did not declare unconstitutional any law currently in effect. Lincoln's House Divided speech of 1858—which Justice Rehnquist ignores—had charged a conspiracy to extend slavery by four "workmen"—Stephen, Franklin, Roger, and James—two presidents, a United States senator, and a chief justice of the United States. It was against this alleged conspiracy, involving all three branches of the government, and not any unilateral action by the Supreme Court, that Lincoln directed his arguments in 1858 and thereafter. Rehnquist quotes from Lincoln's inaugural address as follows.

> The candid citizen must confess that if the policy of the government, upon vital questions affecting the whole people, is to be irrevocably fixed by decisions of the Supreme Court, the instant they are made, in ordinary litigation between parties in personal actions, the people will have ceased to be their own rulers, having to that extent practically resigned their government into the hands of that eminent tribunal.[16]

But Lincoln was not, as Rehnquist seems to think, here attacking the Court for having usurped powers belonging to the Congress. He disagreed with the Court's decision in *Dred Scott*, and his reasons for so doing were developed in virtually all his speeches in and after 1857, especially in his debates with Douglas. In his inaugural address, however, his argument is directed against those in the political community who were attempting to exploit the Court's decision in order to force the extension of slavery upon the country *through* the political process. As we have noted, it was the secession of the delegates from the Deep South from the Charleston Convention, and from the National Democratic party, that set the pattern followed later by those same states in attempting to "secede" from the Union after Lincoln's election. In the secession ordinances, it was the refusal of the North to accept Taney's *obiter dicta* in *Dred Scott* as if they had been the very words of the Constitution that constituted one of the paramount grievances justifying secession. It was this use of *Dred Scott*, rather than *Dred Scott* itself, to which Lincoln objected when he spoke the words Rehnquist quoted. This is plain from what Lincoln says in the immediate sequel.

> Nor is there in this view any assault upon the Court or the judges. It is a duty from which they may not shrink, to decide cases properly brought before them; and it is no fault of theirs if others seek to turn their decisions to political purposes.

To repeat, it was the "political purposes" of "others," not the Court's decision as such, against which Lincoln's argument is directed in his inaugural.

In speaking of the Kansas-Nebraska Act, which repealed the Missouri Compromise restriction of slavery three years before the Court declared it unconstitutional, Rehnquist writes as follows:

> The enactment of the bill was, of course, a victory for the proslavery forces in Congress and a defeat for those opposed to the expansion of slavery. The great majority of the antislavery groups, as strongly as they felt about the matter, were still willing to live with the decision of Congress. They were not willing, however, to live with the *Dred Scott* decision.

Rehnquist's version of antebellum American history is, to speak mildly, confused. We are uncertain as to what he means by the expression "willing to live with." The repeal of the slavery restriction in the Missouri Compromise in the Kansas-Nebraska bill raised the greatest political fire storm the republic has ever known. It brought Abraham Lincoln back into politics, and it led to the formation of the Republican party, which was known for most of its first year of existence simply as the Anti-Nebraska party. Its original purpose, and for some time its sole purpose, was to restore the Missouri Compromise restriction of slavery. We would not call this being "willing to live with the decision of Congress." By 1857, the Republicans, and the free-soil coalition they engendered, already foresaw the victory that had evaded them in the presidential election of 1856. When the *Dred Scott* decision was handed down in 1857, all free-soilers howled their maledictions upon the heads of Taney and his cohorts. But the soberer ones among them, like Lincoln, made no attack upon the Court as an institution, nor did they declare there was anything in the political process they were "not willing . . . to live with . . . " They meant to do no more, nor less, than to have the decision reversed by a future Court by means of electing a president and Congress of their persuasion. It was the proslavery party that could be said to be unwilling to "live with" its purely legal results, but demanded that its *obiter dicta* be accepted by all parts of the political community as rules binding upon their political actions. It was the proslavery groups who, as we have noted, insisted that the political branches end their discussion of slavery in the Territories and accept Taney's opinion as binding upon their political decision-making. Their answer to the refusal of the American people to accept Taney's *dicta* as a political rule was secession. That is what "not willing to live with" something really meant. It had nothing whatever to do with the question of the Court vis-à-vis that of the Congress.

We have noted above Rehnquist's assertion that according to Taney's opinion "Congress was without power to legislate upon the issue of slavery even in a Territory governed by it . . ." But this is inaccurate. Taney said that Congress *did* have the power of legislation, "coupled with the duty of guarding and protecting the owner in his rights."[17] It could legislate *for* slavery in the Territories, but not against it. This was the reverse of the free soil view, which was Lincoln's, that Congress could legislate *against* slavery in the Territories, but not for it. At no point did the dispute take the form which Rehnquist would like to think that it took: which branch of the government, the Congress or the Court, ought to decide the question of slavery in the Territories. Before secession, each side wanted Congress to adopt its view of the legality of slavery in the Territories, and each side wished, if possible, to have its view endorsed by the Court. Abraham Lincoln would have had no objection whatever to any alleged intrusion of the judiciary into political or legislative decision-making had the Taney Court decided *Dred Scott* in accordance with the free soil understanding of the Constitution. Lincoln would have been happy to have the Court decide both that Dred Scott was free and that Congress had the power, coupled with the duty, of guaranteeing freedom in the Territories. Lincoln believed that the natural condition of the Territories was freedom, but that it was prudent for Congress to make explicit what was implicit constitutional law.

What then was the fundamental question in *Dred Scott?* Although I have written often on this subject,[18] what I have written seems not to have penetrated the emanations or penumbrae that surrounded the Meese Justice Department, or its judicial nominees, including Mr. Justice Rehnquist. Briefly, the Fifth Amendment to the Constitution declares that "No person shall be . . . deprived of life, liberty, or property, without due process of law . . . " Taney said that the Constitution recognized the right of property in slaves by declaring in Article IV that

No person held to service or labor in one State, under the laws thereof, escaping into another, shall, in consequence of any law or regulation therein, be discharged from such service or labor, but shall be delivered up on claim of the party to whom such service or labor shall be due.

This represented constitutional recognition of the laws of the slave states that regarded those persons "held to service or labor" (viz., slaves) as chattel property. Moreover, in Article I, Section 9 the Constitution declares that

The migration or importation of such persons as any of the States now existing shall think proper to admit shall not be prohibited by the Congress prior to the year one thousand eight hundred and eight . . .

This unrepealable limitation[19] for twenty years upon the power of Congress "to regulate commerce with foreign nations and among the several states . . ." was evidence, said Taney, that a Negro slave was regarded at the time the Constitution was adopted, as "an ordinary article of merchandise and property." One might cavil that since no other form of property is thus singled out in the text of the Constitution it would have been more proper for Taney to have called it *extraordinary.* Although one might object, as Lincoln did, that the right to property in a slave is not *expressly* affirmed in the Constitution, one can hardly deny that it is affirmed by necessary implication. If the government of the United States is compelled by the Constitution to recognize the validity of those State laws guaranteeing the right of property in a slave and is expressly empowered to assist in the enforcement of those laws, then one can certainly say that the right of property in slaves of the aforesaid States is recognized by the Constitution. But "no person [may] . . . be deprived" of property "without due process of law." To deprive a citizen of a slave State of his particular form of chattel property because he set foot in a United States Territory with it would certainly seem to qualify as a violation of the right to property protected by the Fifth Amendment.

Justice Rehnquist, in a passage already quoted, has declared on the authority of John Marshall, that when "the popular branches of government . . . overstep the authority given them by the Constitution . . . *or invade protected individual rights,*" the Court may act to protect those rights. Now this is precisely what Taney believed the Court was doing in the case of *Dred Scott.* Looked at in this light, a law excluding slavery from a Territory would be as surely unconstitutional as an *ex post facto* law. Whatever one may say of Taney's opinion, at this point, it cannot be censured as a usurpation of power by the judiciary.

What then *was* wrong with Taney's opinion in *Dred Scott?* The heart of Taney's opinion was the judgment that constitutionally the Negro was not a man but a chattel. Everything that Taney had to say about the power of Congress over slavery in the Territories followed from his opinion that the slave was the chattel property of his owner and that the owner's right in that property was protected by the Fifth Amendment. How can Rehnquist object? According to Justice Rehnquist, all moral judgments are merely "value judgments" and take on a "generalized moral rightness" only by being incorporated into a constitution by a people. The constitutions of the slave States in 1857 reflected their peoples' "value judgments" that Negroes—whether free or slave—were "so far inferior that they had no rights which the white man was bound to respect." For this reason they "might justly and lawfully be reduced to slavery . . ." These "value judgments" having been duly incorporated into the State constitutions had, we may presume, "take[n] on a form of moral goodness because they [had] been enacted into positive law." "[I]ndividual value judgments," that is to say moral judgments of any kind, have no "independent virtue . . . [beyond] any particular citizen's own scale of values." That is to say, prior to enactment into positive law, no value judgment (e.g., antislavery) has any more authority than any other value judgment (e.g., proslavery). All moral judgments, according to Rehnquist, are in a Hobbesian state of nature with respect to each other. Apart from positive law (viz., the will of the sovereign) no action (as for example enslaving another human being) is unjust. The opinion that the Negro is subhuman has therefore equal authority *a priori* with the opinion that he is human, and whichever of these opinions gains "sufficiently numerous" adherents will become the positive law and have the authority of the sovereign people behind it. By this fact alone can it be called morally obligatory. The truth is that Justice Rehnquist has no ground whatever to object to Taney's opinion in *Dred Scott*. Indeed, Taney's opinion, as we have restated it, is the only one consistent with Justice Rehnquist's premises.[20]

But Rehnquist and Taney's premises are wrong. That the Negro is a human being is a matter of fact and not of opinion. In the Fugitive Slave Clause of the Constitution, the slave is referred to, not as a chattel, but as a person. He is "a person held to service or labor," but a person nonetheless. The State laws holding him to such service or labor called him a chattel, *but the Constitution does not*. Even the aforesaid State laws were not themselves consistent in holding him a chattel. The very essence of chatteldom is the absence of a rational will. A chattel—e.g., a dog, a cow, or a pig—cannot be held responsible for its actions. Only an adult human being, one who has reached the age of consent, can be held responsible for his actions, *because he is responsible for knowing the difference between right and wrong*. Yet Negro slaves, not to mention free Negroes, were held responsible for a variety of felonies under the criminal codes of all the slave States. As such they were, however inconsistently, "persons" in the sense of the Fifth Amendment. But what about free Negroes? Who ever heard, Lincoln asked, of free horses or free cattle? And what about laws forbidding miscegenation? Who ever heard about laws forbidding the marriage of whites and cattle?

Fundamental to the law of the Constitution was the fact of the Negro's personality—in short, his humanity. But it cannot be repeated too often that a person cannot be a chattel, and a chattel cannot be a person. Viewed in this light, one may say that the antebellum Constitution was self-contradictory, if not schizophrenic. But it is an axiom of constitutional interpretation that a self-contradictory interpretation is a mistaken interpretation, because one cannot obey a self-contradictory law. That the Negro belongs to the species *homo sapiens* is as undeniable as that any white (or yellow, red, or brown) individual belongs to this species. His rationality—his use of the parts of speech which characterize human language—is indicative of the essence of his humanity; the color of his skin, a mere accident. What makes the slaughter of cattle for food not only lawful, but moral, is the subhumanity of their species. What makes the gratuitous killing of a black man murder is the fact that his species is the same as that of the man who murders him. But what makes the killing of a black man murder, makes the enslavement of him theft. For to enslave a man is to steal his labor and the fruit of his labor. This is theft apart from all positive law as much as murder is murder apart from all positive law. Indeed, to take the whole of the fruit of a man's labor for his whole life makes murder and theft, in any final sense, morally indistinguishable. Hence Lincoln denied that the moral condemnation of slavery required any positive law. The ground of this condemnation was antecedent to any positive law or to any human pronouncement whatever.

> Slavery is founded in the selfishness of man's nature—opposition to it in his love of justice. These principles are an eternal antagonism. Repeal the Missouri compromise, repeal all compromises, repeal the Declaration of Independence, repeal all past history, you still cannot repeal human nature.[21]

Taney's opinion in *Dred Scott* was wrong for one paramount reason. He did not see that the Constitution, grounded in the principles of the Declaration of Independence, reflected a standard of justice other than positive law. He did not see that the word "person" meant any human person, whatever his race, creed, or nation.

In December 1860 Lincoln wrote to his old friend Alexander Stephens—who, he hoped, was still a friend and not an enemy—that the South would be in no more danger from his administration than from that of Washington. He would no more interfere with slavery in the slave States than had any president before him. But that, he said, did not meet Southern objections. "You think slavery is right and ought to be extended, while we think it is wrong and ought to be restricted. That, I suppose, is the rub."[22]

That was indeed the "rub" that led to secession and civil war. It was also the "rub" in *Dred Scott*. Until Justice Rehnquist learns this lesson from Abraham Lincoln, he will not understand the original intentions of those who framed and those who ratified the Constitution of the United States.

# Original Intent and Justice Rehnquist

1. *The Declaration of Independence: A Study in the History of Ideas*, New York, Knopf, 1942, p. 277.
2. Ibid., p. xvi.
3. 54 *Texas Law Review*, p. 693 (1976). This is the revised text of the 9th annual Will E. Orgain Lecture, delivered at the University of Texas Law School on March 12, 1976. Reprinted in *Taking the Constitution Seriously: Essays on the Constitution and Constitutional Law*, Gary L. McDowell, ed., Kendall/Hunt, 1981, pp. 69–79. All references to Justice Rehnquist are from this essay.
4. Query XVIII. *The Complete Jefferson*, Saul Padover, ed., Tudor, New York, 1943, p. 677.
5. "Living Constitution," op. cit., citing O. W. Holmes, "Natural Law," in *Collected Papers* (1920), pp. 310, 311.
6. The philosopher cannot lead an absolutely solitary life because legitimate "subjective certainty" and the "subjective certainty" of the lunatic are indistinguishable. Genuine certainty must be "intersubjective."

    *On Tyranny*, by Leo Strauss, revised and expanded edition, edited by Victor Gourevitch and Michael S. Roth, the Free Press, 1991, p. 194.
7. *Marbury v. Madison*, 5 U.S. at 175–176.
8. Commager, *Documents of American History*, Vol. I. to 1898. Henry Steele Commager, 7th edition, Appleton-Century-Crofts, New York, 1963 (Hereafter, *Commager*), p. 107.
9. On July 4, 1776, the Continental Congress, after "appealing to the Supreme Judge of the world for the rectitude of our intentions" declared independence "in the name and by authority of the good people of these colonies . . . " This was a moral act by a moral people.
10. *The Writings of Thomas Jefferson*, Ford ed., Vol. X, p. 4.
11. The words quoted are from the *Notes on Virginia*, but are also cited by Madison in the 48th *Federalist*.

12. *The Collected Works of Abraham Lincoln*, Roy P. Basler, ed., Rutgers University Press, 1953 (Hereafter, *CW*), III, p. 315.
13. Emphasis added.
14. As dexcribed above both in the letter to *Policy Review* and in Appendix A.
15. *Commager*, p. 321.
16. *CW*, IV, p. 268.
17. *Commager*, p. 345.
18. See especially *Crisis of the House Divided* (1959), University of Chicago Press reprint, 1984.
19. Article V of the Constitution reads, in part:

    that no amendment which may be made prior to the year one thousand eight hundred and eight shall in any manner affect the first and fourth clauses in the ninth section of the first article . . .

20. If it were true, as Justice Rehnquist maintains, that there is no basis in reason for moral judgments, then the idea of a rational will in man would be an illusion. This would collapse the distinction between persons and chattels.
21. *CW*, II, p. 279.
22. *CW*, IV, p. 160.

# Three Critiques

# Judicial Conscience and Natural Rights:
# A Reply to Professor Jaffa

BRUCE LEDEWITZ

Professor Jaffa's paper represents an important step in interpreting the United States Constitution.[1] Professor Jaffa demonstrates that the advocates of historical interpretation are in fact descendants of John C. Calhoun rather than of the Framers, that they consider Edmund Burke, but not Abraham Lincoln, a "Defender of the Constitution,"[2] and that they read God and natural rights endowed by man's Creator out of the Constitution.

Professor Jaffa's critique is all the more devastating because he is himself a conservative and a historian. Because he is a conservative, the reader senses his sympathy for what Attorney General Meese, Chief Justice Rehnquist, and Judge Robert Bork are attempting to accomplish. Because he is a historian, Professor Jaffa, like his predecessor in many ways, Edward Corwin, approaches the politically charged field of constitutional interpretation with the trustworthy attitude of the scholar, rather than that of the advocate.

Despite my admiration for both his undertaking and the soundness of his results, I confess an impatience with his paper. I would like to understand his critique at the point of actually interpreting the Constitution. If, as it appears at various points in his text, Professor Jaffa agrees with the votes cast by the Calhounites on current issues before the Supreme Court, how is it that their flawed methodology can yield reliable results? Is *Dred Scott v. Sanford*[3] the last case in which a proper understanding of original intent mattered? Is slavery the last issue on which the Framers may be said to have spoken a word of liberation?

My subject is this gap in Professor Jaffa's paper between the consciousness of the Framers and the practice of judicial review today. The understanding that Professor Jaffa brings to the intent of the Framers is one that opens up the Constitution to the call of justice. Professor Jaffa's Framers are not enemies of the poor and the oppressed, the criminal defendant and the homosexual. Nor are they protecters of the rich and powerful, the washed and the comfortable.

Professor Jaffa begins with *Dred Scott*.[4] For conservatives today, *Dred Scott* represents the unfortunate triumph of moralism in judicial review. Because Chief Justice Taney did not stick to the principles of original intent, but instead responded to the passions of the day, he condemned blacks as mere property, which Congress then must protect as property in the Territories.

Professor Jaffa asserts that this conservative account is false. Taney was in no sense responding to the passions of the day. Taney was in fact interpreting the Constitution precisely in accordance with original intent as Meese and the others understand that concept. In analyzing the rights of black people, Taney considered the Constitution to be no more than positive law.

Here, according to Professor Jaffa, was Taney's great error and the great error of today's conservatives. Though faithful in a sense to the constitutional text and its treatment of slavery, Taney failed to deal with the "genuine principles" of the Constitution that are found in the Declaration of Independence.[5] It is in the light of the equality of all men, a light binding on the constitutional interpretation, that *Dred Scott* stands condemned.

Professor Jaffa's analysis of *Dred Scott* illustrates a fundamental ambiguity about original intent that permeates his paper. In his view, Taney did not rely on any sort of Framers' intent. In determining the Constitution's view of blacks, Taney looked at the text of the Constitution, noted its obvious acceptance of slavery, and concluded from the text that blacks had no rights that the white man was bound to recognize.[6] This approach may be called textual intent, and Taney's account of the text's intent is said by Professor Jaffa to be a plausible one.[7]

In contrast to, or in amplification of, the method of textual intent, one might employ original intent, asking what was the intent behind the text. "Original intent" employed in this fashion might mean the views of the Framers on the issue at hand. For example, their attitude toward blacks. On the other hand, "original intent" might refer instead to the intent of the Framers generally in creating the Constitution. For purposes of this paper, I will call the first, specific intent, and the second, general intent.

Professor Jaffa is criticizing Taney for ignoring the Framers' general intent, not for ignoring the Framers' specific intent concerning the status of blacks as human beings. This criticism may at first seem odd. Taney was wrong in *Dred Scott* in terms of specific intent as Professor Jaffa demonstrates.[8] Madison and Jefferson clearly believed blacks were human beings entitled to the inherent rights of all men. But Professor Jaffa criticizes Taney for misinterpreting the Declaration of Independence, not for ignoring the opinion of those who framed the Constitution's proslavery clauses. For Professor Jaffa, the Declaration of Independence is the lens through which the text of the Constitution must always be studied, however clear the text seems to be. After all, in the case of blacks, the text was relatively clear and could be read fairly as racist. Thus Professor Jaffa is arguing for the method of general intent; he is not proposing to consult the Framers on the specific issues that come before the Supreme Court today.[9]

What was the Framers' general intent as revealed in the Declaration of Independence? Professor Jaffa states that the Framers' primary purpose was the creation of a government that would "secure" certain rights.[10] Indeed, "to secure these rights" was viewed by the Framers as the sole legitimate purpose of any government.[11] The Framers were attempting to establish in positive law "[t]he primacy of rights and of right, understood in the light of the laws of nature . . ."[12] Professor Jaffa describes these rights: "These rights were the unalienable rights with which all men have been equally 'endowed by their creator' under 'the laws of nature and of nature's God."[13] Certain of these rights are denominated in the Declaration of Independence: "Life, Liberty and the Pursuit of Happiness." For Professor Jaffa the Declaration is not merely a precatory document to be trotted out for Fourth of July speeches. Rather, he calls the Declaration "the most fundamental dimension of the law of the Constitution."[14]

Professor Jaffa's major example, *Dred Scott*, illustrates the role that he thinks general intent should play in interpreting the Constitution. The Declaration's assumption of basic human equality represents the Constitution's "genuine" principle on the issue of slavery. The doctrine of the inequality of blacks, strongly supported by hints in the constitutional text, should be considered a mere compromise with transient political forces.

Professor Jaffa's main purpose is to show that neither today's conservatives nor today's liberals understand and follow original intent. The conservatives who claim to embody original intent do not understand "what . . . original intent was."[15] They are "antagonists" of original intent.[16] because, like the apologists for slavery of an earlier time, they "rejected the ground of the Constitution in natural justice. . . ."[17]

At much less length, Professor Jaffa criticizes liberal jurisprudence on precisely the same ground, that liberals reject "natural rights teaching."[18] Because the individual has no inherent rights that the majority is bound to respect, liberals seeking to enhance liberty must refer to an evolving conscience of a future, reformed "scientific" society."[19] Conservatives and liberals, thus "stand upon common ground."[20] That ground turns out, jurisprudentially, to be a positivist vision of law that grounds authority in the will of the people, either today's will or that of tomorrow.

What are the implications of this powerful critique? What sort of jurisprudence would result from a modern commitment to the natural law principles of the Declaration of Independence?

Professor Jaffa does not expressly venture onto this ground. Unfortunately, his implied prescription for conservatives is to accept an antiquated natural rights outlook, and for liberals, to abandon the search for a modern one.

To see the first point, imagine Professor Jaffa addressing Chief Justice Rehnquist, the "pure legal positivist."[21] Chief Justice Rehnquist would assert that there are no "self-evident truths," that there is no accessibility to a divine intention for humankind, and, thus, no endowed rights.[22] Or at least Chief Justice Rehnquist would say that if people disagree about these matters, discussion must be closed. At the point of disagreement, there is nothing more than subjective preference, which may or may not be backed by power.[23]

Professor Jaffa associates the Framers with a different view of the universe. According to this view, political science and law are capable of uncovering a "true understanding"[24] of the individual and her relation to society. There are principles, "truths 'applicable to all men and all times,' " [25] that Chief Justice Rehnquist must accept if he wishes to interpret the Constitution in accordance with original intent.

It is not clear how Professor Jaffa would like Chief Justice Rehnquist to respond to his position. If the chief justice examines modern philosophy, history, anthropology and, yes, even science, as well as his own being and concludes that this claim about eternal truth is incoherent, an echo of a less sophisticated time, he can hardly will himself to believe otherwise. Professor Jaffa obviously agrees with the Framers that their views are self-evident. But Professor Jaffa knows he is addressing an audience in which no one else is persuaded.[26]

This is precisely the dilemma John Hart Ely brilliantly described in *Democracy and Distrust*.[27] In assessing a hypothetical natural law jurisprudence, Ely asked what we would do with a constitutional provision protecting ghosts. How could we who know that there are no such things attempt to interpret the Constitution as if we did believe in ghosts and apply the implications of ghost-belief? Such an undertaking would be self-defeating. Because we do not believe in ghosts, an appropriate application of a ghost provision would be beyond us.

Chief Justice Rehnquist, who does not believe in the ghost of natural law, seems to have two intellectually honest options if he were to accept Professor Jaffa's account of the Framers' views. One option would be to abandon original intent altogether and to find some other basis to interpret the Constitution. Chief Justice Rehnquist would reject this approach because in his view only original intent is a ground beyond subjective judicial will. The second option, the one the Chief Justice usually attempts to utilize,[28] is to find in history the Framers' views, their "personal judgments upon contingent matters," on a particular issue before the Supreme Court.[29] The advantage of this approach is that such specific intent is sometimes reasonably ascertainable and thus serves to limit the judiciary's otherwise plenary power to rule at will.

Professor Jaffa's paper demonstrates that the second option is an illusion because specific intent is not true to the Framers' larger purposes. In that sense, it is not an original intent methodology at all. Thus, even if Chief Justice Rehnquist could establish, for example, that the Framers thought Congress possessed the authority to proscribe abortions, the Supreme Court should not enforce that specific judgment if, under today's circumstances, to do so would violate the Framers' understanding of equality and liberty. We must understand "what principles of moral and political philosophy guided" the Framers[30] before we make legal judgments in which the constitutional text is silent or ambiguous. Furthermore, Chief Justice Rehnquist's underlying and implied idea, that if there is no clear textual prohibition, government may act, is an excellent illustration that specific intent without a larger framework is dangerous. The Framers did not assume that, generally, government could act. They assumed the converse, that, generally, individuals could act. Thus, there is no genuine constitutional presumption against judicial action when the Constitution's text is not a clear guide.

Professor Jaffa does not argue for such specific intent. Nor, of course, is he proposing to abandon original intent. Professor Jaffa wants conservatives to subscribe to the "true" understanding of original intent[31] both because this is a legitimate method of interpretation and, more important, because the Framers' views of man and morality are themselves eternally true.

But what sense does this call for a return to the "true" understanding of original intent make when addressed to people who, in good faith, find original intent to be gibberish? Here we would expect Professor Jaffa to show that the Framers' views are true and that modern critics of natural rights are wrong. He avoids this effort, however. Perhaps he feels that, as a historian, it is not his place. Or perhaps he imagines that once conservatives understand "what the original intent was," they will come to believe it. This is a forlorn hope.

What Professor Jaffa seems to urge, instead, is that judges rely upon the Declaration of Independence whether they believe in self-evident truths or not. It is clear that the Framers were committed to equality, life, liberty, and property. It is also clear that the Framers presumed that individual preferences in these realms would govern even against the pronouncements of majoritarian governments. If we cannot believe what they believed, we can at least follow loyally where the Framers led.

This approach, to act as if we believed, turns today's conservatives into a generation of atheists carrying forward a tradition of theism. And it turns the truths of the Declaration into principles we decide to accept *as if* true. What do such pretenders do, however, with disputes about the implications of equality, liberty, and property? Professor Jaffa provides no answer to this crucial question. But judging from Professor Jaffa's criticism of judicial activism and legislation,[32] his determination to avoid any new applications of the Declaration of Independence, it is obvious that we are to find answers in Aristotle and Cicero, and if not in them directly, in them as interpreted by the Framers' generation.

Professor Jaffa demonstrates this tendency in his reference to racial quotas in appendix A.[33] Attorney General Meese asserts that racial quotas are unconstitutional as a violation of equality. With this Professor Jaffa agrees. But we know this, asserts Professor Jaffa, only from the perspective of "the Declaration's understanding of equality."[34]

I assume that the "Declaration's understanding" means simply the views of Madison and Jefferson, or of their teachers Aristotle and Cicero, regarding the meaning and portent of equality. But this historical approach treats the Declaration as a document frozen in time. The authority of the Declaration's assertions cannot be based on age, but on their truth. But if truth is the ground of their authority, we cannot avoid asking ourselves what is the nature of the equality we may all justly claim from birth and what are its consequences. That is, we must ask this question of ourselves and not just of Aristotle, Cicero, Madison, and Jefferson. I have no love for quotas, but real questions of moral right and political policy cannot be handled by quotes from the ancients about abstractions like equality.

Self-conscious emulation is not natural law. Nor is it true to the Framers' intent. It is an archaeological dig into the remnants of natural law. It is an attempt to hold human understanding still at a certain point in time. Neither a judge nor a legal thinker can be true to the tradition of natural law unless it lives in her. Merely to appeal to equality without commitment to the reality of equality, its self-evident quality, is to celebrate the shell without the substance. And the results that such an antiquated method purports to yield cannot do justice to the living tradition that the Declaration of Independence celebrated. It is not that Aristotle is not to be consulted; it is rather that we have seen and experienced some truth since then. It is dangerous to attempt to apply the insights of old literally.

But Professor Jaffa discourages any contemporary attempt to live within the principles of the Declaration of Independence. He is wedded to antiquity. The problem for Professor Jaffa is that he wishes to be true to an original intent that is revolutionary in its call for natural justice, but also wants to restrict carefully the implications of original intent.

Professor Jaffa takes pains to insulate himself from what he calls judicial activism. His methods of limitation are first, fidelity to the text; second, opposition to judicial "evolutionary conscience"; and third, the requirement of corporate judicial action. For those who consider the principles of the Declaration of Independence to be true, these negative techniques interfere with an attempt to practice the constitutional tradition bequeathed to us by the Framers.

Professor Jaffa makes the textual point in a discussion of Justice Brennan's opposition to the death penalty. Justice Brennan's Constitution is said by Professor Jaffa to represent principles without a text that ignores the Fifth Amendment's clear acknowledgment of capital punishment. If we take original intent as seriously for issues today as Professor Jaffa does for slavery, we see that the Constitution does not support capital punishment.

According to Professor Jaffa, though the Constitution promotes slavery in several respects, it is not a proslavery document. Slavery is a prudent compromise, not a matter of genuine constitutional principles. The genuine principle is said to be human equality as demonstrated by the Declaration of Independence.

But the Declaration of Independence also proclaims the unalienable right of human persons to "life." One may say that the calculated taking of human life is presumptively disfavored under the Declaration of Independence, just as slavery clearly is disfavored.

The Fifth Amendment[35] no more turns the Constitution into a pro-death penalty document than the fugitive slave provision turns the Constitution into a proslavery document. The Fifth Amendment represents a limitation on capital punishment, that it was not to be carried out in the future as it had been in the past. One could hardly call the due process clause an endorsement of capital punishment. It acknowledges that capital punishment was a prevailing practice, but this recognition is similar to the recognition accorded slavery. The genuine principle of the Constitution is "life," just as surely as it is "equality."

In fact, the attack on capital punishment through the Eighth Amendment is much more consistent with the text of the Constitution than is Professor Jaffa's attack on slavery. The constitutional text seems actually to endorse slavery. Conversely, the Eighth Amendment was viewed at the time of its introduction and criticized as an invitation to abolish capital punishment.[36] Reading the reference to deprivation of life in the Fifth Amendment as if it had been intended to quiet the fear of abolition is more weight than this reforming provision will bear. The due process clause is more easily interpreted as quieting the opposite fear: that the death penalty would be widespread and discretionary if the Eighth Amendment were not interpreted to eliminate it. To exclude the due process clause might have suggested that a citizen could be deprived of life without due process.

I do not mean to argue literally that the death penalty and slavery issues are the same. We know on good authority that many of the Framers did oppose slavery, but agreed to its inclusion in the Constitution as the cost of union. There is no reason to think the Framers similarly opposed capital punishment, but refrained from condemning it as an act of compromise. But the Framers' personal views on the death penalty should not matter. Professor Jaffa does not rely primarily on the Framer's personal opinions. He relies instead on the public principles of the Declaration of Independence. Professor Jaffa would say that even if many of the Framers supported slavery (and of course some did, thus requiring compromise), the Declaration of Independence would still condemn it because the Declaration proclaims equality. Similarly, even if the Framers supported the death penalty, which I do not know to be true, the Declaration would still condemn it, for it proclaims the right to life.

Professor Jaffa's textual attack on the abolition of the death penalty is particularly unpersuasive given the Framers' view that a bill of rights was unnecessary.[37] The Bill of Rights was introduced only later to respond to fear of an oppressive federal government. But that must mean that the federal government was barred from violating the principles later embodied in the Bill of Rights even without these express limitations. Such a view would have supposed that Article I did not authorize the federal government to act oppressively or, more generally, that no government could legitimately claim the right to oppress its own people, notwithstanding prevailing doctrines of parliamentary supremacy.

To translate these generalities into a modern context, a German judge in the 1930s or a South African judge today would be entitled, under the Framers' view of legitimate authority, to condemn oppression by their governments whether positive law sanctioned judicial review or not. That is, governments may claim only powers consistent with inherent rights. Since the individual citizen would not, or could not, have ceded[38] the power of tyranny to his government, tyranny is never legitimate.[39]

This is a jurisprudence of liberation, if ever one existed. But we find its expositor, Professor Jaffa, suggesting that a judge in America, where the Framers' views have the authority of positive law as well as inherent right, may not rely on the principles of the ends of legitimate government, but must stay within the text of the Bill of Rights. The Bill of Rights is not a limit on individual liberty. Chief Justice Rehnquist may believe that government may lawfully do anything not prohibited by the Bill of Rights. But Professor Jaffa knows that this was not the Framers' intention. Their intention was to specify some of the limits on government, but not all of them. And this intention was written specifically into the text of the Ninth Amendment.[40] Where should the judge look to see what the rest of the limits on government power are? The judge need look no further than the principles of the Declaration of Independence.

A second aspect of Professor Jaffa's resistance to judicial activism is his attack on "evolutionary conscience"[41] in legal thinking. Professor Jaffa accuses liberal jurisprudence of dismissing the insights of the Framers in the name of new insights said to be based on science.

The heart of this critique is valid. The Framers proposed eternal principles based on an unchanging human nature created by God. Liberal and radical left-wing legal thinkers today reject all such conceptions as epistemologically naive. This is as true of main line consensus thinkers like Owen Fiss,[42] and Harry Wellington,[43] as it is to the Conference of Critical Legal Studies.[44]

Although this criticism may be valid with regard to those who do not accept the Framers' fundamental notions of enduring standards of right and wrong, what of those who share the Framers' commitments? Are they condemned never to learn anything from science or other advances in human thinking?

Consider the issue of protecting developing fetuses under the Fifth and

Fourteenth Amendments. The long term significance of this issue is that when and if *Roe v. Wade*[45] is overruled, a period of state choice with regard to abortion laws will be ushered in unless due process and equal protection are read to *require* protection of the unborn.

The prevailing view of the Court, in fact the only view expressed in *Roe v. Wade,* is that fetuses are not "persons" for purposes of the Fourteenth Amendment and so are not protected. Justice Blackmun's majority opinion utilized the specific intent technique Judge Bork had used to illustrate an argument against the availability of equal protection for gay people.[46] Justice Blackmun argued that the Framers of the Fourteenth Amendment were not considering fetuses when they wrote the word "person."[47]

This is the sort of simplistic original intent analysis that Professor Jaffa has in mind when he says that we are not bound by specific judgments of the Framers on contingent matters.[48] I doubt that the Framers of the Fifth Amendment or the Fourteenth Amendment thought about the rights of the fetus.

Even Professor Jaffa's "true understanding" of the Framers' original intent is little help in evaluating the rights of the fetus. Acknowledgment of individual rights does not tell us whether the fetus is to be recognized as such an individual, as a member of the human family. I admit that the analysis Professor Jaffa attributes to Lincoln concerning whether blacks are human beings seems to me so unerringly applicable to the unborn that it is disconcerting to read (if blacks are not human beings, may masters then eat them?).[49] Nevertheless, given the nature of the question, original intent is a very uncertain guide concerning the unborn.

But science teaches us a great deal. Every act of fetal surgery, every early intervention to improve the health of the developing child, every sonogram proudly displayed by new parents, in short, all that modern science teaches us about developmental biology proclaims the fetus to be our young brother or sister in the human family. And once we know this, we cannot forget it for purposes of a legal argument. These insights do not resolve the abortion dilemma. In fact, they reveal it for the dilemma it is.[50] But the insights of science are as entitled to a hearing as any other claim to truth.

Nor is new learning limited to physical sciences beyond the grasp of the Framers. New learning extends to new insights into older practices with which the Framers were familiar. A good example is the view of the Framers that private property is the "product of a man's labor."[51] It is no secret that high on the political/legal agenda of the Neo-Lockeans, Stephen Macedo, Richard Epstein, the Cato Institute, and all the rest, is an attack on the New Deal and the Welfare State in the name of the Framers' commitment to individual property rights.[52] Since every man is entitled to the fruits of his own labor, progressive taxation, income redistribution, and governmental regulation all become disfavored, if not unconstitutional. But Marxism, as well as the lessons of an interconnected industrial society, should have taught us something about the role of property. Property is never a matter of individual right alone. Property is a social product. This knowledge shapes our understanding of natural rights.

While one may say this is a matter of evolutionary conscience, it reflects simple growth of human understanding. But it does not follow that the starting point of inherent rights grounded in human nature and nature's God is thereby lost.

What did the Framers bequeath to us in the Declaration of Independence? Self-evident truth. The equality of mankind. Certain rights that flow from these insights. It should come as no surprise that people in a later age still committed to self-evident truth and the equality of humankind might think differently about the rights that are thus implied. This bothers Professor Jaffa, but I wonder whether Madison and Jefferson would have objected.

It is important to Professor Jaffa that the Framers' insights be permanent.[53] And they are. Man's creatureliness, his place in the world as one who seeks his purpose, is not subject to change. The equality of persons, the claim of each of us to be recognized as supremely important, is not subject to change. The inherent rights of man, that there are limits to what any individual or majority may rightly do to a fellow human being, are not subject to change. But the particular content as well as the application are subject to change. They have to be if the constitutional tradition is to live.

Does this level of abstraction distort the Framers?[54] I suppose in a way it does. To be true to the Framers' view of reality, we must reject some of the implications they drew from man's equal endowment of rights.

But it is Professor Jaffa's third criticism, that Justice Brennan is willing to act alone in his interpretation of the Constitution, that seems the furthest removed from his explanation of the Framers' original intent. In repeating the textualism point made above, Professor Jaffa adds the following:

> Thus Justice Brennan finds the true meaning of the Constitution, not in the text and not in any interpretation of the text by others, including the entire political community acting through the political process, but in some kind of "striving," albeit "not yet arrived." This "striving" may have the character of a revelation vouchsafed to the Justice, but not to anyone else.[55]

What sort of method does Professor Jaffa think is the appeal of "self-evident" truths if not "revelation vouchsafed" to certain people, in particular, to the Framers? In 1776, most of humankind did not agree that "all men are created equal." Professor Jaffa points out that the South later made precisely the opposite claim.[56] There is no appeal to "others" that can decide the matter of the equality of all men, for it was and is a matter of dispute. If, however, one sees the self-evidence of the statement "all men are created equal," those proclaiming inequality must be viewed as deluded. John Hart Ely makes wonderful fun of the idea that those who disagree with one person's view of natural law are denounced as wrong.[57] He is right that it is an indefensible embarrassment. Nevertheless, show me a Nazi laughing at man's essential equality, and I say the Nazi is either crazy or is denying the evidence of his own being. All natural law, as the Framers understood, rests on some such appeal to self-evident principles. This represents one of the great weaknesses of natural law. But that does not mean natural law is untrue.

Perhaps Justice Brennan is not committed to original intent.[58] Accordingly, Justice Brennan's search for an evolving consensus may in fact be subject to Professor Jaffa's criticism that it represents arrogant subjectivity. But for Professor Jaffa to criticize generally the idea of individual access to truth is an appalling irony. Professor Jaffa believes and is totally committed to the proposition that all men are endowed by their Creator with certain unalienable rights. Now how did this idea come to Professor Jaffa? Certainly, as he admits, the elites of our time do not believe it. Philosophers reject it. Liberal and conservative jurisprudence reject it. It may be that most Americans still believe in inherent rights, but that traditional belief may be fading under the pressure of positivism and modernity.[59] If the day should come that no one else takes the idea seriously that man has inherent rights given by God, would Professor Jaffa then abandon it? No. Because it is true. Why then should a justice of the Supreme Court interpreting fundamental rights be subject to a numbers test?

The Supreme Court has not shied away from judgments based on personal moral insight. Despite some energetic dissents, the Court has condemned conduct that shocks the judicial conscience or violates some similar formula.[60] Even Justice O'Connor, a member of the conservative bloc on the Court, has spoken in this idiom.[61]

When the Court does this, as when, for example, the Court condemns the use of the stomach pump in *Rochin*,[62] it is without regard to interpretations of the constitutional text by others. It is, in fact, with only the vaguest nod toward the text at all. And no nod at all to the political community. The Court was not concerned in *Rochin* with what others thought; such conduct is condemned by any civilized conscience.

Many of our greatest cases rely on such moral insights by the Court. *Brown v. Board of Education's*[63] condemnation of segregation laws can be defended, if one is interested in doing so, by its stabs at history and by the words "equal protection" in the constitutional text. But Professor Jaffa is on sounder ground in asserting that segregation laws were "utterly inconsistent with the ends of free government and hence of the Constitution."[64] Professor Jaffa's implication is that any practice "utterly inconsistent with the ends of the free government" violates the Constitution. And he is right. The Court certainly agreed with this implication when it held that the federal government was also precluded from segregating blacks, despite the absence of both history and text condemning the practice in the Fifth Amendment.[65] The justices simply could not stomach the scandal of federal segregation any longer.[66]

I cannot believe that Professor Jaffa lacks sympathy for a judge confronting a fundamental injustice. He does not condemn *Griswold*,[67] and I doubt he would condemn *Skinner*.[68] Furthermore, the refusal of the justices to countenance oppression is fully in keeping with the spirit of inherent rights that Professor Jaffa celebrates and that the Ninth Amendment embodies. Without any textual support at all, governments have never possessed authority to segregate or otherwise to oppress their citizens. Why then is Professor Jaffa so certain that governments have been given authority to kill their prisoners through capital punishment? While I acknowledge that opinions differ, it is clear to me that killing a citizen in a prison cell is utterly inconsistent with the ends of free government. And if, upon reflection and moral insight, a justice is convinced of this truth, the justice has an obligation to act—even if alone.

Of course, setting oneself up as spokesman for truth against the judgment of the majority of one's fellows is no small thing. But thinkers about the Constitution should not overemphasize the danger. Certainly this context was not unfamiliar to the Framers. They knew that majorities were capable of despotism. I do not doubt, for example, that a large majority would agree today to modest torture for certain murderers, except that we are restrained by the Eighth Amendment. If the Eighth Amendment were removed, Chief Justice Rehnquist believes this protection would vanish.[69] But this view was not the Framers' view. The Framers viewed majorities, even massive majorities, as inherently limited in wielding power.

Moreover, while the justices may each act alone, the Courts act corporately. It is never going to be easy to convince five justices, appointed through the political process, to condemn a generally accepted practice without the comfort of strong textual support. If even without textual support, a majority of the Court finds a practice repugnant to conscience, we can have some confidence in its conclusions. The justices are practicing the tradition of inherent rights that Professor Jaffa supports. When a judicial majority does this, Professor Jaffa should condemn it for being wrong, for being unpersuasive in its reasons, or for giving no reason at all. There have been occasions on which the justices have been wrong, unpersuasive, and willful. But one who believes what Professor Jaffa believes should not condemn the justices for standing against injustice.

I agree with Professor Jaffa that liberals do not follow the tradition of the Declaration of Independence. In the portions of opinions by Justice Brennan quoted by Professor Jaffa, the plea is made to a future consensus. That is, Justice Brennan asserts that one day a majority will agree with him in condemning the death penalty. If this assertion were merely prediction, we could say that truth is powerful and is eventually irresistible. But Justice Brennan is justifying, not predicting. He votes against the death penalty in part on the strength of a future majority. Justice Brennan emerges in Professor Jaffa's quotation as devoted to a sociological jurisprudence similar to that of Chief Justice Rehnquist. Both justices rely on notions of majority consensus. Chief Justice Rehnquist relies on today's majority; Justice Brennan relies on that of tomorrow. Neither man relies on an enduring standard of right.

Professor Jaffa thus shows us an exhausted constitutional tradition, not so much at the level of what judges still do, but what legal thinkers teach about the possibility of a moral law. This exhausted tradition is incapable of addressing the serious issues of the rights of persons and of the nature of free government for it lacks faith that people have such rights or that free government is inherently superior to any other kind. On the conservative side, the tradition drifts toward utilitarian tinkering,[70] on the liberal side, toward alienated individualism. The traditional mainline thinkers fail to ask of law any questions larger than itself.

We are not destined, doomed I should say, to continue on this course. Professor Jaffa has put us in touch in a vital way with a tradition of law much healthier than the one we know today. But Professor Jaffa is not content to let that tradition speak to us. He is justly proud, but at the same time fearful, because the Framers' power may be misread and misused.

From his perspective, Professor Jaffa's fear is well justified. Once we take the rights of persons seriously and the strengthening of free government as law's obligation, we cannot avoid asking about the rest of the rights of man: about economic rights—to shelter, food, clothing, and education; about social rights—to wear religious clothing and to love a person of the same sex; and about corporate rights—to prevent the police from lying to attorneys and to bar unconstitutional actions by our government. The Supreme Court has spoken negatively on all of these matters. In each case, Professor Jaffa seems confident that we have been faithful to the Declaration of Independence. I am certain we have not. But it is clear to both of us that we must strive within our powers to be faithful. For our legal tradition and those who participate in it are judged by enduring standards of right and wrong.

NOTES TO

# Judicial Conscience and Natural Rights

1. Professor Jaffa's paper does not deal with all of the problems that the original intent position, however interpreted, faces. Such questions as "who counts as a framer?" "what is the relevance of the ratification process?" or even "why should intention matter in the first place?" do not occupy him here. In this paper Professor Jaffa deals primarily with a much narrower question, how well do the self-professed advocates of original intent understand the intellectual and political presumptions of the generation they accept as Framers? Surely it is justifiable to deal with an issue of manageable scale rather than to attempt to do all things at once. I will limit my reply to this same issue but from a different, one might say left-wing, perspective.

2. Jaffa, *What Were the "Original Intentions" of the Framers of the Constitution of the United States*, 10 U. PUGET SOUND L. REV. 351 (1987) [herinafter Jaffa].

3. Dred Scott v. Sanford, 60 U.S. (19 How.) 393 (1856) (Congress bound to protect slaveowner's property rights in slaves in federal territories). *Dred Scott* represents Professor Jaffa's starting point. *See* Jaffa, *supra* note 2.

4. Jaffa, *supra* note 2.

5. "[The Declaration of Independence] tells us why slavery must be regarded as an anomaly, a necessary evil entailed upon the Constitution, but not flowing from—or consistent with—its genuine principles." *Id.* at 364; *see also id.* at 408 (appendix A): "[T]he principles of the Declaration of Independence are the principles of the Constitution."

   Unlike today's conservatives, Taney did not deny all authority of the Declaration of Independence. He asserted, however, that in light of the constitutional textual acceptance of slavery, blacks could not have been included in the commitment to the equality of all men. Taney read the Declaration in light of the Constitution, rather than the other way around. *See id.* at 368-69.

6. *Id.* at 353-54.

7. "Plausible" is far too weak a word. Although Professor Jaffa rejects the Taney interpretation, he acknowledges at length that elements of the constitutional

124

text strongly support the Constitution's apparent pro-slavery position. *Id.* at 407-10 (appendix A).

8. *Id.* at 390-93.
9. "In asking what were the original intentions of the Founding Fathers, we are asking what principles of moral and political philosophy guided them. We are not asking their personal judgments upon contingent matters." *Id.* at 386.
10. *Id.* at 355.
11. *Id.* at 378.
12. *Id.* at 384.
13. *Id.* at 355-56.
14. *Id.* at 363.
15. *Id.* at 354.
16. *Id.* at 356.
17. *Id.* at 362.
18. *Id.* at 394.
19. *Id.* at 394-95; *see also id.* at 355-56.
20. *Id.* at 395.
21. *Id.* at 393.
22. This is my conclusion from reading Chief Justice Rehnquist's more ambitious attempts to declare a theoretical approach to constitutional interpretation. *See* Rehnquist, *Government by Cliche: Keystone Address of the Earl F. Nelson Lecture Series,* 45 Mo. L. Rev. 370 (1980) [hereinafter *Government by Cliche*]. As I discuss *infra* note 23, Professor Jaffa views my statement in the text here, as well as similar expressions of mine elsewhere, as overstatements of what Chief Justice Rehnquist has actually said. Thus, although I have not changed my view, I add the next statement in the text as a toned-down alternative. I would urge the interested reader, and since this man is now Chief Justice of the United States it behooves us all to be interested, to read the two articles herein cited. I find revealing, in particular, Chief Justice Rehnquist's argument in *The Notion of a Living Constitution,* 45 Tex. L. Rev. 693, 704-05 (1976), that all moral judgments are only "personal" and "individual" until enacted into law, and his argument in *Government by Cliche,* 45 Mo. L. Rev. at 390-392, that the authority of the Constitution is grounded in majority rule rather than in "any principles of natural law." These expressions are entirely inconsistent with the ideas of self-evident truth and endowed rights. I know it sounds strange to criticize a justice for being an atheist when we usually regard such matters as personal. But I do not mean that Chief Justice Rehnquist attends no church, which I do not know and which is none of my business, but rather that he is a jurisprudential atheist, a man for whom law is grounded in nothing more than the power of the majority. These matters are discussed in great depth in Professor Jaffa's appendix C, *spura* note 2, at 422.
23. Professor Jaffa is kind enough to include in his critique of Chief Justice

Rehnquist in appendix C several references to a short article I wrote in the *Wall Street Journal*, August. 7, 1986, at 20, col. 3. I would say that Professor Jaffa states my criticism of Chief Justice Rehnquist far better than I could, and did, myself.

Professor Jaffa errs, however, in criticizing my characterization of Chief Justice Rehnquist as one "who does not believe there is such a thing as right or wrong." Professor Jaffa argues that what Chief Justice Rehnquist says is that right and wrong cannot be logically demonstrated, not that they do not exist, and thus like Carl Becker, Chief Justice Rehnquist may nevertheless believe in the right as a fundamental reality. The difference between the two cases is that Carl Becker's belief justified action, in his case a willingness to kill or be killed. In the case of Chief Justice Rehnquist, the unavailability of logic to resolve issues of value is an argument for a judge not to act. This unwillingness to act suggests that Chief Justice Rehnquist does not accept the difference between right and wrong as representing a fundamental reality.

For Chief Justice Rehnquist, the world is divided between facts and opinions. Facts are amenable to empirical or logical verification. Opinions are subject to no sort of verification. When I called Chief Justice Rehnquist's commitment to an objective analysis of original intent "unobtainable," I had in mind these categories of empirical or logical verification. Obviously, the views of Madison and Jefferson are subject neither to empirical nor logical verification. One must look at the evidence and make reasoned argument. But, of course, one can proceed in the same way; that is by argument rather than verification when discussing fundamental values, which, Chief Justice Rehnquist says, is the reason for banishing such talk from the courtroom.

It should be noted that Professor Jaffa's category of reason at times seems to go a great deal beyond Chief Justice Rehnquist's idea of how an argument can be justified. Reasons for Professor Jaffa is not always limited to empiricism and logic, but partakes of all the different aspects of human understanding. This approach to reason seems to parallel Edmond Cahn's description of the sense of injustice: "a blend of reason and empathy." *See* Ledewitz, *Edmond Cahn's Sense of Injustice: A Contemporary Reintroduction*, 3 J. LAW & REL. 277, 285 (1985) [hereinafter cited as *Cahn*]. At other times, however, Professor Jaffa treats reason as merely empirical or logical. Consider Professor Jaffa's assertion that a black person's humanity "is a matter of fact and not of opinion. Jaffa, *supra* note 2, at 446 (appendix C). That it is, but not because the slave codes inconsistently treated blacks. For even if the slave codes had consistently degraded blacks, blacks would still have retained their humanity. To put this another way, the humanity of blacks is a "fact" more fundamental than either empirical or logical demonstrations. Professor Jaffa faults Carl Becker for acknowledging this, but what arguments could "objectively prove" the humanity of a person? The category of the real is objectively true, but may not be amenable to the sort of demonstration Professor Jaffa sometimes suggests reason can provide. *Compare* Edmond Cahn's comment about slavery, that it "was doomed to disappear everywhere, for no other reason than that a slave is a man." E. CAHN, THE SENSE OF INJUSTICE: AN ANTHROPOCENTRIC VIEW OF LAW 15 (1949). Even though Cahn did not share Professor Jaffa's confidence in reason alone, he did not abandon the true. Nor did he abandon reasoning about the true.

24. Jaffa, *supra* note 2, at 425 (appendix C).

25. *Id.* at 374.

26. "The crisis of American constitutionalism—the crisis of the West—lies precisely in the denial that there are any such principles or truths. It is no less a crisis in the heart of American conservatism than of American liberalism." *See id.* at 386. *See generally id.* at 415-22 (appendix B).

27. J. ELY, DEMOCRACY AND DISTRUST 38-40 (1980) [hereinafter ELY].

28. I describe briefly Chief Justice Rehnquist's reliance on specific intent, which I call the "historical method" in *Cahn, supra* note 23, at 314-19 n.163.

29. Jaffa, *supra* note 2, at 386.

30. *Id.*

31. *Id.* at 425 (appendix C).

32. *See, e.g., id.* at 356, and 357-59.

33. *Id.* at 402-04 (appendix A).

34. *Id.* at 405 (appendix A).

35. "[N]or shall any prisoner be subject for the same offense to be twice put in jeopardy of life or limb . . . nor be deprived of life, liberty, or property, without due process of law." U.S. Const. amend. VIII.

36. This is the gist of the celebrated objection of Representative Livermore of New Hampshire during consideration of the proposed Eighth Amendment: "[I]t is sometimes necessary to hang a man, villains often deserve whipping, and perhaps having their ears cut off; but we are in the future to be prevented from inflicting these punishments because they are cruel?" 1 ANNALS OF CONG. 754 (J. Gales ed. 1789).

37. Consider the comment of Alexander Hamilton in the 84th FEDERALIST: "I go further, and affirm that bills of rights . . . are not only unnecessary in the proposed Constitution, but would even be dangerous. They would contain various exceptions to powers not granted. . . . For why declare that things shall not be done which there is no power to do?" THE FEDERALIST NO. 84, at 537 (A. Hamilton) (H. Lodge ed. 1888).

38. Professor Jaffa does not attribute to the Framers a social contract into which one might actually enter. As the Virginia Declaration of Rights put it, people "cannot" divest their posterity of inherent rights. Jaffa *supra* note 2, at 385.

39. I should add here a reference to the brave Ghanian judges whose insistence upon the availability of habeas corpus, despite a military constitution that apparently precluded judicial review, ultimately proved fatal to several of them. Cover, *The Supreme Court, 1982 Term—Forward: Nomos and Narrative,* 97 HARV. L. REV. 4, 59 (1983).

40. "The enumeration in the Constitution, of certain rights, shall not be construed to deny or disparage others retained by the people." U.S. CONST. amend. IX.

41. Jaffa, *supra* note 2, at 385.

42. *See* O. Fiss, *Objectivity and Interpretation*, 34 STAN. L. REV. 739 (1982).

43. *See* Wellington, *Common Law Rules and Constitutional Double Standards: Some Notes on Adjudication*, 83 YALE L.J. 221 (1973).

44. *See, e.g.*, Singer, *The Player and the Cards: Nihilism and Legal Theory*, 94 YALE L.J. 1 (1984). I am not suggesting that Joseph Singer's comprehensive statement is representative of Critical Legal Studies thinking in all ways; but insofar as he rejects the Framers' worldview, he is quite representative.

45. 410 U.S. 113 (1973) (*Roe* invalidated state laws prohibiting abortion during the first six months of pregnancy).

46. Bork, *The Constitution, Original Intent, and Economic Rights*, 23 SAN DIEGO L. REV. 823, 828 (1986) [hereinafter Bork].

> Assume for the sake of the argument that a judge's study of the evidence shows that both black and general racial equality were clearly intended, but that equality on matters such as sexual orientation was not under discussion. . . .[The judge] has, therefore, no warrant to displace a legislative choice that prohibits certain forms of sexual behavior.

> I am never sure how literally specific intent proponents intend to be taken. Judge Bork uses the example of sexual orientation to illustrate a group whose rights were "not under discussion." But gays are a politically easy target who have achieved little protection in any event under the Fourteenth Amendment. Would Judge Bork launch the same wholesale attack against *any* judicial protection of the equal rights of women? Surely sexual equality "was not under discussion" when the Fourteenth Amendment was adopted.

47. 410 U.S. at 156-59.

48. Jaffa, *supra* note 2, at 386.

49. *Id.* at 446-48 (appendix C).

50. Professor Jaffa desires the "prudential" morality of the Framers. "But knowing that [slavery] is wrong does not, of itself, tell us what to do about it." *Id.* at 371. The situation with regard to abortion is similar. Although the unborn child is always an innocent victim, even in the cases of rape and incest, it is unthinkable to me that anyone would consider forcing a woman to live with that experience by bringing the pregnancy to term. Even in the so-called "easier" cases of a woman's emotional or financial incapacity, it is relevant to consider the burden society is content to visit on young mothers. By social convention and the resulting laziness of law, society encourages sexual exploits by young men by force or seduction, dependence by women, and irresponsibility as to birth control. Then, after the baby is born, society allows the father to remove himself both physically and financially so that essentially *all*

of the burdens of parenthood remain with the mother. If abortion is to be a crime, one must act with full awareness of society's callousness about young life once it is brought into the world.

51. *Id.* at 380.
52. Stephen Macedo's excellent monograph brings much of this together. S. MACEDO, THE NEW RIGHT V. THE CONSTITUTION (1986). Fittingly, the monograph is published by the Cato Institute with an introduction by Richard Epstein. Macedo argues a theory of original intent very close to that of Professor Jaffa and criticizes the skepticism of Judge Bork and Attorney General Meese on much the same grounds as does Professor Jaffa. Unlike Professor Jaffa, however, Macedo raises the issue of protection of property from government interference. Of course, Professor Epstein has done so with even more vigor. *See* R. EPSTEIN, TAKINGS: PRIVATE PROPERTY AND THE POWER OF EMINENT DOMAIN (1985).
53. "Historical experience means experience in time, but what is permanent is recognized as an intelligible necessity—or as grounded in an intelligible necessity—outside of time." Jaffa, *supra* note 2, at 385-86.
54. Compare Judge Bork's criticism of distorting the Framers' specific intent by over-abstraction. Bork, *supra* note 46, at 827-28.
55. Jaffa, *supra* note 2, at 357.
56. *Id.*, at 392-94.
57. ELY, *supra* note 27, at 48: "Well, what may seem like the truth to you," said the seventeen-year-old bus driver and part-time philosopher, "may not, of course, seem like the truth to the other fella, you know."
    "THEN THE OTHER FELLOW IS WRONG, IDIOT!" (quoting P. ROTH, THE GREAT AMERICAN NOVEL 20 (1973).
58. I am sorry that Professor Jaffa makes so much of an isolated quotation from Justice Brennan's speech in *The Great Debate: Interpreting Our Written Constitution*, THE FEDERALIST SOCIETY 11-25 (1986). Considering the speech as a whole, as well as Justice Brennan's recent comments in the Harvard Law Review, Brennan, *Constitutional Adjudication and the Death Penalty: A View From the Court*, 100 HARV. L. REV. 313 (1986), and, of course, his concurrence in Furman v. Georgia, 408 U.S. 238, 257 (1972) (Brennan, J. concurring), I am not sure that Professor Jaffa has accurately interpreted Justice Brennan's method. This matter is beyond my scope here; I am content to deal with these isolated passages as given.
59. Professor Jaffa in fact complains that "professional philosophers" have "mined and sapped the ordinary man's confidence in the vitality of ordinary language, and of common sense moral judgments. . . ." Jaff, *supra* note 2, at 416.
60. *See generally* Miller v. Fenton, 106 S. Ct. 445, 449 (1985): "This Court has long held that certain interrogation techniques, either in isolation or as applied to the unique characteristics of a particular suspect, are so offensive to a

civilized system of justice that they must be condemned under the Due Process Clause of the Fourteenth Amendment." The classic cases are Rochin v. California, 342 U.S. 165, 172-73 (1952) ("conduct that shocks the conscience" or "afford[s] brutality the cloak of law") and Brown v. Mississippi, 297 U.S. 278, 286 (1936) ("revolting to the sense of justice"). In more recent cases, Court majorities have not used this express language and it has remained for dissents, often by Justice Black, to point out the underlying premise of the majority holding. *See, e.g.,* Boddie v. Connecticut, 401 U.S. 371 (1971) (Black, J., dissenting). "The Equal Protection Clause is no more appropriate a vehicle for the 'shock of conscience' test than is the Due Process Clause" *id.* at 394; and Harper v. Virginia Board of Elections, 383 U.S. 663, 675-680 (1966) (Black, J. dissenting) (criticism of "natural-law-due-process formula"). To its great credit, the Court prevented the State of Texas from denying public schooling to the children of illegal aliens under this natural law tradition. Plyler v. Doe, 457 U.S. 202 (1982): "Even if the State found it expedient to control the conduct of adults by acting against their children, legislation directing the onus of a parent's misconduct against his children does not comport with fundamental conceptions of justice." *Id.* at 220. It is important to note that even when refusing to apply the "shock-the-conscience" test, the Court has never abandoned it. *See, e.g.,* Moran v. Burbine, 106 S. Ct. 1135, 1147 (1986) and Louisiana v. Resweber, 329 U.S. (1947).

61. 329 U.S. 459, 473 (1947) (Burton J., dissenting).

    We do not question that on facts more egregious than those presented here police deception might rise to a level of a due process violation. . . .We hold only that, on these facts, the challenged conduct falls short of the kind of misbehavior that so shocks the sensibilities of civilized society as to warrant a federal intrusion into the criminal processes of the States.

62. Rochin v. California, 342 U.S. 165 (1952) (after the defendant swallowed two capsules containing morphine, the police directed a doctor to force an emetic solution through a tube into the defendant's stomach. Resulting evidence was excluded.)

63. 347 U.S. 483 (1954).

64. Jaffa, *supra* note 2, at 403.

65. Bolling v. Sharpe, 347 U.S. 497 (1954).

66. *Id.* at 500: "In view of our decision that the Constitution prohibits the states from maintaining racially segregated public schools, it would be unthinkable that the same Constitution would impose a lesser duty in the Federal Government." *Id.*

67. Griswold v. Connecticut, 381 U.S. 479 (1968) (conviction for giving birth control instruction to married couple reversed). *Griswold* is discussed by Professor Jaffa with at least an air of sympathy in Jaffa, *supra* note 2, at 402-04 (appendix A).

68. Skinner v. Oklahoma, 316 U.S. 535 (1982) (Equal Protection bars steriliza-

tion for persons convicted two or more times of felonies involving moral turpitude). *Skinner* is generally regarded as a substantive due process case disguised as equal protection. *See* Lupu, *Untangling the Strands of the Fourteenth Amendment,* 77 MICH. L. REV. 981, 1019 (1979).

69. *See Government by Cliche, supra* note 22, at 390-92. This article contains Chief Justice Rehnquist's ultimate anti-natural rights statement. If 70 percent of the American people wish to remove the Bill of Rights from the Constitution, then according to our theory of constitutionalism, this would not be "an illegal, an immoral, or an improper act." Chief Justice Rehnquist added, "[i]t might well be unwise. . . ." Yes, it might.

70. There is nothing hateful about "utilitarian tinkering." If law and economics can help to prevent accidents at lower cost, to better deter crime, or to recognize inconsistencies between goals and means, why would anyone object? It is only the imperial claim to embody all clear-thinking human understanding that makes law and economics a proper object of scorn.

# Professor Harry V. Jaffa Divides the House: A Respectful Protest and a Defense Brief

ROBERT L. STONE

*There are in nature certain fountains of justice, whence all civil laws are derived but as streams.*[1]

*Man's [natural] capacity for justice makes democracy possible, but man's [natural] inclination to injustice makes democracy necessary.*[2]

## I. Introduction

### A. THE CONTEXT

Professor Harry V. Jaffa has done it again. His remarkable essay, "What Were the 'Original Intentions' of the Framers of the Constitution of the United States?" together with his related book, *Crisis of the House Divided*,[3] should help "provoke the most profound and far-reaching debate of our generation about American politics."[4] Both works are required reading for anyone who would know what is this thing called law. Both address the central question in American constitutional law today, which is the same question over which the Civil War was fought: How should the law be interpreted if the Declaration of Independence is correct that it is self-evidently true that all men are created equal?

Science is not egalitarian. In the study of the law there is a natural[5] hierarchy of the importance of the questions asked and answered. If the law is like a house, the Constitution of 1787 is like the foundation of the house in which we Americans live; statutory law is like the supporting walls; and case law is like the roof. To begin legal education, as do many law schools, with case law is like building a house by starting with the roof. Professor Jaffa demands that we proceed from the ground up. In fact, he goes so far as to look to see what lies under the foundation by exploring the nature of obligation: "[E]very human being has the indefeasible right to ask anyone proposing to exercise authority over him, 'Why should I obey [the Constitution or any other law]?' "[6] We are indebted to Professor Jaffa for a profound if passionate elaboration of the enormous consequences to constitutional law of the fact that in American positive law the answer to the question of obligation is found in the same document as the doctrine of the equality of all men and an invocation of natural right: In the Declaration of Independence, the first "organic law" in the current edition of the *United States Code*.[7] Abraham Lincoln showed that some Supreme Court decisions such as *Dred Scott*,[8] which denies the doctrine of natural equality set forth in the Declaration, are not the supreme law of the land. Furthermore, he argues that this is the case because the question of obligation determines not only what the law should be, but also what the law is in concrete practical cases.[9]

Why is it that virtually all Americans say that they honor and obey the Constitution? Is it because the majority ratified it, and we should honor and obey anything for which the majority voted? If so, why? Is it because the majority outnumbers the minority? If so, is this just another way of saying, "Might makes right?" A majority once voted for Hitler and his political program. Do Nazi laws then have the same status as our laws? On the other hand, do we obey and honor the Constitution not because the majority voted for it, but because it is good—and the majority voted for it because it is good? Both reasons are important, but which is more so? If the Constitution is good, it must be because it is good for human beings. What, then, is a truly human being? If the nature of being human, i.e., human nature, is shaped by history or the environment rather than being fixed, then human nature can be adapted to any constitution, even a Nazi constitution or a cannibal constitution, and we must in principle be indifferent to the kind of constitution we have.

However, if human nature cannot change, then the status of the Constitution, and hence also of all subordinate laws, depends upon whether or not the laws adapt themselves to the requirements of human nature. If a law is adapted to the requirements of human nature, it is naturally right or just. If it is not adapted to the requirements of human nature, it is naturally unjust. That is the doctrine of natural right. And if this doctrine is true, then nature or being is the deepest question underlying the science of law—just as it is the deepest question underlying all the other sciences.

Does this doctrine mean that students of the law may not differ on the questions posed by their discipline? Not at all. For an example of the flexibility and undogmatic character of the doctrine of natural right, we should turn to the fullest elaboration of the doctrine in the Anglo-American legal tradition: not the Declaration, but rather Judge William Blackstone's *Commentaries on the Laws*,[10] the "oracle of the common law." (The Constitution of 1787 does not explicitly mention natural right. But Judge Blackstone's understanding of the common law is incorporated implicitly into the Constitution of 1787 through Article III and the Seventh Amendment's reference to the common law.)[11]

Judge Blackstone throughout his work compares the common law with the civil or Roman law, showing how these two very different systems of law adapt themselves to the requirements of nature. For example, in the chapter on family law,[12] Judge Blackstone assumes that, because human nature is invariable, all human societies must provide institutions for the care of the young. Beasts do not care for the young of other members even of their own species, because they cannot reason. Also, because human nature is invariable, all civilized societies must provide for legally appointed guardians when the parents are unable to care for their children. Human nature being what it is, the common law does not permit an infant's heir to be also his guardian. (For the same reason, it may be against public policy for a parent to be the beneficiary of a large insurance policy on the life of his child or otherwise to have a direct interest in his child's death.) The common law seeks to protect the life of the child. However, Roman or civil law does permit an heir to be a guardian, because, human nature being what it is, an heir will take much better care of the infant's property than would a disinterested non-heir.

Both approaches, common law and civil law, assume natural self-interest, and both are coherent and sensible—but there are a strictly limited number of such approaches. Thus nature suggests the questions, although it does not dictate one set of answers. Judge Blackstone does not claim that the common law is the only natural law. But any legal arrangement that does not adapt itself both to nurturing of the young and to self-interest would not make sense or be respected. Hence, it would be unnatural and could not endure. Judge Blackstone states the general relationship between positive law and natural right as follows:

> This law of nature, being co-eval with mankind and dictated by God himself, is, of course, superior in obligation to any other. It is binding over all the globe, in all countries, and at all times; no human [positive] laws are of any

validity, if contrary to this; and such of them as are valid derive all their force, and all their authority, mediately or immediately, from this original.[13]

Therefore, "Aristotle himself has said, speaking of the laws of his own country, that jurisprudence of the knowledge of those laws is the principal and most perfect branch of ethics."[14] However, as mentioned above, the Constitution of 1787 does not mention explicitly natural right. Is it thereby rejected, or is it thereby assumed? As important as this question is, many lawyers today would be hard pressed to answer it. Professor Jaffa provides a most cogent and eloquent reminder that the foremost American source of natural rights that is recognized as law is the Declaration of Independence.

Professor Jaffa's argument is that the deepest and most characteristic division in American politics is the debate between Abraham Lincoln and John C. Calhoun[15] (Stephen A. Douglas was standing in for Calhoun)[16] on the question of slavery or states' rights. The earlier debate between Alexander Hamilton and Thomas Jefferson did not represent opposite poles, because they were not as clear in their thought and took both sides of the fundamental question: Is the ground beneath the foundation of our law ultimately morality or force—the natural rights of man or majority rule? (A third possible position, associated with the Critical Legal Studies movement, is that law is basically fraud,[17] but this doctrine is similar to Calhoun's.) In this debate, Lincoln and Calhoun stand in for Aristotle and Machiavelli, respectively. One of the deepest issues at stake in this titanic conflict is the question of the status of nature: Aristotle teaches that the world is naturally so ordered that good men tend to prevail in the end. Machiavelli teaches[18] that force and fraud are justified because the world is naturally so ordered that good men finish last.

Professor Jaffa argues incisively that *Dred Scott*[19] is an application of Calhoun's doctrine to the question of the legal status of slavery in the territories. Calhoun held that the Constitution of 1787 established a government of concurrent majorities composed of the State governments and the federal government, with the States enjoying the rights of veto (or nullification) and secession. Furthermore, Calhoun held, the rights of the Southern States were violated by the Missouri Compromise,[20] which excluded slavery from the territories north of 36 degrees 30 minutes. *Dred Scott* held that the Missouri Compromise was unconstitutional because it deprived slaveowners of their property without due process of law. The Missouri Compromise had been replaced by the Kansas-Nebraska Act of 1854,[21] which was sponsored by Stephen

Douglas, and which provided for popular majority sovereignty on the question of slavery in each Territory. Lincoln argued that a decision by the majority in a Territory to legalize slavery would not have the authority of true law because it violates the natural rights doctrine of the Declaration. Calhoun's argument at its core is that majority rules, and majority must be the local majority in the area in question and not all men in the world. "Majority rules," if it is the only legal principle, is another way of saying, "Might makes right."[22]

Another aspect of Professor Jaffa's argument is more obviously relevant for lawyers today. He points out that the doctrine of "legal realism,"[23] the doctrine that asserts "the law is what the judges say it is,"[24] is yet another way of saying, with Calhoun, that "might makes right." And the temporary ascendancy of this doctrine in American law schools[25] represents "a victory of Richmond over Washington." Furthermore, Professor Jaffa's most pointed argument is that conservative thinkers, while seeking to defend American law against attempts to purge it of morality, have done this by invoking states' rights and majority rule. (Conservatives who would rely only on the words of the text of the Constitution would do so because that, not the ideology of activist judges, is what has been ratified by the people. But the principle of majority rule cannot stand alone.) On this fundamental question, Lincoln prevailed over Douglas: There are only two viable positions. Of course, this is not to say that majority rule is not a proper principle, in accord as it is with both natural equality and positive law. Rather, it is to say that the principle of majority rule cannot stand alone because it has no moral content. It is mere procedure without substance. In the words of Thomas Jefferson,

> All too will bear in mind this sacred principle, that though the will of the majority is in all cases to prevail, that will to be rightful must be reasonable; that the minority possess their equal rights, which equal law must protect, and to violate would be oppression.[26]

The problem that Professor Jaffa emphasizes may be found in the work of Willmoore Kendall. In his review of Jaffa's *Crisis of the House Divided*,[27] Mr. Kendall writes that,

> it was the Southerners [Calhoun] who were the anti-Caesars of pre-Civil War days, and . . . Lincoln was the Caesar Lincoln claimed to be trying to prevent; and . . . the Caesarism we all need to fear is the contemporary liberal movement, dedicated like Lincoln to egalitarian reforms sanctioned by mandates

emanating from national majorities—a movement which is Lincoln's legitimate offspring.[28]

And about the meaning of the equality clause in the Declaration, Kendall and Carey opine as follows:

> Our best guess is that the clause simply asserts the proposition [not truth] that all peoples who identify themselves as one—that is, those who identify themselves as a society, nation, or state for action in history—are equal to others who have likewise identified themselves . . . . [E]quality is not listed among those ends to be secured by government . . . . That Lincoln held a markedly different conception of the equality clause is beyond dispute . . . . That he considered equality a value or goal to be promoted . . . seems clear from the Gettysburg Address. If there be any doubts on this score, the Lincoln-Douglas debates, Lincoln's speech at Springfield, Illinois (June 26, 1857), and, among other items, his Message to Congress in Special Session (July 4, 1861) ought to dispel them.[29]

There is some evidence that Mr. Kendall, late in life, was won over to Lincoln's position, probably by Professor Jaffa himself, and that he decided that Lincoln was not responsible for the later mistakes (such as the "one person, one vote" rule)[30] that were made in the name of the Declaration's equality clause. But taking Mr. Kendall's published works as they stand, Mr. Kendall stands convicted under Professor Jaffa's passionate indictment. Woe to the citizen upon whom this public prosecutor focuses his searingly critical eye.

## B. THE INDICTMENT HAS THREE FLAWS

In this essay, Professor Jaffa sharply criticizes several prominent thinkers on the law, including Robert H. Bork, Jeane Kirkpatrick, Martin Diamond, and Irving Kristol, all of whom have risked the prosecutor's wrath by agreeing with him that the old and tried is preferable to the new and untried.[31] Lewis E. Lehrman, in the first paragraph of his Foreword to Professor Jaffa's essay, implies that this prosecutorial indictment lacks "the temperament of a lawyer" and "the profession of a judge." This reviewer will show that Professor Jaffa's method throughout his indictment has three flaws. First, he takes statements of sensible political compromises—such as support for judicial restraint, British traditions, and local self-government—and treats them as if they were philosophical statements.

Second, he assembles a composite indictment, which in law is appropriately applied only to an indictment against a proven conspiracy, the existence of which Professor Jaffa has not proved. (If the argument from Machiavelli for slavery had four steps, and each of four authors says one or two of the four steps, it does not follow that any one of the four authors intends the whole argument.) Third, this reviewer will show in detail that each of the statements of the four steps almost certainly was not intended as such by its author. Professor Jaffa's indictment therefore fails to meet its burden of proof. A decent respect to the opinions of mankind requires that I should declare the causes which impel me to these observations. To prove them, let facts be submitted to "our candid countrymen."[32]

## II. He has Refused his Assent to the Works of the Honorable Robert H. Bork, Which Are Wholesome and Necessary for the Public Good

Professor Jaffa alleges that Judge Bork teaches that there is no general theory of constitutional law, and that this void is good because "our constitutional liberties arose out of historical experience."[33] He alleges that Judge Bork denies that our colonial charters were based on the "immutable laws of nature" and alleges that Judge Bork claims that public opinion and the opinion of the Framers was not antislavery at the time of the writing of the Constitution of 1787.[34] All of these allegations are supposed to be evidence that Judge Bork is, whether he knows it or not, like all the other members of "the whole tribe of conservative publicists," a Calhounian apologist for legal realism, slavery, and states' rights.[35]

I have been unable, after a search of Judge Bork's published works, to find any claim that the opinion of the Framers was not antislavery at the time of the Founding or that our colonial charters were not based on the immutable laws of nature. This shifts the burden of proof back to the prosecution.

It is true that the phrases quoted by Professor Jaffa, if examined in isolation, do seem to support his allegation that Judge Bork denies natural right. But when the phrases are seen in context, a more even-handed interpretation suggests itself. Judge Bork's writings on constitutional law are intended as contributions to the current debate in American law schools and courts on the question of whether federal judges are bound by the text of the Constitution.[36] In "The Impossibility of Finding Welfare

Rights in the Constitution,"[37] Judge Bork argues that we the people in the several States are legally free to increase or decrease charitable payments to the poor. He says that his opponents (certain ultra-liberal teachers at Harvard of the doctrine of "representation-reinforcement")[38] argue that we as a community do not have this freedom—that we may increase but may not decrease such payments, because to decrease them would, under the First, Fourteenth, and Fifteenth Amendments, abridge the rights of the poor or of blacks to speak and to vote, and might make them feel "stigmatized." The opponents' argument prevailed to a limited extent in several Supreme Court decisions during the 1960s and 1970s.[39]

On this and similar questions, Judge Bork is vexed by the tendency of his opponents not to rely on textual or legal arguments but, refusing to abide by the rules laid down, to resort to an "abstract, philosophical style."[40] Justice Holmes made a similar point in his dissent in *Lochner v. New York*,[41] which held that the people of New York as a community do not have the freedom under the Constitution to prohibit the employment of bakery employees for more than ten hours a day or sixty hours a week. Holmes states what for us is obvious: "The Fourteenth Amendment does not enact Mr. Herbert Spencer's Social Statics."[42] Does a hostility to saying that the Fourteenth Amendment enacts the Harvard doctrine of representation-reinforcement mean that Judge Bork is hostile to philosophy? Or are such reservations justified because "[t]he consequence of this (so-called) philosophical approach to constitutional law almost certainly would be the destruction of the idea of the law"? [43] Judge Bork properly refrains from *obiter dicta*—from deciding questions that are not ripe for adjudication. Should a good judge say, "The Harvard doctrine of representation-reinforcement is wrong because, for the following reasons, it is incompatible with the original intention of the Framers," which is what Judge Bork indicates in other words? Or should he, as Professor Jaffa urges him to do, say that "The Harvard doctrine is wrong because it is incompatible with original intent, and, by the way, I know of another doctrine that is compatible"? For example, from the point of view of the discipline of the law, one of the many objectionable aspects of *Dred Scott* is that Chief Justice Taney reaches out in a dictum to discuss the Declaration of Independence at all—when the case should have been decided on the narrower ground of the Territory Clause of Article IV, Section 3, parag. 2. If a reluctance to follow Taney's example is part of what it means to be a judge, then it is not fair to assume that a judge's silence about the Declaration means either agreement or disagreement. To the extent that the Framers of the Constitution of 1787 were successful and we are bound by their work, the philosophical questions have been settled and do not come before a judge.[44] This is an indication that the system is working well, not badly. As Judge Bork explains,

> What is important about the non-interpretivists is not that they added moral philosophy but that moral philosophy displaces such traditional sources as text and history and renders them unimportant.[45]

Professor Jaffa refers us to Judge Bork's "Tradition and Morality in Constitutional Law"[46] as evidence that he teaches that the academic study of constitutional law has very little theory of its own. Therefore, judges are compelled to turn for guidance, when the text is ambiguous, to "the common sense of the community,"[47] i.e., to "American traditions" or history, which Judge Bork indicates are distinct from "morality." However, according to Professor Jaffa, American "traditions" in 1787 most conspicuously included slavery.[48] Are these facts evidence that Judge Bork would defend slavery? For example, to apply Judge Bork's method of reliance upon historical context, the same way any lawyer interprets any statute, we seek the answer to the question, "Does the Republican Form of Government Clause forbid slavery in the States?" If I may presume, for the sake of the argument, to speak for Judge Bork, the answer would be, "No, because the Southerners who wrote the Constitution of 1787 believed that their States were republican forms of government in 1787, and in 1787 they had slaves." But this is not the end of the answer. "Therefore, emancipation should have been accomplished by an act of Congress under the Commerce Clause or by amendment."[49] What is wrong with this argument? Does the fact that Calhoun would have used at least part of it mean that it is wrong? Does the fact that Calhoun would have used part of it mean that Judge Bork is a Calhounian?

Again, the context of Judge Bork's remarks are decisive for understanding them. True, Judge Bork, in "Tradition and Morality in Constitutional Law,"[50] says that the academic study of constitutional law has very little theory of its own. But he makes it clear that he deplores this lack of theory and the resultant appeals to mere "tradition" or history. He defends them only as preferable to appeals to "contractarian [libertarian] or utilitarian or what-have-you philosophy rather than . . . to the Constitution"—because such "philosophies" are outside "our most basic compact."[51]

> [C]onstitutional law has very little theory of its own and hence is almost pathologically lacking in immune defenses against the intellectual fevers of the

larger society as well as against the disorders that were generated by its own internal organs.[52]

It is the stubborn refusal of Anglo-American law before the twentieth century to impose upon the people a "philosophy" that does not have the consent of the people in their basic social compact that distinguished the American from the French Revolution. And to the extent that judges impose any such external philosophy, no matter how good it be, we are no longer "a free people."[53] To read this profound critique of American constitutional law as taught in most law schools today as a hostility to philosophy in general and an antipathy to natural rights in particular is to go beyond the text.

One of the important truths that Professor Jaffa is asserting is that the legal realists are wrong when they argue that law is basically force or fraud (which are two of the three possible answers to the question, "Why do We Obey the Law?"). Rather, the ground of all positive law is morality. And on this decisive question Judge Bork and Professor Jaffa are in complete agreement. Thus, Judge Bork can endorse the observation that,

> Whatever else law may be, it is . . . stubbornly entangled with beliefs about right and wrong. Law that is . . . legitimate is related to the larger universe of moral discourse . . . . If law is not . . . a moral enterprise, it is without legitimacy or binding force [i.e., it is not truly a law].[54]

No logically consistent legal realist or Calhounian could indicate that an immoral law is not fully a law. What Judge Bork is doing is showing us why there is a critical need in the science of law for a moral ground[55] and then why that ground must be found in the texts—and why constitutional law will remain "diseased" and "fevered" until such a ground is recognized. It will remain diseased for lack of theory because, "mere tradition carrie[s] no authority."[56] Judge Bork:

> I recall one evening listening to a rather traditional theologian bemoan the intellectual fads that were sweeping his field . . . . I remarked with some surprise that his church seemed to have remarkably little doctrine capable of resisting these trends. He was offended and said there had always been tradition. Both of our fields purport to rest upon sacred texts, and it seemed odd that in both the main bulwark against heresy should be only tradition. Law is certainly like that . . . . As Alexander Bickel observed, all we ever had was a tradition, and in the last 30 years that has been shattered.

Now we need theory, theory that relates the framers' values to today's world. That is not an impossible task by any means, but it is ... complex. ...[57]

Now we need theory, theory that relates the Framers' prudence to today's world. That is precisely what Professor Jaffa offers. He and Judge Bork are natural allies.

## III. He has Refused his Assent to the Works of Jeane Kirkpatrick, Which Are Wholesome and Necessary for the Public Good

Professor Jaffa quotes from the works of Mrs. Kirkpatrick:

> The freedom of the American people is based not on the marvelous and inspiring slogans of Thomas Paine but, in fact, on the careful web of restraints, of permission, of interests, of tradition woven by the Founding Fathers into the Constitution and explained in *The Federalist Papers*. And rooted, of course, in our concrete rights as Englishmen.[58]

Then he denies that she believes that one should "look for the principles of the Constitution [in] the Declaration of Independence."[59] He alleges that she denies the natural rights of man.[60] He alleges also that she denies that public opinion at the time of the Founding was antislavery.[61] Further, as with his allegations against Judge Bork, Professor Jaffa argues that these alleged opinions are evidence that the defendant, knowingly or unknowingly, is a Calhounian defender of legal realism and states' rights, and thereby slavery.[62] As in his indictment of Judge Bork, Professor Jaffa provides us with very few quotations, and some of the allegations are unsupported by references to any text, so I will have to refer to works in addition to those cited by the prosecution.

The selection quoted above by Professor Jaffa is from Mrs. Kirkpatrick's speech, "The Reagan Phenomenon and the Liberal Tradition."[63] Taken alone it could reasonably be interpreted the way Professor Jaffa uses it. But taken in context, a different and more favorable interpretation suggests itself. This passage is used by Professor Jaffa in support of his allegation that Thomas Paine is a surrogate for Thomas Jefferson in the works of Mrs. Kirkpatrick and that she rejects the Declaration[64] in favor of the "rights of

Englishmen." But this passage, when published later in final, book form, appears within two pages of the following explanation of what these rights are:

> The government of the United States was founded squarely and explicitly on the belief that the most basic function of government is to protect the rights of its citizens. Our Declaration of Independence states, "We hold these truths to be self-evident: that all men are created equal, that they are endowed by their creator with certain unalienable rights, that among these are life, liberty and the pursuit of happiness." It adds, "To protect these rights, governments are instituted among men, deriving their just powers from the consent of the governed."
>
> These notions—that the individual has rights which are prior to government, that protection of these rights is the purpose of the very existence of government, that the just powers of government depend on the consent of the governed—are the core of the American creed. That being the case, we naturally believe that the United Nations has no more important charge than the protection or expansion of the rights of persons.[65]

So the Declaration is the core itself of what America means, and Mrs. Kirkpatrick uses it to interpret not only American law but international law as well. How could Professor Jaffa ask for more? Lest someone allege that she does not understand the implications of natural rights for the attitude of the law to relations among blacks and whites, another speech in the same volume, which addresses itself to relations between American and sub-Saharan Africa, leaves no doubt on this question. Mrs. Kirkpatrick rejoices in the advantage in world affairs that America has because of the federal government's uncompromising stance against both public and private "discrimination." America's position as the only large successful multiracial society in the West with a democratic government gives us a tremendous moral advantage in dealing with African and Asian countries. It is clear that Mrs. Kirkpatrick is proud of our achievements in civil rights and wishes the efforts of the federal government to continue.

How do we reconcile these two apparently contradictory texts? One says that Americanism is the traditional rights of Englishmen, and the other says that Americanism is the rights of man. The simplest way is to suppose that the two are understood to be one. The rights of Englishmen are the rights of Englishmen as understood by the American Founding generation; and Jefferson claimed that the Declaration was nothing new but rather represented the common sense of the subject. Mrs. Kirkpatrick is simply correct to identify the rights of Englishmen with the natural rights of man. Judge Blackstone writes that the common law on this question follows "the law of nature and reason":

> The three origins of the right of slavery assigned by Justinian, are all of them built upon false foundations. As, first, slavery is held to arise "*jure gentium*," from a state of captivity in war . . . . But it is an untrue position . . . that, by the law of nature or nations, a man may kill his enemy: he has only a right to kill . . . for self-defence . . . . [S]econdly, it is said that slavery may begin "*jure civili*," when one man sells himself to another. . . . [But,] every sale implies a price, a *quid pro quo* . . . : but what equivalent can be given for life, and liberty . . . ? Lastly, we are told, that . . . slaves . . . may also be hereditary . . . , *jure naturae* . . . . But this being built on the two former rights must fall together with them.[66]

Blackstone, having demolished on natural-rights grounds the arguments for slavery, goes on to state the absolute rule, and cites the famous *Somerset* case by Lord Mansfield.[67] In the words of Judge Blackstone,

> Upon these principles the law of England abhors, and will not endure the existence of, slavery within this nation: so that when an attempt was made to introduce it, by statute 1 Edw. VI. c.3. which ordained, that all idle vagabonds should be made slaves, and fed upon bread, water, or small drink, and refuse meat; should wear a ring of iron round their necks . . .[etc.]; *the spirit of the nation could not brook this condition, even in the most abandoned rogues; and therefore this statute was repealed in two years afterwards.* And now it is laid down, that a slave or negro, the instant he lands in England, becomes a freeman; that is, the law will protect him in the enjoyment of his person, his liberty, and his property. . . . Hence too it follows, that the infamous and unchristian practice of withholding baptism from negro servants, lest they should thereby gain their liberty, is totally without foundation, as well as without excuse. The law of England acts upon general and extensive principles: it gives liberty. . . .[68] [emphasis added]

In other words, slavery is contrary to the "extensive principles" of natural right and is incompatible with the spirit of the common law. This means that it can exist only by positive law. If any legislature does legalize it, that statute should be interpreted as narrowly as possible by judges and will soon be repealed. What happened in the colonies was, therefore, an aberration. Professor Jaffa exaggerates the differences between England and New England, and Virginia, when he dives through the surface to deal only with theory. In theory the Parliament *can* do anything that is not naturally impossible. But what the British mean by that is that, of course, it *will* not do anything contrary to natural right. If it tries to do so, the offending statutes will be repealed.

Another difficulty remains with the practice of diving through the surface of the law to deal only with natural law. Even assuming *arguendo* that Mrs. Kirkpatrick and Judge Blackstone are wrong about the "general and extensive" character of the rights of Englishmen, and somehow both secretly reject natural-rights teachings, it still does not follow that they must agree with Chief Justice Taney in *Dred Scott*. There almost always is a narrower ground on which a judge should decide such questions. For example, the Fifth Amendment, when it says that no person shall be deprived of his property (in slaves or in something else) *without* due process of law, necessarily implies thereby that any person may be deprived of his property *with* due process. Therefore, there is nothing in the Constitution of 1787 to prevent Congress from abolishing slavery in all of the territories pursuant to Article IV, Section 3, para. 2.[69] We need refer to first principles only when the text is ambiguous. On the question of the broad authority of Congress to regulate property and liberty, there is little ambiguity.[70] Likewise, hardly ambiguous is Mrs. Kirkpatrick's understanding that the Declaration of Independence is the "core" of not only American law but of the entire "American creed." It is like Blackstone's "spirit of the nation," which is so powerful that it can repeal acts of Parliament within two years time. If this is the case, the difference between Mrs. Kirkpatrick and Professor Jaffa dissolves down to a disagreement over the status of Thomas Paine. And that question is not worth discussing here.

# IV. He has Refused his Assent to the Works of Martin Diamond, Which are Wholesome and Necessary for the Public Good.

Professor Jaffa notices that the late Martin Diamond has written that the Declaration provides "no guidance whatsoever" for the construction of the Constitution of 1787—that the Declaration is "neutral" on this question.[71] This statement is alleged to be evidence that Mr. Diamond, like Judge Bork and Mrs. Kirkpatrick, and like all the other members of the "whole tribe,"[72] is a Calhounian apologist for legal realism and states' rights and, therefore, slavery.

The passage in question bears consideration at some length:

What wants understanding is precisely how [not whether] our institutions of government sprang from the principle of the Declaration . . . . And what more had to be added actually to frame those institutions?[73]

Mr. Diamond found in Lincoln's 1861 "Speech in Independence Hall"[74] evidence for a tentative answer to the question of precisely how our institutions of government sprang from the Declaration:

> All the political *sentiments* I entertain have been drawn, *so far as I have been able to draw them*, from the *sentiments* which originated, and were given to the world from this hall in which we stand. I have never had a *feeling* politically that did not spring from the *sentiments* embodied in the Declaration of Independence.[75]

It is interesting to note that the sentiment that Lincoln drew from the Declaration was not equality but liberty:

> I have often inquired of myself, what great principle or idea it was that kept this Confederacy so long together. It was not the mere matter of the separation of the colonies from the motherland; but something in the Declaration giving liberty, not alone to the people of this country, but hope to the world for all future time . . . . This is the sentiment embodied in that Declaration of Independence.[76]

What is the meaning of this interpretation of the Declaration? Mr. Diamond:

> We must take careful heed of Lincoln's remarkable stress, throughout this speech from which we are quoting, on the words feeling and sentiment. He carefully limits his indebtedness to the Declaration only to certain sentiments and feelings, that is, to the spirit of liberty within which he conceives American government and its institutions. Indeed, he could not have done otherwise . . . .[77]

Mr. Diamond reminds us that, according to the Declaration, equality is not said to be an unalienable right. Rather it is a truth which precedes the rights and may be the logical precondition for the three unalienable rights listed: life, liberty, and the pursuit of happiness:

> . . . for there is nothing in the Declaration which goes beyond that sentiment of liberty . . . . [N]oble document that the Declaration is, indispensable source of the feelings and sentiments of Americans and of the spirit of liberty in which

their institutions were conceived, the Declaration is devoid of guidance as to what those institutions should be.[78]

Mr. Diamond then quotes from a letter from James Madison to Thomas Jefferson which assumes that the works of John Locke, from which Jefferson drew the Declaration, are likewise insufficient guides to interpret the Constitution.[79]

There is no doubt that Mr. Diamond in the above passage has made himself vulnerable to Professor Jaffa's allegations. Professor Jaffa has an instinct for the jugular. But should not the advocate distinguish between the holding of a case and mere *obiter dictum*, by examining not the rhetorical flourish ("devoid of guidance") but the facts of the concrete case at hand? The concrete questions that Mr. Diamond is addressing are the following: If the American people, by means of the procedures set forth in the Constitution of 1787, were to amend the Constitution to provide for an hereditary executive office and a House of Lords, would that be unconstitutional because of the Declaration of Independence?[80] And, did the Declaration make property qualifications for the franchise unconstitutional?[81] Mr. Diamond's answer to both questions is, "No." I believe that Mr. Diamond is right.

Is it not true that the Declaration attacks tyranny—not monarchy? If it is only "a Prince whose Character is thus marked by every act which may define a tyrant" who is "unfit to be the Ruler of a free People," the implication is that a prince whose character is not so marked would be fit to rule a free people. Why would not a Whig monarchy, like England today, in which the form of government is very democratic, in which the hereditary executive is merely another public servant serving at the pleasure of Parliament, be consistent with the Declaration? Professor Jaffa says that the

> American Whigs were willing to pretend that the monarchical . . . features of the British constitution were compatible with their natural rights, as a concession that any people might prudently make "while evils are sufferable," rather than "abolishing the forms to which they are accustomed." But when evils were no longer sufferable and revolution became necessary, prudence no longer dictated restraint to Americans in making their institutions wholly republican.[82]

However, the Declaration says that it is the right of the people to institute their government, laying its foundations on such principles, and organizing its powers not in republican form but in whatever form, as to them shall seem most likely to effect their safety and happiness. Again and again during the Federal Convention, when the Framers were speaking in private and when the prerevolutionary fear of persecution was long past, several leading Framers warmly described the British government as "the best in the world."[83] In accordance with Judge Bork's method of inference from historical context, can we not agree with Mr. Diamond that it is unlikely that the Founding generation would have signed and subscribed to a Declaration of Independence that is incompatible with the best government in the world? If so, slavery may be an untypical case—one of the few institutions that cannot be reconciled with the Declaration. If the Declaration is open even to constitutional monarchy, would it not then be open to almost any other institution that is likely to come before the courts—provided that the institution in question has the consent of the people?

With regard to the question of property qualifications on the franchise, the purpose of Mr. Diamond's argument is to show that such qualifications by the states could be compatible with the Constitution and the Declaration—if they are reasonable and mild and have the consent of the people. Mr. Diamond recognizes, of course, that such qualifications are abhorrent to American law today. However, he asserts that the present situation is caused more by the Constitution of 1787 than by the Declaration of Independence. The Constitution of 1787 is the more democratic of the two documents because it is the one that specifies our democratic institutions.[84] This thesis is intended as a salutary refutation of those who argue that the Constitution of 1787 is conservative while the Declaration is liberal, hence the Constitution represents the revolution betrayed:

> These are the two great charters of our national existence, representing the beginning of our Founding and its consummation; in them are incarnated the two principles—liberty and democracy—upon the basis of which our political order was established, and upon the understanding of which in each generation our political life in some important way depends.[85]

This, then, is the "holding" of Mr. Diamond's essay. The dictum is "devoid of guidance," but the holding is that, just as Professor Jaffa would say, our entire "political life," which must include all of our laws, "depends" on the Declaration. The "democratic" "sentiment" of the Declaration works on the law to prohibit property qualifications on the franchise, and it does this by working through a Constitution that does not specifically forbid such qualifications.

What, then, is the difference between the teachings of Professor Jaffa and of Mr. Diamond? It seems that they agree that the Declaration is the core of the American creed, that it means what it says that all men are created equal, that the positive laws somehow "depend" upon it, that Lincoln interpreted the Declaration correctly, and that Lincoln's political project of emancipation was correct because it was naturally right. They disagree only as to how the Declaration acts upon the positive law.

On two crucial occasions the Supreme Court has directly invoked the Declaration to invalidate positive law. In *Dred Scott* it held that Negroes are not "men."[86] In *Gray v. Sanders* (1963) it held that "The conception of political equality from the Declaration of Independence . . . can mean only one thing—one person, one vote."[87] There can be no doubt that the method specified in the Constitution for electing United States senators does not square with the "one person, one vote" approach. It is not obvious why, if the Declaration can serve as the basis for striking down the State statute in *Gray v. Sanders*, it cannot also operate to nullify the provision in Article I, Section 3, that the Senate of the United States shall be composed of two senators from each state, regardless of the number of voters in each state. Since it is obvious that this result was not intended by the Framers of the Constitution, is it not correct to say that the result in *Gray v. Sanders* cannot rest upon the Declaration directly but requires an act of Congress to enforce the Declaration (under the Republican Form of Government Clause,[88] as Justice Frankfurter suggested in *Baker v. Carr*)[89]—just as emancipation of the slaves required either a constitutional amendment or a statute? The obvious fact that slavery is incompatible with the Declaration does not mean that slavery was illegal prior to 1865. It merely means that Congress was authorized to outlaw it when it saw fit. Mr. Diamond seems correct in arguing that the Declaration works only indirectly upon American law.

But what of Professor Jaffa's remaining allegation, that Mr. Diamond is a legal realist? In all his writings, Mr. Diamond, like Professor Jaffa, keeps before his readers the "philosophical question of what human nature is."[90] But we should let the defendant speak for himself:

> The modern idea of human nature is democratic. No difference among us can reach so far as to alter our naturally equal humanness, and *that* is the crucial fact . . . . Now a democracy derived, so to speak, from the natural equality in depravity (or at least mediocrity) of all mankind is obviously a democracy in need of moderation . . . . And the means for achieving this moderation, obviously, would have to be drawn from that same human nature, the universal fallibility of which had justified democracy in the first place. The scheme . . . is nowhere stated more thoughtfully, nor more chillingly, than by James Madison in *Federalist* 51 . . . using one person's passion or interest to check

another's [and] to emancipate acquisitiveness to a degree never contemplated by traditional political thought.[91]

In summary, Mr. Diamond's account of the significance of the Declaration of Independence shows the "chilling" necessity of the relationship between the Declaration and the Constitution and is thoroughly compatible (with the possibly minor exception of whether the Declaration operates directly or indirectly upon the positive law) with the account provided us by Professor Jaffa. One would expect such a compatibility, because these men are intellectual brothers who openly acknowledge their indebtedness to their intellectual father, Leo Strauss.[92]

# V. He has Refused his Assent to the Works of Irving Kristol, Which are Wholesome and Necessary for the Public Good

Professor Jaffa quotes from the works of Irving Kristol:

> To perceive the true purposes of the American Revolution it is wise to ignore some of the more grandiloquent declamations of the moment . . . .[93]

In the heat of debate, people do say all kinds of things. According to Mr. Kristol, one should ignore especially the excesses of Thomas Paine:

> Tom Paine, an English radical who never really understood America, is especially worth ignoring . . . [L]ook [instead] at the kinds of political activity the revolution unleashed. This activity took the form of constitution-making, above all. In the months and years immediately following the Declaration of Independence, all of our states drew up constitutions. These constitutions are terribly interesting in three respects. First, they involved relatively few basic changes in existing political institutions and almost no change at all in legal, social, or economic institutions; they were, for the most part, merely revisions of the preexisting charters. Second, most of the changes that were instituted had the evident aim of weakening the power of government, especially of the executive; it was these changes—and especially the strict separation of powers—that dismayed [the French revolutionaries], who understood revolution as an expression of the people's will-to-power rather than as an attempt to circumscribe political authority. Thirdly, in no case did any of these state constitutions tamper with the traditional system of local self-government. Indeed, they could not, since it was this traditional system of local self-government which created and legitimized the constitutional conventions themselves.[94]

Reservations about Tom Paine have been discussed in Section III above with regard to Mrs. Kirkpatrick.[95] The nub of this question is whether the texts that Professor Jaffa quotes support his allegation that criticisms of Tom Paine are intended as veiled attacks on the Declaration of Independence—which Mrs. Kirkpatrick and Mr. Kristol allegedly do not dare to attack openly. Likewise, the advantages of the method of reliance on historical context to discern the original intent of a law—notwithstanding Chief Justice Taney's misuse of the method in *Dred Scott*—are discussed above in Section II on Judge Bork. Mr. Kristol's contribution to the debate is the thesis of the continuity of the colonial institutions and charters with the Declaration. Is his point that the Declaration is thereby rendered less democratic, or that the preceding institutions are seen as more democratic?

> In short, the revolution reshaped our political institutions in such a way as to make them more responsive to popular opinion and less capable of encroaching upon the personal liberties of the citizen—liberties which long antedated the new constitutions and which in no way could be regarded as the creation or consequence of revolution. Which is to say that the purpose of this Revolution was to bring our political institutions into a more perfect correspondence with an actual "American way of life" which no one even dreamed of challenging.[96]

What is the essence of that "American way of life which no one even dreamed of challenging"? Does Mr. Kristol say that it included slavery, or does he say that it included "local self-government"? Does defense of "local self-government" represent a covert defense of slavery?

Professor Jaffa's second allegation against Mr. Kristol is that the above passage indicates that he rejects the natural right teaching of the Declaration in favor of the traditions of the American people:

> What these pristine documents of the revolution assert is in direct contradiction of Calhoun, as it is of Kristol, Bork, Kirkpatrick, and the whole tribe of present-day conservative publicists ... in reading the Declaration of Independence—and its reasoned teaching of equal and universal natural and human rights—out of the American political tradition.[97]

The third allegation against Mr. Kristol is that the thesis of the continuity of the colonial and revolutionary institutions reveals this defendant as a Calhounian defender of legal realism and states' rights and thereby slavery.

To believe what Kristol believes about this unquestioned American way of life, one would have to read the documents of the period— including the Constitution—the same way Chief Justice Taney did in *Dred Scott*.[98]

The second and third allegations both rest upon the first. The decisive question, then, with regard to the allegations against Mr. Kristol, is whether defense of "the American way of life," seen essentially as a deep commitment to "local self-government," necessarily implies rejection of universal rights and a defense of slavery.

Mr. Kristol's thesis that the Americans were a self-governing, free people from the beginning, and that as such they were fundamentally different from the Europeans who remained in Europe, is not a new thesis. Alexis de Tocqueville[99] made the same point:

America, as Marx observed in the same spirit as Tocqueville, did not have a "feudal alp" pressing down upon the brow of the living. During one hundred and seventy years of colonial life the *stuff* of American life was thus quietly being prepared in the direction of democracy.[100]

The context of Mr. Kristol's remarks is an attempt to distinguish the American from the French Revolution. It is obvious that the one suc- ceeded and the other failed to perpetuate itself in law.[101] What accounts for this difference? Are not de Tocqueville and Kristol correct to point to the centuries-old tradition of self-government in America? The success of the American Revolution, then, is because it is a much easier task to remove a monarchical lid on underlying democracy than it is to impose democracy upon a people that have never had it. It is impossible here to decide this historical question.

But even a cursory reading of "A Coppie of the Liberties of the Massa- chusetts Colonie in New England," reproduced for the convenience of the readers as an Appendix, indicates that the burden of proof remains upon Professor Jaffa to show that de Tocqueville and Kristol are wrong. If we look to the famous Virginia Bill of Rights of 1776, the continuity with both the Declaration and the Bill of Rights of 1791 is obvious. But the Massa- chusetts Body of Liberties is the most difficult case from Mr. Kristol's point of view. This document was the earliest New England code of laws and was adopted in 1641, forty-seven years before the Glorious Revolution and 135 years before the Declaration of Independence. It was adopted by the General Court of the Colony of Massachusetts Bay after having been considered by the freemen of the several towns and then revised and voted by the General Court. There are numerous parallels to the Magna Carta and the English common law. If the thesis that the colonial charters and the Declaration are in essence alike, and that all are intended primarily to protect local self-government and civil liberties, is correct, then Professor Jaffa surely does not want to argue that this thesis is Calhounian. Does he mean to argue that defense of local self-government necessarily implies defense of "squatter sovereignty" and hence defense of slavery and/or segregation?

There is evidence in Professor Jaffa's text that he would concede the above argument. He does admit that Mr. Kristol's thesis "may be regarded as true—if somewhat hyperbolic"—but only if "the American way of life" is understood to mean not what Americans *did* in practice (which included slavery)[102] but what they *said* in the Declaration and the colonial charters.[103] But this is exactly what Mr. Kristol indicates in the passage quoted above by Professor Jaffa. This is precisely why Mr. Kristol refers us to the colonial charters and to the revolutionary constitutions in the thirteen states.

If Professor Jaffa then admits that Mr. Kristol's thesis "may be regarded as true—if somewhat hyperbolic," then one should wonder what all the passion is about. Perhaps there is evidence that Mr. Kristol is influenced by the teachings of Machiavelli, whose works like those of his student, Thomas Hobbes, are "justly decried." In his Appendix A, Professor Jaffa tells us that one's position on the works of Machiavelli is a litmus test of whether one believes in the natural-right doctrine of the Declaration.[104] It is much to Mr. Kristol's credit that he has published an excellent essay, "Machiavelli and the Profanation of Politics,"[105] on just this question. Here Mr. Kristol rejects the legal-realist argument that Machiavelli simply tells it as it is, or in the words of Francis Bacon,

> We are much beholden to Machiavel and others, that write what men do, and not what they ought to do.[106]

Mr. Kristol touches the heart of the difference between the followers of Aristotle on the one hand and the followers of Machiavelli and Hobbes on the other hand, with regard to politics and the law. Aristotle, Mr. Kristol tells us, teaches that the world is naturally ordered in such a way that truly good men tend to prevail in the long run.[107] Machiavelli teaches:

> If you watch the ways of men, you will see that those who obtain great wealth and power do so either by force or fraud, and having got them they

conceal under some honest name the foulness of their deeds. Whilst those who through lack of wisdom, or from simplicity, do not employ these methods are always stifled in slavery or poverty. Faithful slaves always remain slaves, and good men are always poor men. Men will never escape from slavery unless they are unfaithful and bold, nor from poverty unless they are rapacious and fraudulent, because both God and Nature have placed the fortunes of men in such a position that they are reached rather by robbery than industry, and by evil rather than by honest skill.[108]

Mr. Kristol then classes Machiavelli not with the scientific teachers of politics as it really is but with Nietzsche and de Sade, the teachers of immorality.[109] Mr. Kristol leaves no doubt which teacher he believes is the better, more effective, guide for rulers (or for lawyers). And there can be no doubt which teacher presents the traditional doctrine of natural law.

# VI. Conclusion

For the reasons stated above, this reviewer respectfully submits that Professor Jaffa has failed to meet his burden of proof. We have appealed to Professor Jaffa's native justice and magnanimity. We conjure him by the ties of his common kindred with his intellectual brethren to disavow the terms of this debate, which would inevitably interrupt our connections and correspondence. It remains to be seen what his response will be to the voice of justice and of consanguinity.

# Professor Harry V. Jaffa Divides the House

1. F. Bacon, of the "Proficience and Advancement of Learning, Divine and Human," Book II (1605).
2. R. Niebuhr, *The Children of Light and the Children of Darkness. A Vindication of Democracy and a Critique of its Traditional Defense* xiii (1944).
3. H. JAFFA, CRISIS OF THE HOUSE DIVIDED (1959).
4. Harry V. Jaffa's CRISIS OF THE HOUSE DIVIDED is: (1) a political history of the United States through the years preceding the Civil War; (2) an analysis of the political thought of the spokesmen (Abraham Lincoln and Stephen A. Douglas) for two of the alternative courses proposed during those years; and (3) a creative venture in political philosophy that—unless the United States be as sick intellectually as some of us believe it to be—will provoke the most profound and far-reaching debate of our generation about American politics. W. KENDALL, THE CONSERVATIVE AFFIRMATION 249 (1963).
5. "Nature: from *natus*, born; the essential character of a thing; qualities that make something what it is; essence; in-born character; inherent tendencies of a person." WEBSTER'S NEW WORLD DICTIONARY OF THE AMERICAN LANGUAGE (1974) s.v. "nature." For an explication of the meaning of "nature," see L. STRAUSS, NATURAL RIGHT AND HISTORY (1953); J. Klein, "On the Nature of Nature," in LECTURES AND ESSAYS 219–239 (1985); H. Jaffa, "Is Political Freedom Grounded in Natural Law," Claremont Institute for the Study of Statesmanship and Political Philosophy (February 1984); H. JAFFA, THOMISM AND ARISTOTELIANISM (1952); G. ANASTAPLO, HUMAN BEING AND CITIZEN: ESSAYS ON VIRTUE, FREEDOM, AND THE COMMON GOOD (1975) Ch. IV: "Natural Right and the American Lawyer," Ch. V, "Liberty and Equality," which is a review of Professor Jaffa's EQUALITY AND LIBERTY: THEORY AND PRACTICE IN AMERICAN POLITICS (1965); and Ch. VI: "Law and Morality," which is a review of Lord Devlin's THE ENFORCEMENT OF MORALS (1965) and Jacob Klein's A COMMENTARY ON PLATO'S MENO

(1965); and G. Anastaplo, *Introduction, A Conversation with Harry V. Jaffa at Rosary College*, in H. JAFFA, AMERICAN CONSERVATISM AND THE AMERICAN FOUNDING (1984): the "minority belief that [is] fundamental to sensible political science and to a decent life as a community is a general respect for natural right and what is known as natural law. This means, among other things, that discrimination based on arbitrary racial categories cannot be defended, especially by a people dedicated to the self-evident truth that 'all men are created equal.' It also means that the family as an institution should be supported."

6. Jaffa, *What Were the 'Original Intentions' of the Framers of the Constitution of the United States?*, 10 U. PUGET SOUND L. REV. 351, 363, 367 (1987).
7. 1 U.S. CODE xxxv-xxxvii (1982 ed.). The other "organic laws" include the Northwest Ordinance of 1787 and the Constitution of 1787, with the Bill of Rights. The relevant portion of the Declaration is the second paragraph:
   "We hold these Truths to be self-evident, that all Men are created equal, that they are endowed by their Creator with certain unalienable Rights, that among these are Life, Liberty, and the Pursuit of Happiness—That to secure these Rights, Governments are instituted among Men, deriving their just Powers from the Consent of the Governed, that whenever any Form of Government becomes destructive of these Ends, it is the Right of the People to alter or to abolish it, and to institute new Government, laying its Foundation on such Principles, and organizing its Powers in such Form, as to them shall seem likely to effect their Safety and Happiness."
   1 U.S. CODE xxxv (1982 ed.).
8. Dred Scott v. Sanford, 60 U.S. [19 How.] 393, 15 L.Ed. 691 (1857).
9. CREATED EQUAL? THE COMPLETE LINCOLN-DOUGLAS DEBATES OF 1858, 3–7, 28–29, 36–37, 77–79, 120, 217–18, 256, 309–11, 328–29, 337–38, 377–78 and 394 (P. Angle ed. 1958); H. JAFFA, CRISIS OF THE HOUSE DIVIDED (1959).
10. W. BLACKSTONE, COMMENTARIES ON THE LAWS (1st ed. 1765–1769), 4 vols [hereinafter COMMENTARIES]. For a beginning of an interpretation of the COMMENTARIES and for an explanation of why the first edition of 1765–1769 is more authoritative than later American editions for some questions of American Constitutional law, *see* R. Stone, *Review of Blackstone's Commentaries*, 8 HASTINGS CONST. L.Q. 923 (1981). A few examples of Judge Blackstone's influence on the Framers of the Constitution of 1787 include the following. His advocacy of the doctrine of "separation of powers" is persuasive. His writings on the importance of the writ of habeas corpus and of a free press, and his disavowal of all prior restraints on the press contributed to the establishment of these fundamental constitutional rights on American shores. Similarly, the Framers assumed that the relevant public was generally familiar with Blackstone's discussion of the nature of "the executive power" when they drafted Article II. In fact, W. W. Crosskey, in POLITICS AND THE

CONSTITUTION (1953), 2 vols., points out that the enumeration of some of the powers of Congress in Article I, Section 8, of the Constitution of 1787 is best understood as, in part, an amendment of the list set forth in the COMMENTARIES, transferring certain powers from the executive to the legislative branch of government. Moreover, Judge Blackstone's elucidation of the principles of sovereign immunity gained wide currency among the various colonies and became part of American law. Of course, Judge Blackstone's doctrine of natural right helped inspire the American Revolution. R. Stone, *id*. at 925.

11. For a compelling elaboration of this thesis, see W. W. CROSSKEY, POLITICS AND THE CONSTITUTION (1953 and 1980), 3 vols. Of course, as T. S. Schrock & R. C. Welsh point out in *Reconsidering the Constitutional Common Law*, 91 HARV. L. REV. 1117 (1978), none of this means that federal judges are free to make up or create laws.

12. 1 COMMENTARIES, *supra* note 10 at 448–450 ch. 17.

13. 1 COMMENTARIES, *supra* note 10 at 41.

14. 1 COMMENTARIES, *supra* note 10 at 27.

15. *See* J. CALHOUN, A DISQUISITION ON GOVERNMENT (1853). *See also* R. Lerner, *Calhoun's New Science of Politics*, 57 AMERICAN POL. SCI. REV. 918–932 (1963).

16. Douglas would take exception to any characterization of him as standing in for Calhoun. His career, as Professor Jaffa points out in CRISIS OF THE HOUSE DIVIDED, was devoted to avoiding the Civil War by finding a middle course between Lincoln and Calhoun. He did not agree with Calhoun that slavery is a positive good or that the Constitutional rights of the South were violated by the Missouri Compromise. But Lincoln is right when he saw that, on the question of the natural rights of man, there are only two viable opinions.

17. For one example, *see* Duncan Kennedy, *The Structure of Blackstone's Commentaries*, 28 BUFF. L. REV. 205 (1979): "[All] legal thinking . . . has a double motive. On the one hand, it is an effort to discover . . . social justice. On the other, it is an attempt to deny the truth . . . about the actual . . . social world. . . . In its second aspect, it has been . . . an instrument of apology—an attempt to mystify . . . by convincing [us] of the "naturalness," the "freedom" and the "rationality" of a condition of bondage . . . something like chaos." (at 210–211).

18. For an interpretation of the works of Machiavelli that touches the heart of his disagreement with Aristotle, *see* I. Kristol, *Machiavelli and the Profanation of Politics*, in REFLECTIONS OF A NEO-CONVERVATIVE (1983), discussed in this review *infra* at 499.

19. *See supra* note 8.

20. The Missouri Compromise, effective 1820 and repealed in 1854, comprised two statutes. One provided that Maine would enter the Union as a free State. Act of April 7, 1820, 16th Cong. Sess. 1, ch. 19, 3 *U.S. Statutes at Large* 544.

The other statute provided that Missouri would enter as a slave State, with slavery prohibited elsewhere in the Louisiana Purchase north of 36 degrees 30 minutes. Act of March 6, 1820, 16th Cong. Sess. 1, ch. 22, 3 *U.S. Statutes at Large* 545. The Kansas-Nebraska Act, effective May 30, 1854, repealed the Missouri Compromise. Southerners wanted no territory west of Missouri to become free and so had prevented attempts to organize Kansas and Nebraska as one territory. The Act was sponsored by Stephen A. Douglas and provided for two separate territories, each of which would decide the slavery question for itself according to the principle of "popular sovereignty." The practical result was that both pro- and antislavery forces sent money and armed settlers into Kansas to influence the vote by means of force. The results of this "squatter sovereignty" were "bleeding Kansas" and the formation of the Republican party, which sought to repeal the Act.

21. Act of May 30, 1854, "An Act to Organize the Territories of Nebraska and Kansas," 33d Cong. Sess. 1, ch. 59, 10 *U.S. Statutes at Large*, 277.

22. *Cf.* A. Lincoln's Address, at Cooper Union, New York (February 27, 1860). "Let us have faith that right makes might, and in that faith, let us, to the end, dare to do our duty as we understand it." 3 THE COLLECTED WORKS OF ABRAHAM LINCOLN 550 (R. Basler ed. 1953).

23. The origin of legal realism is T. HOBBES, THE LEVIATHAN (1651). Before Hobbes, no thinker on the law had dared to take explicitly such an antimoral position. In Plato's *Republic*, legal realism is argued by Thrasymachus, who asserts that justice is the interest of the stronger. But Thrasymachus is shamed into silence by Socrates. In American legal science, the most revered exponent of legal realism, or legal positivism, is Oliver Wendell Holmes, Jr. "What Marshall had raised, Holmes sought to destroy. The natural constitution behind the written constitution, characteristic of Marshall's jurisprudence and the object of the court's solicitude, was to give way to the will of society and the competitive conditions for its appearance." FAULKNER, THE JURISPRU-DENCE OF JOHN MARSHALL. "There is no meaning in the rights of man except what the crowd will fight for." Letter, Holmes to Harold Laski (July 28, 1916), 1 HOLMES-LASKI LETTERS 8 (1953).

24. "We are under a Constitution, but the Constitution is what the judges say it is." Charles Evans Hughes, Speech at Elmira, New York (May 3, 1907). "Just so far as the aid of the public force is given a man, he has a legal right, and this right is the same whether his claim is founded in righteousness or iniquity." O. W. HOLMES, JR., THE COMMON LAW 169 (M.D. Howe ed. 1963).

25. The doctrine of legal realism is for the most part confined to the law schools. The crucial defect in American Legal Realism is that it stops at the courthouse door. It has no meaning for either an advocate or a judge. The judge trying to decide a case will not be helped by the reflection that the law is anything he says it is, nor will the lawyer serve his clients' cause by arguing it in those terms. R. RHODES, THE LEGAL ENTERPRISE 20 (1976).

26. The inaugural address of Thomas Jefferson, quoted by Jaffa, *supra* note 6 at 359.
27. H. JAFFA, CRISIS OF THE HOUSE DIVIDED (1959).
28. W. KENDALL, THE CONSERVATIVE AFFIRMATION 252 (1963).
29. W. KENDALL AND G. CAREY, THE BASIC SYMBOLS OF THE AMERICAN POLITICAL TRADITION 155–156 (1970). For a refutation of Kendall and Carey, *See* H. Jaffa, *Equality as a Conservative Principle*, in HOW TO THINK ABOUT THE AMERICAN REVOLUTION: A BICENTENNIAL CELEBRATION 13–48 (1978).
30. "The conception of political equality from the Declaration of Independence . . . can mean only one thing—one person, one vote." Gray v. Sanders, 372 U.S. 368, 381 (1963), which struck down Georgia's county-unit system of voting for statewide offices. If the principle of this case were correct, the present system of electing United States senators, in which one vote in Wyoming counts the same as about sixty-five votes in California, would be incompatible with the Declaration.
31. "What is conservatism? Is it not adherence to the old and tried, against the new and untried?" A. Lincoln's Address, at Cooper Union, New York (February 27, 1860), 3 THE COLLECTED WORKS OF ABRAHAM LINCOLN 537 (R. Basler ed. 1953).
32. Jaffa, *supra* note 6 at 379.
33. Jaffa, *supra* note 6 at 373.
34. Jaffa, *supra* note 6 at 385, 394.
35. Jaffa, *supra* note 6 at 373, 380, 385, 391. We are dealing here with an entire "legion of present-day Conservative epigones" of Calhoun. Jaffa, *supra* note 6 at 377.
36. Of course, to be bound by a text does not mean that one is not supposed to consider the history of the text and the purpose of the text in context. "Original intention" means original context, and that must include history secondarily. In the words of Judge Bork,

> I represent that school of thought which insists that the judiciary invalidate the work of the political branches only in accordance with an inference whose underlying premise is fairly discoverable in the Constitution itself. That leaves room, of course, not only for textual analysis, but also for historical discourse and interpretation according to the Constitution's structure and function.

> The latter approach is the judicial method of McCulloch v. Maryland, for example, and it has been well analyzed by my colleague Professor Charles Black in his book, STRUCTURE AND RELATIONSHIP IN CONSTITUTIONAL LAW [1969].

37. R. Bork, *Commentary: The Impossibility of Finding Welfare Rights in the Constitution*," (1979) WASH. U. L.Q. 695.
38. *Id.* at 700.
39. G. STONE, SEIDMAN, SUNSTEIN, AND TUSHNET, CONSTITUTIONAL LAW (1986), assert that the doctrine of representation-reinforcement is, to use a

phrase those authors would eschew, the "final cause" of Roe v. Wade, 410 U.S. 113 (1973).

40. R. Bork, *supra* note 37 at 701.
41. 198 U.S. 45 (1905).
42. Holmes's opinion bears further quotations:

     It is settled . . . that . . . state laws may regulate life in many ways which we as legislators might think as injudicious . . . and which . . . interfere with the liberty to contract . . . . Sunday laws and usury laws are ancient examples. A more modern one is the prohibition on lotteries. The liberty of the citizen to do as he likes so long as he does not interfere with the liberty of others to do the same, which has been a shibboleth for some well-known writers, is interfered with by school laws, by the Post Office, by every state or municipal institution which takes his money for purposes thought desirable, whether he likes it or not. The Fourteenth Amendment does not enact Mr. Herbert Spencer's Social Statics.

     198 U.S. At 75. The force of Justice Holmes's dissent is not diminished by recognition that he, unlike Judge Bork, was a "legal realist."
43. R. Bork, *supra* note 37 at 696.
44. "Indeed, in one important respect the American Revolution was so successful as to be almost self-defeating: It turned the attention of thinking men away from politics, which now seemed utterly unproblematic, so that political theory lost its vigor, and even the political thought of the Founding Fathers was not seriously studied." I. Kristol, *The American Revolution as a Successful Revolution*, AMERICA'S CONTINUING REVOLUTION 9 (1975).
45. R. Bork, *Styles in Constitutional Theory*, 26 S. TEX. L.J. 383, 394 (1955).
46. R. Bork, *Tradition and Morality in Constitutional Law*, in VIEWS FROM THE BENCH: THE JUDICIARY AND CONSTITUTIONAL POLITICS 166 (M. Cannon and D. O'Brien Eds.) (1985) (cited by Jaffa, *supra* note 6 at 373).
47. *Id.* at 167.
48. Jaffa, *supra* note 6 at 376.
49. There is no evidence whatsoever that Judge Bork would include slavery in the traditions of Anglo-American law or in the common sense of the community. Judge Bork knows the common law, and Blackstone makes it clear that slavery is wholly incompatible with the common law, that it can exist only by statute, and that judges should restrict it whenever and however possible. The common sense of the community is the common law for most purposes. 1 COMMENTARIES ON THE LAW *supra* note 10, at 412–413 (1st ed. 1765–1769). For another argument that slavery is un-American, see *infra* note 102 of this brief.
50. *See supra* note 46.
51. *Id.* at 169.
52. *Id.* at 167.
53. *Id.* at 170.
54. *Id.* at 171 (quoting R. NEUHAUS).

55. With regard to moral ground, Professor Jaffa implies that one's position on
what used to be called the Negro Question is the litmus test of American
politics. Judge Bork, in CONSTITUTIONALITY OF THE PRESIDENT'S BUSING
PROPOSALS (1972), argues—against some reputable students of the law—
that Congress is granted, by section 5 of the Fourteenth Amendment, signifi-
cant power to regulate the use of busing as a remedy in desegregation decrees.
On the other hand, Judge Bork also argues that Congress does *not* have the
authority to except all busing cases from the jurisdiction of the Supreme
Court, a tactic that Congress was at one time considering to stop busing.
Nominations of Joseph T. Sneed to Be Deputy Attorney General and Robert
H. Bork to Be Solicitor General: Hearings before the Committee on the
Judiciary, 93rd Cong. 1st Sess. 22–23 (1973) (exchange between Mr. Bork
and Senator Hart). Senator Hart responds, "I wish the full committee were
here to hear that."
56. Jaffa, *supra* note 6 at 379.
57. See *supra* note 46 at 171.
58. JAFFA, *supra* note 6 at 375, (quoting from an article in the *National Review*).
The same passage appears in book form in a collection of essays. *See The
Reagan Phenomenon and the Liberal Tradition*, THE REAGAN PHENOMENON
AND OTHER SPEECHES ON FOREIGN POLICY 3–45 (1983).
59. Jaffa, *supra* note 6 at 377.
60. Jaffa, *supra* note 6 at 380, 382, 385.
61. Jaffa, *supra* note 6 at 391.
62. Jaffa, *supra* note 6 at 385.
63. *Supra* note 58 at 44.
64. "The truth, however, is that it is Jefferson who is being depreciated in the
slighting of Paine. But he [Jefferson] is too large a figure to be attacked
directly. And it is not the *Rights of Man*, but the Declaration of Independence,
which by indirection is the object of their patronizing condescension." Jaffa,
*supra* note 6 at 375–76.
65. Statement before the Third Committee of the United Nations General Assembly (November 24, 1981), *reprinted* in *Human Rights and Wrongs in the
United Nations*, in THE REAGAN PHENOMENON AND OTHER SPEECHES ON
FOREIGN POLICY 46 (1983).
66. 1 COMMENTARIES *supra* note 10 at 411–412.
67. Somerset v. Stewart, 20 How. St. Tr. 1, Easter Term, 12 Geo. 3, K.B. (May 14,
1772).
68. 1 COMMENTARIES *supra* note 10 at 412–413.
69. U.S. CONST. Art. 4 section 3, cl. 2 U.S. Code xxxvii (1982): "The Congress
shall have power to dispose of and make all needful rules and regulations
respecting the territory or other property belonging to the United States; and
nothing in this Constitution shall be so construed as to prejudice any claims of
the United States . . . ."

70. For a most instructive commentary on the text and context of the Constitution of 1787, *see* G. Anastaplo, *The Constitution of 1787: A Commentary* (Baltimore and London: The Johns Hopkins University Press, 1989). *Cf.* Lochner v. New York, 198 U.S. 45 (1905), which nullifies a New York statute fixing maximum hours of work for bakers. The Supreme Court, defending liberty from what is conceived as a mere meddlesome interference, asked, "[A]re we all . . . at the mercy of legislative majorities?" 198 U.S. at 59. The correct answer, especially when the majority is in the United States Congress and not the Assembly of New York, is "Yes." R. Bork, *Neutral Principles and Some First Amendment Problems*, 47 IND. L.J. 1, 11 (1971).

71. Jaffa, *supra* note 6 at 373, 386.

72. Jaffa, *supra* note 6 at 380, 377.

73. M. DIAMOND, *The Revolution of Sober Expectations*, in AMERICA'S CONTINUING REVOLUTION, 27 (1975).

74. 4 THE COLLECTED WORKS OF ABRAHAM LINCOLN 240–241 (R. Basler, Ed. 1953).

75. *Id.* at 240 (quoted with emphasis added by Mr. Diamond, *supra* note 73 at 27).

76. *Id.*

77. M. DIAMOND, *supra* note 73 at 27.

78. *Id.* at 27–28.

79. Letter, James Madison to Thomas Jefferson, February 8, 1825, 9 THE WRITINGS OF JAMES MADISON 218–219 (G. Hunt ed. 1900), discussed in M. DIAMOND, *supra* note 73 at 28–30.

80. M. Diamond, *supra* note 73 at 31–36.

81. *Id.* at 37–38.

82. Jaffa, *supra* note 6 at 387.

83. *See, e.g.*, (A. Hamilton) J. MADISON, NOTES OF DEBATES IN THE FEDERAL CONVENTION OF 1787, 134 (Ohio University Press ed. 1966).

84. "Article I, Section 2 . . . establishes the then broadest possible democratic franchise as the basis of the federal election . . . . To this may be added the total absence of any property qualifications, contrary to existing state practices, for any federal office, and also the clause barring the introduction of any titles of nobility. Finally, we may note the provision for payment of salaries to federal officeholders . . . ." M. DIAMOND, *supra* note 73 at 38.

85. M. DIAMOND, *The Declaration and the Constitution: Liberty, Democracy, and the Founders*, in THE AMERICAN COMMONWEALTH 39, 45–46 (1976).

86. 15 L.Ed. at 703 "[I]t is too clear for dispute, that the enslaved African race were not intended to be included [in] this Declaration."

87. 372 U.S. 368, 381 (1963).

88. U.S. CONST., at IV, § 4: "The United States shall guarantee to every state in this union a Republican form of government, and shall protect each of them against invasion . . . ."

89. 369 U.S. 186, 301 (1962) (Frankfurter, J., dissenting, joined by Harlan, J.).

90. This is the opening phrase of Mr. Diamond's essay, *The American Idea of Man: The View from the Founding*, THE AMERICANS: AN INQUIRY INTO FUNDAMENTAL CONCEPTS OF MAN UNDERLYING VARIOUS U.S. INSTITUTIONS (I. Kristol and P. Weaver eds. 1976).

91. *Id.* at 7–14.

92. L. STRAUSS, NATURAL RIGHT AND HISTORY (1953), remains the definitive study of the modern natural-right doctrine of Hobbes and Locke.

93. I. Kristol, *The American Revolution as a Successful Revolution*, in AMERICA'S CONTINUING REVOLUTION 1, 13 (1975).

94. I. KRISTOL, *supra* note 93 at 13–14, quoted by Jaffa, *supra* note 6 at 373, 375–376, 380, 386.

95. *See infra* at 485–488.

96. I. KRISTOL, *supra* note 93 at 14.

97. Jaffa, *supra* note 6 at 380.

98. Jaffa, *supra* note 6 at 376.

99. ALEXIS DE TOCQUEVILLE, DEMOCRACY IN AMERICA (G. Lawrence trans. 1969).

100. M. Diamond, *The Revolution of Sober Expectations*, AMERICA'S CONTINUING REVOLUTION 23, 36 (1975).

101. The laws of the American Revolution are still in force more than two centuries after the Declaration. And they are in force not merely on paper but in the hearts and minds of Americans. The laws of the French Revolution, which had been purchased at the enormous cost of the Terror, endured only fifteen years until Bonaparte restored the absolute executive. And France became a democratic republic only about eighty years after the French Revolution.

102. "It is by no means settled that the American way of life . . . in 1776 and 1787" included slavery. JAFFA, *supra* note 6 at 376. *Cf.* Jaffa, *supra* note 6 at 364 (where he describes slavery as an anomaly). Few New Englanders or Pennsylvania Quakers would have agreed with him. Americans at the Feast of Thanksgiving, their most characteristic holy day, stubbornly persist in revering as their ancestors the Pilgrims of what soon became Massachusetts, not the dashing, wealthy cavaliers that settled Jamestown in Virginia—in spite of the embarrassing facts that Jamestown was settled earlier, that the first Thanksgiving was celebrated at Jamestown, and that Governor Bradford's famous diary is silent about the supposed first Thanksgiving at Plymouth. A plausible explanation for this apparent anomaly is that Americans have for centuries seen themselves as belonging to Massachusetts and not to Virginia. Massachusetts was the leader in the Revolution and the leader in agitation for emancipation. It is no accident that Thanksgiving was instituted as a national holiday by Abraham Lincoln during the Civil War. The Virginian way of life, including slavery and the oligarchic traditions it made possible, was correctly perceived as being un-American—for the reasons Professor

Jaffa and Mr. Kristol point out. R. STONE, CIVIC EDUCATION, HOLIDAYS, AND THE UNITED STATES' REGIME 358–380 (1986).

103. Jaffa, *supra* note 6 at 389.

104. Jaffa, *supra* note 6 at Appendix A, p. 398.

105. I. KRISTOL, *Machiavelli and the Profanation of Politics*, REFLECTIONS OF A NEOCONSERVATIVE 123 (1983).

106. 2 F. BACON, OF THE PROFICIENCE AND ADVANCEMENT OF LEARNING, DIVINE AND HUMAN (1605).

107. I. KRISTOL, *supra* note 105 at 123–125, citing Aquinas: "Eventus sequens no facit actum malum qui erat bonus, nec bonum qui erat malus."

108. N. MACHIAVELLI, HISTORY OF FLORENCE AND OF THE AFFAIRS OF ITALY FROM THE EARLIEST TIMES TO THE DEATH OF LORENZO THE MAGNIFICENT (1532), (quoted in I. KRISTOL, *supra* note 105 at 129).

109. I. KRISTOL, *supra* note 105 at 134.

# Seven Questions for Professor Jaffa

## GEORGE ANASTAPLO

*We must not expect that liberal education can ever become universal education. It will always remain the obligation and the privilege of a minority. Nor can we expect that the liberally educated will become a political power in their own right. For we cannot expect that liberal education will lead all who benefit from it to understand their civic responsibility in the same way or to agree politically. Karl Marx, the father of communism, and Friedrich Nietzsche, the stepgrandfather of fascism, were liberally educated on a level to which we cannot even hope to aspire. But perhaps one can say that their grandiose failures make it easier for us who have experienced those failures to understand again the old saying that wisdom cannot be separated from moderation and hence to understand that wisdom requires unhesitating loyalty to a decent constitution and even to the cause of constitutionalism. Moderation will protect us against the twin dangers of visionary expectations from politics and unmanly contempt for politics. Thus it may again become true that all liberally educated men will be politically moderate men. It is in this way that the liberally educated may again receive a hearing even in the market place.*

—LEO STRAUSS[1]

## Prologue

The reader who has had the privilege of studying the essays by Harry V. Jaffa collected in his "Original Intentions" article in the Spring 1987 issue of the *University of Puget Sound Law Review* should be able to appreciate what has long been evident about the work of a scholar whose considerable learning is surpassed only by his dedicated passion.[2] It should be evident as well why Professor Jaffa has been able to enlist as he has, for some years

167

now, so many talented young people for an unrelenting crusade to save our country from the deadly follies of liberals and conservatives alike.

My longstanding assessment of Mr. Jaffa's work is indicated in the Introduction I made of him for a "Conversation" at Rosary College on December 4, 1980 (while I was still teaching there).[3] That Rosary College Introduction and the interesting colloquy which followed between Mr. Jaffa and his audience have been published by Mr. Jaffa in his next book.[4] My 1980 Introduction of him went something like this:

It is my privilege to introduce on this occasion a friend of a quarter century and a distinguished political scientist, Harry V. Jaffa, of Claremont Men's College and Claremont Graduate School. Professor Jaffa, whose appearance at Rosary College has been made possible by the support of him by the Intercollegiate Studies Institute, is available this afternoon for an extended conversation with us about matters ancient and modern.

Mr. Jaffa is, to my mind, the most instructive political scientist writing in this country today. The things he writes about range from Socrates and Aristotle to Thomas Aquinas and William Shakespeare, from the Founding Fathers to Abraham Lincoln, from Tom Sawyer and Winston Churchill to contemporary politics and the joys of cycling.

I am reminded, when I encounter Mr. Jaffa, of another provocatively influential American, a great woman who died only this past weekend, Dorothy Day of the *Catholic Worker* movement (whom I was privileged to see close-up only once). It was true of Miss Day, as it is true of Mr. Jaffa, that it was virtually impossible for her not to be interesting about whatever she wrote. Intelligence, hard work, and a gift for language no doubt contributed to this capacity to invest every discourse with significance. But fundamental to such influence is a certain integrity, even a single-minded moral fervor. Thus, it could be said of Miss Day in her obituary in the *New York Times* on Monday of this week that she had sought "to work so as to bring about the kind of society where it is easier for people to be good." Much the same can be said about Mr. Jaffa. Indeed, Miss Day, in the way she lived her life, in an unrelenting effort to better the lives of the downtrodden, could be said to have put into practice the much-quoted proposition by Mr. Jaffa which was used by Senator Goldwater in his Acceptance Speech upon being nominated for the presidency by the Republican party in 1964, "I would remind you that extremism in the defense of liberty is no vice. And let me remind you also that moderation in the pursuit of justice is no virtue."

A little more should be said by me about Mr. Jaffa now, if only to suggest matters that we might want to talk about on this occasion. A few differences between us, of which I was reminded when I heard him speak yesterday at Loyola University, could usefully be indicated.

Mr. Jaffa not only makes far more of exercising than I do—I limit myself to walking whenever possible and to the avoidance of elevators for ascents or descents of less than five floors—but he also is a much more vigorous moralist than I am, both in regulating his own conduct and in judging the conduct of others. I believe that I allow more than he does for good-intentioned errors, for inefficiency on the part of people, and for circumstances which account for, sometimes even justify, what seem from the outside to be moral aberrations. Compassion can be almost as important as moral indignation in these matters, particularly with respect to domestic relations, whether the subjects be abortion, divorce, or homosexuality. Perhaps also I make more than he does of the importance—if only out of respect for the sensibilities of others and for the moral tone of the community—of discretion, if not even of good-natured hypocrisy.

We differ as well with respect to the conduct of foreign relations. We do share an abhorrence of tyranny, whether of the Right or of the Left. But we sometimes part company on assessments of how constitutional government and American republicanism can best be defended abroad. Thus, he was much more hopeful than I could ever be that our involvement in the Vietnam War (however noble in intention that involvement might have been, and *that* it surely was, in some respects)—he was much more hopeful than I was that our Vietnam involvement could do the American or the Indo-Chinese people some good. Today we differ as to precisely what kind of a threat the Russians pose to us. I see them as much more vulnerable (both politically and militarily) than does he; and I consider all too many calculations about nuclear-war "scenarios" to depend too much on game theories and not enough on political judgment. I believe, for example, that Russian leaders are much more constrained by domestic public opinion (by a pacific, even though patriotic, public opinion) and by other factors than many of us recognize. They have suffered, at home and abroad, a considerable setback in Afghanistan; we can only hope that they, and we, do not suffer an even greater setback by a Russian invasion of Poland. But whatever happens in Poland, it is now evident that the cause of freedom is bound to be in better shape in Eastern Europe than it has been since the Second World War—in part because of what Polish workers have done in showing the world how things really stand there. The only question may be what price the Polish people will have to pay, and this may depend, in part, on their prudence and on ours.

Perhaps at the heart of the differences between Mr. Jaffa and me—whether the differences be as to the status of exercise or as to assessments of the Russians—is with respect to how much one should be concerned with the preservation of one's life. An immoderate cherishing of what happens to be one's own can lead, it seems to me, to psychic paralysis or to undue combativeness: either can undermine that relaxed competence which makes healthy statesmanship more likely. Certainly, Mr. Jaffa responds much more than I do to the apocalyptic as against the comic and somewhat less than I do to "liberty" as against "equality." Obviously, we touch here on questions about the nature of human existence, of virtue, and of happiness.

On the other hand, at the heart of our deep affinities—besides the fact that we were both fortunate enough to share a great teacher in Leo Strauss—is our minority belief that fundamental to sensible political science and to a decent life as a community is a general respect for natural right and what is known as natural law. This means, among other things, that discrimination based on arbitrary racial categories cannot be defended, especially by a people dedicated to the self-evident truth that "all men are created equal." It also means that the family as an institution should be supported.

I mention in passing that we do differ with respect to the Equal Rights Amendment—but here I believe that Mr. Jaffa, even though he puts what he says in terms of nature in his opposition to that amendment, has allowed himself to be unduly influenced by the antics and "principles" of a minority of the proponents of that largely symbolic grace note for our Constitution.

Be all this as it may, an informed study of nature in human things is perhaps the most pressing demand in education today—and for this Mr. Jaffa, with his profound grasp of the classical writers, of Shakespeare's thought, and of the career of Abraham Lincoln, is an invaluable guide.

Permit me to close these introductory remarks by returning to something else that has been said about Dorothy Day, something which (with appropriate adjustments) can be applied to the tireless dedication that Mr. Jaffa devotes to his "conservative" creed and to his graduate students. We are reminded by Dorothy Day's *New York Times* obituary that Church officials in New York were "often sorely tempted to rebuke Miss Day—her ardent support of Catholic cemetery strikers a number of years ago especially irked Cardinal Spellman—but they never could catch her in any breach of Church regulations." Besides, the editor of *Commonweal* has observed, one of the bishops she fought with, James Francis McIntyre (who later became a cardinal himself), "was afraid he just might be dealing with a saint." "He was alluding to what has been called Miss Day's 'indiscriminate and uncompromising love of the Mystical Body' as well as to her courage and her care for the poor in hospices she established in New York and elsewhere."

But enough of this canonization of Harry Jaffa, who does remind me in certain ways of St. Augustine. Any effort at canonization, you recall, requires that the devil's advocate have his say also. As you can see, I have had to take on more than one role in introducing to you a gifted colleague whom we are privileged to have with us today.

Some of you must have questions—but first, Mr. Jaffa may have something to say in response to the remarks I have made in an effort to guide the conversation I look forward to in the hours and years ahead.[5]

Several of the issues touched upon in this 1980 Rosary College Introduction continue to interest me. They are reflected in the questions inspired at this time by the four "Original Intention" essays collected by Mr. Jaffa in the 1987 *Puget Sound Law Review*.6 I offer, in addition to fresh reflections upon these questions, three appendices of my own which bear upon various of the matters touched upon by Mr. Jaffa. These previously prepared appendices are entitled,

IIIA. The Founders of Our Founders: Jerusalem, Athens, and the American Constitution

IIIB. The Ambiguity of Justice in Plato's *Republic*

IIIC. Private Rights and Public Law: The Founders' Perspective.

I offer as well, in my Epilogue to this article, the informed observations of a scholar who comments upon differences between Mr. Jaffa and myself.

The questions inspired by Mr. Jaffa testify to the instructive challenges he generously lavishes upon those who are fortunate enough to know his work. Wisdom, according to Leo Strauss, consists more in clarifying the fundamental problems and alternatives than in providing answers and solutions.7 My seven questions are accompanied by suggestions about some of their presuppositions and implications. The seven questions, which shall be developed in turn, are the following:

1. What more should be said on behalf of Attorney General Meese with respect to the matters touched upon by Mr. Jaffa?

2. Does Mr. Jaffa recognize sufficiently the shortcomings of the equality which he so eloquently extols?

3. Does Mr. Jaffa mean to leave the impression that theory alone determines political practice?

4. Is there not an inevitable tension, because of the very nature of things, between philosophy and the city?

5. Does Mr. Jaffa mean to leave the impression that "the Consent of the Governed" is for the Declaration of Independence, as well as for himself, a necessary basis for legitimate government in all circumstances?

6. Does Mr. Jaffa recognize sufficiently the merits of that freedom which he routinely subordinates to equality?

7. What more should be said on behalf of Chief Justice Rehnquist and Associate Justice Brennan with respect to the matters touched upon by Mr. Jaffa?

# I.

What more should be said on behalf of Attorney General Meese with respect to the matters touched upon by Mr. Jaffa?

Mr. Meese is given a hard time by Mr. Jaffa because he ventured to suggest (in advocating "original intent") that "the Supreme Court under Chief Justice Roger B. Taney [in the *Dred Scott* case] read blacks out of the Constitution in order to invalidate Congress' attempt to limit the spread of slavery." Mr. Jaffa's immediate response is, "Unfortunately for Mr. Meese's argument, no one, on or off the Court, has ever expounded the theory of original intent with greater eloquence or conviction than Chief Justice Taney in the case of *Dred Scott*." It is difficult for me, however, to acclaim as "eloquent" or to concede as "conviction" an argument which is patently false. Critical to the highly questionable Taney argument is his finding of what the general opinion was as to the status of Africans for the statesmen who had insisted that "all Men are created equal."

Indicative of the 1776 opinion with respect to slavery is what had been said by William Blackstone in 1765:

> I have formerly observed that pure and proper slavery does not, nay cannot, subsist in England; such I mean, whereby an absolute and unlimited power is given to the master over the life and fortune of the slave. And indeed it is repugnant to reason, and the principles of natural law, that such a state should subsist any where.[8]

Blackstone then exposes the "false foundations" upon which various arguments for "the right of slavery" are based. Whatever "the necessity of the case" obliged Americans to put up with in 1776 and 1787–1789, the decisive case against slavery was known, and respected, by thinking men in all of the thirteen states during the Founding Period.

Mr. Meese is correct in sensing that chief justice Taney did not truly believe in "original intent," or else he would have approached the slavery question quite differently. The chief justice had already been shown by John C. Calhoun that the only way to get around the true original intention of the Declaration of Independence on the issue of the status of slavery was to disavow the Declaration. Taney could not do this in his circumstances; he was reduced instead to trying to reinterpret the Declaration. One can see in Taney, as in Calhoun, how reason can be subverted by passion.

Mr. Jaffa points out (in his criticisms of Mr. Meese) that "Taney's opinion in *Dred Scott* did not invalidate any attempted action of the Congress," since "the Missouri Compromise restriction of slavery" had been repealed in 1854. But since Dred Scott's owner had taken him before 1854 into jurisdictions presumably covered by congressional restrictions, it could very much matter whether those restrictions *had* been valid. The Taney opinion was also important, as Mr. Jaffa recognizes, for what it said about the Republican party platform.

Nor should one accept as readily as Mr. Jaffa seems to do the Taney proposition that the Constitution is friendly to slavery. Rather, the Constitution of 1787 can be read as reflecting a grudging accommodation to slavery, as may be seen even in the terms of the 1808 Clause in Section 9 of Article I. In addition, it is recognized in the Fugitive Slave Clause that persons claimed as slaves are held thus only by the positive laws of the states; they are not spoken of, as other persons on the run are, as fugitives from justice. These are, I believe, readings of the Constitution consistent with Abraham Lincoln's.[9]

Two other dubious features of the Taney opinion in *Dred Scott*, which Mr. Jaffa seems to acquiesce in, should be noticed. One is that Congress could not act to restrict slavery in the Territories if slaves were regarded as merely property. But constitutional provisions such as the Due Process Clause should not be taken to mean that particular kinds of property cannot be singled out for special legislative treatment (and even complete suppression) in various circumstances. It is hardly likely that the state legislatures that abolished slavery from 1776 on violated the due process clauses in their respective constitutions.

The other dubious feature in the Taney opinion to be noticed here is the assumption that what the Court said in defining the powers of Congress with respect to the Territories was binding upon Congress, and that the only way to get around the Court's reading was by constitutional amendment. The propriety of judicial review in such matters should not be taken for granted—and I believe there are indications that Lincoln did not do so, however prudent he may have thought it to acquiesce (at least for the time being) in what the Court had done in a particular case.[10]

## II.

Does Mr. Jaffa recognize sufficiently the shortcomings of the equality which he so eloquently extols?

Mr. Meese can perhaps be chided for not appreciating the full implications of the insistence by the Declaration of Independence that "all Men are created equal." Dedication to equality can no doubt contribute to justice and the common good, standing as a bulwark against tyranny. But it can also lead to an emphasis upon self-centeredness and upon private right—and these in turn can promote relativism, if not even nihilism, and hence another kind of tyranny. Certainly, mediocrity can easily become the order of the day when equality is made too much of. Perhaps it is this prospect that moves Mr. Meese and his cohorts to be as apprehensive as they sometimes seem to be about current egalitarian movements. In any event, is it not "freedom," even more than "equality," which appeals to mankind in the noblest opposition to slavery. May not this be seen in Winston Churchill's greatest speeches during the Second World War?

## III.

Does Mr. Jaffa mean to leave the impression that theory alone determines political practice?

Not enough seems to be made by Mr. Jaffa of nature (or personal temperament) and of circumstances in everyday political life. If he did make more of these, he might not be as apt as he is to subject political men to the most exacting philosophical scrutiny.

The fact remains that men can be fairminded and effective statesmen without having much in the way of philosophical astuteness. It is imprudent to regard as radically flawed human beings those political men who hold dubious theoretical opinions. To do so leaves the philosopher without allies—and, even worse perhaps, subverts the ability of decent men to do good. Such an attitude can be discerned to have been critical to the intolerance both of the Inquisition and of Stalinism.

Too much of an emphasis upon the theoretical may even be seen in Mr. Jaffa's insistence upon the natural-right tradition of the Declaration of Independence to the virtual exclusion of the prescriptive rights of the English-speaking peoples. This is to ignore the central place given in the Declaration to the grievances grounded in the British Constitution.

## IV.

Is there not an inevitable tension, because of the very nature of things, between philosophy and the city?

Of course, Mr. Jaffa recognizes this tension, but one must wonder whether he gives it sufficient weight. The limitations of the city, and of political life, may be seen in the ambiguity of justice, and of political life itself, in Plato's *Republic*.

Perhaps the most instructive essay in Mr. Jaffa's 1987 *Puget Sound* "Original Intentions" collection is what he has to say about Leszek Kolakowski. But Professor Kolakowski, as a professional philosopher, can properly be subjected to a degree of theoretical scrutiny which may be inappropriate in dealing as Mr. Jaffa does with such political men as Attorney General Meese, Chief Justice Rehnquist, and Associate Justice Brennan.

I dare to venture the opinion that even Mr. Jaffa's beloved Abraham Lincoln is not the great theoretician that he is sometimes taken to be. There is about Mr. Jaffa's passion in these matters the *eros* of the political man rather than that of the philosopher—of the political man who is driven to consider as the very best whatever happens to be his own.

It may well be that underlying Mr. Jaffa's passion here is his deep concern for the survival of philosophy itself. But both philosophy and the city may be misconceived, and ill-served, if they are brought together in the rationalistic fashion of the Enlightenment. On the limitations, and even perils, of the Enlightenment Mr. Jaffa can be most instructive.

## V.

Does Mr. Jaffa mean to leave the impression that "the Consent of the Governed" is for the Declaration of Independence, as well as for himself, a necessary basis for legitimate government in all circumstances?

Perhaps "the Consent of the Governed" associated with the Declaration of Independence can be translated into the terms used by Plato and Aristotle, but not without significant distortion. Certainly, Plato and Aristotle, as well as the Bible, recognized the possibility of just regimes that do not depend on the consent of the governed. Mr. Jaffa, in his stance here, seems more in the spirit of Rousseau, if not of the Enlightenment, than in the spirit either of the Bible or of Classical Thought, both of which he nevertheless looks up to.

To make too much of the consent of the governed may even run the risk of enthroning positive law (in the form of the will of the people) at the expense both of natural right and of divine revelation (itself an exalted form of positive law?). Mr. Jaffa does warn against this substitution—but his polemical thrusts sometimes move in a different direction from his warning.

The Framers of the Constitution spoke again and again of the merits of the British Constitution, a constitution which was not grounded in that sense of "the Consent of the Governed" that Mr. Jaffa finds to be demanded by the Declaration of Independence. Leo Strauss insisted again and again upon the superiority today of liberal democracy, even as he recognized its critical limitations—and hence its inferiority to certain regimes (not available, as a practical matter, in our time) which do not depend upon consent of the governed.[11]

I myself was obliged to recognize these reservations almost two decades ago, in the opening note of my *Constitutionalist*: "The tension evident in this study may be inevitable for anyone who tries to 'live with' both the *Apology of Socrates* and the *Declaration of Independence*—for anyone, that is, who finds himself drawn to two public declarations which are, despite their superficial compatibility, radically divergent in their presuppositions and implications. Thus, an attempt is made herein to see American constitutional law and political thought from the perspective of our ancient teachers."[12]

## VI.

Does Mr. Jaffa recognize sufficiently the merits of that freedom which he routinely subordinates to equality?

Of course, it is possible to see "freedom" and "equality" in terms of each other. Even so, freedom tends to look more to excellence, or virtue (and hence philosophy), while equality tends to make more of private interests (and hence of certain kinds of revelation). It is for this reason that Plato and Aristotle can be said to have been more open to claims based on freedom than to those based on equality, something which Leo Strauss himself pointed out on more than one occasion.

That is not to deny that freedom can deteriorate into simply living as one likes. This makes essential that liberal education which helps equip free men to make proper use—and to want to make proper use—of their freedom.[13]

## VII.

What more should be said on behalf of Chief Justice Rehnquist and Associate Justice Brennan with respect to the matters touched upon by Mr. Jaffa?

Justice Brennan does stand for the rule of law.[14] The misreadings of the Constitution that Mr. Jaffa laments have the merits of an attempt to look beyond the Constitution to the principles, or aspirations, which breathe life into our constitutional enterprise.

The chief justice, on the other hand, exhibited (as associate justice) respect for the primary purpose of the free-speech guarantee of the First Amendment. I have had occasion to say of him that "he can well become, among the members of the Court during the next decade, perhaps the closest on First Amendment issues (except on the issue of obscenity) to Hugo L. Black, the first (and probably the greatest) of the New Deal justices."[15]

In any event, it is difficult to see what practical differences there are likely to be, in terms of how cases should be decided, between Mr. Jaffa and the chief justice, whatever theoretical shortcomings Mr. Jaffa may discern in the chief justice. It is to be hoped that the chief justice will not so forget himself, and his high calling, as to subvert the teaching function of his office by proclaiming from the bench what one of his predecessors did (in order to justify packing some Communist party leaders off to jail in 1951):

> Nothing is more certain in modern society than the principle that there are no absolutes, that a name, a phrase, a standard has meaning only when associated with the considerations which gave birth to the nomenclature. . . . To those who would paralyze our Government in the face of impending threat by encasing it in a semantic straitjacket, we must reply that all concepts are relative.[16]

It is politically salutary to acknowledge what is good about both the chief justice and Justice Brennan. Thus, Justice Brennan could say, upon the recent elevation of Justice Rehnquist, "He's going to be a splendid chief justice." Decent conservatives and decent liberals do have much in common. Our regime depends upon the constant recognition by political men of their affinities, despite their respective theoretical shortcomings.[17]

I confess, that is, that I am not in these matters the purist that Mr. Jaffa is. This is, I suppose, another way of saying that I may yet have a great deal to learn from him.

# Epilogue

The reader may better grasp the questions I have posed for Mr. Jaffa (as well as for myself) if he should be reminded of how differences between us have developed heretofore. Those differences are hinted at in the 1980 Rosary College Introduction reprinted in my Prologue to this article.

Our differences (and, of course, our affinities) are further spelled out in a recent article by a scholar who has known Mr. Jaffa and me for decades and who was also privileged to study with Leo Strauss.[18] Consider Laurence Berns's instructive 1987 survey of our situation:

> The most impressive attempt known to me to combine classical thought with the principles of the American polity is to be found in the work of Harry V. Jaffa. I will for the most part confine myself here to his discussion of the Declaration of Independence in the essay, "What is Equality? The Declaration of Independence Revisited."[19] Jaffa builds on George Anastaplo's observation that the references to God in the Declaration of Independence portray him in terms of the three powers of constitutional government.[20] "All men are created equal" is interpreted by Jaffa in an Aristotelian mode placing man between beasts and God. The respects in which men are equal or the same is understood "as much by understanding what he is *not*, as by understanding what he *is*. . . . Man in not either beast or God." The three powers of government are properly united in God, but never in human hands; that is, they are properly united in a being that is the perfection of reason, justice, and mercy. It is the very definition of tyranny to unite them in fallible creatures like men, whose partial perfections are subject to corruption by passionate self-love and other such influences. "The equality of mankind is an equality of defect, as well as an equality of rights." The qualitative distinction between animals that possess reason and beasts that do not is more fundamental than any distinction of quantity or intensity of possession between the possessors of reason. Just government presupposes sufficient enlightenment among human beings to recognize that no rational animal is the proper subject of despotic rule, and no man is sufficiently godlike to be entrusted with despotic rule. Reciprocal with these equalities of superiority and defect is the notion that consent is the only just basis of government. Jaffa anticipates the objection that consent is not an adequate replacement for wisdom as the ground upon which rule can be legitimated. The claims of wisdom have dubious political value because of "the fact that it is not the wise who advance under the banners of wisdom but rather pretenders to wisdom." Leo Strauss's account of the classical position in a way admits this last point. The classics favored the rule of gentlemen, that element of society that through its wealth and leisure had the greatest opportunities to acquire a liberal education, which means an education that among other things fosters civic responsibility. This points to the ultimate justification of the rule of gentlemen: the rule of gentlemen is the political reflection of the, for almost all political purposes, impossible rule of the philosophers, the rule of "the men best by nature and best by education."[21] Jaffa is aware of the impoverishment that would attend the removal of such political reflections.

An interesting contrast to the classicism of Harry Jaffa [Professor Berns continues] is to be found in the classicism of George Anastaplo. While Jaffa emphasizes the natural equalities of superiority and defect upon which the moral principles governing the American polity are based, the central consideration for Anastaplo's "Constitutionalist" are the blessings of liberty. He reviews Jaffa's *Equality and Liberty* in an article entitled "Liberty and Equality."[22] Civil liberties, in contrast to civil rights, make for popular influence over, as well as protection against, government. But most importantly during "a time of effective popular rule," they provide for the protection of minorities from the encroachments of majorities, for the protection within democratic government for natural aristocracy.[23] While Jaffa's rhetoric emphasizes the transformation of self-evident truth into "living faith," the sacramental character of our moral and political principles,[24] Anastaplo recurs to the distinctions between human being and citizen, politician and scholar, thoughtful man and partisan, and nature and circumstance.[25] The inevitable partiality and relativity of any effective political statement point to prudence and moderation as indispensable political virtues—even in the pursuit of justice.[26]

The most useful way of beginning to account for these differences may well be in terms of different judgments about the needs of our situation, about "the crisis of liberal democracy," about the political conditions for philosophizing, on the one hand, and the reliability of nature, on the other.

The moral fervor of the political savior is not usually associated with the cool deliberation of the man of prudence. And yet both Jaffa and Anastaplo find their paradigms in Abraham Lincoln. After a careful line-by-line analysis of the Emancipation Proclamations, "recreating" the complex of problems Lincoln had to deal with, Anastaplo reflects on prudence in general:

> We see, of course, what prudence can mean in a particular situation—and hence what prudence itself means. One must adjust to one's materials, including the prejudices and limitations of one's community. Such adjustment often includes settling for less than the best. But the most useful adjustment is not possible unless one *does* know what the very best would be, . . . how important chance is in human affairs—and hence how limited we often are in what we can do, even when we know what should be done.
>
> We should . . . guard against that fashionable opinion which dismisses what is reasonable and deliberate as cold-blooded and calculating. It is also important, however, if one is to be most effective as a reasonable, deliberate and deliberating human being, to seem to be other than cold-blooded and calculating . . . That is, it is important to be a good politician. . . . We are reminded of the importance in political things of appearances, of a healthy respect for the opinions (and hence for the errors as well as the sound intuitions) of mankind.
>
> Certainly self-righteousness should always be held in check, but not always a show of indignation. Still, indignation even in a good cause should be carefully watched. Consider, for example, the famous

Abolitionist William Lloyd Garrison's 1831 promise, "I *will* be as harsh as truth, and as uncompromising as justice. On this subject I do not wish to think, or to speak, or write, with moderation." Such passion may be useful, even necessary, if great evils are to be corrected, but only if a Lincoln should become available to supervise what finally happens and to deal prudently with others (zealous friends and sincere enemies alike) with a remarkable, even godlike, magnanimity.[27]

Last but not least, [Professor Berns concludes] the classical emphasis on the ethical implications of all political arrangements reminds us conversely that every political arrangement presupposes certain qualities in the populace that is to live under that arrangement. Free government based on enlightened consent is not going to survive if its citizens are regarded as unworthy of such government and if they are incapable of making it work. The cultivation of excellence, or, more euphemistically, liberal education for leadership, may be indispensable for the survival of such government. If it should be that capacities for liberal education are not created equal in all men, religious education for all the people must supplement liberal education. Did the Founding Fathers rely on the virtues of a religiously trained populace without taking provision for the continuance of that training?[28] However that may be, although they did concentrate more on the structures of government, they did not forget the character of the people. "As there is a degree of depravity in mankind which requires a certain degree of circumspection and distrust, so there are other qualities in human nature which justify a certain portion of esteem and confidence. Republican government presupposes the existence of these qualities in a higher degree than any other form."[29] Classical and American thought seem to come together most in their reliance on "moral principles grounded in thoughtfulness," political prudence, that is, the avoidance of unreasonable expectations, and the concern for enlightenment, for liberal education.

. . . [I have dealt here] with two thinkers who have, with the aid of Leo Strauss and others, liberated themselves from the powerful dogma that a return to classical thought is impossible and devoted themselves to studies in depth of American thought and institutions. In interesting and complementary ways the principles, problems, and virtues of the modern American polity have been shown to require for their clarification not only modern philosophy but also the "premodern thought of our western tradition." We note that when Strauss speaks of our western *tradition,* he refers not only to classical philosophy but also to the Bible. This side of the tradition is more conspicuous in the work of Jaffa, but it is not ignored by Anastaplo.[30]

Is it not evident from this 1987 survey by Laurence Berns why we should all be grateful to Professor Jaffa? He does oblige us to think about the most important things, and to try to do so in a way worthy of our greatest teachers.

# The Founders of Our Founders: Jerusalem, Athens, and the American Constitution[31]

## GEORGE ANASTAPLO

*Behold, I have taught you statutes and judgements, even as the Lord my God commanded me, that ye should do so in the land whither ye go to possess it. Keep therefore and do [these statutes and judgements]; for this is your wisdom and your understanding in the sight of the nations, which shall hear all these statutes, and say, Surely this great nation is a wise and understanding people.*

—MOSES, *DEUTERONOMY* 4: 5-6

## I.

The Bicentenary of the Founding of these United States as an independent community has stimulated interest in our fundamental constitutional documents. This stimulation of interest has not been limited to American constitutional documents. The dependence of the Founding Fathers upon British constitutional experience has been noticed, with special attention having been paid by the Congress of the United States to Magna Carta, an original copy of which has been lent to this country by the British Parliament.

But in order to understand what we have come to be and how, one should look beneath, if not beyond, both American and British constitutional statements to what can be considered the underpinnings not only of the Anglo-American development but of Western civilization itself. That is, one must look to those influences, rooted in Jerusalem and in Athens, which appeal to the human being in us all, to human beings who find themselves allocated to one of the political subdivisions of what we know as the West. Those influences find authoritative expression in the books of the Bible and in the dialogues of Plato. These divergent influences have found literary expression in such works as John Bunyan's *Pilgrim's Progress* and William Shakespeare's plays, helping to shape thereby American opinion.

To regard the Bible and the Platonic dialogues as contributors to our constitutional development is to recognize that any analysis one might attempt of that development must be anything but comprehensive. It is to say that one must attempt to plumb the depths of Western Civilization. However inaccessible those depths may ultimately be, a preliminary survey of our great heritage should be of some use.

# II.

When one looks at Jerusalem, one confronts two principal sets of doctrines—the Judaic and the Christian—with the latter claiming to be the destined fulfillment of the former. (A third set, that of Islam, proclaims itself in turn the true completion of the other two.) It is the Christian set of doctrines which has had, and continues to have, the more immediate influence upon the West, and it is with this that we will primarily concern ourselves on this occasion in thinking about Jerusalem and its relation to Athens.

When one looks at Athens, one confronts several sets of doctrines, the various schools of thought that all trace their origins to Socrates as somehow the founder of a way of life rooted in moral philosophy. There has been in the West, for almost two thousand years now, an uneasy, yet often fruitful, relation between Athens and Jerusalem (or perhaps Jerusalem's pagan counterparts). This tension may have been in large part responsible for the remarkable accomplishments of the West—as well as for its curious psychic vulnerability. Of course, there have been minds in whom thoughtful accommodations between philosophy and religion have been made. One thinks of Xenophon, Maimonides, Averroes, Alfarabi and, at times, Thomas Aquinas. But even in those cases, there did remain the question as to which is ultimately sovereign, philosophy or religion.

In men of ordinary understanding—mere mortals like the rest of us—thoughtful accommodations are much harder to come by. Thus, we are familiar with free-thinking intellectuals who call into question the religious traditions (or, as they might even call them, the superstitions) of their time—so much so in our own time as to threaten the continued appeal and influence of organized religion. Thus, also, we are familiar with men of faith who confidently put pretenders to worldly wisdom in their place. A professor of church history (he happens to be in a Greek Orthodox college, but it could be the college of any standard Christian sect) is asked, "Are there any fundamental differences between Jesus and the great Greek philosophers like Socrates, Plato and Aristotle?" The following answer is given:

> There are many fundamental differences. Socrates and others taught the uncertain philosophical conclusions of their own limited and finite minds. Jesus taught infallible and divine truth. The fruit of the teachings of these philosophers is a temporary proficiency in an imperfect human knowledge. The fruit of the knowledge of Jesus Christ is eternal happiness. In themselves these great Greek philosophers were men, but Jesus was God. His words are infallible and eternal and have their value in all climates and centuries.

Yet, as I have indicated, thoughtful men have worked out responsible accommodations between these contending approaches. But however smooth and enduring such an accommodation may be, it cannot help but regard one or the other of the two approaches as ultimately authoritative.

## III.

The most interesting—that is to say, the most dramatic—times are those in which religion and "philosophy" struggle for supremacy, in which whatever longstanding accommodation there has been between them has (for one reason or another) broken down. One such period was that in which Socrates lived, especially in the closing years of his life, a time very much unsettled by the trials and ultimate defeat of Athens during the Peloponnesian War. That time of stress culminated, for Socrates, in his prosecution, conviction, and execution on charges which turned around his supposed refusal to acknowledge the gods of his city. Plato's *Apology of Socrates* remains the most instructive account of what happened to Socrates on that occasion.

Indeed, the *Apology* (or, rather, the combination of the *Apology*, which reports the trial of Socrates, and the *Crito*, which reports his refusal to accept the escape plan offered him)—this combination of the *Apology* and the *Crito* is *the* public document among the dialogues of Plato. It is this pair of dialogues which is most widely known and which has had the greatest direct influence upon public opinion with respect to the Socratic (or philosophic) way of life. This is as it should be, since this pair of dialogues—perhaps more than any others in the Platonic corpus—is directed to the general public. One dialogue shows Socrates speaking to the Athenian people, the other shows him providing Crito arguments that Crito can thereafter make in explaining to others in Athens why he had not been able to use his money to secure his friend's escape.

It is instructive to notice just how the dialogues can be seen by the public-spirited man of Christian inclinations. It is instructive, that is, to notice just how the Socratic experience, as related by Plato, can appear to pious men in the West. The bearing of all this on Anglo-American constitutional developments can be somewhat more immediate if we consider what is made of Socrates by the great English-speaking champion of ordered liberty, John Milton (the author of, among other things, the *Areopagitica*). Particularly instructive is the ambiguous status of Socrates in Milton's epic poem, *Paradise Regained*. This ambiguity reflects not only the natural tension between religion and philosophy but also the related tension between the citizen and the human being.

Most of *Paradise Regained*—the sequel to *Paradise Lost*, in which Adam and Eve had been tempted by Satan to their mortal doom—is devoted to the temptations of Jesus by Satan, temptations which are stoutly resisted by Jesus to the ultimate salvation of mankind. We see, in Book III, the efforts by Satan "to awaken in Jesus a passion for glory, by particularizing various instances of conquests achieved, and great actions performed, by persons at an early period of life." Jesus replies by showing the vanity of worldly fame, and the improper means by which it is generally attained. He contrasts with it the true glory of religious patience and virtuous wisdom, as exemplified in the character of Job. Thus, Jesus says ( *P.R.*, III, 88-95),

> But if there be in glory aught of good,
> It may by means far different be attain'd,
> Without ambition, war, or violence;
> By deeds of peace, by wisdom eminent,
> By patience, temperance; I mention still
> Him whom thy wrongs with Saintly patience borne,
> Made famous in a Land and times obscure;
> Who names not now with honor patient *Job*?

Jesus then adds in this reply by him to Satan's temptation ( *P.R.*, III, 96-99):

Poor Socrates (who next more memorable?)
By what he taught and suffer'd for so doing,
For truth's sake suffering death unjust, lives now
Equal in fame to proudest Conquerors.

In Book IV, the Tempter, proposing to Jesus the intellectual gratifica-
tions of wisdom and knowledge, points out to him the celebrated seat of
ancient learning, Athens, with its musicians, poets, orators, and philosophers of the different sects. Satan's tempting description of philosophy
hearkens back to, and tries to exploit, what Jesus had said about Socrates in
Book III (*P.R.*, IV, 272-280):

To sage Philosophy next lend thine ear,
From Heaven descended to the low-rooft house
Of *Socrates*, see there his Tenement,
Whom well inspir'd the Oracle pronounc'd
Wisest of men; from whose mouth issued forth
Mellifluous streams that water'd all the schools
Of Academics old and new, with those
Surnam'd *Peripatetics*, and the Sect
*Epicurean*, and the *Stoic* severe . . .

Thus, Satan is displayed as aware not only of the Socratic source for the
various schools of philosophy but also of what those various schools consist
of. (One must wonder how much Satan can truly be aware of, especially
anyone who holds with Socrates that vice is the result of ignorance.) There
then follows, upon Satan's display of the intellectual treasures of ancient
Athens, this "sage" reply by Jesus (*P.R.*, IV, 286-292):

Think not but that I know these things; or think
I know them not; not therefore am I short
Of knowing what I ought: he who receives
Light from above, from the fountain of light,
No other doctrine needs, though granted true;
But these are false, or little else but dreams,
Conjectures, fancies, built on nothing firm.

Notice that whoever "receives/Light from above, from the fountain of
light,/No other doctrine needs." That is a sufficient reply to Satan. But
there still follows upon this a critique by Jesus of the various schools of
philosophy, a critique which is preceded by a tacit exemption for the
Socrates who had earlier been extolled by Jesus (*P.R.*, IV, 293-294):

The first and wisest of them all profess'd
To know this only, that he nothing knew . . .

Presumably, it is Socrates' insistence upon this truth—that he recognized the limits of his, and consequently other men's, knowledge—which led to his fate as one who "For truth's sake suffer[ed] death." (*P.R.*, III, 98)

The Socratic insistence is taken to repudiate worldly wisdom, thereby pointing up the need in men, even in the wisest of men, for "Light from above, from the fountain of light." (*P.R.*, IV, 289) Indeed, one might add, what makes Socrates particularly noteworthy from the perspective of the Christian writer may be that he *suffered* for the sake of the truth, more than the truth for which he happened to suffer. Certainly, there seems tension in Milton's poem between respect for Socrates, the sufferer for the sake of truth, and suspicion of the philosophers emanating from Socrates, philosophers who consider natural reason sufficient, to say nothing of those who more directly threaten the faith that men have in illumination "from above." Such threateners, it would seem, are as vulnerable to the armed guardians of received doctrines as the Socratic way of life itself was before it came to be invested with the respect for divinity provided it by Plato. (Plutarch's *Nicias* is instructive here.) Thus, there seems to have been both in pagan times and in Christian times tension, if not even a necessary conflict, between philosophy and an established religious life.

Jesus is presented in *Paradise Regained* as decisively repudiating the schools derived from Socrates. These successive repudiations, which themselves draw upon perceptive characterizations of each school, address themselves, in turn, to Socrates himself (as we have seen), to Plato, to the Skeptics, to the Aristotelians, to Epicurus, and to the Stoics (*P.R.*, IV, 293-308):

The first and wisest of them all profess'd
To know this only, that he nothing knew;
The next to fabling fell and smooth conceits;
A third sort doubted all things, though plain sense;
Others in virtue plac'd felicity,
In corporal pleasure he, and careless ease;
The Stoic last in Philosophic pride,
By him call'd virtue; and his virtuous man,
Wise, perfect in himself, and all possessing
Equal to God, oft shames not to prefer,
As fearing God nor man, contemning all
Wealth, pleasure, pain or torment, death and life,

Which when he lists, he leaves, or boasts he can,
For all his tedious talk is but vain boast,
Or subtle shifts conviction to evade.

It might be noted in passing that the Stoics are considered at greater length than the others, perhaps because they resembled in some ways the Christians themselves.

Jesus is then shown dismissing all the philosophers with criticisms that the philosophers' more pious-patriotic critics in Athens (and later, in Rome) might also have applied to them (*P.R.*, IV, 309-330):

Alas! what can they teach, and not mislead;
Ignorant of themselves, of God much more,
And how the world began, and how man fell
Degraded by himself, on grace depending?
Much of the Soul they talk, but all awry,
And in themselves seek virtue, and to themselves
All glory arrogate, to God give none,
Rather accuse him under usual names,
Fortune and Fate, as one regardless quite
Of mortal things. Who therefore seeks in these
True wisdom, finds her not, or by delusion
Far worse, her false resemblance only meets,
An empty cloud. However, many books
Wise men have said are wearisome; who reads
Incessantly, and to his reading brings not
A spirit and judgment equal or superior
(And what he brings, what needs he elsewhere seek)
Uncertain and unsettl'd still remains,
Deep verst in books and shallow in himself,
Crude or intoxicate, collecting toys,
And trifles for choice matters, worth a sponge;
As Children gathering pebbles on the shore.

Notice the question that is posed about the advisability of any reading at all in the books of these worldly men. The reader remains "uncertain and unsettl'd," no matter how much he reads, unless he brings to that reading a "spirit and judgment equal or superior"—and, it is asked, if he already has that spirit and judgment to bring to his reading of the philosophers, "what needs he elsewhere seek"? Thus, the self-sufficiency, both for understanding and for a virtuous life, of the doctrines of true religion, is insisted upon. On the other hand, the philosopher, who cannot help but be somewhat skeptical even when he is not something of a materialist, poses a constant threat to the good order of the community. That is to say, we again see that the lifelong civic vulnerability of Socrates was not accidental.

Of course, Socrates himself can be understood to have tried to refine and otherwise to correct religious opinions which had become all too questionable and which, consequently, were doomed to fall before the criticisms of others who would not be as responsible as he was in reforming them. On the other hand, Jesus is presented as rooted in religious doctrines and institutions which provide men all they need, thereby making superfluous for them the arts and sciences of ancient Athens. Thus, Jesus says to the Tempter (*P.R.*, IV, 331-364),

Or if I would delight my private hours
With Music or with Poem, where so soon
As in our native Language can I find
That solace? All our Law and Story strew'd
With Hymns, our Psalms with artful terms inscrib'd
Our Hebrew Songs and Harps in *Babylon*,
That pleas'd so well our Victors' ear, declare
That rather *Greece* from us these arts deriv'd;
Ill imitated, while they loudest sing
The vices of their Deities, and their own
In Fable, Hymn, or Song, so personating
Their Gods ridiculous, and themselves past shame.
Remove their swelling Epithets thick laid
As varnish on a Harlot's cheek, the rest,
Thin sown with aught of profit or delight,
Will far be found unworthy to compare
With *Sion's* songs, to all true tastes excelling
Where God is prais'd aright, and Godlike men,
The Holiest of Holies, and his Saints;
Such are from God inspir'd, not such from thee;
Unless where moral virtue is express'd
By light of Nature, not in all quite lost.
Their Orators thou then extoll'st, as those
The top of Eloquence; Statists indeed,
And lovers of their Country, as may seem;
But herein to our Prophets far beneath,
As men divinely taught, and better teaching
The solid rules of Civil Government
In their majestic unaffected style
Than all the Oratory of *Greece* and *Rome*.

In them is plainest taught, and easiest learnt,
What makes a Nation happy, and keeps it so,
What ruins Kingdoms, and lays Cities flat;
These only, with our Law, best form a King.

A double claim seems to be made here, that the stories told among the Jews (and, it would seem, among the Christians-to-be) about the divine are sounder than those told by the Greeks; and that "our law" provides a better basis for statecraft and hence for the happiness of nations than what came out of Greece and Rome. That is to say, "our" way is held out as being both more true and more salutary.

Certain of the philosophers might have been inclined to ask whether that which is *not* true may nevertheless be employed by conscientious men in the promotion of that which is salutary. They might even have been inclined to suggest (in language later used by George Washington) that whatever may be conceded to the influence of refined education on minds of peculiar structure, both reason and experience forbid us to expect most people to be moved with respect to matters divine by anything more reliable than noble fables, so much so that even when the truth is presented to them about such matters, they can receive them with no other or no more assurance than that with which others like them in other times have received what is now recognized to have been error. Or, put another way, did not Plato himself know that he "to fabling fell, and smooth conceits"? (*P.R.*, IV, 295) And if so, how did he justify it?

We are warned, as we have seen, against "Philosophic pride." (*P.R.*, IV, 300) This seems to be something that philosophers are easily believed to indulge themselves in, Socrates not the least in this respect, despite the characterization of him in Milton's poem as "Poor Socrates," as one who had "for truth's sake suffer[ed] death," as one who knew only "that he nothing knew." (*P.R.*, III, 96–97, IV, 294. See, also, the opening pages of Judah Halevi's *The Kuzari.*) One truth that Socrates *did* know, and for which he suffered, was that he was markedly superior to most people he had come to know. His unwillingness, or inability, to conceal this truth from other finally contributed to his death at the hands of his fellow-citizens. But in thus arriving at the truth, and at other truths upon which this fatal truth rested and to which it leads, Socrates did achieve that fulfillment as a human being—that profound moral and intellectual development of embodied reason—to which all citizens, whether they know it or not, can be understood to have dedicated their communal life. It may well be that it is because citizens have such an implicit dedication that they can act as they do against anyone who is perceived to be threatening the received and cherished opinions (religious and otherwise) upon which virtue and the meaningfulness of things depend.

## IV.

Socrates, we have noticed, does not seem to have been of the opinion that what he happened to be capable of, many others would be likely to achieve as well. What the community *is* and is not capable of is suggested by the *Apology* and the *Crito*, that pair of dialogues provided by Plato for the training of the general public. (See Anastaplo, *Human Being and Citizen*, Essays No. 2 and No. 16.)

What, then, is the teaching of these dialogues which can be said to bear on our constitutional development? That teaching takes men much as they are: it points to the best possible regime (which is transitory), not to an "ideal" regime. An ideal regime may be seen in the Christian Paradise. The ideal may be realized there, with a redeemed or transformed human nature. From *that* something permanent or eternal can be expected. Consider how that transformation is celebrated, as Jesus is honored by angels after his triumph over the Tempter (*P.R.*, IV, 606–617):

> [N]ow thou hast aveng'd
> Supplanted *Adam*, and by vanquishing
> Temptation, hast regain'd lost Paradise,
> And frustrated the conquest fraudulent:
> He never more henceforth will dare set foot
> In Paradise to tempt; his snares are broke:
> For though that seat of earthly bliss be fail'd,
> A fairer Paradise is founded now
> For *Adam* and his chosen Sons, whom thou
> A Savior art come down to reinstall,
> Where they shall dwell secure, when time shall be
> Of Tempter and Temptation without fear.

The devout Christian is transformed, it would seem, in anticipation of his Heavenly condition—and this is transformation into a state far superior to anything mere reason can provide man. It is available, furthermore, for anyone who *will* believe.

Socrates, on the other hand, assumes that most people will continue to be much as they are. How *are* they? They are susceptible to prejudice and envy; they are incapable of understanding much, which makes the reputations assigned to men rather suspect; they are much more interested in survival and self-gratification than they are in virtue. One consequence of all this is that it is dangerous for the thoughtful man, at least in the ordinary regime, to go into political life: he is not apt to last long, thereby being of little use either to himself or to others.

There is also a certain inevitable folly to political life, if only because would-be leaders (who must try, as they become more and more "successful," to anticipate and regulate the doings of more and more people) find it difficult really to know what is going on. Consider a prosaic illustration I draw from an occasion in April 1973 when a half dozen of us, of different political inclinations and of considerable interest in politics (including several political scientists), predicted who would be the presidential *candidates* of the major parties in 1976. Although this was only three years ago, none of us happened upon any man who was nominated this past summer for either president or vice-president by any political party! It is difficult to lead a meaningful life in politics partly because it is all too often next to impossible to plan sensibly for oneself even in "the short run."

The role of chance in politics is all too evident to the thoughtful man—and this cannot help but curtail his interest in it. This is not to say, however, that there are no enduring standards which apply to what one should or should not do, either in public life or in response to the demands of politicians. It is evident that Socrates believed that there are such standards—and that they very much bear on what the best possible regime is like. There are standards which make far less of the threat or possibility of death than most people are apt to do. Thus, Socrates is shown in both the *Apology* and the *Crito* as relatively unaffected by the prospect of death. He can even wonder whether life is better than death. Certainly, according to him, a vicious life is worse than death. Certainly, also, there is not in him the concern about death that is evident in the designation, by God Himself, of Sin and Death as "the two grand foes." (*P.R.*, I, 159)

Socrates may well see sin—or rather, the ignorance from which vice follows—as the grand foe of mankind. The typical city, on the other hand, sees death as the evil especially to be guarded against—and much of what it does and says takes that for granted (including its usual alliance with religion). But then, the typical city—and hence the typical citizen—is a prisoner of unexamined habits and distorted opinions.

Even in the best possible city, there would be a necessity to distinguish between the few who understand and the many who have no more than sound opinions. For these many, poetry (including religious prophecy) is necessary for a decent life. That is to say, the limitations of human nature must be taken into account; the distribution of talents and differences in temperament, however mitigated by efforts to control both breeding and nurture, very much affect what can be done to develop and preserve a just order, especially an order which permits that philosophic life to which the city is somehow dedicated and in which all can be said somehow to participate.

The philosopher, on the other hand, recognizes his need for the city and the duties consequent upon that need. He also recognizes that there are better cities and worse, useful institutions and harmful ones.

## V.

No doubt, chance developments (including the emergence of gifted men as founders) can determine whether a city is blessed with institutions that promote moral virtue and permit intellectual virtue. We can see in the *Apology* and the *Crito* various duties, standards, and institutions deemed by Socrates to contribute to the perpetuation of *decent* cities. Some I have already touched upon. We need to do little more, in this effort to indicate how the Platonic dialogues bear on our constitutional development, than notice a few of the suggestions Socrates made. Many of these suggestions, which affect our notions of what a humane regime is like, we now take for granted—even though there are many peoples in the world today who have never enjoyed them. One major objective of these suggestions is to develop and maintain a city which, even while it insists upon its necessary prerogatives, is aware of its limitations—and conducts itself accordingly. Some Socratic suggestions, as evident in the *Apology* and the *Crito*, follow:

There is no question, first of all, but that the city should be concerned with those opinions of citizens which bear upon morality and citizenship, and these include opinions about the divine and about the condition of the soul after death. The education of the young and some lifelong supervision of all citizens with respect to these matters are called for, as are efforts to suppress corrupting influences and to promote those influences which make or keep men good. For this nurture and care, something is due in return.

So, next (in this list of Socratic suggestions about the proper ordering of cities), the citizen has a variety of duties, including military service in distant lands and civic service at home. This does not mean, however, that one is obliged, as a soldier or as a civilian, to do everything one is ordered to do. We learn of Socrates' refusal to comply with orders which would have had him perform unjust acts in Athens. Would he not have responded the same way to a clearly unjust war abroad? But whatever one's duties with respect to military or civic service, there are all too often moral ambiguities which may keep a sensible man from volunteering for either.

Next, we can see that the city, too, has duties which can be translated into various rights of citizens. The city should conduct itself in certain ways in exercising the considerable power with which it is entrusted. Orderly procedure is called for in trials; time for careful deliberation should be provided; cross-examination of accusers and witnesses is taken for granted. It also seems to be taken for granted in much of what Socrates says in the *Apology* and the *Crito* that the rule of law should be relied upon—and this means that laws should be clear and known in advance, that citizens should have an opportunity to criticize them, and that there should be means for having them changed. (Something of what we know as freedom of speech is implied.) That is to say, the laws which call upon citizens to respect them should themselves measure up to reasonable standards of "conduct."

Central to the constitutional arrangements and laws that any city may have are those which attempt to deal with the opinions of citizens and others about how the whole of things is to be understood. There should be authoritative customs with respect to impiety (and disloyalty); but these customs and laws should not, in their application, destroy the occasional Socrates. Certainly, considerable tolerance for conscientious, even though sometimes mistaken, dissent, is sensible. But a city does need to stand for something, even as it allows people such as Socrates to challenge an often mistaken public opinion.

Next, the city must permit those who are not under indictment to leave whenever they wish to do so. Those who remain, when they have the privilege of emigration, imply that they are willing to abide by the laws of the city—and that they are willing to be judged and punished according to those laws. On the other hand, the city which recognizes that dissatisfied citizens can leave is much more likely to restrain itself than is one which erects a Berlin Wall. Of course, tyrannies will arise from time to time (including those which do not allow free movement in or out)—and these, it would seem, may be overthrown. The standards of justice which exist independently of regimes provide a basis for judging all regimes—and may be seen in the right of revolution, rooted in nature, found in the Declaration of Independence. This can usefully be understood as a natural-right legacy of the Socratic assessment of the regimes of his day; it complements his salutary stand for law-abidingness even in the face of death.

Next, private property is taken for granted. Should it not be understood to extend not only to physical possessions but also to family associations? The importance of property is reflected in the privilege of emigration, for that privilege includes the right to take with one whatever is one's own. Of course, what *is* one's own—whether possessions or relatives—does depend in large part upon what the laws have provided for, such laws as those regulating marriages, estates, and burials. Of course, also, there are in Socrates' opinion things more important than property, as property is ordinarily understood. Even so, property does reaffirm the importance of one's own—and may even move the thoughtful human being to consider what should truly be one's own. Certainly, there is something reassuring about private associations and about the useful friendships that property makes possible: people can vouch for, and protect (and in the best cases elevate), one another. Certainly, also, property means leisure—and that *can* mean the proper cultivation of one's soul. Or, as Milton's Jesus says of the Aristotelians, "[They] in virtue plac'd felicity,/But virtue join'd with riches and long life." (*P.R.*, IV, 297-298)

Finally, in this catalogue of suggestions drawn from the *Apology* and *Crito* about the ordering of cities, there are the implications of Socrates' modest proposal that the most fitting "punishment" for him, as one who has neglected his own fortunes in his tireless advancement of the common good, would be his maintenance in the Prytaneum for the rest of his life at public expense. A well-ordered city, he seems to say, is one which has been able to work its way to sound judgments in these matters: it is somehow aware of what cities are really for and how someone such as Socrates contributes to the very best a city can aspire to.

In the well-ordered city, names (as well as property and honors) are distributed properly; for example, those who judge justly are truly called "judges." In such a city those who shape the authoritative opinions of the community know what they are talking about. In such a city it is recognized (if only tacitly) that a true flowering of the human spirit, even though it can be manifested in only a few at a time, is the city's ultimate reason for being—and this flowering includes a constant effort to determine the truth about things, including about what divinity is like and what happens to the human soul upon death.

This effort, it should again be noted, is consistent with "fabling . . . and smooth conceits" (*P.R.*, IV, 295), lest the discoveries that a few are privileged to make should be harmful to the many who provide the social support for such discoveries and who (for one reason or another) may not be able to understand them properly. The two dialogues we have had under consideration contributed to Plato's deliberate efforts to make "Philosophic pride" (*P.R.*, IV, 300) socially acceptable thereafter—to establish a place in the community for the occasional man or woman who, for good reason, may be more a human being than a citizen.

## VI.

We return now, after this survey of some of the influences upon our constitutional development which can be traced back to dialogues such as the *Apology* and the *Crito*, to that other great set of influences—to the Biblical, and specifically to the Christian, influences—upon our way of life. Those influences, which have been evident in what I have said about Jesus' response to philosophy in *Paradise Regained*, are apparent even in skeptical times. Some of those influences are of the sort that other religions would exert also, since almost all, if not all, serious religions dictate moral conduct and provide social restraints. Various Biblical influences may be seen among us in the Mayflower Compact, in the Gettysburg Address, and even in that noble product of a somewhat rationalistic age, the Declaration of Independence.

The religion of a people provides the "philosophical" setting for that people's political and legal arrangements. It looks beyond (or provides a foundation for) the life of the city (even when "the separation of Church and State" is religiously insisted upon). Thus, a moral influence is exerted, both with instruction in what is right and wrong and with forecasts of what rewards and punishments can be expected and when. For these purposes, there can be quite specific rules of conduct about such matters as diet, marriage, and worship. Thus, also, a sense of purpose for the community, and for human life itself, is provided. Things are made meaningful; life is depicted as rich, or at least as significant, not as sterile, empty, hopeless.

Limits to temporal authority are suggested whenever a concern for the soul is put before a concern for the body (with the body's natural appetite for mere survival and for sensual gratification). Indeed, concern for the soul—for the proper ordering of the soul—can be taken in some circumstances to authorize resistance to temporal authority; and it can, for better as well as for worse, inhibit political activity.

Those bound to particular religious sects are citizens of *those* "principalities or republics." They are different in their citizenship, one from another, according to the particular sects they are associated with. On the other hand, educated human beings, insofar as they are not bound by such allegiances, tend to be like one another. But it should be recognized that most men do need particular associations, religious as well as political. One can even say that religion (or certain kinds of patriotism) can do for the many something of what philosophy does for a few.

But there is a critical distinction between religion and philosophy which should be of enduring significance for us: the salutary moral concerns of citizenship (religious as well as political) do tend to be pressed at the expense of genuine inquiry. That is, as we have seen, why Socrates was inevitably vulnerable. True, he was not prosecuted until his old age; but he had been placed under clouds for decades, and not only by public opinion, as someone who had gone his own way, a threat to the associations which most men naturally hold dear.

# VII.

Whatever the ancient quarrel between the Socratic way of life and the religious-political way of life—between, that is, the human being and the citizen, between (in a different form) philosophy and poetry—both ways of life are vulnerable today. These two ways of life have, in the face of certain modern developments, more in common than they have dividing them. One can argue that only within the social context provided by a decent religious faith is a thoughtful philosophical effort likely to maintain itself. Perhaps this has always been true—but it seems particularly apparent today.

Religious faiths are peculiarly vulnerable at the hands of intellectuals— that is, at the hands of those who have inherited from the philosophers an openness to inquiry but not a recognition of the need for self-restraint. Self-restraint—a salutary restraint which takes account not only of one's vulnerability but also of the needs of others—may be seen in the deeper meanings of the *Apology* and the *Crito*, and I suspect in the deeper reaches of Milton's great religious poems as well. Explicit examinations of such further teachings must be reserved for an appropriate occasion.

I have been concerned on this occasion with the landscape (or surface meanings) of these works, with a view to indicating some of the influences of Jerusalem and of Athens upon American constitutional developments. These have been, I have suggested, sometimes conflicting influences.

One set of influences, associated more with the interests of the citizen, makes for piety and hence stability; the other, associated more with the interests of the human being, makes for speculation and hence change.

One can degenerate into either stultification or harshness, the other into either irrelevance or irresponsibility. How to combine properly these divergent influences is the work of either the truly inspired prophet or the inspiringly prudent statesman.

In any event, both Jerusalem and Athens remind us of something which is critical to American constitutionalism, the necessity of returning again and again to authoritative texts for guidance.

# The Ambiguity of Justice in Plato's *Republic*[32]

## GEORGE ANASTAPLO

> *That which gives to human Actions the relish of Justice is a certain Noblenesse or Gallantnesse of courage, (rarely found,) by which a man scorns to be beholding for the contentment of his life to fraud or breach of promise.*
>
> —THOMAS HOBBES, *LEVIATHAN*, XV

## I.

The oddness of the passage in Book IV of Plato's *Republic* where the virtue of justice is hunted (*Rep.* 432B *sq.*) has been noticed in this fashion by Leo Strauss in *The City and Man* (at pp. 105–106):

> After the founding of the good city is completed, Socrates and his friends turn to seeking where in it are justice and injustice and whether the man who is to be happy must possess justice or injustice. They surely succeed in stating what justice is. This is perhaps the strangest happening in the whole *Republic*. That Platonic dialogue which is devoted to the subject of justice answers the question of what justice is long before the first half of the work is finished, long before the most important facts without the consideration of which the essence of justice cannot be possibly determined in an adequate manner, have come to light, let alone have been duly considered. No wonder that the definition of justice at which the *Republic* arrives determines at most the genus to which justice belongs but not its specific difference (cf. 433a3). One cannot help contrasting the *Republic* with the other dialogues which raise the question of what a given virtue is; those other dialogues do not answer the

question with which they deal; they are aporetic dialogues. The *Republic* appears to be a dialogue in which the truth is declared, a dogmatic dialogue. But since that truth is set forth on the basis of strikingly deficient evidence, one is compelled to say that the *Republic* is in fact as aporetic as the so-called aporetic dialogues. Why did Plato proceed in this manner in the dialogue treating justice as distinguished from the dialogues treating the other virtues? Justice, we may say, is the universal virtue, the virtue most obviously related to the city. The theme of the *Republic* is political in more than one sense, and the political questions of great urgency do not permit delay: the question of justice must be answered by all means even if all the evidence needed for an adequate answer is not yet in. . . .

I am particularly interested on this occasion in the description of the hunting down of justice, with the discovery of this virtue as lurking "from the beginning" in obscurity underfoot. How is this to be understood? The passage begins in this way (*Rep.* 432B-433D):

"All right," I [Socrates] said. "Three [forms of virtue—courage, wisdom, and moderation] have been spied out in our city, at least sufficiently to form some opinion. Now what would be the remaining form thanks to which the city would further partake in virtue? For, plainly, this is justice."

"Plainly."

"So then, Glaucon, we must, like hunters, now station ourselves in a circle around the thicket and pay attention so that justice doesn't slip through somewhere and disappear into obscurity. Clearly, it's somewhere hereabouts. Look to it and make every effort to catch sight of it; you might somehow see it before me and could tell me."

"If only I could," he said. "However, if you use me as a follower and a man able to see what's shown him, you'll be making quite sensible use of me."

"Follow," I said, "and pray with me."

"I'll do that," he said, "just lead."

"The place really appears to be hard going and steeped in shadows," I said. "At least it's dark and hard to search out. But, all the same, we've got to go on."

"Yes," he said, "we've go to go on."

And I caught sight of it and said, "Here! Here! Glaucon. Maybe we've come upon a track; and, in my opinion, it will hardly get away from us."

"That's good news you report," he said.

"My, my," I said, "that was a stupid state we were in."

"How's that?"

"It appears, you blessed man, that it's been rolling around at our feet from the beginning and we couldn't see it after all, but were quite ridiculous. As men holding something in their hand sometimes seek what they're holding, we too didn't look at it but turned our gaze somewhere far off, which is also perhaps just the reason it escaped our notice."

"How do you mean?" he said.

"It's this way," I said. "In my opinion, we have been saying and hearing it all along without learning from ourselves that we were in a way saying it."

"A long prelude," he said, "for one who desires to hear."

"Listen whether after all I make any sense," I said. "That rule we set down at the beginning as to what must be done in everything when we were founding the city—this, or a certain form of it, is, in my opinion, justice. Surely we set down and often said, if you remember, that each one must practice one of the functions in the city, that one for which his nature made him naturally most fit."

"Yes, we were saying that."

"And further, that justice is the minding of one's own business and not being a busybody, this we have both heard from many others and have often said ourselves."

"Yes, we have."

"Well, then, my friend," I said, "this—the practice of minding one's own business—when it comes into being a certain way, is probably justice. Do you know how I infer this?"

"No," he said, "tell me."

"In my opinion," I said, "after having considered moderation, courage, and prudence, this is what's left over in the city; it provided the power by which all these others came into being; and, once having come into being, it provides them with preservation as long as it's in the city. And yet we were saying that justice would be what's left over from the three if we found them."

"Yes, we did," he said, "and it's necessarily so."

"Moreover," I said, "if one had to judge which of them by coming to be will do our city the most good, it would be a difficult judgment. Is it the unity of opinion among rulers and ruled? [Moderation] Or is it the coming into being in the soldiers of that preserving of the lawful opinion as to which things are terrible and which are not? [Courage] Or is it the prudence and guardianship present in the rulers? [Wisdom] Or is the city done the most good by the fact that—in the case of child, woman, slave, freeman, craftsman, ruler and ruled—each one minded his own business and wasn't a busybody?" [Justice]

"It would, of course," he said, "be a difficult judgment."

"Then, as it seems, with respect to a city's virtue, this power that consists in each man's minding his own business in the city is a rival to wisdom, moderation and courage."

"Very much so," he said.

I have long wondered about this passage, especially about the condition and location of justice. I now attempt to suggest how one might begin to think about the place of justice in the *Republic*.

## II.

One massive fact about the *Republic* should be noticed at the outset—and that is that hundreds of pages of dialogue are required to establish that justice is choiceworthy for its own sake. (Serious questions remain, of course, whether this proposition is truly established.) Justice, it is evident, is quite different in this respect from "wisdom, moderation, and courage," each of which can be fairly easily shown to be worth having for itself alone, aside from considerations either of reputation or of the responses of others.

It is said in the dialogue that the intrinsic choiceworthiness of justice had never been established before. (See *Rep.* 358C-D, 366D-E.) The problem with justice is reflected in the fact that, first, Thrasymachus, and then Glaucon and Adeimantus, can make the powerful arguments they do against justice (as commonly understood) being desirable for its own sake, aside from the opinions of others.

Everyone knows that justice is intimately related to the uses and effects of laws. (The *Laws* of Plato, too, has to be a very long dialogue. See Anastaplo, *The American Moralist*, Essay No. 3.) Laws, we also know, vary from place to place, from time to time; it is not difficult to see that they often serve the interests of rulers. (See, e.g., *Rep.* 338C, 339A.) We know as well that laws very much depend upon force and that can be troublesome. The prospect of a resort to force in the organization of a community may even be seen in the first "argument" used in the opening lines of the *Republic*, when Polemarchus "threatens" to compel Socrates and an all-too-willing Glaucon to remain in the Piraeus for the evening's festivities. Thus, there is something compulsory in the "founding" of the community from which this great conversation emerges. It is hard to deny that this threatened recourse to violence was most salutary and, in more than one way, in the interest of justice.

## III.

I count some seven hundred uses of one form or another of the term *dikaiosyne* (justice) in the *Republic*. There are three principal clusters in the uses of words of this family (which include, in almost one-half of the instances, references in the dialogue to "injustice" and "unjust"). The first, and by far the largest, cluster is in Book I and the first part of

Book II (with two-thirds of the total uses in the first seventh of the dialogue). The second cluster (about one-tenth of the total uses) is in Book IV, part of which I have quoted. The third cluster (another one-tenth) is at the end of the dialogue, in the closing pages of Book X. I draw upon each of these clusters in my remarks on this occasion.

We have seen that when justice is hunted down, in Book IV, it turns out to have been there all along: in fact, it had been used in the very construction of the city from the outset. Such use is reflected in the division of labor, which is obviously advantageous in everyday life. (This suggests that the utility of "justice" can be apparent to common sense.)

It is said that the city has its origins in need. (*Rep.* 369B) At the inception of Socrates' city-building, the allocation of tasks and duties according to people's natural capacities is made explicit. (*Rep.* 369A *sq.*) This mode of allocation is again and again referred to thereafter. (See, e.g., *Rep.* 433A, 443B-C.) This principle had been anticipated during Socrates' exchange with Polemarchus, when the specialized virtue of the pruning knife had been recognized. (*Rep.* 333D)

Thus, justice is natural for men to rely upon. And yet it can be obscure, or difficult to locate and to justify, with its questionableness indicated in the fact that justice can be called another's good. (*Rep.* 343C, 367C)

# IV.

We have noticed that the other three principal virtues are much more readily identified and justified. Why is justice so hard to come by?

Although justice is naturally useful for a community, it can still be said of this virtue that it was providential that it had been relied upon in the founding of Socrates' city. (*Rep.* 443B: "through some god") Where some might say "providence," others might say "nature" or "chance." Certainly, there is something accidental (at least in appearance) in the way justice comes into this conversation, for it is introduced not by Socrates but by Cephalos. (*Rep.* 330D)

There are four uses of "unjust" by Cephalos before he makes his single use of "just"—and *his* single use comes only when he draws upon lines from Pindar. Cephalos, it can be said, is primarily concerned to avoid the consequences (particularly the personal consequences after death) of one's injustice; he is not moved primarily by justice itself. That is, he is not drawn to justice for its own sake. His repeated sacrifices to the gods are designed to serve him in the hereafter which he, as a "very old" man, recognizes is for him near at hand. (See *Rep.* 328C, 331D.)

Socrates, too, draws five times on some form of "justice" in his exchange with Cephalos: but Socrates reverses Cephalos' distribution, using "just" (or "justice") four times to one use of "unjust." Socrates, we come to see, is more interested than is Cephalos in justice itself, singling out that term from the speeches of Cephalos—and the great conversation we do have can thereafter be generated. (Polemarchus [War Lord] is not altogether his father's son: he never uses "unjust" in *his* five uses of some form of "justice." There are in the Socrates-Polemarchus exchange two dozen uses of "just" before the first use of "unjust." Should not the military-minded be exposed mostly to justice if they are to be reliable?) But however interested Socrates may appear to be in justice on this occasion, we also come to see that neither justice nor the political life dedicated to justice is ultimately what moves him.

# V.

Scoundrels, we are reminded, are obliged to have some semblance of justice among them if they are to maintain a profitable association. (See *Rep.* 351C-D, 352C.) Since they want to avoid the disruptive consequences of injustice, they are obliged to be, or at least to appear to be, not unjust to one another. Instinct, or a kind of shrewdness, seems to be at work here. Is there not something of this, also, in Cephalos' pious respect for justice?

Even the bold Thrasymachus shrinks from calling justice a vice; rather, he concedes, it is high-minded innocence. (*Rep.* 348C. See *Rep.* 409A-B.) This reflects the fact that justice *is* invoked all the time, that the appearance of it *is* powerful, that people somehow respect it (even though they might personally subvert it clandestinely when they believe they can safely do so). (See, e.g., *Rep.* 361A.)

# VI.

All this points up the problem put by Glaucon, a problem that we now associate with Immanuel Kant. Is justice choiceworthy for its own sake? (See, e.g., *Rep.* 361B-C. See, also, Anastaplo, *The American Moralist,*

Essay No. 2-B.) What would be needed truly to establish that? Or is this too much to ask for, especially since justice is the most social of the principal virtues? Is an emphasis upon justice only for its own sake likely to distort justice itself, partly because it discourages use of that prudential judgment which helps determine what should be done in varying circumstances?

In any event, we know that Kant wants justice to be aboveboard and splendid, not something underfoot and obscure. Certainly, any reliance upon deception and subterfuge is condemned by him. Compare the necessary recourse to noble lies that Socrates takes for granted. (See, e.g., *Rep.* 414B-415D.)

Less prosaic than justice is the moderation that Socrates describes: moderation manifests, in its harmonious aspect, the elevated features we commonly associate with justice. (See *Rep.* 431E-432B.) Perhaps this helps explain why Socrates wanted to skip dealing with moderation (Rep. 430D): it can make justice (at least as defined in the *Republic*) seem rather drab by comparison.

# VII.

Something of the Kantian splendor of justice may be seen in the closing references to justice in the *Republic*, both in the Myth of Er (at the very end of the dialogue) and in the passage just before that Myth is resorted to.

Socrates (in an exchange with Glaucon) describes what happens, or at least what is most likely to happen, to both the just man and the unjust man toward the end of their respective lives, however much each of them had been long misjudged by the community (*Rep.* 613B-614A):

> ". . . Don't the clever unjust men do exactly as do all those in a race who run well from the lower end of the course but not from the upper? At the start they leap sharply away but end up by becoming ridiculous and, with their ears on their shoulders, run off uncrowned? But those who are truly runners come to the end, take the prizes, and are crowned. Doesn't it also for the most part turn out that way with the just? Toward the end of every action, association, and life they get a good reputation and bear off the prizes from human beings."
>
> "Quite so."
>
> "Will you, then, stand for my saying about them what you yourself have said about the unjust? For I shall say that it's precisely the just, when they get

older, who rule in their city if they wish ruling offices, and marry wherever they wish and give in marriage to whomever they want. And everything you said about the unjust, I now say about these men. And, again, about the unjust, I shall say that most of them, even if they get away unnoticed when they are young, are caught at the end of the race and ridiculed; and when they get old, they are insulted in their wretchedness by foreigners and townsmen. As for being whipped and the things that you, speaking truly, said are rustic— that they will be racked and burned—suppose that you have also heard from me that they suffer all these things. But, as I say, see if you'll stand for it."

"Very much so," he said. "For what you say is just."

"Well, then," I said, "such would be the prizes, wages, and gifts coming to the just man while alive from gods and human beings, in addition to those good things that justice itself procured."

"And they are," he said, "quite fair and sure ones."

Thus, the just man is shown as finally vindicated, even here on earth. But are we not meant to remember the fate of Socrates? Does not what is supposed to happen eventually to the unjust man sound distressingly like what did happen to Socrates at the end of his own life? Socrates, in talking at the outset of the *Republic* to Cephalos, had said that *perhaps* he too would take the road Cephalos had taken. (*Rep.* 328C) But the reader knows that Socrates does not become "very old," something which is further anticipated by Socrates's use of "for the most part" in the passage I have just quoted.

Of course, the truly philosophical man may not be concerned about such an "accident" as Socrates's earthly fate. (See, as indicative of what philosophers are like, *Rep.* 476A, 480A, 494B, 500C. See, on something greater than justice and the three other virtues, *Rep.* 504D.) But such lack of concern is hardly likely to lend much support to a popular argument for justice as praiseworthy for its own sake.

Thus, the Myth of Er may be crucial for the general effect of the dialogue. Mankind is thereby told of the divergent fates of the unjust and of the just in the afterlife, which fates seem to compensate for the things that go wrong here (that is, for the misallocations of rewards and punishments on earth). Adeimantus's instinct may have been sound in these matters: he had insisted upon considering as well the significance of the afterlife in any proper assessment of justice. The central uses of "justice" in the dialogue seem to be in the course of his elaboration (in Book II) of that significance (turning around *Rep.* 363D). Even so, Socrates at the end of the *Apology* remains uncertain about whether there is life after death; this suggests how he probably regards such things as the Myth of Er.

The Myth of Er is also of use in that it reflects the need to account for the apparent role of chance in the shaping of men's lives (as seen in the natural capacities one may have, or in the circumstances in which one is born, or in the training and other experiences that happen to be available to one). This Myth suggests that one's life is truly of one's choosing, leaving in obscurity the ultimate origins of one's "personal" sequence of lives and afterlives.

Both of these uses of, if not needs for, the Myth of Er remain to trouble us about justice, however noble or gallant it may be for a man to be open to justice without regard for its demonstrable consequences.

# Private Rights and Public Law: The Founders' Perspective[33]

## GEORGE ANASTAPLO

*He came here as a Representative of America; he flattered himself he came here in some degree as a Representative of the whole human race; for the whole human race will be affected by the proceedings of this [Federal] Convention. He wished gentlemen to extend their views beyond the present moment of time, beyond the narrow limits of place from which they derive their political origin.*
—GOUVERNEUR MORRIS, JULY 5, 1787

## I.

Private rights—which may be a refined way of saying "self-interest"—private rights are said by some to be at the heart of the American regime. If this should be so, how does having private rights at its core affect the American way of life? Does it mean that a concern for private rights is critical to the ends and doings of government and hence to the public law that is developed? Does it mean that the public, as public, has no independent status or dignity but rather is something derivative from, and ultimately limited by, private rights and that looking-inwardness which an emphasis upon private rights suggests?

The importance of private rights—of the rights of men prior to or otherwise independent of government—may be seen in our founding document, the Declaration of Independence. You must all recall those famous sentences in the Declaration of Independence upon which Abraham Lincoln, here on the plains of Illinois and later in his first inaugural address, grounded his decisive policies some one hundred and twenty-five years ago:

> We hold these Truths to be self-evident, that all Men are created equal, that they are endowed by their Creator with certain unalienable Rights, that among these are Life, Liberty, and the Pursuit of Happiness—That to secure these Rights, Governments are instituted among Men, deriving their just Powers from the Consent of the Governed, that whenever any Form of Government becomes destructive of these Ends, it is the Right of the People to alter or to abolish it, and to institute new Government, laying its Foundation on such Principles, and organizing its Powers in such Form, as to them shall seem most likely to effect their Safety and Happiness.

It is, we are told, to secure these rights—*such* rights as those to life, liberty, and the pursuit of happiness—it is to secure these rights that "Governments are instituted among Men." All are somehow equal: either all are equal and hence have such rights, or they all have such rights and hence are equal.

Men, it seems, have such rights prior to, or otherwise independent of, government: for, we are told, governments are instituted among men in order to secure these rights. No other reason, it seems, is as important as this for instituting governments, for judging them once instituted, and for replacing them when the required securing of such rights fails.

We must notice that other (sometimes complementary) reasons have been given by mankind (including by many Americans) for instituting government: thus it has been said that social relations, and hence government to order such relations, are natural to mankind; or it has been said that virtue (whether for one's own personal good, temporal or eternal, or for the good of all, or for virtue's own sake)—that the promotion of virtue is why governments are instituted; or it has been said that it is for the common good (whether the good of some community or of mankind) that governments are instituted.

But the Declaration of Independence seems to take it for granted—finds it to be self-evident—that governments are instituted to secure the rights that all men have inasmuch as they are created equal. It is with this relation—the relation of private rights to public law—that I am primarily concerned on this occasion. My discussion will include consideration of the status of slavery and of citizenship, both matters of deep concern for the often-troubled Roman Republic to which the American Founders looked for guidance.

## II.

The rights with which men are endowed seem quite varied, even if one limits oneself to those which are listed in the Declaration of Independence. (Others *are* indicated, since the ones listed are introduced, "that among these . . .") Is there not likely to be conflict (as well as diversity) among these rights? Thus, for example, those measures which secure one's right to life may interfere with the exercise of liberty.

Is there a natural hierarchy among the inalienable rights of men? Is there a principle of ordering them which permits us to see and to say that one is to be preferred to the others? What is the bearing on this question of the right of revolution? I will return to this at the end of this talk.

Is the variety among the rights such, and is the even-handedness with which they are asserted such, that it is difficult to insist on any hierarchy among them? (Is there any indication, in the ways that violations of various rights are spoken of in the list of grievances in the Declaration of Independence, what kind of rights is taken most seriously?) One people may prefer one right to all the others; another people may prefer another right to all the others.

If preferences differ from one people to another, if not even from one man to another, would it not make sense to provide for a variety of ways (or forms of government) for securing these rights? The more variety, the greater the opportunity people have to gather with those who are like-minded, thereby securing in the way they prefer the rights that matter most to them.

If a premium is placed upon such variety—and does not this make sense if the securing of rights, variously arranged in order of personal preference, is the principal end of government?—then local governments become more important, those governments which can respond to diverse conditions in various localities within a large union. A political union may be large in part because it alone can provide the protection needed against foreign interference with being allowed to live as people happen to desire from one locality to the other.

And so it was recognized by the Founding Fathers that the states reflected different manners, preferences, perhaps even ways of life. Experiments of one kind and another had led to some diversity among the regions of the United States. Governments dedicated to those regions could be expected to be more respectful of, and more intimately related to, the diversity to be found there, including diversity with respect to which of the inalienable rights was cared most for. (Thus, for example, one community could care more than another for property in preference to liberty.)

A government for all of the United States, on the other hand, tends to reflect, perhaps even to impose, one set of preferences over another for the Union as a whole. Is it apt to do so on the basis of a more elevated opinion as to which is truly to be preferred? Or is it apt to settle upon those preferences which can most easily be made to have a general appeal, irrespective of their intrinsic merits?

With these observations about the importance of the States because of their closeness to local manners and opinions, we move into the Federal Convention, that remarkable assembly which met in 1787. One of the issues which divided the Convention during that hot Philadelphia summer was what the status of the States should be under the constitution that was being drafted. This was, at least in part, the issue of which private rights were to be made most of in devising the fundamental public law of the United States.

# III.

It is again and again evident, whenever one studies the accounts we have of the proceedings of the Federal Convention of 1787, that there is a significant relation between the private and the public. Respect for the private, or a restraint upon the public, may be seen in the very way the convention was conducted: it was a closed (a closed, *not* a clandestine) convention. But, it should at once be added, this was done more for the sake of the public than for the sake of the private. It was decided by those experienced men of 1787 that the public interest was best served by permitting conscientious delegates to explore fully the issues before them, to make trial runs, and to back off when persuaded. Such maneuvers are much harder to execute whenever everything one says immediately becomes a matter of public record and when constituents line up behind this or that position. (Is this, one might well wonder, as near as one can hope to get to "philosophy" in practical discourse on public matters?)

Furthermore, is a proper respect for the private vital to a healthy public life? If things are made public prematurely, or improperly, does not the private become perverted by public considerations? I mention in passing that these questions may be at the heart of the obscenity issue and of the issue about whether confidential deliberations by courts and others should be exposed to public view, both of which are current issues. (Consider the implications in all this of the opinion, such as seems to be found in Hobbes's *Leviathan*, that the private, or personal, is somehow real, whereas the public is somehow artificial.)

Benjamin Franklin indicated, at the end of the Federal Convention, that he had reservations about parts of the Constitution which they had just written but that these reservations would die with him. Does this raise a question whether James Madison should have provided for the publication of his notes? That remarkable record does instruct us as to what men *are* capable of in such circumstances. But would they be equally capable in the future if it is *known* that a publishable record is being made? (Still, it must have been obvious to the Convention delegates that Madison *was* making elaborate notes. Was anyone else doing so also—and, if so, what became of *those* notes?

## IV.

The importance of private rights is reflected in what was said in the Federal Convention about what it is that government should aim at. Or, perhaps it should be said, the importance of private rights may best be seen in the repeated insistence in the convention upon what government should *not* aim at. Glory and empire should not be the primary ends of government; military conquest and the use of force abroad should be discouraged.

The ends of government, various delegates indicated, should be much more modest. (It is a nice question whether those who believed this most strongly tended to be those who made much of the states as against the Union.) Such delegates probably were most concerned about domestic tranquility and an assured (and ever-growing?) prosperity. Is it thus that one's pursuit of happiness is best secured? (Is there not something Hobbesian about this too? Is a thirst for glory's illusory in its object, if not simply mad?)

But even these men, who can be said to have made so much of the securing of private rights, were aware of the significance of what they were doing, for which, if they should prove successful, they would be celebrated widely and for generations to come. It was observed several times in the Convention that they were deciding perhaps forever the fate of republican government for all mankind. They were concerned lest they so conduct themselves that they would be objects of enduring reproach.

Thus, these men sought, and seemed to enjoy prospectively, the somewhat private satisfaction of becoming public benefactors who would be recognized to be such. (Consider the youthful Abraham Lincoln's reflections on ambition in his Perpetuation Speech, a half century later. Harry V. Jaffa provides an instructive exposition of that speech in his *Crisis of the House Divided*.)

## V.

I have been talking about how a concern for private rights and private interests have determined, or at least have very much affected, such things as public law and the goals of government. The concern for private rights predisposes Americans toward a critical role for the States, toward "modest" government, and toward encouraging local institutions, private as well as public. This is one element in our constitutional development.

Another element in that development, and evident throughout the Convention proceedings, was the recognition of the limitations placed upon the delegates by the country's circumstances. It was again and again said by delegates that they should not try to write the very best constitution; the circumstances simply were not right for that. It takes time, they said, to develop the conditions which make the best possible: a certain kind of people is needed for the very best constitution; since the American people are not yet that kind, the form of government appropriate to them has to be a compromise with the best. (This is one thing, by the way, which it would have been difficult to face up to, and to say, if the convention proceedings had been public.)

The best constitution previously known to mankind, at least in modern times, was evidently that found in Great Britain—in that very country from which the American colonists had been obliged to separate themselves! That the British Constitution was indeed the best was several times acknowledged during the Convention without, so far as I know, ever having been contradicted at length. (There is a critical problem here which I can barely touch upon in this investigation of the relation between private rights and public law: *is* "the best constitution in the world" one that was itself considered by the British people, or by students of that constitution, to have been instituted to secure the rights of men? Or was it instituted for some other purpose? Liberty *was* regarded by Blackstone as vital to the British Constitution.)

# VI.

The British Constitution (it was again and again lamented in the Federal Convention) is simply not feasible for the American people, at least for a century or two. But it is not only because the people of the United States are not constituted as the British are that a British-style constitution is not now feasible, although this difference in peoples was made the most of.

Also of some importance was a concern, especially among delegates from the smaller States, that the prerogatives of all of the States be respected, prerogatives which the Articles of Confederation had indeed respected but which a unitary British-style constitution would override. Each state under the Articles had one vote; but delegates from the larger States complained that they had had to agree to that kind of equality during the Revolutionary War because of the dangers facing the Union; and, such delegates added, they were no longer under such duress, and so would not allow all States to continue to have an equal voice in Congress.

The smaller States spoke of the integrity of their communities, of their equal status among the States, and of the state of nature in which all the States had been (with respect to one another) before forming the Union. Their opponents, although they would not speak so bluntly in the Convention, considered any major concern about protecting the prerogatives of States primarily the concern of local political men of little talent but of established appetites who were afraid they would be pushed aside if American politics became truly national.

It is likely that some selfishness was exhibited here in defense of the interests of states as states. But there must also have been considerable concern about respecting differences due to geography, "history," and so forth. On the other hand, the very things that made the States important (as champions of the private rights of men) also made them a hindrance to the formation of a national government with sufficient powers to secure those private rights effectively. (Perhaps it can be said that to rely upon the prerogatives of the smaller States was, in effect, the most critical defense of the prerogatives of states as states, since the larger States could be considered as tending, in their size and hence in their approach to government, toward the perspective of a national government.)

The Convention debated this State-equality issue extensively. It may be true (as some argued) that the small State-large State difference was not the fundamental one that summer, but it certainly was important and it had to be resolved. Resolution took the form, as we know, of the now-familiar differences between the two Houses of Congress, with the Senate (based upon equal votes for all States) being in this respect more like the one-house legislature under the Articles of Confederation. Even the name "Congress" for our national legislature reflects its origins in a body which was made up under the Articles of Confederation of deputations from States, just as would be a Congress in which sovereign nations are represented, with each participant equal *as State* to the others. (There are other features of the Constitution which still respect the claims of the small States to be treated as equals to the large: consider, for example, how States vote in the House of Representatives in the event no president is elected by presidential electors or how States vote on proposed constitutional amendments.)

The States continue to be recognized as significant elements under the Constitution, so much so that all new States admitted to the Union come in with the prerogatives of the original thirteen.

# VII.

To make much of the States and the way things happened to be arranged under the Articles of Confederation and otherwise *is* to defer considerably to chance developments. Is this inevitable in public life? A private person can become, if he is fortunate in his training, natural gifts, and circumstances, less susceptible to chance than can any public person or perhaps any community. Does not the life of philosophy mean, in effect, a temporary conquest of chance, both with respect to the mode of one's life and with respect to the primary end of one's life (a comprehensive, however temporary, understanding of the meaning of things)?

And yet, leading members of the Federal Convention could insist that, for Americans at least, reason is to govern, not chance alone. (See, on this, the opening passage of *Federalist* No. 1.) Such a response was made, for example, when it was suggested that a lottery be relied upon to choose among certain candidates for public office. (Compare ancient Athens, where democratic principles were carried to this "logical" extreme.) The insistence upon reason, rather than upon chance, was in opposition to sentiments (such as those by John Dickinson) which presupposed that the most useful political things have evolved among men by accident. It is not an accident, perhaps, that Dickinson had been reluctant to invoke the right of revolution against the British. Does not that right and its invocation make more than he was inclined to do of deliberate appraisals and of the systematic refashioning of one's government? Should one expect also that those who made more of chance would also make more of the States as against a strong national government which ignored arbitrary State lines as much as possible?

We do see a remarkable reliance upon reasoning in the Federal Convention. Is not this related to the assumption in the Declaration of Independence itself that reasons should be given for the action the colonists were taking, that a people should at least try to explain itself? Is there not a natural openness in man to reasoning, especially in political relations? Perhaps significant here is the fact that anyone who tries to rule is likely to advance *some* plausible title to rule. (See Plato, *Laws* 690A *sq.* See, also, Anastaplo, *The American Moralist*, Essay No. 3.)

# VIII.

Among the things that reasonable men in politics know—among the things that *prudent* men know (for that is what reason-in-the-life-of-action comes down to)—is that statesmen are indeed limited by their circumstances.

We have already noticed the account that had to be taken of the established prerogatives (and expectations) of the States. We have already noticed as well the inadvisability of contemporaneous public discourse on the sensitive matters discussed in the Federal Convention.

But more critical, and perhaps at the root of all such circumstantial restraints, are the limitations of the people themselves. (This is aside from what was noticed in the convention about the differences between the American people and the British people or between one State and another in the American Union.) The limitations of the people are particularly important here, since the American emphasis upon equality and upon the determination to be republican made so much of the people.

It is again and again indicated in the Federal Convention that the people can be easily led astray, that their understanding is limited, and so forth. This can be said even though the constitutional system to be devised is one that will ultimately rest upon the people's will.

# IX.

The limitations of the people are not restricted to their capacities as citizens, including the productive or private lives with which citizenship has to be somewhat concerned.

We are reminded here of another people, with *its* peculiar limitations, those second-class (or three-fifths class) citizens who made up the considerable body of African slaves in the United States in 1787.

Their limitations, due in large part both to the way of life from which they had been wrenched and to the way of life to which they had been condemned, affected what could be done with *them*. In addition, slavery (with its attendant investments, costs, and discipline) affected the prosperity and happiness of the whites among whom the slaves lived.

And yet all the time, there was the continuing awareness that the principles of the regime (as seen in the "created equal" language of the Declaration of Independence) raised questions about the institution of slavery. Northerners and Southerners alike were aware of slavery as a problem. (Consider, for example, how bitterly so hard-headed a commerce-minded man as Gouverneur Morris could condemn slavery. Consider, also, James Madison's reluctance to have it explicitly recognized in the Constitution itself that there could be such a thing as property in men—and so circumlocutions were resorted to.)

The importance of this issue can be seen, of course, in the Civil War and what led up to it. But the issue was vital from the beginning—and so it could be said by Madison and by others in the Federal Convention that the slavery issue was what really divided the States, not such differences as those between large States and small States.

# X.

One can see in the slavery issue that deep conflict among private rights which I touched upon at the beginning of these remarks. There are, of course, the rights of Africans to their lives and liberty. (Notice how Chief Justice Roger B. Taney and Senator Stephen A. Douglas dealt with this: they simply read the African out of the Declaration of Independence.) Then there were the rights of the Southern white man—his right to his property (duly paid for) and his right to self-preservation (which was threatened by emancipation): it was widely believed that wholesale emancipation would bring bankruptcy for whites in the South, a general breakdown of law and order, and the misery of helpless Africans. It is important for us to appreciate why and how good men of considerable political talent "had to" acquiesce in slavery. (See, on the painful accommodations required by a system of slavery, Plutarch, *Life of Titus Flamininus*, XIII, 3-6; Anastaplo, *The Constitution of 1787*, Lecture No. 13. See, also, *The Amendments to the United States Constitution*, Lectures No. 10, No. 11, and No. 12.)

The slavery issue (an issue which would not die and the aftereffects of which continue among us in various forms) reminds us of the fundamental tension between expediency and justice. Still, it was recognized in the Federal Convention, at least by some members, that unless a political arrangement is just, it cannot be expected to endure.

Does recourse to *expediency* tend to respect private rights and the limitations of people? It may be seen in the use of extraordinary measures in perilous times (which recourse to the Federal Convention can itself be understood to have been).

Does a concern for *justice*, on the other hand, tend to make more of universal standards of the common good, perhaps even of the requirements of humanity at large? Does it not tend to discourage an emphasis upon private rights? Is it not a concern for "the whole human race" (to use Gouverneur Morris's phrase) a concern for more than the mere amalgamation of everyone's private rights? A concern for private rights is not as likely (at least in our circumstances) to look to Nature for guidance as is a concern for the common good: "the common good" implies, more than do "private rights," the ascendancy of an enduring perfection over transient satisfactions in our judgments both as human beings and as citizens.

# XI.

The problem of reconciling expediency and justice may be seen as well in the problem (recognized again and again in the Federal Convention) of dealing with avarice and with ambition. The concern *was* to deal with avarice and ambition, not to eliminate them. Avarice *is* useful in the commercial life of the community and ambition *is* useful in its political life.

Does an efficient commercial life, especially on a continent-wide basis, tend to promote certain desires, to break down State barriers, and to make people more or less uniform? Does it also tend to discourage the arbitrary, shortsighted, and foolish by making them vulnerable both in the marketplace and before a national (if not also international) public opinion?

It was indicated in the Convention that the most effective way of dealing with avarice, and perhaps with ambition—a way which does not require constant governmental intervention but depends much more on people to police themselves—is to allow vice to counter vice. This is not an appeal to higher principles, but rather to the natural workings of self-interest. This may be seen in Douglas's position with respect to the spread of slavery: there was, he believed, no need for the American people at large publicly to condemn slavery, which would antagonize the South against the North; rather, he depended on (among other things) white prejudices—the prejudices of free labor against Africans and thus against slavery—to keep slavery from taking root in the Territories.

The use, as well as the limits, of vice to counter (and hence control) vice may be seen in a playful illustration by Franklin. The Scottish lawyers, he reported to the Federal Convention, manage to keep the quality of their courts high by always choosing as judges those of their colleagues who are most successful—and this they do, he explained in order to be able to divide their prosperous colleagues' practice among themselves. But, it should be noticed, this approach can operate to produce judges of quality only so long as successful lawyers, whose competition is thereby eliminated by their colleagues, *are* successful for the right reasons and in the right way.

## XII.

There is a further problem with any substantial reliance upon vice to counteract vice. When vice is set against vice, are not both of the vices involved somehow legitimated? What are the consequences of such legitimation? May it not lead to a failure, in some circumstances, to recognize vice *as* vice? If something should come *not* to be recognized as a vice, may not people neglect to set another vice against it? (Is this problem critical to any appraisal of the moral and political implications of economic theories?)

Besides, if these are indeed vices, are they not ultimately irrational? If so, would it not be a matter of chance who or what did prevail when vices contend with one another? (Is there for this approach no natural hierarchy among vices, just as there is no natural hierarchy among rights?) If vices are to be used intelligently (and to be discarded or rearranged as need requires), must there not be higher principles by which one should be guided (in making use of vices) and to which one can appeal (in opposition to certain vices)? That is, must not one sometimes raise people above considerations of mere self-interest?

Consider in this connection the suggestion made by Franklin at a critical point in the Federal Convention when an impasse had been reached: he suggested that the delegates open each day's session thereafter with prayer, for they were obviously in need of divine help. Franklin's proposal seems to have troubled some of the more freethinking delegates; yet it could not be simply voted down: not only would this have been an affront to the venerable Franklin, but not a few of the more pious Convention delegates would have been offended. The proposal was allowed to fade away without a vote on it, reflecting perhaps a sensitivity on each side to the sensibilities of the other side.

What did the prayer proposal really come down to? Was it not a way of inducing members to step back, to get outside their particular, divisive interests? To pray—or, indeed, to call for prayer—is to ask, in effect, "How would all this look to someone whose good opinion you cherish?" Did, for Franklin (who was, to say the least, not conventionally pious)— did, for Franklin, the *proposal* itself matter most, not any prayer thereafter? Did he not succeed therefore in what he attempted, even though public prayers were never resorted to in the Convention?

The decision of Franklin to proceed thus does suggest that self-interest (or an overriding concern for private rights) cannot always be enough. Much *should* be made of self-interest, sensibly pursued (that is, what we call enlightened self-interest), but it must itself be subject to principles grounded in Nature which regulate reliance upon it. In any event, an emphasis upon personal virtues is more likely than is an emphasis upon private rights to aim at excellence, an excellence which tends to be public (if not even philosophical) in its orientation. An emphasis upon private rights, on the other hand, easily leads to an insistence upon an undiscriminating equality, to a recourse to private lives, perhaps even to a suppression of liberty (so long as all are similarly restrained).

# XIII.

The need to rely (in the Franklin mode) upon higher principles is reflected in the observation, made in the Federal Convention, that since the sentiments of the people are hard to know it is best simply to do the right thing and depend upon the people eventually to recognize and ratify this.

It is also difficult to be sure of what the enduring interests of any people are: circumstances are so varied and so changeable, that those interests may not truly be what they seem at the moment. Thus, it was pointed out in the Convention, for the delegates to make much of the immediate interests of their States, or to establish special privileges for the thirteen original States, or to place limitations upon the new Western States would be shortsighted, since the delegates themselves could not know where their own descendants would live and what they would do. (Bearing upon all this are the prohibitions placed in the Constitution of 1787 upon the granting, either by the United States or by the States, of any "Title of Nobility.")

Besides, what is truly in one's interest if one's soul is big, if one is open to the noble? Is it not better to aim at what is good and right, not just for the moment but on a permanent basis, not just for individuals but for the whole human race?

With these observations we can return to the Declaration of Independence passage with which we began on this occasion. If this securing of rights (and private rights at that) is the primary end of our government, and if there is no natural hierarchy among such rights, then our way of life can easily deteriorate into hedonism or mere selfish gratification. (There *is* much in our way of life that encourages self-indulgence, especialy since our remarkable material abundance naturally tempts us in that direction.)

It is instructive to notice, therefore, that the Declaration does conclude with an emphasis upon "our sacred Honor," which points us to something outside ourselves. At the least, "Honor" suggests a community response, preferably that of self-sacrifice in the interest of something elevated.

It is instructive to notice as well that the right of revolution is the only right in the Declaration of Independence that also is referred to as a duty. If rights were all that mattered, one would be left the choice of *whether* to insist upon them. One can "legitimately" neglect one's rights. Why not do so if one is comfortable and self-absorbed?

But where duty is involved, it is different. To speak of duty is to presuppose standards. At the very least, it would seem from the Declaration; men have the obligation to insist that governments respect those rights which attest to and permit full development of their humanity, in private as well as in public. That humanity is reflected in the self-evident truth that "all Men are created equal."

What *did* the Founders believe about all this, especially about whether a concern for private rights should take precedence over respect for public law (when these are in conflict with one another)? We have been considering what various members of the Federal Convention thought about this subject. But, as we have seen, the opinions of the people at large may have been different. This is reflected in what has been noticed about the limitations of the people. Indeed, one suspects, the people might have been less "sophisticated" than some of their leaders about the primacy of private rights. That is, do not a healthy people tend to be patriotic? Do they not tend to believe that there are eternal principles superior to private rights and interests, whatever they might settle for in practice? Does the American openness to justice, as commonly understand, indicate that private rights might not be fundamental among us? Certainly, one of the most exalted of rights, freedom of speech, has a decidedly public cast to it.

Are not the people of the United States the true founders of this regime, that people for whom the delegates in the Federal Convention of 1787 acted and in the name of whom the Constitution itself is proclaimed? Americans do seem to remain a people who, whatever self-centeredness there is in their increasing absorption with private life, still by and large naturally consider public law, or the concern for justice and the common good, as ultimately taking precedence over private rights. In this they resemble the Roman Republic in its prime.

With these observations I suggest that the apparent emphasis in the Declaration of Independence upon the primacy of private rights may have been unnaturally influenced by political theorists. But then, I further suggest, the enduring appeal of the Declaration of Independence for the American people, as well as for many peoples around the world, may not truly have been because of any emphasis therein upon private rights but rather because of the public-spirited nobility (also somewhat Roman in its accent) that that Declaration displays in its appeal to justice, to the sacred, and to the common good—a prudent appeal which all human beings are expected to be able to respond to by nature.

# Seven Questions for Professor Jaffa

1. Leo Strauss, *Liberalism Ancient and Modern* (New York: Basic Books, 1968), p. 24. See, on liberal education, note 13, below.
2. All quotations in "Seven Questions" from Professor Jaffa are, unless otherwise indicated, from his article, "What Were the 'Original Intentions' of the Framers of the Constitution of the United States?" *University of Puget Sound Law Review*, vol. 10, p. 351 (1987). See, for a recent discussion by Mr. Jaffa of related issues, his article on Abraham Lincoln in *Encyclopedia of the American Constitution* (L. W. Levy, K. L. Karst, and D. J. Mahoney, eds.) (New York: Macmillan Publishing Co., 1986), vol. 3, pp. 1162–66. See, for additional discussion by Mr. Jaffa of these issues, notes 4, 19, and 21, below.
3. Other assessments by me of Mr. Jaffa's work may be found in Anastaplo, "Prophets and Heretics," *Modern Age*, vol. 23, p. 314 (1979) (which I quote from in note 30, below) and in those things of mine cited in notes 19, 22, and 27, below. Mr. Jaffa has spoken kindly, in public, of my article on the Declaration of Independence (see note 20, below), of my article on the Emancipation Proclamation (see note 27, below), of my Commentary on the Constitution of 1787 (see note 9, below), and of my essay on the Nixon-impeachment campaign (see Anastaplo, *Human Being and Citizen: Essays on Virtue, Freedom and the Common Good* (Chicago: Swallow Press, 1975), p. 160).
4. See Harry V. Jaffa, *American Conservatism and the American Founding* (Durham: Carolina Academic Press, 1984), p. 48. The transcript of this two-hour 1980 conversation at Rosary College had been previously published by Mr. Jaffa in the December 1981 issue of the *Claremont Review of Books*.
5. Anastaplo, *The Artist as Thinker: From Shakespeare to Joyce* (Athens, Ohio: Ohio University Press, 1983), p. 476. Mr. Jaffa's immediate response to my introductory remarks was, "Well, thank you very much, Professor Anastaplo. I must say that that is the most remarkable introduction I have ever had or that I am ever likely to have." Two hours later, at the end of the general discussion (see note 4 above), he concluded, "Thank you for your introduction, which

certainly inspired me, or gave me a sense of responsibility to live up to."
Mr. Jaffa subsequently spoke well of this introduction to many others.
See, on Leo Strauss himself, *The Artist As Thinker*, p. 250.

6. By "four essays" I mean Mr. Jaffa's introductory article and its three appendices (as found in the *University of Puget Sound Law Review*, vol. 10, p. 355 (1987):

   [1] What Were the "Original Intentions" of the Framers of the Constitution of the United States?

   [2] Appendix A: Attorney General Meese, the Declaration, and the Constitution

   [3] Appendix B: Are These Truths Now, or Have They Ever Been, Self-Evident? The Declaration of Independence and the United States of America on Their 210th Anniversary

   [4] Appendix C: Original Intent and Mr. Justice Rehnquist.

7. See Victor Gourevitch, "A Reply to Gildin," in *The Crisis Of Liberal Democracy: A Straussian Perspective* (K. L. Deutsch and W. Soffer, eds.) (Albany: State University of New York Press, 1987), p. 110. See, also, note 11, below.

8. William Blackstone, *Commentaries on the Laws of England*, vol. 1, p. 411 (1765). See also *id.*, vol. 1, p. 123: "And this spirit of liberty is so deeply implanted in our constitution, and rooted even in our very soil, that a slave or a negro, the moment he lands in England, falls under the protection of the laws, and with regard to all natural rights becomes *eo instanti* a freeman."

9. See, for my discussion of slavery and the Constitution, "The American Alcibiades?" *Modern Age*, vol. 25, p. 106 (1981); "Mr. Crosskey, the American Constitution, and the Natures of Things," *Loyola University of Chicago Law Journal*, vol. 15, p. 181 (1984), "Slavery and the Constitution: Explorations," *Texas Tech Law Review*, vol. 19, p. 677 (1989); *The Constitution of 1787: A Commentary* (Baltimore: Johns Hopkins University Press, 1989); those things of mine cited in note 3, above, and in notes 10, 12, 19, 20, 26, and 27, below; and Appendix C, above. See, on the Confederate Constitution of 1861, the Emancipation Proclamation, and the three Civil War amendments, Anastaplo, *The Amendments to the United States Constitution: A Commentary* (to be published by the Johns Hopkins University Press).

10. See, for my discussions of the Constitution, "How to Read the Constitution of the United States," *Loyola University of Chicago Law Journal*, vol. 17, p. 1 (1985); "Political Philosophy of the Constitution," *Encyclopedia of the American Constitution*, vol. 3, pp. 1417–20 (I preferred the title, "Principles of the Constitution"); *The Constitution of 1878*; those things of mine cited in notes 3 and 9, above, and in notes 12, 14, 15, 19, 20, 22, 26, and 27, below; and Appendices A and C, above.

11. "That Leo Strauss and the classics, for all practical purposes, favored the rule of law rather than of men and were averse to arbitrary government is not plain

to all. That is because although their support of the rule of law was unhesitating, their approval of it was not unqualified." Hilail Gildin, "Leo Strauss and the Crisis of Liberal Democracy," in *The Crisis of Liberal Democracy*, p. 95. "A Communist society cannot regard anything as more sacred than itself, except perhaps some future condition of itself. The plausibility of the case for liberal democracy depends on the extent to which there are to be found, among the things that it regards as higher in dignity than itself, things that truly are higher than it in dignity. Liberal democracy continues to be the troubled repository of the great western tradition at the same time that it harbors within itself tendencies that undermine it: thoughtless conformism and mass culture are equally inimical to Biblical religion and to genuine philosophical thought. . . . Liberal democracy gives the effort to preserve the western tradition, in a manner worthy of that tradition, a fighting chance. This is another one of the essential differences between it and communism that made Strauss give liberal democracy his unhesitating support even though his approval of it was not and could not be unqualified." *Id.*, p. 100. "I [have] tried to explain why, according to Strauss, constitutional democracy comes closer today to what the classics require than does any feasible alternative to it. This is very different from affirming that democracy is the simply just political order, a view that I do not think he held." *Id.*, pp. 122–23. See note 30, below.

12. Anastaplo, *The Constitutionalist: Notes on The First Amendment* (Dallas: Southern Methodist University Press, 1971), p. 420, n. 1. See, on the limitations of modern egalitarianism, Section II, above, and the passage quoted from my "Prophets and Heretics" article in note 30, below. See, also, Appendix C (e.g., Section XII), above.

13. See on liberal education, the passage from Leo Strauss used as the epigraph to this article and the passage from Laurence Berns used in the epilogue to this article. See, for my discussions of liberal education, the essays on Plato's *Apology*, on Plato's *Meno*, and on Plato's *Crito* in *Human Being and Citizen*; "What Is a Classic?" in *The Artist as Thinker*; "Notes Toward an *Apologia pro vita sua*," *Interpretation*, vol. 10, p. 319 (1982); "Aristotle on Law and Morality" and "The Teacher as Learner: On Discussion" in Anastaplo, *The American Moralist: On Law, Ethics and Government* (Athens, Ohio: Ohio University Press, 1992); "On How Eric Vogelin Has Read Plato and Aristotle," *Independent Journal of Philosophy* vol. 5, p. 85 (1988); and Appendices A and B, above. See, also, the Bibliography provided in *Law and Philosophy: The Practice of Theory* (J. A. Murley, W. T. Braithwaite, and R. L. Stone, eds.) (Athens: Ohio University Press, 1992). *The Artist as Thinker* includes discussions of Shakespeare, Milton, and Bunyan. See Appendix A, Section I, above.

14. See Anastaplo, "Justice Brennan, Due Process and the Freedom of Speech: A Celebration of *Speiser* v. *Randall*," *John Marshall Law Review*, vol. 20, p. 7 (1986). See, also, Anastaplo, "Justice Brennan, Natural Right, and Constitutional Interpretation," *Cardozo Law Review*, vol. 10, p. 201 (1988).

15. Anastaplo, "William H. Rehnquist and the First Amendment," *Intercollegiate*

*Review*, Spring 1987, p. 31. See, for my discussions of freedom of speech, Anastaplo, "Freedom of Speech and the Silence of the Law," *Texas Law Review*, vol. 64, p. 443 (1985) (reviewing Frederick Schauer, *Free Speech: A Philosophical Inquiry*); and those things of mine cited in notes 5, 9, 10, 12, and 13, above, and in notes 19, 20, 27, and 30, below. See, on obscenity, Anastaplo, *Human Being and Citizen*, Essay No. 10.

16. *Dennis* v. *United States*, 341 U.S. 494, 508 (1951) (Vinson, C.J.). Such sentiments are regarded as respectable today among sophisticated people. See, e.g., Theodore J. St. Antoine, "Integrity and Circumspection: The Labor Law Vision of Bernard D. Meltzer," *University of Chicago Law Review*, vol. 53, p. 78, opening paragraph (1986); William H. Rehnquist, "The Notion of a Living Constitution," *Texas Law Review*, vol. 54, pp. 693, 704–706 (1976). Mr. Jaffa is properly concerned lest the moral underpinnings of the American regime be undermined by the thoughtlessness of people who should know better and who *do* "feel" better than they (in their sophistication) say. In any event, it is salutary that "sophisticated" jurisprudential speculations (if to be indulged in at all) should be interred in the law review articles that judges write. See, on the unnecessary costs of the Cold War, note 33 (end), below.

17. For the Brennan quotation, see Glenn Elsasser, "Senate Groups Cram for Rehnquist Quiz," *Chicago Tribune*, July 27, 1986, p. 5. See, also, "Justice Brennan, Due Process, and the Freedom of Speech," p. 10, n. 8.

Much is to be said for magnanimity if there is to be a healthy polity. The most eloquent (and encouraging) recognition of the longstanding grievances of American racial minorities that I heard during the recent mayoral contest in Chicago was made (at the University of Chicago, on February 27, 1987) by an "ethnic" candidate (Edward Vrdolyak) who has been in recent years the bitterest opponent of the incumbent mayor (Harold Washington, an African-American). Mr. Vrdolyak's testimonial to the enduring claims among us of equality can easily be dismissed as mere politics. It can even be said that these stated convictions do not come from the heart. However that may be, the passions are not all that count: such a public recognition as I heard from Mr. Vrdolyak, if "only" in words, of the plight of minorities in this country reflects an informed awareness even as it appeals to the passions (including the speaker's passions) through the reason. Thus, we have come a long way in these matters from John C. Calhoun and Roger B. Taney. In short, a useful magnanimity requires that one's opponents' merits (apparent as well as genuine) be acknowledged and thereby reinforced. See the text at note 27, below. See, also, note 32, below.

18. The scholar drawn upon here is Laurence Berns, a senior member of the faculty of St. John's College, Annapolis, Maryland. His publications include "Aristotle's *Poetics*," in *Ancients and Moderns: Essays on the Tradition of Political Philosophy in Honor of Leo Strauss* (J. Cropsey, ed.) (New York: Basic Books, 1964); "Rational Animal-Political Animal: Nature and Convention in Human Speech and Politics," in *Essays In Honor Of Jacob Klein* (Annapolis,

Maryland: St. John's College Press, 1976), p. 29; "Francis Bacon and the Conquest of Nature," *Interpretation*, vol. 8, p. 1 (1978); "Speculations on Liberal and Illiberal Politics," *Review of Politics*, vol. 40, p. 231 (1978); Book Review, *Interpretation*, vol. 10, p. 322 (1982). See, also, Anastaplo, *The Constitutionalist*, p. 362; Berns, "Two Old Conservatives Discuss the Anastaplo Case," *Cornell Law Review*, vol. 54, p. 920 (1969) (reprinted in *Law and Philosophy*) (this is the last article cited to by Professor Berns in the article from which I quote at length here in my epilogue).

My notes 19 through 29 in this article are taken (except for the bracketed material therein) from notes 33 through 43 in Professor Berns's article, cited in note 30, below.

19. [This is note 33 in the Berns article from which I am quoting here.] Harry V. Jaffa, *The Conditions of Freedom: Essays In Political Philosophy* (Baltimore: Johns Hopkins University Press, 1975), pp. 149–60. I shall not discuss here Jaffa's remarkable book on Lincoln, *The Crisis of the House Divided*. For a criticism and appreciation of Jaffa's Lincoln book, which moves on a philosophical plane commensurate with Jaffa's plane, see George Anastaplo, "American Constitutionalism and the Virtue of Prudence: Philadelphia, Paris, Washington, Gettysburg," in *Abraham Lincoln, the Gettysburg Address and American Constitutionalism*, ed. Leo Paul S. de Alvarez (Irving, Texas: University of Dallas Press, 1976), pp. 165–68, n. 64.

20. [This is note 34 in the Berns article from which I am quoting here.] See George Anastaplo, "The Declaration of Independence," *St. Louis University Law Journal*, vol. 9, p. 390 (Spring 1965). [See, also, note 30, below.]

21. [This is note 35 in the Berns article from which I am quoting here.] Leo Strauss, *Liberalism Ancient and Modern* (New York: Basic Books, 1968), pp. 11–16. Cf. Harry V. Jaffa, *Equality & Liberty* (New York: Oxford University Press, 1965), pp. 50–52. Cp. Hamilton's arguments against ancient political thought and practice in Harvey Flaumenhaft, "Alexander Hamilton on the Foundation of Good Government," *Political Science Reviewer*, vol. VI, pp. 143–214 (Fall 1976).

22. [This is note 36 in the Berns article from which I am quoting here.] George Anastaplo, *Human Being and Citizen* (Chicago: Swallow Press, 1975), Essay No. 5. Cf., also, Anastaplo, *The Constitutionalist: Notes on the First Amendment* (Dallas: Southern Methodist University Press, 1971), Chapter 8.

23. [This is note 37 in the Berns article from which I am quoting here.] See Anastaplo, *The Constitutionalist*, Chapter 8, Section ix, and Thomas Jefferson's letter to John Adams, October 28, 1813.

24. [This is note 38 in the Berns article from which I am quoting here.] Harry Jaffa, *Equality & Liberty*, p. 139; Jaffa, *Crisis of the House Divided* (New York: Doubleday and Co., 1959), pp. 227, 232, and 239.

25. [This is note 39 in the Berns article from which I am quoting here.] Anastaplo, *Human Being and Citizen*, Essays No. 3, No. 10, and No. 16.

26. [This is note 40 in the Berns article from which I am quoting here.] See George Anastaplo, "Citizenship, Prudence and the Classics," *The Artist as Thinker* (Chicago: Swallow Press, 1983), pp. 279–83. See, also, Leo Strauss, *Natural Right and History* (Chicago: University of Chicago Press, 1953), Chapter 4. [See, as well, Appendix B, above.]

27. [This is note 41 in the Berns article from which I am quoting here.] George Anastaplo, "Abraham Lincoln's Emancipation Proclamation," in *Constitutional Government in America*, ed. Ronald K. L. Collins (Durham: Carolina Academic Press, 1980), p. 439. In the context of a discussion of the right and the wrong way to argue against censorship, Anastaplo gives voice to what has become a growing concern in his recent writings: "Indeed, we may have more to fear from a lack of concern about abuses of our considerable liberties than we have from threats of immediate restrictions upon them." Anastaplo, "Human Nature and the First Amendment," *University of Pittsburgh Law Review*, vol. 40, p. 746 (1979). Cf. Anastaplo, "Censorship," *Encyclopedia Britannica, Macropedia* (15th ed. 1988), vol. 15, pp. 634–41.

28. [This is note 42 in the Berns article from which I am quoting here.] "Heaven grant that it may be the glory of the United States to have established two great truths, of the highest importance to the whole human race: first, that an enlightened community is capable of self-government; and, second, that the toleration of all sects does not necessarily produce indifference to religion." Daniel Webster, speech, reception at Pittsburgh, July 8, 1833. Cf. Alexis de Tocqueville, *Democracy in America*, Book 2, Chapter 15, and Xenophon, *Memorabilia*, Book IV, Chapter 3.1 and 3.2. See, also, the remarkable biologist's account of "the distress of the modern soul" by Jacques Monod, *Chance and Necessity* (New York: Vintage Books, 1972), pp. 164–73.

29. [This is note 43 in the Berns article from which I am quoting here.] *The Federalist*, No. 55, end.

30. Laurence Berns, "Aristotle and the Moderns on Freedom and Equality," in *The Crisis of Liberal Democracy* (Deutsch and Soffer, eds.), pp. 156–59 (1987). My notes 19 through 29 in this article have been taken in their entirety (except for the bracketed material therein) from notes 33 through 43 in the 1987 Berns article.

    Mr. Berns notices (at note 20, above in my text, which is at note 34 in his 1987 text) my 1965 observations about the references to God in the Declaration of Independence. I have recently developed further those observations in *The Constitution of 1787*, pp. 21–22:

> The affinity between the Declaration of Independence and the Constitution of 1787 is further suggested by certain implications of the separation-of-powers approach in the Constitution, a principle that had been severely compromised in the Articles of Confederation.
>
> Various of the grievances in the Declaration of Independence, and the

way government itself is spoken of there, presuppose a separation-of-powers approach much like that made explicit in the Constitution. We can even see in the references to divinity in the Declaration of Independence an oblique anticipation of the qualified separation of powers found in the Constitution itself. There are four references to divinity in the Declaration. The first reference, and perhaps the second as well, regarded God as legislator; it is He that orders things, ordaining what is to be. That is, he first comes to view as lawgiver. Next, God is seen as judge. Finally, He is revealed as executive, as One Who extends protection, enforcing the laws that have been laid down, with a suggestion as well of the dispensing power of the executive. Thus, the authors of the Declaration portrayed even the government of the world in the light of their political principles.

In this way, at least, a republican regime is implied by the Declaration of Independence, such a regime as may be seen in various of the State constitutions of that period, in the Constitution of 1787, and even (however distorted in some respects) in the British Constitution. Among the features of the republicanism endorsed by the Declaration are the consent of the governed, a qualified separation of powers, and a proper respect for the inalienable rights of mankind.

I referred in Section VI of Lecture No. 1 [of *The Constitution of 1787*] to the natural constitutionalism of the Declaration of Independence. Is it not appropriate that the deference in the Declaration to "the Laws of Nature and of Nature's God" should be reflected in the understanding that the best ordering of human things should take as its model the divine ordering of the world?

The Constitution of 1787 can plausibly be taken, then, as an incarnation of the principles revealed in the Declaration of Independence. It is a form of government appropriate for the people of the Declaration—that is, for a people who could produce such a declaration. It is also a form of government that had to defer to circumstances, particularly the long-established institution of slavery. This accommodation left the Constitution deeply flawed, but not without hope of eventual redemption.

These observations can be taken to provide qualified support for one aspect of the position taken by Mr. Jaffa during the past decade against Walter Berns, Martin Diamond, and Irving Kristol. This aspect of Mr. Jaffa's position, with respect to the relation between the Declaration of Independence and the Constitution, is glanced at by me in the third paragraph of the following comment upon his work some years ago ("Prophets and Heretics," pp. 315–16):

> Whatever differences I may have with Mr. Jaffa can, it seems to
> me, be reconciled, especially since we do share certain critical opinions

about the dominant relativism and historicism among political scientists today. But, then, his differences with Mr. Diamond and Mr. Kristol . . . also seem to me to be less serious than he likes to make them out to be.

Consider, for instance, the concern expressed by Mr. Diamond and Mr. Kristol about the tendencies of egalitarianism toward utopianism, levelling and populism. An equality hedged in as Mr. Jaffa hedges it need not arouse their concern—except as to whether such hedges can be maintained in these times. Mr. Jaffa does tacitly recognize their concerns, in the way he places his hedges—concerns which go back to at least Tocqueville.

Or consider Mr. Jaffa's extended critique of Mr. Diamond for presuming to say that the Declaration of Independence "is devoid of guidance" for the institutions of government under the Constitution. Is it not evident that Mr. Diamond meant that considerable leeway was left by the Declaration, that the institutions to be established by a people depend to a considerable extent on circumstances? There may have been something careless in Mr. Diamond's rhetorical flourish here. But is it not evident that Mr. Diamond agreed with the substance of what his tougher-minded critic has said on this score? And, indeed, has not Mr. Jaffa himself said things, in his *Conditions of Freedom* (e.g., pp. 114, 154–55, 158–59), which sound very much like what Mr. Diamond has now been so vigorously rebuked for saying on this point? See, on the limitations of an emphasis upon equality, Section II, above. See, on the continuing importance of the right of revolution, Anastaplo, "What Is Still Wrong with George Anastaplo? A Sequel to 366 U.S. 82 (1961)," *DePaul Law Review*, vol. 35, p. 551 (1986). See, also, note 33, below.

See, on the relation of religion and politics, Anastaplo, "The Religion Clauses of the First Amendment," *Memphis State University Law Review*, vol. 11, p. 151 (1981); Anastaplo, "On Speaking to and for Mankind: The *Laborem Exercens* Encyclical of Pope John Paul II," *Catholicism in Crisis*, September 1983, p. 6 (reprinted in *The American Moralist*); Anastaplo, "On Trial: Explorations," *Loyola University of Chicago Law Journal*, vol. 22, p. 765 (1991); Anastaplo, "Church and State: Explorations," *Loyola University of Chicago Law Journal*, vol. 19, p. 61 (1987); Appendix A, above. I anticipate, in my "Notes Toward an *Apologia pro vita sua*," pp. 341–42, "a series of inquiries into the divine based upon a recognition of that question which is fundamental to much of philosophy as well as to theology—the question *quid sit deus*." See, also, Laurence Berns, "The Relation Between Philosophy and Religion," *Interpretation*, vol. 19, p. 43 (Fall 1991); note 31, below.

31. This talk, "The Founders of Our Founders: Jerusalem, Athens, and the American Constitution," was given by George Anastaplo at Wake Forest University, Winston-Salem, North Carolina, October 8, 1976. The quotations from *Paradise Regained* (cited as *P.R.* in the text) are taken from John

Milton, *Complete Poems and Major Prose* (Merritt Y. Hughes, ed.) (Indianapolis: Odyssey Press, 1957). See, also, Anastaplo, "Rome, Piety, and Law: Explorations," *Loyola Law Review* (New Orleans), vol. 39 (1993) (including essays on St. Paul, Tertullian, Julian the Apostate, St. Augustine, and Justinian). See, on what Socrates did know, Anastaplo, "Freedom of Speech and the First Amendment," *Texas Tech Law Review*, vol. 21, pp. 1945–58 (1990).

This talk is dedicated to the memory of James A. Steintrager of the University of Chicago and Wake Forest University.

32. This talk, "The Ambiguity of Justice in Plato's *Republic*," was given by George Anastaplo at a staff meeting of the Basic Program of Liberal Education for Adults, The University of Chicago, Chicago, Illinois, February 22, 1987. The quotations from Plato's *Republic* (cited as *Rep.* in the text) are taken from the Allan Bloom translation (in the Basic Books edition). See, also, Anastaplo, *The Constitutionalist*, pp. 278–81.

33. This talk, "Private Rights and Public Law: The Founders' Perspective," was given by George Anastaplo at Illinois State University, Normal, Illinois, April 17, 1983. See, also, Anastaplo, "Natural Law or Natural Right? An Appreciation of James V. Schall, S.J.," *Loyola Law Review* (New Orleans), vol. 38, p. 915 (1993); Anastaplo, "On Freedom: Explorations," *Oklahoma City University Law Review*, vol. 17, p. 465 (1992).

Special thanks are due to Martha J. Schaeffer who, as an enterprising and sensitive editor-in-chief of the *University of Puget Sound Law Review* (encouraged by Professor Ronald K.L. Collins), devoted the Spring 1987 issue of her journal to "Framers' Intent: An Exchange" (with Lewis F. Lehrman, Harry V. Jaffa, Bruce Ledewitz, Robert L. Stone, and George Anastaplo). That collection, now published in book form by Harry V. Jaffa, has been supplemented by (among other things) his reply, "Seven Answers for Professor Anastaplo," *University of Puget Sound Law Review*, vol. 13, p. 379 (1990) (reprinted in *Law and Philosophy: The Practice of Theory*). A response by George Anastaplo, "Professor Jaffa and That Old-Time Religion," was prepared in 1993 for the Jaffa book version, eliciting in turn his reply with the splendid title, "Our Ancient Faith." See, also, Studs Terkel, "We Must Not Be Afraid To Be Free: Interviews with George Anastaplo," *Law and Philosophy*, pp. 504–38 (1992).

Bearing on various matters discussed here and in Anastaplo, "Professor Jaffa and That Old-Time Religion," is the following excerpt from an interview of George Anastaplo conducted by Andrew Patner on WBEZ-FM, the National Public Radio affiliate station in Chicago, Illinois, August 14, 1992. This excerpt has been adapted for use here:

A.P.: ... So you were asked, upon appearing before the character committee as an applicant for admission to the bar, whether members of the Communist Party should be able to have a license to practice law in the State of Illinois?

G.A.: That's right. I was asked that here in Chicago is November, 1950. I answered, in effect, that I didn't see why Communists should not be permitted to practice law. (This was a test question that they were asking other applicants. I wasn't the only one asked that.) The response to my answer by the two Commissioners who were examining me was, "Don't Communists believe in revolution?" From then on the fat was in the fire. [Laughter] It didn't matter after that what I said. They asked me, "Are you a Communist? You must be a Communist," and I answered, "That's not a proper question." Later on they asked me if I was a Nazi or a Fascist and I told them that that was also an improper question. They even asked me at one point, when they got really exasperated, if I was a Republican or a Democrat. I suggested that even they could see that that was not a proper question. [Laughter] Once all this started there was no way for any of us to back off. I was twenty-five years old. They were much older in years, but in some ways even Less mature than I was. They stuck by their position, insisting that I had to answer such questions in order to be admitted to the bar. The litigation that resulted lasted about ten years. I finally lost, of course, in the Supreme Court of the United States in 1961 [366 U.S. 82], but it was a great adventure.

A.P.: It *was* a great adventure, with at least that segment culminating in your arguing your own case as a non-lawyer before the United States Supreme Court. You lost five to four, but if you were to look at who voted which way—

G.A.: —the good guys were on the right side.

A.P.: [Laughter] The good guys voted for you?

G.A.: Sure.

A.P.: And the opinion authored by Justice Black on that occasion was one of his most distinguished dissenting opinions. In fact, a portion of that opinion was read, at Justice Black's request, at his funeral service.

G.A.: That's right. It concludes with that wonderful sentence, "We must not be afraid to be free."

A.P.: You stood accused of being a free man.

G.A.: Another use of the Black dissent is that its concluding sentence, "We must not be afraid to be free," was featured as the slogan for an exhibition in the Soviet Union, in Leningrad and Kiev, of photographs of American and Soviet dissidents in opposition to their respective regimes. My photograph was included in the exhibition. This Soviet exhibition was before the changes of recent years over there. Thus the Black dissent in my case provided a rallying cry against efforts to suppress dissent in the Soviet Union and may even have contributed to the revolution there.

See Anastaplo, *The Constitutionalist*, Appendix F; Anastaplo, "What Is Still Wrong With George Anastaplo? A Sequel to 366 U.S. 82 (1961)," *DePaul Law Review*, vol. 35, p. 551 (1986). See, also, Harry V. Jaffa, "Our Ancient Faith," note 10, below. See, for a sensible assessment of "the Soviet threat," James Burnham, "Through the Mirror: The Protracted Conflict," *National Review* November 11, 1972, p. 1299.

# PART IV

# Jaffa Replies to His Critics

# Judicial Conscience and Natural Rights: A Reply to Professor Ledewitz

## HARRY V. JAFFA

I am grateful to Professor Ledewitz for the kind words with which he both prefaces and concludes his critique. There are, I should add, many welcome expressions of agreement in between. I am heartened to believe that we are not going to talk past each other, and that continued—but candid—discussions of our differences will not so much intensify those differences, as expand the areas of agreement between us.

Let me begin with the note attached to the asterisk following Professor Ledewitz's name on his title page. In it he says that my paper

> does not deal with all of the problems that the original intent position . . . faces. Such questions as "who counts as a framer," "what is the relevance of the ratification process," or even "why should intention matter in the first place," do not occupy him . . .

According to Professor Ledewitz, I dealt

> primarily with a much narrower question, how well do the professed advocates of original intent understand the intellectual and political presumptions of the generation they accept as Framers?

Professor Ledewitz says that it was quite right for me to have limited myself to a question of manageable scale. He says that his reply will be similarly limited, but from a different, one might say left-wing, perspective.

Professor Ledewitz says, also correctly, that he

> senses a sympathy [on my part] with what Attorney General Meese, Chief Justice Rehnquist, and Judge Robert Bork are attempting to accomplish.

Yet he generously concedes that I have approached

> the politically charged field of constitutional interpretation with the trustwor-
> thy attitude of the scholar, rather than the advocate.

It is true that I addressed myself primarily to conservatives, because I shared with them *a priori* a commitment to the idea of "original intent" jurisprudence. I set out to prove—as Professor Ledewitz agrees that I have proved—that their jurisprudence does not, in the most important respect, correspond with the intent of those who framed and those who ratified the Constitution. I felt that these conservatives would be obliged by their own premises to "alter or abolish" whatever was manifestly inconsistent with the intent to which they professed themselves committed.

But "a man convinced against his will is of the same opinion still." I am well aware that however great is the obligation of men to their premises, they are seldom as attached to those premises as they are to their conclusions, whether or not those conclusions actually follow from the premises. My larger purpose, however, was to illuminate the profound break with the thought of the Founding Fathers that is represented by the "mainstream" of American conservatism (including most particularly neo-conservatism). The legal positivism of Rehnquist has much in common with Calhoun. It has nothing in common with the political philosophy—or jurisprudence— of a Jefferson or a Madison.

What Ledewitz fails to notice, however, is that the Brennanite (or left-wing) perspective that he shares is one that is in its essentials the same as that of the conservatives, with whom, he mistakenly thinks, he differs. For what is most important about left- and right-wing jurisprudence today, is not that they are of the Right or of the Left, but that they are "result oriented." Their so-called principles are not in their premises but in their conclusions. They differ in the particulars of their "value judgments," but not in the subjectivity of what they propose as the ground of constitutional law. Calling their subjective preferences "traditional moral-ity," on the one hand, or "human dignity," in the other, does not make them less "value judgments," or less subjective. But if the basis of law is believed to be subjective, then the basis of law is believed to be will, not reason. The goal or perfection of the law, according to the whole tradi-tion of Western civilization, is that it should be, in Aristotle's words, "reason unaffected by desire."[1] This is what law means, according to the natural rights and natural law teaching of the Declaration of Independence. But law that rests upon nothing but "value judgments" is desire unaffected by reason.

Professor Ledewitz is mistaken in supposing that I did not deal with "who counts as a framer" or "what is the relevance of the ratification process." The political philosophy of natural rights and natural law, expressed in virtually all the great documents of the revolutionary and Founding period—but quintessentially in the Declaration of Independence—was the common ground for both Framers and Ratifiers. It is in the rejection of this common ground that we see the common ground of both Left and Right today. Professor Ledewitz, in his delight at my exposure of the inconsistencies of present-day conservatism, fails to notice that the same inconsistencies characterize his own "left-wing perspective."

Professor Ledewitz is also mistaken in supposing that I did not address the question of "why should [original] intention matter in the first place." I pointed to the fact that Madison and Jefferson agreed that the principles of the Declaration of Independence are the principles of the Constitution. But I also argued—notably but not exclusively in Appendix B—that the principles of the Declaration are the true principles of the rule of law, and the ground of political justice. Original intention ought then to govern because "ought" refers to what is right or just.

But these principles, being governed in their application by "the dictates of prudence," do not of themselves determine the conclusions that the people of the United States or their representatives ought to draw from them. They are a necessary, but not a sufficient condition for just judgment. Professor Ledewitz is thus correct when he writes that I am not "proposing to consult the Framers on the specific issues that come before the Supreme Court today." It is of the essence of the idea of prudence, to which the Founding Fathers appealed, that it be directed to the particular circumstances in which it is to be applied. And our circumstances are not in all respects those of two hundred years ago. (Neither, of course, are they altogether different.) Justice Brennan, and his partisans, have a field day in declaiming against the utility of any appeal to the opinions of the Framers. But in thus declaiming they—like their conservative adversaries—fail to distinguish between principles and their prudent or wise application. That is because their conception of principles is always, at bottom, that they are "value judgments." But "value judgments" are essentially nonrational, and the ends of prudence are and must be essentially rational. Hence the very idea of "value judgments" as the principles or ends of law excludes the idea of prudence, properly understood.

Professor Ledewitz's seems to accept, for the most part, my interpretation of "original intent" as historically authentic. But he cannot accept the authority of that intention because he believes that in the decisive respects the thought of the present is wiser than the thought of the past. He agrees—as do I—with Aristotle's dictum that what is intrinsically desirable is not the old but the good.[2] I think that Professor Ledewitz is justified, as any man is justified, in arguing for the superiority of one idea to another. He would be justified, for example, in arguing that the central idea of the Communist Manifesto ("that all history is the history of class struggle") is a wiser and better ground for political understanding than the central idea of the Declaration of Independence ("that all men are created equal"). But he would not be justified in so arguing on the ground that the Communist Manifesto was written later than the Declaration; or that the Manifesto, as a by-product of the historical school, was intrinsically superior to the Declaration, because the latter reflected the anachronistic belief in eternal categories. In truth, nothing ought to be more thoroughly discredited today, in the eyes of intelligent human beings, than any such belief in progress. Both National Socialism and Marxism-Leninism (International Socialism) justify themselves on this ground. However, as I pointed out above, Alexander Stephens, in his cornerstone speech of April 1861, justified the Confederate States of America as a form of government superior to all others because it was based upon the newly discovered scientific truth of Negro inferiority. This alleged scientific truth (which Stephens compared, among other things, to Harvey's discovery of the circulation of the blood) had replaced the old doctrine of human equality in the Declaration of Independence.

I do not mean here to argue for one or another version of the *reductio ad Hitlerum*. Hitler, or Stalin, or Stephens, must be refuted. We are not entitled to say that they are wrong because we have different "value judgments." That an argument leads to conclusions we do not like does not mean that it is a bad argument. I believe, however, that the opinions and actions of Hitler and Stalin and Stephens can be proved wrong by arguments founded upon the doctrines of the Declaration of Independence, doctrines which are consistent with reason and experience, and which are intrinsically truthful and just.

*     *     *

Professor Ledewitz imagines a dialogue in which I exhort Chief Justice Rehnquist to abide by the self-evident truths of the Declaration of Independence. But the chief justice would reply to me, says Professor Ledewitz,

> that there are no "self-evident truths," that there is no accessibility to a divine intention for humankind, and, thus, no endowed rights . . . [Furthermore] Chief Justice Rehnquist would say that if people disagree about these matters, discussion is closed. At the point of disagreement, there is nothing more than subjective preference, which may or may not be backed by power.

And again:

> Professor Jaffa associates the Framers with . . . [a] view [according to which] political science and law are capable of uncovering a "true understanding" of the individual and her [sic] relation to society. There are principles, "truths 'applicable to all men and all times,' " that Chief Justice Rehnquist must accept if he wishes to interpret the Constitution in accordance with original intent.
>
> It is not clear how Professor Jaffa would like chief justice Rehnquist to respond to this position. If the chief justice examines modern philosophy, history, anthropology and, yes, even science, as well as his own being and concludes that this claim about eternal truth is incoherent, an echo of a less sophisticated time, he can hardly will himself to believe otherwise. Professor Jaffa knows he is addressing an audience in which no one else is persuaded.

Professor Ledewitz next cites John Hart Ely, who asks what would we do with a constitutional provision protecting ghosts.

> How could we who know that there are no such things attempt to interpret the Constitution as if we did believe in ghosts and apply the implications of ghost-belief? Such an undertaking would be self-defeating. Because we do not believe in ghosts, an appropriate application of a ghost provision would be beyond us.

And Chief Justice Rehnquist—for whom Professor Ledewitz now speaks unreservedly—like John Hart Ely,

> does not believe in the ghost of natural law . . .

I believe, with Jefferson, that "Almighty God hath created the mind free." Hence I do not believe a man or woman—not even a law professor or a

Supreme Court justice—can be expected to believe anything of which he or she is unpersuaded. I can therefore only hope to persuade them of what reasonable men and women ought to be persuaded. I can only marvel, however, that someone can, at one and the same time, deny that there are self-evident truths, and yet speak of the accessibility or inaccessibility of such truths "for humankind." For the assertion of the self-evidence of the proposition "that all men are created equal" means nothing more nor less than what Professor Ledewitz himself means when, answering in behalf of the chief justice, he speaks of what is accessible or inaccessible "for humankind."

What is that "humankind?"[3] Is it not the human species, distinguished from the nonhuman? How is it that Professor Ledewitz can speak of this humankind without argument or evidence that there is such a thing? To speak thus is to assume that his meaning is self-evident.

I would remind Professor Ledewitz of the interlocutor described in my essay who denied that there were any self-evident truths and, consistently with this denial, denied that he knew that he was not a dog. Here we come to the real meaning of the logical positivists when they speak of the ghosts of natural law. These ghosts are not the immaterial realities of Gothic novelists (or Gothic theologians). To paraphrase a famous cartoon character, "We have met these ghosts and they are us!" Thus positivism denies the reality of the knowledge that we ourselves exist and have identities in an external reality—a nature of which human nature is a part. In this nihilistic dispensation—where the ground of thought becomes an infinite regress—we ourselves thus become imaginary creatures of our own imaginations!

Recently, the entire nation, from the president of the United States to every farm or factory worker, clerk, or shoe salesman, held its breath while drilling and rescue teams worked around the clock to save an eighteen-month-old girl who had fallen to the bottom of an abandoned well. Why this tremendous concern for this tiny bundle of earth, air, fire, and water? A puppy or a kitten might also have been an object of concern, but not of the same magnitude or kind. "One touch of nature makes the whole world kin." It was the *nature* of the child that brought the entire country together, as if it were a single family. After all, none of us knew her as an individual. Some of us believed that hers was an immortal soul loved by God. But whether or not we believed that God loved her, we knew that we did.

Why? Does Professor Ledewitz really believe that the evidence of such experience—which is the root in the ground of natural law—is something to be put aside as something unscientific, a kind of superstitious hang-up? We know of course that human beings can be dehumanized to the point that they can kill human children as if they were microbes. The minions of Hitler and Stalin and Pol Pot did so in great genocidal convulsions. But when we speak of dehumanization, we imply a norm in nature by which we can recognize and characterize in appropriate terms what is degenerate and immoral.

By the logic of this debased philosophical positivism, whatever is not "verifiable" by "scientific" canons is not known at all. But we should consider that all scientific verification presupposes prescientific categories. The scientist who verifies an hypothesis by experimental means presents his evidence to another scientist. In doing so he must believe in the reality of his own existence and that of his fellow scientist. But he makes no attempt to verify the truth of his own identity—as man and scientist—in the way he attempts to verify the hypothesis that is the subject of his experiment. In fact, such a demonstration of his own existence is an impossibility. I will not now reconstruct the technicalities of this argument, but refer the reader to the title essay of *The Conditions of Freedom*.[4] Suffice it to say every attempt at demonstration presupposes the existence of the demonstrator. Our own existence is a self-evident truth, because there can be no evidence stronger than what is implicit in the assumption that enables us to consider evidence. Without the assumption of the reality of our own existence, without the assumption of the reality of our individual identities—which means our existence as individuals of a species—all rationality would be impossible. Scientific rationality is a subspecies of human rationality, but it has no life or being apart from that prescientific rationality which is the condition of its existence.

*       *       *

Professor Ledewitz says that Chief Justice Rehnquist, examining the claims of the Declaration of Independence to "eternal truth" in the light of modern philosophy and modern social science, must conclude that such claims are "incoherent, an echo of a less sophisticated time." But it is modern philosophy and modern social science that lead Mr. Rehnquist to think that all moral judgments are "value judgments." It is modern philosophy and modern social science that, on his own premises, would require a judge to enforce Nazi law, once he had been satisfied that the "original intention" of the legislator had been to enshrine Nazi "value judgments" into law. It is mere accident, and nothing in the nature of law itself, as the chief justice himself understands the nature of law, that places

Mr. Rehnquist's judicial skills in the service of Jefferson's—and not of Hitler's or Stalin's or Pol Pot's—"value judgments." And we would remind Professor Ledewitz that it is also modern philosophy and modern social science that disable an otherwise intelligent human being from knowing that he is a human being—and not a dog. But it is precisely because some disciples of logical positivism do not know that they are not dogs, that other disciples of that same positivism do not know that, for example, black men are not monkeys, and that Jews are not termites.

Professor Ledewitz concludes that I, in indulging in exhortations by the canons of a by-gone age, am "addressing an audience in which no one else is persuaded." It may seem strange to Professor Ledewitz, but it is nonetheless true, that I have unfailingly persuaded student audiences for all of the forty-three years of my teaching career, that they really do know that they are not dogs, that black men are not monkeys, and that Jews are not termites. And I have not only persuaded them that such knowledge is genuine knowledge, but that the ground of such knowledge is what Abraham Lincoln called "an abstract truth, applicable to all men and all time." I have, moreover, found that it is relatively easy to persuade students of this, if they are young enough and have not been duped by the superstitions of that relativism, positivism, and nihilism that are the reigning modes of thought in this new dark age. Once they have been persuaded—as my anonymous (but genuine) interlocutor was—that it is sophisticated to say that you do not know that you are not a dog, then the task of persuasion is much more difficult. Difficult—but not impossible. In the long run we all have a much greater interest in being thought human than in being thought sophisticated. I certainly do not despair of persuading Professor Ledewitz.

Professor Ledewitz asks

> what sense does this call for a return to the "true" understanding of original intent make when addressed to people who, in good faith, find original intent to be gibberish? Here we would expect Professor Jaffa to show that the Framers' views are true and that modern critics of natural rights are wrong. He avoids this effort, however. Perhaps he feels that, as a historian, it is not his place.

On the contrary, however; I have consistently argued—as I do here—that the Framers' intent is authoritative for no other reason than that it is true. What did Professor Ledewitz think I meant when I showed that "the modern critics of natural rights" could not discover any epistemological foundation for their own humanity, for what distinguished them "from the beasts of the field that perish"? What did he think I was doing when I argued, with Lincoln, that, for the positive law to treat a black man as a chattel was against the natural law, because a black man possessed a rational will, which a chattel cannot possess? I was not making this argument as an historian. While I am a student of history, my vocation is that of a political scientist. I turned to Lincoln's argument not as an historical curiosity, but because it revealed more clearly than any other single example the disjunction of positive law and natural law within the Constitution itself. And while Lincoln's argument conceded a prudential obligation to the positive law arising from "necessity," it pointed to the contrary obligation arising from "freedom."[5]

Among the fundamental texts of my vocation are Aristotle's, as when he says that "we are inquiring not in order to know what virtue is, but in order to become good . . ."[6] Right action, morally and politically, is the end or purpose of political science, rightly understood. Nothing I have ever written has been unrelated to this end. The only explanation I can imagine, for Professor Ledewitz so to misunderstand me, is that looking to the past for wisdom is alien to him. I grant that it ought to be alien to anyone who is justifiably confident of the wisdom of the present. However, I see little justification for such confidence. The subjective confidence of the lunatic is not less than that of the philosopher—indeed, not only have many lunatics imagined that they were philosophers, but great numbers have been successful in persuading others that they were! Of course, in an age in which the most radical subjectivity receives academic certification the distinction between lunatics and philosophers tends to vanish. We should never forget that both Hitler and Stalin demanded public recognition for themselves as the undisputed sources of philosophic wisdom in their regimes.

What then passes for wisdom with Professor Ledewitz? Oddly enough, while rejecting my uses of it, Professor Ledewitz himself patronizes the natural law. As I have already pointed out, that was already implicit in his appeal to "humankind." However, in the following he clearly establishes himself as the true representative of "the tradition of natural law."

Self-conscious emulation is not natural law. Nor is it true to the Framers' intent. It is an archaeological dig into the remnants of natural law. It is an attempt to hold human understanding still at a certain point in time. Neither a judge nor a legal thinker can be true to the tradition of natural law unless it lives in her [sic]. Merely to appeal to equality without commitment to the reality of equality, its self-evident quality, is to celebrate the shell without the substance.

One must marvel at how Professor Ledewitz can speak of the ghost of the natural law doctrine of the Declaration of Independence at one moment, and of the self-evident reality of its substance at the next! But there is not a word of the foregoing with which we are not in complete agreement. In the sequel, however, Professor Ledewitz writes that

> The problem for Professor Jaffa is that he wishes to be true to an original intent that is revolutionary in its call for justice, but also wants to restrict carefully the implications of original intent. Professor Jaffa takes pains to insulate himself from what he calls judicial activism. His methods of limitation are first, fidelity to the text; second, opposition to judicial "evolutionary conscience"; and third, the requirement of corporate judicial action.

According to Professor Ledewitz, these

> negative techniques interfere with an attempt to practice the constitutional tradition bequeathed to us by the Framers.

It is good to know that the question is not *whether* but *how* we should go about having a constitutional jurisprudence of original intent! Professor Ledewitz makes the issue of capital punishment the centerpiece for his discussion of my "negative techniques." He argues that the Constitution is no more presumptively in favor of capital punishment than it is in favor of slavery.

> According to Professor Jaffa, though the Constitution promotes slavery in several respects, it is not a pro-slavery document. Slavery is a prudent compromise, not a matter of genuine constitutional principles. The genuine principle is said to be human equality as demonstrated by the Declaration of Independence. But the Declaration of Independence also proclaims the unalienable right to "life." One may say that the calculated taking of human life is presumptively disfavored under the Declaration of Independence, just as slavery is clearly disfavored. The Fifth Amendment no more turns the Constitution into a pro-death penalty document than the fugitive slave provision turns the Constitution into a pro-slavery document ... The genuine principle of the Constitution is "life" just as surely as it is "equality."

Professor Ledewitz is, however, simply wrong in his premises. The rights proclaimed in the Declaration are rights which we are bound to respect in others only insofar as others respect them in us. The right to life which we are bound to respect is, as such, a right of innocent life. The right of a murderer—or tyrant—is not on a level with that—for example—of an unborn child. Professor Ledewitz should reflect on the fact that the Declaration was issued in the midst of a war—a just war—-in which the "one people" who made the Declaration were taking the lives of some of those who would forcibly deprive them of the enjoyment of their natural rights. That "the great principle of self-preservation" was "the transcendent law of nature and of nature's God"—as James Madison declared in the forty-third *Federalist*—and that this might justify the taking of human life, was axiomatic for the Founding Fathers. The very text whose words resonate in the Declaration—Locke's *Second Treatise of Civil Government*—defines "political power" to be "a right of making laws with penalties of death, and consequently all less penalties . . . " (Chapter One) Locke says, moreover, that we ought when our

> own preservation comes not in competition . . . to preserve the rest of mankind and not, *unless it be to do justice on an offender*, take away or impair the life, or what tends to the preservation of the life, the liberty, health, limb or goods of another [Chapter Two, emphasis added].

Now I challenge Professor Ledewitz to find anywhere a document of the thought of those who framed and those who ratified the Constitution, disagreeing with the foregoing definition of legitimate political power, a definition itself derived from the right to life. I challenge him to find anywhere a denial of the right, under certain circumstances, of doing justice to an offender by taking away the offender's life.[7] Moreover, to cite Locke is not "an archaeological dig." Ledewitz has himself cited the Declaration as authority for the Constitution. And Madison and Jefferson, in that same correspondence in 1825 in which they agreed upon the Declaration as the guide to the principles of the Constitution, also agreed upon Locke's *Second Treatise* (together with Sidney's *Discourses on Government*) "for the general principles of liberty and the rights of man, in nature and society." And the doctrines of Locke and Sidney, Madison and Jefferson said, were those approved by the American people.[8] Translated into a more modern idiom, they are the doctrines still approved—and I would say rightly approved—by the American people. Professor Ledewitz's argument that the principles of the Declaration—which we agree condemned slavery—also condemned capital punishment is simply without foundation. Hence his attempt to ground an objection to capital punishment in the "original intent" of the Constitution—seen as an expression of the principles of the Declaration of Independence—is without foundation.

Concerning my objections to Justice Brennan's (or anyone else's) "evolutionary conscience" superseding the words of the Constitution in the interpretation of the Constitution, Professor Ledewitz says that

> Professor Jaffa accuses liberal jurisprudence of dismissing the insights of the Framers in the name of new insights said to be based on science. *The heart of this critique is valid.* The Framers proposed eternal principles based on an unchanging human nature created by God. Liberal and radical left-wing thinkers today reject all such conceptions as epistemologically naive. This is true of main line consensus thinkers like Owen Fiss and Harry Wellington, as it is of the Conference on Critical Legal Studies [emphasis added].

I am glad that Professor Ledewitz and I stand together here. I take it as evidence that he recognizes, as I do, that the worst tyrannies of human history—notably those of Hitler and of Stalin—rested on assertions of scientific validity for their thought, as well as a denial of the moral relevance of "an unchanging human nature." And, as I have shown from Alexander Stephens' "cornerstone" speech, this was also true of the "positive good" defense of slavery in the antebellum South.

Proceeding from this point, however, Professor Ledewitz seems to impute to me the opinion that because there are "eternal principles" there is no such thing as new knowledge! It would be very strange indeed, for someone who holds both Aristotle and Jefferson in the regard that I do, to deny that "the insights of science are as entitled to a hearing as any other claim to truth." But, of course, the assertion that something is "new knowledge" does not make it such. There is always at least ten thousand times as much new quackery as there is new knowledge. Professor Ledewitz writes that "modern science teaches us [that] developmental biology proclaims the fetus to be our young brother or sister in the human family." With great respect, I submit that, while the "proclamation" is true, it does not emanate directly from the evidence supplied by modern science, or from developmental biology. It is true only in the light of an assumption brought to that evidence. That assumption—which is contradicted by the theory of evolution, in any of its contemporary versions—is the permanent moral significance of the distinction of species.

I would be the last one to exclude any evidence from any source that might assist us in legislating wisely on the extraordinarily difficult question of abortion. Professor Ledewitz and I seem to agree very largely upon the main question: that it was a judicial atrocity—unsurpassed since *Dred Scott*—for the Supreme Court in *Roe v. Wade* to set aside the legislative protection of innocent human life provided by the laws of the States. Professor Ledewitz's discussion of the need for prudential morality in dealing with the question of abortion is nothing less than a brief for denying courts jurisdiction over what is clearly a legislative question. But the right of innocent human life to the protection of law—the first of the rights proclaimed in the Declaration—is here the ground of the legislative prudence that he and I call for.

Professor Ledewitz's call for "new learning" extends, he says,

> to new insights into older practices with which the Framers were familiar. A good example is the view of the Framers that private property is the "product of a man's labor." It is no secret that high on the political/legal agenda of the Neo-Lockeians . . . is an attack on the New Deal and the Welfare State in the name of the Framers' commitment to individual property rights . . . But Marxism, as well as the lessons of an interconnected industrial society, should have taught us something about the role of property. Property is never a matter of individual right alone. Property is a social product. This knowledge shapes our understanding of natural rights.

Let us observe, first of all, that Neo-Lockeianism is not the same thing as the Lockeianism of the Founding Fathers. I cannot speak of the Neo-Lockeans mentioned by Professor Ledewitz. However, many of those going under that description place an overriding emphasis upon individual freedom, defined merely as doing what one likes, without regard to objective norms of human behavior. They are in this very far from recognizing the moral claims that were paramount for a Washington, a Jefferson, or a Madison. Jefferson once wrote (to Spencer Roane, in 1819) that "Independence can be trusted nowhere but with the people in mass. They are inherently independent *of all but moral law*" (emphasis added). That qualification was, however, fundamental. For Locke himself, the law of reason—which was the law of nature—was a moral law. In Locke's comprehensive understanding of property, the claims of property and the claims of morality coincide. Adultery, no less than murder, theft, perjury, and covetousness, is an offense against property. Samuel Johnson was very much the Lockeian in replying to Boswell's query, as to why chastity in the female was so much more important than chastity in the male: "Because, sir, all our laws of property depend upon it." The humor in this remark should not detract from its seriousness. Marx's hatred of private property reflected a hatred of morality, as an enemy of human freedom. In this Marx had much in common with the Neo-Lockeians, and in general with present-day libertarianism.

Professor Ledewitz thinks that we should have learned from Marxism and an "interconnected industrial society" that "property is never a matter of individual right alone." Property, he says, is a social product. In fact, the labor theory of value is something Marx simply took over from John Locke. The link between economy and society (and polity) is to be found in the division of labor, a leading argument of Plato's *Republic*, but one Marx certainly learned from Adam Smith, if not from Smith's predecessors. Once civil society is formed—according to Locke, no less than Marx—property is "never a matter of individual right alone." Each individual in joining with others to protect his natural rights surrenders to civil society, acting by the majority, the right to regulate property in whatever way shall best contribute to the common good. What that way is becomes a matter of legislative prudence.

Marx's "contribution" was his alleged discovery that the common good is best served by the total abolition of private property. If Marx had demonstrated—or if experience had shown—that the regulation of private property for the common good was best served by its abolition, then indeed we would have something to learn from him. But Professor Ledewitz should bear in mind that the abolition of private property, in Marx, extends to everything—including the family. If he has any doubts on this point, let him reread the Communist Manifesto. Marx knew—as did Socrates in the *Republic*—that the indefeasible basis of private property, within civil society no less than within the state of nature, was the pleasure and pain felt by individual bodies, and the souls thereof. The generation of children, although a social act, is also the ground of an indefeasible individualism. Property and family are indissolubly linked. Men—and women—care more for their own children than for good children (however much they may wish their own children to be good). The argument for the prudence of having property remain essentially private in civil society, according to Locke (as well as Aristotle in his critique of the *Republic*), is that the property will thereby be better cared for and more industriously increased. For both Locke and Aristotle the argument for private property is the advantage to the common good—not the good of individuals as such. I know of nothing either of theory or of practice to contradict this judgment. To quote Sir Winston Churchill, "The vice of capitalism is the unequal distribution of its blessings. The virtue of socialism is the equal distribution of its misery." Or as John Locke put it:

> There cannot be a clearer demonstration of anything [viz., of the connection between private property and productive labor and the common good] than several nations of the Americans [that is to say, the precolonial natives] are of this, who are rich in land and poor in all the comforts of life, whom nature having furnished as liberally as any other people with the materials of plenty . . . yet for want of improving it by labor, have not one-hundredth part of the conveniences we enjoy. And a king of a large and fruitful territory there, feeds, lodges, and is clad worse than a day-laborer in England [*Second Treatise*, Chapter 5].

Except for the status of communism's "kings" (viz., the upper echelons of the Communist party and the bureaucracy, which sees to it that its highly privileged members are supplied with Western goods and services denied to at least 95 percent of their society), these words could apply today to the comparison between communist and capitalist societies.[9] The Lockeian argument for private property has always rested upon its comparative benefits to the poorest members of society. When James Madison wrote in the famous tenth *Federalist* that "the first object of government" was the "protection of the different and unequal faculties of acquiring property," he was faithfully reflecting the teaching of John Locke. But he was in this arguing for a widespread and diverse ownership of property (in an "extended republic") as an absolutely necessary condition of democratic constitutionalism. It should be hardly necessary to say at this time that collective ownership of property means such a monopoly of economic power as to make democratic government an impossibility. I do not therefore think that there is any wisdom to be gained from Karl Marx concerning the nature of property.

In what I regard as his decisive argument, Professor Ledewitz makes a determined effort to enlist me—as I have all along wished to enlist him—in a crusade for justice, as understood within the framework of the natural rights and natural law doctrines of the American Founding. He writes:

> Perhaps Justice Brennan is not committed [as Professor Ledewitz concedes he ought to be] to original intent. Accordingly, Justice Brennan's search for an evolving consensus may in fact be subject to Professor Jaffa's criticism that it represents arrogant subjectivity. [It is!] But for Professor Jaffa to criticize generally the idea of individual access to truth is an appalling irony. Professor Jaffa believes and is totally committed to the proposition that all men are endowed by their Creator with certain unalienable rights. Now how did this idea come to Professor Jaffa? Certainly, the elites of our time do not believe it. Philosophers reject it. Liberal and conservative jurisprudence reject it. It may be that most Americans still believe in inherent rights, but that traditional belief may be fading under the pressure of positivism and modernity. If the day should come that no one else takes the idea seriously would Professor Jaffa then abandon it? No. *Because it is true.* Why then should a justice of the Supreme Court interpreting fundamental rights be subject to a numbers test [emphasis added]?

Professor Ledewitz may rest assured that that "appalling irony" of which he writes is altogether imaginary. Never have I "criticized . . . the idea of individual access to truth." In a famous passage that I often quote, George Washington in 1783 wrote that

> The foundation of our empire [viz., forms of government] was not laid in the gloomy ages of ignorance and superstition; but at an epoch when the rights of mankind were better understood and more clearly defined, than at any other period.

Washington did not mean to say that "the rights of mankind" were then perfectly understood. He himself was then pressing urgently toward the formation of "a more perfect union." But of course Washington implied that in the "gloomy ages of ignorance and superstition" free government would be impossible. In such times, mankind's only options are among forms of despotism. If then "the day should come" of which Professor Ledewitz speaks, constitutional government would be an impossibility. And that day may indeed not be far distant, if as Professor Ledewitz says, "the elites of our time do not believe in" the doctrine of the rights of man, if "philosophers reject it," and if "liberal and conservative jurisprudence reject it." These new dark ages may be darker than any which have preceded them, and more impervious to the light of reason. "No light but only darkness visible," Milton's Satan said of Hell. It is far more difficult to attack superstitions masquerading as science, than superstitions masquerading as faith.

When Professor Ledewitz, however, asks why a Supreme Court justice, interpreting fundamental rights, should be "subject to a numbers test," what he is really asking is why a Supreme Court justice should be subject to the principles of free government, as those principles are set forth in the Declaration of Independence and embodied in the Constitution. Professor Ledewitz should consider how the Constitution itself represents, not "numbers," but fundamental rights. Because "all men are created equal" the "just powers" of government are derived "from the consent of the governed." And just because every human being counts, every human being has a right to be counted. Having the right to be counted means having the right to be part of the political process, which is primarily and essentially the legislative process. The principle of majority rule—the "numbers test" which Professor Ledewitz unwittingly disparages—arises from the principle of human equality. That those who live under the law make the laws they live under is an essential implication of the doctrine of the Declaration. When judges take it into their hands to act as legislators they are introducing an element of despotism into legislation as surely as if they were kings or dictators.

Majority rule—the use of "numbers" in the political process—arises from the unanimous consent by which civil society is understood to be constituted. In understanding this argument one cannot have too "frequent recurrence to fundamental principles." As the Massachusetts Bill of Rights tells us, "all men are born free and equal." Because of this natural freedom and equality,

> The body politic is formed by a voluntary association of individuals; it is a social compact by which the whole people covenants with each citizen and each citizen with the whole people that all shall be governed by certain laws for the common good.[10]

Majority rule—the *lex majoris partis*—arises from, and is practical surrogate for, the unanimity by which the body politic is first formed. Jefferson in his inaugural address called the right of the majority to rule "sacred" because it is the necessary means for implementing the rights with which all men have been equally endowed by their Creator. But majority rule is governed by a qualitative no less than a quantitative principle.

> All too will bear in mind this sacred principle that though the will of the majority is in all cases to prevail, that will to be rightful must be reasonable; that the minority possess their equal rights which equal law must protect, and to violate would be oppression.[11]

Jefferson did not expect the will of the majority always to be rightful and reasonable. The Jefferson we have quoted had been elected president largely because of his (and Madison's) indictment of the Alien and Sedition Acts as unconstitutional. And the political process, as a means of correcting the unconstitutional enactments of one constitutional majority, was vindicated by a new, and as Jefferson believed, more just constitutional majority. Certainly the Jefferson who had called the slaves "one half the citizens" of his native state ( *Notes on Virginia,* Query XVIII) knew that the Constitution was very far from the equal protection of the rights of minorities. But the recourse of oppressed minorities was either to the political process, or to the right of revolution. In the case of slavery, one might say that neither recourse was genuinely available to the slaves themselves. This, however, is not how Jefferson himself looked at the matter. In the same *Notes on Virginia* he predicted that unless the problem of slavery was dealt with on the basis of the principles of the Declaration, there would be a civil and servile war, in which God would take the side of the slaves.

> Indeed, I tremble for my country when I reflect that God is just; that his justice cannot sleep forever; that considering numbers, nature and natural means only, a revolution of the wheel of fortune, an exchange of situation is among possible events; that it may become probable by supernatural interference. The Almighty has no attribute which can take side with us in such a contest.[12]

The right of revolution, we see, is an ever-present element of political public opinion in a free society founded (and maintained) on the basis of the principles of the Declaration. That "firm reliance upon the protection of divine Providence" with which the Declaration concludes is something to which all mankind—including the American slaves—are equally entitled. Jefferson warned that the very Providence that supported their cause in the Revolution would be against them in any struggle over slavery. "I tremble for my country when I reflect that God is just" was repeated many times by Lincoln in his antislavery speeches in the 1850s. It explains why Lincoln ended his Cooper Institute speech, with

> Let us have faith that right makes might, and in that faith, let us, to the end, dare to do our duty as we understand it.[13]

Jefferson's prediction of a civil war was uncanny. Yet one would also have to say that that prediction, as an element of the policy of Abraham Lincoln, went a long way both to bring about the crisis it predicted, and to lift the cause of Union and emancipation to victory. Lincoln's second inaugural address—perhaps the greatest political speech in the history of mankind—with its interpretation of the Civil War as a divine punishment for the sin of slavery, is also a Jeffersonian interpretation of the right of revolution. From this interpretation we see how consciousness of the right of revolution can become an active element in the political process by which opinions favorable to human freedom are brought to bear upon that very process.

The antislavery cause did finally prevail by reason of the fact that a constitutional majority elected an antislavery president. Professor Ledewitz should reflect that in the crisis brought on by that election, it was the proslavery faction—buoyed and driven by a decision of the Supreme Court—that revolted against the principles of the right of revolution! Professor Ledewitz's idea that the justices of the Supreme Court should look directly to the idea of natural justice in deciding what is constitutional would pervert the very essence of the idea of the right of revolution. The right of revolution resides in the people as a whole. The Constitution itself is an expression of the right of revolution—as Madison makes plain in the forty-third *Federalist*. To suggest that this great exertion of the authority of the people resides in their agents, chosen to carry out certain high but limited functions, is absurd. Above all is it absurd because in the name of equal natural rights it denies the right of self-government in and through the consent of the governed. The words of Locke here are of the highest authority.

> [The] freedom of men under government is to have a standing rule to live by, common to everyone of that society, and made by the legislative power erected in it; a liberty to follow my own will in all things wherein that rule prescribes not; and not to be subject to the inconstant, uncertain, unknown, arbitrary will of another man . . . [*Second Treatise*, Chapter 4].

The "arbitrary will of another man" is not less arbitrary for being the will of a judge. It is no less arbitrary when intrinsically or naturally right, if it is imposed without that process—the legislative process—whereby the consent of the governed enters into the making of the laws that the governed are to live under.

"Our government rests in public opinion," declared Lincoln. "Whoever can change public opinion can change government practically so much." The heart of the governmental process is the process of forming opinion. If the opinion of the public is simply and unequivocally unfavorable to the rights of man under the laws of nature and of nature's God, there is no possibility of free government. But the public's opinion may be committed to the institution of such a government—as ours was at the time of the Founding and as it is today—without being fully aware of what is logically and morally implied in that commitment.

But let us reflect that this commitment, however perfect or imperfect, is always of a twofold character. It is on the one hand a commitment to "these ends," viz., "to secure these rights," the rights with which all men have been equally "endowed by their Creator." On the other hand, however, it is equally a commitment to secure these rights by "the consent of the governed." Logically, equal rights and consent of the governed are reciprocals, one of the other. Practically, they are in tension with each other, and may sometimes be in flat opposition.

In the crisis over slavery, the seceding states characteristically took their stand on "the consent of the governed." They withdrew their consent to remain in a Union in which a constitutional majority held in moral abhorrence an institution—chattel slavery—which they believed to be vital to their safety and welfare. They did not see that the principle of consent, by which they justified the action they were taking, itself had no validity apart from the principle of equality, whose authority they denied!

I am sure that Lincoln's opposition to slavery is well known to Professor Ledewitz. Perhaps less well known is his opposition to abolitionism. But Professor Ledewitz's call for judicial activism directly parallels the abolitionists call—before and during the Civil War—for direct federal action to abolish slavery. Lincoln held, however, that there was no federal jurisdiction, authorized by the Constitution, for federal action against the domestic institutions of any State. That is to say, in ratifying the Constitution, the citizens of the several States did not consent to grant the federal government authority over their domestic institutions. To employ the power of the federal government to alter or abolish any of the domestic institutions of the slave States would have been usurpation of power never consented to; it would be government without the consent of the governed. The abolitionists in their appeal to equality would have disregarded the requirement of consent which followed from it. The proslavery secessionists asserted their right to be governed only with their own consent, and denied the equality which justified that right. The error of the one side was to appeal to equality and ignore consent; that of the other was to appeal to consent, and ignore equality.

In January of 1838 Lincoln gave a speech, "On the Perpetuation of Our

Political Institutions," to the Young Men's Lyceum of Springfield, Illinois. I have written at length about this speech in *Crisis of the House Divided* (Chapter IX, pp. 182—232). Its muted theme is the danger to the future of the republic from the presence of slavery. A less muted theme is the danger arising from those supremely able and ambitious human characters, those who are of "the family of the lion or the tribe of the eagle." Lincoln speaks of the dangers of "an Alexander, a Caesar, or a Napoleon." This triumvirate were the great destroyers of republics. They were men of the greatest political genius, who used that genius to rise to power by espousing the claims of the people. Having used that power to destroy the enemies of the people—and their own enemies—they then established absolute despotisms, surpassing in evil anything they had overcome. Lincoln saw clearly, with a clairvoyance given to few men, that the power that might destroy slavery in the United States, might destroy freedom at the same time. Lincoln's life was dedicated to placing American slavery "in course of ultimate extinction." But it was dedicated to securing freedom for the slaves without destroying the freedom of the free.

Judicial activism may appear to be a "soft" form of authority, compared to that of a Napoleon. (Or, we might add, of a Lenin or a Hitler, who were also essentially Caesarian demagogues.) It is well to remember that the greatest tyrannies in the world today—and some of the worst of all time—are called "people's republics." Napoleon also represented his authority to be that of the rights of man. But he saw these rights as the ground, not of government by the consent of the governed, but of "enlightened despotism." But whether enlightened or not, the rule of a Napoleon—or of unelected judges usurping legislative authority—is still despotism.

James Madison, speaking in the fifty-first *Federalist* of the means of preventing the tyranny of the majority, says that there

> are but two methods of providing against this evil: the one by creating a will in the community independent of the majority—that is, of society itself; the other by comprehending in the society so many separate descriptions of citizens as will render an unjust combination of a majority of the whole very improbable . . .

Of course, tyranny of the majority is to be prevented by the whole system of constitutional government, in which an independent judiciary is a vital element. But one alternative is firmly excluded: that is "a will in the community independent . . . of the society itself." It is precisely such a will that Professor Ledewitz advocates, an uncontrolled will to discover rights to be vindicated, and one that imposes judicial remedies for alleged violations of those rights, without any antecedent constitutional consent by those governed by those remedies.

Professor Ledewitz writes that

> Many of our greatest cases rely on such moral insights by the Court [viz., that there is "conduct . . . condemned by any civilized conscience"]. *Brown v. Board of Education*'s condemnation of segregation laws can be defended, if one is interested in doing so, by stabs at history and by the words "equal protection" in the constitutional text. But Professor Jaffa is on sounder ground in asserting that "segregation laws were utterly inconsistent with the ends of free government and hence of the Constitution." And he is right.

While I am loathe to disclaim a compliment, Professor Ledewitz here utterly mistakes me, the Constitution, and the principles of the Declaration of Independence. *Brown* was a correct decision, but the opinion accompanying it was so contemptuous of principled constitutionalism as to lay the groundwork of future evils as grave as any it was directed against. It is altogether a disservice to the cause of human freedom for Professor Ledewitz to speak patronizingly of making "stabs" at the history or at the "words . . . in the constitutional text" as if such exercises were merely academic or theoretical. It was precisely this unprincipled approach that made such a judicial monstrosity of Chief Justice Warren's opinion in *Brown*. For consider. The heart of Warren's opinion was an affirmative answer to the question:

> Does segregation of children in public schools solely on the basis of race . . . deprive the children of the minority group of equal educational facilities?

In support of his affirmative answer to this question Warren cites a finding by a Kansas court, that

> Segregation of white and colored children in public schools has a detrimental effect upon the colored children . . . for the policy of separating the races *is usually interpreted* as denoting the inferiority of the Negro group. A sense of inferiority affects the motivation of a child to learn . . . [emphasis added].

Warren then concludes that

> Whatever may have been the extent of psychological knowledge at the time of *Plessy v. Ferguson*, this finding is amply supported by modern authority.

Then follows the famous footnote, citing those ethically neutral, "value free" psychologists and sociologists who, according to Warren, constituted "modern authority" for the moral substance of the Constitution.

I wonder if Professor Ledewitz has reflected upon the resemblances between the foregoing opinion of Earl Warren and Alexander Stephens' cornerstone speech, in which Stephens contended that the Confederate Constitution of 1861 was superior to the United States Constitution of 1787, because it was based upon the "modern authority" which declared that slavery was in the best interests of the Negroes as well as of the whites. I wonder whether Professor Ledewitz has reflected how easily a future Court might overrule *Brown* on the same ground that Warren here (ostensibly) overrules *Plessy*—namely, on the ground that still newer and later experiments in psychology testify to the advantages of segregation to both races. Suppose that we are confronted with a situation in which black children are a majority, and white children a minority. Suppose the attorneys for the white children "prove" on the basis of a new round of "doll tests" that integration causes "a sense of inferiority" in the white children. Suppose circumstances arise in which the blacks themselves demand segregation as best fitting their sense of what makes them feel dignified. This last question is not merely hypothetical. It is not long since that the demand for black dormitories and black studies centers wracked the universities. I myself was on the losing side of a faculty vote to resolve a confrontation in which it was alleged that ours had been a white college giving a white education. This, incidentally, was not the accusation of the blacks, but the *nostra culpa* of the white faculty. It was contended by both whites and blacks that "equal opportunity" meant that blacks were entitled to an institutional structure providing black dormitories, and a curriculum featuring black history, black literature, black economics, etc., taught by black instructors. In short, it was demanded that equal rights dictated an education equally segregated, socially and intellectually, as that which guilty whites had so long enjoyed.

The test—in the light of *Brown*—was not what was objectively right or wrong, on the ground of the Constitution, but how black people were made to feel. The authority of science could support any conclusion, since science has turned out to be the method of discovering how people feel—although it can also be the method of discovering how to make people feel what you want them to feel. The Warren Court could have reached the opposite conclusion it did reach in *Brown* merely by ordering as a remedy (instead of desegregation) a psychological conditioning (or "brainwashing") program, designed to overcome feelings of inferiority. I can assure Professor Ledewitz that it was well within the competence of the psychologists upon whom Warren relied to have come up with such a program had they been directed to do so, a program that would—on the premises—have made segregated schools perfectly constitutional. In fact, Warren's opinion for the Court did not, contrary to a common opinion, reverse *Plessy* at all in the most important respect. To have done so, it would have had to adopt the first Justice Harlan's dissenting opinion in that case, in which he held that the Constitution was color-blind. Warren's opinion was based upon the subjective feelings of black people, rather than upon their objective rights as human beings.[14]

How should *Brown* have been decided? A brief "stab at history" and a consideration of what, in the light of history, "equal protection" ought to be understood to mean will carry us a long way. Consider the first sentence of the Fourteenth Amendment.

> All persons born or naturalized in the United States, subject to the jurisdiction thereof, are citizens of the United States and of the State wherein they reside.

The Thirteenth Amendment had overruled whatever in Taney's opinion in *Dred Scott* concerned slavery and property in slaves. But it had not overruled that part of his opinion which declared that a Negro, whether free or slave, could not be a citizen of the United States. In completing the reversal of *Dred Scott*, the Fourteenth Amendment must be understood to reverse as well the reasoning upon which Taney depended when he declared that free Negroes could not be citizens of the United States. At the center of that reasoning was his assertion that—for the purpose of interpreting the Constitution of the United States—the proposition "that all men are created equal" was not to be understood to include members of the Negro race. It was his understanding that Negroes were excluded from the rights enunciated in the Declaration of Independence which authorized Taney, in his own mind, to say that according to the Constitution Negroes were so far inferior that they had no rights which the white man was bound to respect.

In short, the intention of the Fourteenth Amendment was the completion of the reversal of Taney's opinion for the Court in *Dred Scott*. Hence the "equal protection" clause of the Fourteenth Amendment must be read in the light of the unequivocal constitutional inclusion of black men and women into the proposition of universal human equality. This is just another way of saying that the Constitution is color-blind, as Mr. Justice Harlan (but not Chief Justice Earl Warren) truly said. This would have been the just ground for outlawing school segregation.

\*　　　\*　　　\*

Professor Ledewitz wishes my critique of our "exhausted constitutional tradition" to be the occasion to "take the rights of persons seriously," and to be the occasion for the "strengthening of free government as law's obligation." We cannot, he says,

> avoid asking about the rest of the rights of man: about economic rights—to shelter, food, clothing, and education; about social rights—to wear religious clothing and to love a person of the same sex; and about corporate rights—to prevent the police from lying to attorneys and to bar unconstitutional actions by our government.

Let me begin here by saying that there is no difference between us on the general question of whether or not the courts should "bar unconstitutional actions by our government." Even here, however, one must recognize the distinction between those questions bearing on the rights of persons, which are subject to litigation, and those that are not. President Lincoln denied—rightly, I believe—the right of Chief Justice Taney to issue a writ of *habeas corpus*, when Lincoln had suspended the use of that writ. Let us suppose a taxpayer's suit for an injunction against President Roosevelt in 1941 to prevent the transfer of fifty destroyers to the British navy. A court would have to be insane to take such a case, although Roosevelt himself knew (as did Lincoln) that what he was doing might be considered an impeachable offense. These constitutional questions are so clearly political questions that they cannot be resolved in the courts.

When Professor Ledewitz speaks of "economic rights" as being among "the rest of the rights of man" he simply misunderstands the natural rights doctrine. There are no "economic rights" which are "unalienable" in the sense of those mentioned in the Declaration of Independence. A government devoted to securing these rights—viz., such as those mentioned in the Declaration of Independence—is one which will give great security to private property. This security has always proved to be the greatest incentive for the production and hence the availability of "shelter, food, clothing, and education." There just is no way in which the law can declare a right to economic goods, and thereby make these goods available.

> GLENDOWER. I can call spirits from the vasty deep.
> HOTSPUR. Why, so can I, or so can any man;
>    But will they come when you do call for them?
> (*Henry IV*, Part I, Act III, Sc. 1, lines 53 ff.)

A court of law—or the court of Caesar—decreeing that the people shall be supplied with cabbages or doctorates, are like Owen Glendower calling spirits from the vasty deep. What reason is there to think that they will come? The problem that broke the back of the Soviet economy was that, as the typical worker said, "We do imaginary work for imaginary wages."

When Lenin decreed his New Economic Policy in 1921 he unleashed the productive capacities of the Russian peasants. Not only did they enjoy an unprecedented prosperity in the late 1920s, but the USSR enjoyed an abundant food supply. When Stalin decreed the collectivization of agriculture, he guaranteed that for some sixty successive years there would be poor harvests in the Soviet Union! What is the point of guaranteeing food, if there is no food—as was the case in Ukraine in 1931? What is the point of guaranteeing medical care and education, if the one is rotten and the other is nothing but propaganda (except in the case of the sciences needed to maintain the military power of the regime)? The Soviet Union was an outstanding example of what happens when a government treats "economic rights" as if they were "human rights." The end result is no respect for human rights and poverty for the masses. By this I do not mean to say that there ought not to be entitlements to economic welfare. We have many examples of such around us: social security, unemployment insurance, student loan programs, etc. I personally am opposed to anything that might be called socialized medicine, but the question of how to optimize the health care of the American people is certainly a proper political and legislative concern. The point here, however, is that *it is a political and legislative concern. It is not a judicial concern.* Every so-called "economic right" involves a levy upon the resources of society. The exercise of such rights requires taxes. Neither courts of law, nor courts of kings, ought to have the power to levy taxes. That is what the American Revolution was all about!

Professor Ledewitz asks

> Why ... is Professor Jaffa so certain that governments have been given authority to kill their prisoners through capital punishment? While I acknowledge that opinions differ, it is clear to me that killing a citizen in a prison cell is utterly inconsistent with the ends of free government.

Once again, Professor Ledewitz's premises are altogether mistaken. Someone convicted of first degree murder is *not* a citizen. Here is how John Locke—and all of the Founding Fathers, and I myself—understand this question.

For by the fundamental law of nature, man's being is to be preserved as much as possible, when all cannot be preserved, the safety of the innocent is to be preferred; and one may destroy a man who makes war upon him . . . for the same reason that he may kill a wolf or a lion; because they are not under the ties of the common law of reason, have no other rule but that of force and violence, and so may be treated as a beast of prey, those dangerous and noxious creatures that will be sure to destroy him whenever he falls into their power.

I cite only two examples from recent crimes in the Los Angeles area. In neither case was there capital punishment, although I for one believe there should have been. In one case, a man kidnaped, raped, and strangled a two-year-old girl. In another, two men, working together over a two-year period, abducted, raped, and strangled at least seventeen young women. They tape-recorded their victims' death agonies to amuse themselves during the otherwise boring intervals between murders. To call such persons "citizens" is technically inaccurate, as well as being a travesty upon the meaning of words.

Locke makes it clear that what unites us as human beings, in respect for each other's rights, is the possession and the use of reason. That is ultimately why we may lay claim to the right to be governed with our own consent. But those who, not by mere words, but by deadly deeds, refuse to abide by the law of reason, have thereby placed themselves outside the bounds of humanity, and of the rights of humanity. This, I believe, is of the essence of the common sense of the very idea of the rights and the law of nature.

Finally, I come to Professor Ledewitz's strange notion that among the rights to be enunciated and enforced by the judiciary is the right "to love a person of the same sex." I presume he does not mean by this the love of a father for his son, or a son for his father, or of mothers and daughters, or brothers or sisters. Nor do I think he has in mind the love of friends celebrated by Aristotle in the ninth book of the *Nicomachean Ethics.* I presume that he means sexual love, that is, sodomy and lesbianism. If so, I can assure him that these are unnatural acts and, being unnatural, the very negation of anything that could be called a right according to nature. The very root of the meaning of nature is generation. What marks off one species from another is the ability of individuals of opposite sexes to generate new individuals of the same species. Marriage is possible, therefore, only between men and women, members of the species *homo sapiens*. To conceive of marriage apart from the possibility of the generation and regeneration of human society is *contra naturam*. Incest and sodomy both represent vices that strike at the root of the family, and at the human institutions that represent the moral no less than the physical self-preservation of mankind. To deny the relevance of nature as a standard in this most fundamental of all respects, is to deny its relevance in all other respects as well.

Why do we regard the slaughter of beasts for food lawful, but not the slaughter of other human beings? Why do we regard it moral to make of beasts, beasts of burden? Why do we not speak of enslaving horses or mules? What ground do we have to condemn slavery, except that it violates the order of nature, by treating men as if they were beasts? But using men as if they were beasts is no more against the order of nature than using men as if they were women, or women as if they were men. Nor is such use less unnatural for being voluntary. Human beings have been and can be persuaded to accept slavery, whenever they can be persuaded that natural distinctions are no longer to be thought the basis of moral distinctions. Nor is there any difference here between the moral understanding of reason and of revelation. In the first chapter of *Genesis* the Bible tells us that

> God created man in his own image, in the image of God he created him; male and female he created them. (Verse 27)

By this it is implied, I believe, that the creative power of God, no less than the generative power of nature, resides in the distinction between male and female. And if nature is the ground of all our rights, as the Declaration of Independence affirms, then maleness and femaleness is the ground of nature. In 1779 Jefferson drafted "A Bill for Proportioning Crimes and Punishments." Like many other measures that Jefferson advanced in this period, it was designed to promote the cause of general reform and improvement in civil society. In it Jefferson speaks out against the promiscuous use of capital punishment which, he says, "should be the last melancholy resource against those whose existence is become inconsistent with the safety of their fellow citizens." More generally, he observes that

> the experience of all ages and countries hath shown, that cruel and sanguinary laws defeat their own purpose, by engaging the benevolence of mankind to withhold prosecutions, to smother testimony, or to listen to it with bias,

when, if the punishment were only proportioned to the injury, men would feel it their inclination, as well as their duty, to see the laws observed.

In this humane temper, Jefferson's bill proposed nonetheless that

> Whosoever shall be guilty of rape, polygamy, or sodomy with man or woman, shall be punished, if a man, by castration, if a woman by cutting through the cartilage of her nose a hole of one half inch in diameter at the least.[15]

Whatever one may think of the proportionality of the punishments, I see no reason to doubt—more than Jefferson did—the criminality of the offenses, one more than another, under "the laws of nature and of nature's God."

NOTES TO

# Judicial Conscience and Natural Rights: A Reply to Professor Ledewitz

1. *Politics*, 1287 a 32. The Greek says that "nomos" (law) is "nous" (mind or reason) without desire. That "nous" and "nomos" are cognate indicates linguistically an affinity of mind and law that is lost in the translation.
2. *Politics*, 1269 a 5. "In general, all men seek not what their fathers had [*to patrion*] but the good."
3. The Declaration of Independence, in its very first sentence, speaks at once of "the separate and equal station to which the laws of nature and of nature's God entitle them," and that "decent respect to the opinions of mankind" required of them by those same laws. It is the recognition of the existence of "mankind" and of the rights and duties implicit in that recognition, which is the ground of "the laws of nature." Professor Ledewitz appeals to the very same "mankind" while denying the existence of the very same laws of nature. He is no different in this than the man who denies his own existence, which must be affirmed in order to be denied!
4. The Johns Hopkins University Press, 1975.
5. See "On the Necessity of a Scholarship of the Politics of Freedom," Introduction (by the present writer) to *Statesmanship: Essays in Honor of Sir Winston Spencer Churchill*, Carolina Academic Press, 1981.
6. *Nicomachean Ethics* 1103 b 27ff.
7. Professor Ledewitz asserts that "the Eighth Amendment was viewed at the time of its introduction and criticized as an invitation to abolish capital punishment." This, he says in his note 36, "is the gist of the celebrated objection of Representative Livermore of New Hampshire during consideration of the proposed Eighth Amendment. He quotes Livermore: "It is sometimes necessary to hang a man, villains often deserve whipping, and perhaps having their ears cut off; but are we in the future to be prevented from

266

inflicting these punishments because they are cruel?" *Annals of Congress* (J. Gales ed. 1789). We observe that Ledewitz's only witness is one who is anxious *not* "to be prevented" from inflicting "these punishments." Where is the witness who *wants* these punishments to be prevented? As Professor Ledewitz himself notes, there are no such witnesses against capital punishment, among the generation of the Founders, as there are against slavery. He thinks, however, that we should be bound by the principles of the Declaration, rightly understood, even when the Founders did not understand them rightly. His citation does not constitute a shred of evidence that those who adopted the Eighth Amendment believed that it would authorize the *Supreme Court* to abolish capital punishment. Of course Congress—or state legislatures— might do so as an exercise of legislative power. Certainly, changing opinions of the people as to what constitutes "cruel and unusual punishments" might be the occasion for changes in the law. Professor Ledewitz knows, however, that popular support for capital punishment is today probably as strong as at any time in our history. Consider the 1972 constitutional initiative in California sanctioning the death penalty, which was passed by a majority of 67.5 percent of the voters; and consider as well the rejection in 1986 by 66.16 percent of the voters of Chief Justice Rose Bird. (Official statements of the vote by the Secretary of State of California.) Justice Bird's defeat has been almost uniformly attributed to her "nullification" of the death penalty initiative, by voting to reverse every death sentence that came before her on appeal. For Justice Brennan, or Professor Ledewitz, to maintain that the Supreme Court, on its own authority, might abolish capital punishment, in opposition to the express language of the Constitution—in the Fifth and Fourteenth amendments—is simply inadmissible. This would set a precedent that might indeed turn the Constitution into a sheet of blank paper.

8. ". . . the doctrines of Locke . . . and of Sidney . . . may be considered as those generally approved by our fellow citizens of this [viz., Virginia] and of the United States . . ." *The Complete Jefferson*, Padover ed., p. 1112.

9. This sentence was written before the collapse; and disintegration of the USSR.

10. *Commager*, p. 107.

11. From Jefferson's inaugural address, *Commager*, p. 187.

12. Jefferson, Padover ed., p. 677.

13. *CW*, III, 550.

14. On this whole subject see "Sowing the Wind: Judicial Legislation and the Legacy of *Brown v Board of Education*" by Edward J. Erler. *Harvard Journal of Law and Public Policy*, Vol. 8, Spring 1985, pp. 399–426.

15. Jefferson, Padover ed., p. 97.

# "Who Killed Cock Robin?"
## A Retrospective on the Bork Nomination
## and
## A Reply to "Jaffa Divides the House"

### HARRY V. JAFFA

I am indebted to Dr. Robert L. Stone for his eloquent testimonial to my efforts, over more than forty years, to

> address the central question in American constitutional law today, which is the same question over which the Civil War was fought.[1]

At the same time, I find myself puzzled at his charge against me for "dividing the house." The argument to which he takes exception is in principle—I believe—the same as that of Abraham Lincoln in his immortal speech of June 16, 1858.

In an utterance that may be said to have changed the history of the United States (and of the world) Lincoln argued that the grounds upon which one opposed the extension of slavery into the Territories was inseparable from the opposition to slavery itself. And so I maintain that the ground upon which one argues for a constitutional jurisprudence of "original intent" today is inseparable from such a jurisprudence. As I have already pointed out, no one has ever formulated the doctrine of "original intent" jurisprudence with greater perspicacity or eloquence than did Chief Justice Taney in his opinion in *Dred Scott*. Nor was his judgment that property in slaves in the Territories was guaranteed by the "original intent" of the Constitution unreasonable if one took the text and history of

269

the Constitution—apart from its moral grounding in the principles of the Declaration of Independence—as the guide to that intent. Although the words "slave" and "slavery" do not occur in the text of the Constitution of 1787, no one doubted that the protection of property in slaves was the purport of a number of its clauses. No one could tell from the text, however, whether such protection was extended to something regarded as a necessary evil, something regarded as a positive good, or something that was neither good nor evil until enacted into positive law (like driving on the right side of the road).[2]

In the Congress of 1857-1858, the Southern Democrats, led by President Buchanan (himself a Northern man, but of a species known as "Dough-face") had attempted to give slavery a permanent foothold in Kansas, by admitting Kansas as a state under the Lecompton Constitution. Lecompton was, however, defeated in the House of Representatives by a political coalition of Republicans and free-soil Democrats, under the leadership of Douglas. In the spring of 1858 many in the Republican party—in particular its Eastern wing—were now willing to accept Douglas as an authentic free-soil leader. It was against this acceptance of Douglas by Republicans that Lincoln's House Divided speech was primarily addressed. Here is the precedent that—I believe—I rightfully follow today in opposing certain views of my fellow conservative Republicans. These— represented in particular by our chief justice—hold that constitutional "safeguards to individual liberty" have "no intrinsic worth" and are not grounded in any "idea of natural justice" and derive whatever "moral goodness" they are alleged to have "simply because they have been incorporated into a constitution by a people." Surely this comes very close to, if it is not identical with, Douglas's belief that the people may either vote slavery up, or vote it down, and that whether it is to be lawful or not depends exclusively upon their will.

The Lecompton Constitution would have guaranteed security and permanency to any property in slaves already in Kansas in 1858, whether or not other slaves might later be brought in from other slave States. However, Douglas had opposed Lecompton—not because of any concessions it made to slavery—but because it had been adopted in a rump election marred by fraud. Therefore, he maintained, it was not a valid expression of the will of the people of Kansas. Lincoln also opposed Lecompton, not however because of the fraud which had accompanied the voting (although he certainly objected to voting fraud as much as Douglas) but because of the concessions to slavery. Lincoln did not think that the people of the Territory of Kansas should vote at all on the question of whether to admit slavery among their domestic institutions. Keeping slavery out of the Territories should, he thought, be a matter of national policy, and enacted as such by Congress. The wrongfulness of slavery, he held, was grounded in "an abstract truth, applicable to all men and all times." Like Judge Douglas and his followers, the very idea of such a truth, instructing us as to what is right and what is wrong, is rejected today by Mr. Justice Rehnquist, when he writes that there is "no conceivable way that I can demonstrate to you that the judgments of my [e.g., antislavery or anti-Nazi] conscience are superior to the judgments of your [proslavery or pro-Nazi] conscience." According to Lincoln—and what is indeed the truth of the matter—free political institutions presuppose an agreement on certain principles in regard to right and wrong. These principles are set forth in the second paragraph of the Declaration of Independence, wherein it is said, "We hold these truths to be self-evident. . . ." Voting does not legitimize these principles; the principles are what legitimize the voting. As Lincoln said in the course of the joint debates,

> [Judge Douglas] contends that whatever community wants slaves has a right to have them. So they have, if it is not a wrong. But if it is a wrong, he cannot say that people have a right to do wrong. (CW, III, p. 315.)

Those of Dr. Stone's mind—in 1858—did not want Lincoln to oppose Douglas for reelection to the Senate in that year. They considered that he was "dividing the house" of the free-soil coalition. They thought Douglas had proved his practical effectiveness as an antislavery leader in the fight against Lecompton. Like Dr. Stone, they deprecated theoretical objections to what appeared to them to be Douglas's practical effectiveness. Horace Greeley—among others—did not see what difference it made whether slavery was defeated under the aegis of popular sovereignty, by a vote of the people of Kansas, or excluded (as Lincoln wished) by Congress.

Lincoln continued to insist upon the reenactment of the Missouri Compromise restriction upon slavery, which had provided (in 1820) that in all the remaining Louisiana territory north of 36 degrees 30 minutes (the southern border of Missouri)—not already incorporated into a state—slavery should forever be prohibited. This restriction had been repealed by the Kansas-Nebraska Act of 1854, of which Senator Douglas was the author and chief sponsor. Douglas replaced the congressional prohibition of slavery in the 1820 law by a policy of "nonintervention by Congress with slavery in the states and Territories." Henceforth, according to the language Douglas incorporated in the Kansas-Nebraska Act, the people of each Territory (like the people of each State) would be "perfectly free to form and regulate their domestic institutions in their own way . . ." This meant that the people of a Territory would decide by their votes whether to include slavery among their domestic institutions. The spirit of the Kansas-Nebraska Act is sufficiently indicated by the following passage from Douglas's speech in the Alton joint debate with Lincoln.

> We in Illinois . . . tried slavery, kept it up for twelve years, *and finding that it was not profitable we abolished it for that reason* . . .

For Lincoln, the Kansas-Nebraska Act had from the outset represented an

> open war with the very fundamental principles of civil liberty—criticising the Declaration of Independence, and insisting that there is no right principle of action but *self-interest*.[3]

For Lincoln, to fix the principle of the wrongfulness of slavery as the basis of all policy dealing with it was as important as the Missouri Compromise or any other particular limitation upon the spread of slavery. For Lincoln—as for Madison and Jefferson—the wrongfulness of slavery and the rightness of constitutional government were but two sides of the same coin. The requirement that "the just powers of government" be derived from "the consent of the governed" is grounded upon the prior recognition "that all men are created equal." It is *human beings* whose consent is required, not horses or dogs or oxen or asses. This is not—as Mr. Justice Rehnquist supposes—a "political value judgment." "Value judgments" *qua* "value judgments" are subjective. But the difference between man and beast is not subjective but objective. Hence the moral judgments consequent upon the recognition of this difference are not subjective but objective. Because men are not beasts, they may not be ruled as men may rule beasts. Nor may they have toil imposed upon them, according to the uncontrolled discretion of another, as such toil is imposed upon a horse or an ox or a mule. Nor is it a "value judgment" to refuse to equate the stockyards where cattle are slaughtered with the extermination pens of Buchenwald and Auschwitz.

"Thou shalt not kill" has never been understood to refer to beef cattle or to hogs or to sheep. "Thou shalt not steal" has never referred to the goods produced by the labor of horses or of oxen. It is because it is an objective and self-evident truth, and not a "value judgment," that no man is by nature a beast, that none may arbitrarily be excluded from the class of those whose consent is necessary for the powers of government to be just. It is because it is an objective and self-evident truth—and not a "value judgment"—that the nature of a man is different from the nature of a beast, that every human being has, in Lincoln's words, "a natural right to put into his mouth the bread that his own hand has earned." And it is this antecedent natural right to the product of one's labor that is the foundation of the constitutional right, that declares that the product of that labor may only be taxed with our consent.

If it is true as a general rule that no human beings are to be regarded as so far inferior as to deserve to be treated as beasts, so also is it true—by that same rule—that no human beings are to be regarded as so far superior as to be deferred to as gods. Hence the just powers of government are not only derived from the consent of the governed, but are defined and circumscribed by that same consent. Each one of those who lives under the law has the same right to participate in the political process whereby the laws he lives under are made. And each and every one of those who makes the laws has an identical obligation with everyone else to live under the laws he has had a share in making. It is not simply the will of the people that is to be paramount under the Constitution, but the rational and moral will, formed in accordance with "the laws of nature and of nature's God." This is the argument of the Declaration of Independence, the argument of the American Revolution and of the American Founding: of an essential, original, intrinsic, natural right, a right moral and rational no less than constitutional, that informs the jurisprudence of a free people. As such it embodies, *a fortiori*, the "original intent" of the jurisprudence of the Framers and Ratifiers of the American Constitution.

For Dr. Stone to say that I am "dividing the house" by insisting upon this ground for a jurisprudence of original intent, is to stultify the very idea of such a jurisprudence. Mr. Justice Rehnquist's jurisprudence—which is accepted either implicitly or explicitly by the others whose doctrines Dr. Stone finds "wholesome and necessary for the public good"—is that of legal positivism built upon moral relativism. But without the authentic and genuine morality of the true doctrine of "original intent," there is no principled ground upon which to resist liberal judicial activism, and there can be no house to divide.

Since Dr. Stone's defense of Judge Bork, Judge Bork has been nominated for the Supreme Court by President Reagan, and that nomination has been rejected by the United States Senate. The lengthy and bitter struggle over the Bork nomination involved the Supreme Court in the political process more profoundly than any event since President Roosevelt's "court-packing" plan of 1937.

What I believe to be the truth—although not the whole truth—about that struggle was well expressed by Suzanne Garment in "The War Against Robert H. Bork" in the January 1988 issue of *Commentary*. I regarded Judge Bork's enemies to be the enemies of my understanding of the Constitution no less than of his. While Judge Bork defended the conception of "original intent" in interpreting the Constitution, his opponents believed the Constitution—or at least all those clauses of the Constitution open in any way to interpretation—had virtually no fixed meaning. Anything they regarded as wrong was a wrong to be righted by the judicial process no less than by the legislative process. The question of whether to use the courts or the legislatures to gain a particular end was only a question of expediency, a question of which offered the greater chance of success. The Constitution was deemed to be a vehicle for justice, and whatever was said to be justly claimed was said to be claimed lawfully and constitutionally. That courts are not legislative bodies, and that they neither may (nor ought to) levy taxes, that they have no constitutional authority to transfer wealth (except in the case of lawfully imposed fines) did not seem to restrain the demand for judicial activism on the part of Judge Bork's enemies. The liberal judicial activist's "justice agenda" redefined what had hitherto been understood to be the rule of law. A dramatic example of how this agenda operates has been furnished by the order of a federal court to the city of Yonkers, New York, requiring it to build low cost housing as a remedy for what the court found to be a pattern of discrimination. The city would have had to impose very substantial taxes upon itself to carry out the order, taxes vehemently opposed by a large majority of its citizens. The court thereupon imposed fines both on the city and it officials, fines that would in a relatively short time bankrupt both. City officials were also subject to imprisonment for contempt of court. The order illustrates dramatically that usurpation of legislative authority—including the taxing power—by the judiciary that Judge Bork and I both oppose. It also illustrates why I think it important to have justices on the Supreme Court who—like Judge Bork—would vote to overrule such judicial tyranny. A constitutional jurisprudence of "original intent" has been viewed as a reactionary obstacle to justice by those anxious to carry out "reform" (Yonkers style) through the judiciary. In opposition to the dead hand of "original intent," they call for a "living Constitution."

I publicly supported Judge Bork's nomination,[4] and even contributed money to his cause. As a matter of practical politics, I no more "divided the house" by opposing Judge Bork than Lincoln "divided the house" by opposing the cooperation of Republicans and Douglas Democrats in the struggle to defeat Lecompton.[5] Yet Bork's nomination failed precisely because his conception of "original intent" was flawed. He was never able to command the moral high ground that belonged to the genuine doctrine as held by Jefferson and Madison. For his enemies looked upon "original intent" in the light, not of Lincoln's, but of Taney's espousal of it. They saw "original intent" as having once sanctioned slavery, and even later as having sanctioned racial discrimination of the most odious kind. Judge Bork did nothing to contradict this opinion. In fact, in the course of the hearings Senator Metzenbaum read to Judge Bork the identical passages on "original intent" I had cited from Taney's opinion in *Dred Scott*.[6] Judge Bork's response was only to say that "the Devil can quote Scripture," thereby conceding the accuracy of Taney's characterization of "original intent." He then went on to repeat what Mr. Justice Rehnquist (and Attorney General Meese) had said about *Dred Scott*: that the Court's great error was to usurp the power of Congress by declaring unconstitutional the limitation upon the extension of slavery in the Missouri Law of 1820. I have pointed out, however, that a hopelessly divided Congress, in the Compromise of 1850, had itself remanded the question of the constitutional status of slavery in the Utah and New Mexico Territories to the Supreme Court. As I noted, it had "laid the baby [of the Territorial question] on the doorstep of the Supreme Court, rang the bell, and then disappeared." And three years before *Dred Scott*, in the Kansas-Nebraska Act of 1854, Congress had repealed the Missouri law's restriction upon the extension of slavery. This was at least open to the interpretation— espoused, among others, by Senator Stephen A. Douglas—that Congress itself had come to regard the Missouri law's restriction as a wrongful policy. It certainly did not preclude the view that the Supreme Court, in *Dred Scott*, was merely following Congress and not usurping its powers. The attempt by Bork no less than Rehnquist (or Meese) to treat *Dred Scott* as primarily a matter of judicial usurpation, shows as profound an ignorance of constitutional history as Taney himself displayed in his opinion for the Court in that case.

During the Bork hearings, I had occasion in a public discussion to confront someone who had been a prominent member of the Meese Justice Department, and who was a zealous advocate of Bork's views on "original intent" and the limits of judicial power. In a discussion of *Dred Scott* he too insisted that the abiding sin of the Court in that case was declaring unconstitutional an act of Congress. I put the following hypothetical question to him. Let us contemplate, I suggested, the *Dred Scott* case in reverse. Let us suppose that John C. Breckenridge (not Abraham Lincoln) had been elected president in 1860, and that he had been elected on the platform of the Southern Democratic party, calling for a federal slave code for all the Territories. Let us suppose that Congress, acting upon this platform, passed just such a law. Now let us suppose that Abraham Lincoln—not Roger B. Taney—was Chief Justice, and that a majority on the Court held Lincoln's (not Taney's) opinion concerning the constitutionality of slavery in the Territories. Let us further suppose that Dred Scott sued for his freedom, on the ground that the law Congress had passed enforcing slavery in the Territories was unconstitutional. How did he think that Lincoln—now Chief Justice, writing for the majority—would decide the case? Our Bork disciple had no doubt that Lincoln, no less than Taney, would have upheld the constitutionality of an act of Congress guaranteeing slavery in the Territories. He did not think that Lincoln—or any sound constitutionalist—would interfere with the legislative discretion of Congress "to dispose of and make all needful rules and regulations respecting the Territory . . . belonging to the United States" (Article IV, Section 3). He saw no reason why Dred Scott, in these circumstances (appealing from a Territorial Court to the Supreme Court), should not have remained a slave.

But this is preposterous. Lincoln as a Supreme Court justice would have said that Congress had no lawful power under the Fifth Amendment to deprive any person—whether white or black—of his liberty who had not been lawfully convicted of a crime. Taney had used the Fifth Amendment to say that Congress had no lawful power to deprive any owner of his slave property in a Territory. To reach this conclusion, however, he had first to decide that a Negro was not a person within the meaning of the Fifth Amendment. This he did when he said that Negroes (whether free or slave) were "beings of an inferior order . . . and so far inferior that they had no rights which the white man was bound to respect. . ." Because Lincoln held that the Negro was a human being, and that all human beings—according to the Declaration of Independence—had the same natural rights, he held that a Negro was a person within the meaning of the Fifth Amendment. Lincoln would have had no hesitation in pronouncing unconstitutional any law passed by Congress which was based upon the premise that the Negro was essentially a chattel, and not a human person. But our Borkian could not see that. Such blindness certainly had much to do with Bork's defeat.

It cannot be repeated too often that the central question in *Dred Scott* was whether the Negro was primarily and essentially—that is to say, under "the laws of nature and of nature's God"—a human person, and therefore entitled to that personal liberty guaranteed to all persons in the Fifth Amendment. The Borkians today are as unable as Taney in 1857 to say that *anyone* white or black has natural rights. Hence they are unable to see any foundation for civil rights outside of positive law. That they may themselves be in favor of civil rights, without discrimination on the basis of race, is simply a matter of personal preference (or as the chief justice would say, "a political value judgment") which as such has no constitutional standing. Judge Bork's inability to see the centrality of man's humanity—of his natural rights—as the *constitutional* issue in *Dred Scott* is the reason he was unable to endow his version of "original intent" with any moral authority. For Robert Stone to say that Bork's jurisprudence is "wholesome and necessary for the public good" in the light of such a defect is simply inconsistent with any respect whatever for the constitutionalism of Jefferson, Madison, or Lincoln.

Because of this resemblance of Bork's version of "original intent" to Taney's, Bork's critics could insist with some plausibility that the authority of the Constitution had to be derived not from the reactionary past, but from the liberal future. The principles of the Constitution, they held, were to be found in an "evolving" sense of justice. Just as Darwinian evolution displayed higher biological forms of life emerging out of lower forms, so also with the conceptions of morality and of justice that distinguish, and that ought to distinguish, those of 1987 from those of 1787. A judge, in their view, should not be bound by "original intent," because such intent is irrelevant to and inconsistent with what we the American people—the source of all constitutional authority—expect and ought to expect from our Constitution today. In arguing against "original intent," Bork's opponents also maintained that—whether desirable or not—it was a useless concept, because no one could ever know what that intent was, or how it could be applied to problems the Framers and Ratifiers could never have even imagined. The following is characteristic of the language they used.

> The text of the Constitution, as anyone experienced in words might expect, is least precise where it is most important . . . History can be of considerable help, but it tells us much too little about the specific intentions of the men who framed, adopted, and ratified the great clauses. The record is incomplete, the men involved often had vague or even conflicting intentions, and no one foresaw, or could have foreseen, the disputes that changing social conditions and outlooks would bring before the Court . . . One begins to understand

why so many judges, lawyers, and legal scholars have despaired of the very possibility of neutral principles of constitutional law and have succumbed to the temptations of the interest-voting philosophy. What else is there?[7]

The author of the foregoing, however, was not Justice Brennan in 1987 but Judge Bork in 1968. We mention, only in passing, that "interest voting" and an "evolving" standard of justice are in today's political vocabulary only two names for the same thing. One simply identifies one's own interests—or one's own passionately held opinions—with the higher standard. How this happens is shown by the ease with which so many in the civil rights movement have passed over into the black power movement—that is to say, from a movement against racial discrimination (based upon the "neutral principle" of equal rights for all human persons) into a movement for racial discrimination (preferential treatment for "discrete and insular minorities"). This they have done without any apparent consciousness of, much less admission of, any change of principles.

In 1968, however, Judge Bork saw "two alternative philosophies" to that of judicial "interest voting." One led to "a relatively restrained Court, the other to a relatively activist Court." The restrained Court would simply leave to others—for the most part, to the political branches through the political process—the definition of the Constitution. A restrained Court should not be merely passive, but should do much to "improve the quality and performance of the American political process," (e.g., as by ordering redistricting, when the electoral process cannot reform itself) without itself attempting to achieve substantive ends of government. In 1968, however, this basically nonactivist approach to the work of the Supreme Court was very far from commending itself to Bork unequivocally.

A desire for some legitimate form of judicial activism is inherent in a tradition that runs strong and deep in our culture, a tradition that can be called "Madisonian." We continue to believe there are some things no majority should be allowed to do to us, no matter how democratically it may decide to do them. A Madisonian system assumes that in wide areas of life a legislative majority is entitled to rule for no better reason than that it is a majority. But it also assumes there are some aspects of life a majority should not control, that coercion in such matters is tyranny, a violation of the individual's natural rights. Clearly, the definition of natural rights cannot be left to either the majority or the minority. In the popular understanding upon which the power of the Supreme Court rests, it is precisely the function of the Court to resolve this dilemma by giving content to the concept of natural rights in case by case interpretations of the Constitution.[8]

As I propose to show, there is much that is flawed in this understanding of a jurisprudence of natural rights. Let us, however, say that had Bork propounded it during the hearings on his nomination, he would almost certainly have been confirmed. Much of the controversy during the hearings surrounded his objections to the discovery by the Supreme Court of a "right to privacy" in the *Griswold* case. Senators on the Judiciary Committee could not understand his objection to a decision holding unconstitutional a Connecticut statute forbidding the prescription by a physician of contraceptives to a married couple. It was in this case that Mr. Justice Douglas, speaking for the Court, discovered a "right of privacy" among the "penumbras formed by emanations" from the First, Third, Fourth, Fifth, and Ninth Amendments. Douglas conceded that no such right was explicit in the Constitution, but he felt "the notions of privacy surrounding the marriage relationship" were so "sacred" as to deserve constitutional protection. At his hearings—in 1987—Judge Bork conceded that the Connecticut law was preposterous, ridiculous, absurd, "loony," etc., but he would not concede that these were reasons for regarding it unconstitutional. Besides, he asked, might not a right of privacy extend constitutional protection to otherwise illegal acts, as drug use, wife abuse, child abuse, etc.? In 1968, however, Bork took a very different view of the *Griswold* case. In accordance with his then belief in the plausibility of a "legitimate form of judicial activism," he found "a warrant for the Court to move beyond the limited range of substantive rights that can be derived from traditional sources of constitutional law." Such a warrant he found "persuasively argued" in Mr. Justice Goldberg's concurring opinion in *Griswold*, an opinion based upon the Ninth Amendment (whose author, Bork remarks, was James Madison). This amendment says that

> The enumeration, in the Constitution, of certain rights, shall not be construed to deny or disparage others retained by the people.

Goldberg had written that

> . . . the Ninth Amendment shows a belief of the Constitution's authors that fundamental rights exist that are not expressly enumerated in the first eight amendments . . . and an intent that the list of rights included there not be deemed exhaustive.

In 1968, Bork patronized this version of what was in effect "original intent" jurisprudence (although he did not then use the expression) and was willing to concede that there was a natural and constitutional "right of privacy in marriage." He then assumed—correctly—that it was an innocent right, and not one that might give protection to vicious or immoral acts because done in private. Like Goldberg, he did not see it as an "emanation" from any of the first eight amendments, but as one of the unenumerated rights protected by the Ninth Amendment. Yet he did not see that the doctrine of unenumerated rights itself flowed from the social contract theory of the American Revolution. He did not understand that civil society was understood by the Framers and Ratifiers of the Constitution as being the result of contract, and that only those rights were surrendered to civil society that were necessary for the carrying out of the purpose of that contract. All other rights were reserved. This is the very basis of the idea of limited government and the rule of law, which underlies the entire constitution. As the Massachusetts Bill of Rights of 1780 puts it:

> The body politic is formed by a voluntary association of individuals; it is a social compact by which the whole people covenants with each citizen and each citizen with the whole people that all shall be governed by certain laws for the common good.[9]

The premise upon which the right of contract (or compact) rests is that

> All men are born free and equal . . .[10]

It is this freedom and equality which vests in every human being the natural right to make contracts—including the basic contract creating civil society. But the resulting power of government extends only so far as the original contract authorizes. It is this understanding of the ground of constitutionalism that is embodied in the Ninth Amendment. All this escaped Judge Bork in 1968, and he has not caught up with it yet. In 1968, however, he did see that the protection of marital privacy conformed with the "popular understanding" of what was the Court's function. In the hearings on his nomination, however, he no longer seemed to regard this as a constitutional consideration. This was a fatal flaw in the eyes of senators who thought—as Bork once had done—that the popular understanding deserved high consideration.

What in 1968 Judge Bork called the "Madisonian" alternative was in fact no more—nor less—characteristic of Madison than of his contemporaries. Madison himself would never have dreamed of calling the "concept of natural rights" Madisonian. Nor would these natural rights, as the ground of the Constitution, have been regarded by Madison (or any of his contemporaries) as an optional alternative, any more than they would have regarded human nature as an option for human beings. Being natural, these rights constituted the only possible ground of a genuine jurisprudence of "original intent."

We have cited the correspondence between Madison and Jefferson[11] in which they concurred in commending to the law faculty of the University of Virginia that the first of the "best guides" to the principles of the governments, of both Virginia and of the United States, was "the Declaration of Independence as the fundamental act of union of these states." Neither Madison nor Jefferson thought, however that these principles implied any *a priori* knowledge (as with Kant's categorical imperative) of what particular judgments these principles entailed. The morality of natural rights, as the Declaration of Independence itself makes clear, is a morality of prudence. The principles are the necessary, but not the sufficient ground of wise judgment. The whole Constitution is a bundle of compromises, representing what was believed to be the greatest good, and the least evil, attainable in the actual circumstances of the United States in 1787. These principles, while telling us that slavery was an evil, also tell us that (as Lincoln would say) the concessions to slavery in the Constitution were intended to be (however paradoxical it may seem) in the service of human freedom. Without the concessions—without the prudence that dictated the concessions—there would have been no stronger (more perfect) Union. Without these prudent concessions, there would have been no union strong enough to accomplish what this union in fact did accomplish, within fourscore and seven years, in placing slavery "in course of ultimate extinction."

Nothing in human affairs, held Jefferson, "is unchangeable *but the inherent and unalienable rights of man*."[12] It is irrelevant that we do not know how the Framers and ratifiers of the Constitution and its amendments would have applied each or any of its provisions in our circumstances, in circumstances that they could not have foreseen. "Original intent" means they intended us to understand their handiwork in the light of its enduring principles, not in the light of either their or our own transient circumstances. When Bork writes, as he did in 1968, of a jurisprudence "of natural rights" arrived at "in a case by case interpretation of the Constitution" he is, without apparently knowing it, referring to a jurisprudence of "original intent." However, Bork in 1968 qualified his call for such a jurisprudence, as follows.

This requires the Court to have, and to demonstrate the validity of, a theory of natural rights. A Court without such a theory should candidly admit its lack, eschew policy questions, and practice restraint. Otherwise it will inevitably deny the majority some of its legitimate power to rule, thus abetting a tyranny of minorities.

But why should the Court "demonstrate the validity" of "a theory" which already constitutes the "original intent" of the Framers and Ratifiers? If it is true, as Madison and Jefferson believed it to be, that the Declaration of Independence is "the fundamental act of union of these states," then its principles are *a fortiori* those of the Constitution. Nor can we see why Bork would think that any court of law should be considered either legally or philosophically competent to make such a demonstration. This goes beyond even Justice Brennan's "evolutionary" conscience. There never has been any need for the Court to engage in a philosophical justification assumed by the Constitution itself. That assumption is the "original intent" of "original intent"! John Marshall, in his dissenting opinion in *Ogden v. Saunders* (1827), in considering the "obligation of contracts" clause of the Constitution, wrote as follows.[13]

When we advert to the course of reading generally pursued by American statesmen in early life, we must suppose that the Framers of our Constitution were intimately acquainted with the writings of those wise and learned men, whose treatises on the laws of nature and nations have guided public opinion on the subjects of obligations and contracts. If we turn to those treatises, we find them to concur in the declaration that contracts possess an original intrinsic obligation, derived from the acts of free agents, and not given by government. We must suppose that the Framers of our Constitution took the same view and the language they have used confirms this opinion.[14]

Madison and Jefferson in 1825, in the requirements for the law faculty of the University of Virginia referred to above, had also declared that

. . . as to the general principles of liberty and the rights of man, in nature and society, the doctrines of Locke, in his "Essay concerning the true original extent and end of civil government," and of Sidney in his "Discourses on government," may be considered as those generally approved by our fellow citizens of this, and of the United States . . .

Marshall does not name the "wise and learned men." We may be certain, however, that on the subject of "an original, intrinsic obligation derived from the acts of free agents and not given by government"—that is to say, of natural rights as the ground of constitutional rights—he and Jefferson (however great their other differences) had in mind the doctrines propounded in Locke and Sidney, whether or not they had been disseminated—as they were—by other authors as well. It deserves especial attention, moreover, that Marshall supposed that these doctrines had "guided public opinion" while Madison and Jefferson understood that the same doctrines were those "generally approved" by their fellow-citizens. Hence what we may with propriety call Lockeian natural rights and Lockeian contractualism were deemed to be elements equally of the framing and of the ratification processes.

Some two decades later, however, Bork had apparently abandoned any thought that the Supreme Court—or anyone else—could "demonstrate the validity of a theory of natural rights." In his celebrated 1984 lecture "Tradition and Morality in Constitutional Law"[15] he wrote that

> constitutional law has very little theory of its own and hence is almost pathologically lacking in immune defenses.

But this reflects Judge Bork's own abandonment of the "original intent" of the "Madisonian system" based upon a "theory of natural rights." The pathology lies in his own jurisprudence, not in the Constitution. In the same lecture he also declared that

> judges have no mandate to govern in the name of contractarian or utilitarian or what have you philosophy rather than according to the historical Constitution.

But the "Madisonian system" *does* embrace a "contractarian" philosophy. One wonders whether Bork has ever read an opinion of John Marshall, not to mention any of the relevant writings of Madison.

Absent the demonstration of the theory of natural rights, Bork has turned—as in effect the only alternative to "the interest voting philosophy"—to recommending that the Court "eschew policy questions, and practice restraint." By an amazing mutation of terminology,

Bork has come to call "original intent" the very doctrine that he had proposed in 1968 as a substitute to the system he had called "Madisonian"!

In fact, however, Bork never understood what was meant by a "Madisonian system." In 1968, he commended it—not because it was true but because it reflected "a tradition which runs strong and deep in our culture." But the tradition of equal natural rights does not run more strongly in our culture than very different traditions run in other cultures: e.g., the tradition of stratified classes, with untouchables at the bottom, or the tradition of suttee, in Hindu culture. There is hardly any absurdity—e.g., of polygamy, slavery, human sacrifice, self-mutilation, public prostitution—which is not "sacred" ("strong and deep") in the tradition of some culture. Bork does not seem to recognize any objective basis for evaluating cultures and their different traditions. It was, however, of the essence of the American form of government, as understood by its Founders, that it began a new order of the ages (*novus ordo seclorum*), rejecting thereby all traditions inconsistent with what it regarded as reason and nature. One cannot repeat too often Washington's pronouncement that the foundations of our governments were

> not laid in the gloomy ages of ignorance and superstition; but at an epoch when the rights of mankind were better understood and more clearly defined than at any other period.

For the Founding Fathers, the natural rights of mankind were inherently different from the principles of any tradition—however powerful—that reflected "ignorance and superstition." In fact, however, the natural rights tradition of the Founding was largely abandoned in the South in the generation before the Civil War. The South Carolina doctrines, formulated during the struggle over Nullification (1828-1833), came to dominate the antebellum South. The states which would form the Confederacy came almost completely under the influence of the political thought of John C. Calhoun. And in Calhoun's thought the reasoning which connected political sovereignty—including state sovereignty—with the natural rights— the *equal* natural rights—of individual human persons was entirely abandoned. In Calhoun's thought, the rights of the "Madisonian system," which were the rights of individuals, became the rights of groups. But the rights of groups—in Calhoun's thought—are indistinguishable from the interests of those same groups. This is most clear in the fact that the collective right of slaveholders to preserve and protect slavery is in no way gainsaid by any individual rights to freedom of the slaves.[16] The interest of the slaveholders in slavery constituted their moral right to slavery. Although Calhoun himself would not have used the term, any claim of right in behalf of the slaves would have been what Justice Rehnquist calls "a political value judgment." The effective veto demanded by Calhoun for the slaveholding interest upon any action of the federal government that might tend to put slavery "in course of ultimate extinction" was, according to Calhoun, equally a moral and a constitutional right. Bork's jurisprudence in 1968, although on the surface Madisonian, in fact is Calhounian—and this notwithstanding the loathing of the historical Madison for the historical Calhoun.[17]

We have observed Bork declare that in certain areas a majority has a right to rule "for no better reason than that it is a majority." Without knowing it, Bork has again delivered himself of an opinion that is the very negation of Madisonianism. By it Bork shows that he is unaware of the logic of the relationship connecting majority rule with minority rights. For that logic we turn to Madison himself, writing in the light of that same wisdom and learning that John Marshall had praised. The following is an essay on "Sovereignty," written near the end of Madison's life.

> To go to the bottom of the subject let us consult the Theory which contemplates a certain number of individuals as meeting and agreeing to form one political society, in order that the rights the safety & the interest of each may be under the safeguard of the whole.
>
> The first supposition is, that each individual being previously independent of the others, the compact which is to make them one society must result from the free consent of *every* individual. But as the objects in view could not be attained, if every measure conducive to them required the consent of every member of society, the theory further supposes, either that it was part of the original compact that the will of the majority was to be deemed the will of the whole, or that it was a law of nature, resulting from the nature of political society itself, the offspring of the natural wants of man.
>
> Whatever be the hypothesis of the origin of the *lex majoris partis*, it is evident that it operates as a plenary substitute of the will of the majority of the society for the will of the whole society; and that the sovereignty of the society as vested in & exercisable by the majority, may do anything that could be *rightfully* done by the unanimous concurrence of the members; the reserved rights of individuals (of conscience for example) in becoming parties to the original compact being beyond the legitimate reach of sovereignty, wherever vested or however viewed.[18]

We see again that the right—and limits of the right—of the majority to rule must be understood first and foremost in the light of that "original compact" by which political society is formed. The ground of that compact (or contract) is the equal natural right of every individual to become a member of the body politic by his own consent. This is but another expression of the thought embodied in the great proposition "that all men are created equal." Political authority in society thus formed then devolves upon the "majority." And the majority is the "plenary substitute" for the will of the whole society. It is, however, such a "plenary substitute" *only* for those purposes to which unanimous consent has already been given. The unanimous consent that gives rise to government would be self-defeating if it could act only by unanimous consent. The majority is that substitute for unanimity that makes effective government possible and that does not derogate from the equality of the original contracting or consenting parties. But the very fact that the authority of the majority derives from those purposes—and only those purposes—to which all have unanimously consented, both specifies the purposes and limits the authority of the majority. The majority *never* rules—as Bork mistakenly supposes—merely because it is a majority. It is also the case that in instituting government by unanimous consent "to secure these rights" civil society authorizes the majority—which is primarily and essentially the legislative power—to specify the means by which the rights are to be secured. In short, the "Madisonian system" of natural rights is a system for authorizing legislation, and only derivatively does it provide a role for the judiciary. The will of the people, in the exercise of their natural rights, is to be sovereign; but the judiciary, as the seventy-eight *Federalist* declares, is itself supposed to exercise, not will but judgment. In short, the theory of natural rights, while providing a strong argument for the protection by the courts of the reserved rights of individuals, nonetheless provides a much stronger (because principled) argument *against* proto-legislative judicial activism than that of any of the latter-day "originalists."

Madison says that the majority acts as the substitute for the whole society. But he goes beyond this when he declares that the majority "may do anything that could be *rightfully* done by . . . unanimous concurrence. . ." We see that the reserved rights of individuals control the scope of the authority of the majority—and direct the majority to those objects which represent a common interest of all the citizens. That is why every elected official is deemed to represent those who voted against him no less than those who voted for him. However, not even unanimous consent may authorize the exercise of powers over subjects which are understood by the original contract to remain among the reserved rights of individuals. As an example, Madison mentions the right of conscience. We might here recall that the community of Jonestown committed suicide by unanimous consent—although we may question whether the children who died ought to be supposed to have consented. We certainly ought not to suppose that parents can represent the interests of their children when they themselves have been under delusions that render them irrational. But the right to act upon unanimous consent, no less than the right of the majority, is confined to ends which are rational and moral. Madison himself placed the emphasis upon *rightfully*. To understand the full and inner meaning of a jurisprudence of "original intent" we are reminded that independence was declared in 1776, not merely by a people, but by a "good people," who had confidently and conscientiously affirmed the "rectitude of their intentions" to the "supreme judge of the world."

Jefferson, writing to Spencer Roane in 1819, said that the ultimate authority for the meaning of the Constitution must always rest in the people as a whole, not in the judiciary, or in any branch of government as such.

> Independence can be trusted nowhere but with the people in mass. They are inherently independent of all but moral law.

We see that the exception is the very ground of the rule! Without the moral law, the people is not a people. No less than for any classical or Christian or Jewish writer, for Jefferson and Madison a people is distinguished from a band of robbers. Civil Society is not collective selfishness (or irrationality). It is the moral code of civilized society as such, which must be understood to underlie the jurisprudence of a free people. Positive law, and especially constitutional law, must be seen in its relationship to the natural moral law.

Dr. Stone found that I had also "divided the house" with respect to the allegedly wholesome doctrines of Jeane Kirkpatrick, Irving Kristol, and Martin Diamond. I believe that my differences with these worthies are essentially the same as those I have elaborated with respect to Judge Bork, and it would be merely weaving Penelope's web to repeat them.

For those of unsated appetite, however, I would recommend "Jeane

Kirkpatrick: Not Quite Right," by Charles Kesler, in the October 29, 1982, *National Review*. I would here add only that nothing in my or Professor Kesler's critiques in any way diminishes our admiration for Ambassador Kirkpatrick as a peerless spokesman for American interests in the international arena.

# "Who Killed Cock Robin?"
# A Retrospective on the Bork Nomination
# and a Reply to "Jaffa Divides the House"

1. See above, p. 125.
2. For a review of the pro-slavery clauses, see, pp. 60–63.
3. *CW*, II, p. 255. Emphasis by Lincoln.
4. See my article in *National Review*, March 4, 1988.
5. The pro-slavery constitution for Kansas, supported by President Buchanan.
6. See above, p. 13.
7. "The Supreme Court Needs A New Philosophy," *Fortune*, December 1968, p. 141. This article was brought to my attention by my colleague, Professor Leonard Levy.
8. Ibid., p. 170.
9. *Commager*, p. 107.
10. Ibid.
11. See above, p. 22.
12. *The Writings of Thomas Jefferson*, H. A. Washington, ed., Vol. VII, p. 359. Emphasis added.
13. Article I, section 10. "No State shall ... pass any ... law impairing the obligation of contracts ..."
14. *Wheaton*, 12, p. 351.
15. A lecture at the American Enterprise Institute, reprinted in *Views from the Bench: The Judiciary and the Constitution* (M. Cannon and D. O'Brien editors, 1985).
16. "I am a Southern man and a slaveholder—a kind and merciful one, I trust— and none the worse for being a slaveholder. I say, for one, I would rather meet any extremity upon earth than give up one inch of our equality—one inch of

what belongs to us as members of this great republic! What acknowledge inferiority! The surrender of life is nothing to sinking down into acknowledged inferiority!" Calhoun in *Union and Liberty*, p. 520.

Calhoun could not see any contradiction in preferring death to "acknowledged inferiority" for himself, while demanding—in the name of "equality"—full recognition of his right to impose slavery on others. Slaves simply were not human beings, because they lacked the power to demand the recognition of their rights, as Calhoun did his.

17. See Madison's "Notes on Nullification" and his "Advice to My Country" written at the end of his life. *The Writings of James Madison*, Hunt ed., Vol. IX, pp. 573 and facing p. 610. It is almost certain that in the latter "the serpent creeping with his deadly wiles into Paradise" is Calhoun!

18. Ibid., pp. 570, 571. Emphasis in the original.

# The Closing of the Conservative Mind: A Dissenting Opinion on Judge Robert H. Bork*

## HARRY V. JAFFA

It is difficult to remember when conservatives have been so nearly unanimous in according a book something approaching a neoscriptural status as they have been with respect to Judge Robert H. Bork's *The Tempting of America: The Political Seduction of the Law*. (Bork himself has invited the scriptural analogy by speaking of the "creation" of the Constitution, and of an ensuing "temptation" by the apple of natural law and substantive due process, followed by a "fall" into judicial activism.)[1] The December 8, 1989, *National Review* featured as its main cover article, "Our Captive Courts: How Political Judges Have Perverted the Constitution," which the editors have described as Judge Bork's own adaptation of his book.

There is also, however, a second article by Judge Bork, encapsulated within the first in the same issue, entitled "Why Do the Liberals Rage?" One can summarize the two articles by saying that the liberals rage because Judge Bork says that judges should stick to the law—including the law of

---

* This essay, in slightly different form, was published in the July 9, 1991 issue of *National Review*. "Who Killed Cock Robin?" was written after the Senate hearings on Judge Bork's nomination to the Supreme Court, but before Judge Bork had published *The Tempting of America*. His astonishing mis-reading of the Constitution in that book, especially in relationship to the issues in *Dred Scott*, adds substantially to the critique based upon his previous writings and published statements. I apologize to the reader for the repetition of some of the material previously presented. It was unavoidable in the orderly application of the previous argument to the new material.

the Constitution—in their judging. He thinks—or so he says—that judges should not substitute their opinions of what the law of the Constitution *ought* to be. It is emphatically their job—whether they like the results or not—to say what the law *is*.

The liberals assert, however, that there is nothing but ambiguity and uncertainty in many key phrases of the Constitution (e.g., "general welfare," "due process," or "equal protection"). No one really knows what they "originally" meant, and even if one did know, one could find little guidance in applying them in present-day circumstances. They insist therefore that there is no alternative but to say what the Constitution ought to mean, here and now, rather than what it might have meant when it was framed and ratified. The favorite liberal posture is to call for a "living Constitution," freed from the "dead hand" of the past, one which "evolves" over time, adapting itself to new circumstances in and through the "creative" interpretations by judges sensitive to the needs of society.

In point of fact, Judge Bork replies, these judges, by discovering judicial remedies for what different interest groups claim to be "injuries," but which are really problems of society at large, are usurping powers proper to the political branches of government, and subverting the right of the people to be governed by their elected representatives.

Judge Bork has indeed presented his case against liberal jurisprudence cogently and passionately. He has convinced his conservative followers—and up to a point he has convinced me—that it is unanswerable. He has moreover convinced his followers that the campaign of vicious misrepresentation against him—especially during the fight over his nomination to the Supreme Court—is due mainly if not solely to the fact that they cannot meet him on the ground of the argument. That argument, in a nutshell, is that judicial activism is usurpation, denying to the political processes of democracy their rightful role in governance. His disciples believe—quite rightly—that the American public, by and large, still thinks that the function of judges is to interpret the law, not invent it. His critics on the Left supported their war against him by appealing to highly organized and highly motivated interest groups—especially advocates of group rights (especially those of race, color, and sex) which are not recognized by the Constitution—as opposed to the rights of individuals, which are. These critics blinded the public to the nature of their attack by declaring Judge Bork to be "out of the mainstream." His votaries are confident that the public would have been mightily indignant at his critics had they known the real character of the attack upon him.

In the minds of Judge Bork's partisans—and no doubt in his own mind—he has taken on something of the status of a martyred saint of conservatism. The tone of triumphant martyrology is particularly marked in Senator Orrin Hatch's hosanna in the December 8, 1989, *National Review*, the issue following the publication of Judge Bork's two articles. Hatch's review begins as follows:

> When President Reagan nominated Robert H. Bork to the Supreme Court in the summer of 1987, a carefully staged firestorm of opposition erupted, although no question was ever raised about Judge Bork's qualifications. But those who would manipulate the law to their own political ends knew that they would have no friend in Bob Bork were he confirmed. Their misrepresentations of his record denied Bork a seat on the Court, but their short-term victory is Pyrrhic. Bork is back.

The theological implications of the review might have been better rendered by "Bork is risen." Hatch ends as follows.

> It is rare that those at the center of history happen also to be great scholars or writers of a talent sufficient to explain momentous events. Churchill is the outstanding exception to the rule. Now we know that Judge Bork is another.

Surely hyperbole can go no further! Comparing Bork's prose to Churchill's is approximately on a level with comparing Andy Warhol's Campbell's soup can to Leonardo da Vinci's *Last Supper*. That Judge Bork was treated ill by his critics on the Left may certainly be granted. But the March 8, 1988, *National Review* carried an article by the present writer entitled "Judge Bork's Mistake." In it I accepted everything Judge Bork had said about the necessity and desirability of a constitutional jurisprudence of "original intent." But I denied that what Bork had *called original intent" was* "original intent." I referred my readers to a monograph I had published in the *University of Puget Sound Law Review*, Spring 1987, entitled "What Were the 'Original Intentions' of the Framers of the Constitution of the United States?" where I had argued at great length and with copious documentation that a genuine jurisprudence of "original intent," with respect to the Constitution, would have to recognize the principles of the Declaration of Independence as the principles of the Constitution. The Constitution of 1787, as every beginning student knows, is a bundle of compromises. There is no way, from the text of the Constitution alone, that one can distinguish those provisions which are consistent with its principles, and which implement those principles (e.g., the provisions for the election of Congress and president), from those that are compromises with those same principles (e.g., the security given to property in human chattels). This distinction between the principles of the Constitution and its compromises is one Judge Bork has studiously ignored. His critics have exploited the fact to persuade the general public—not without reason—that Judge Bork really has no principles. That judges should be neutral interpreters of the law is one thing: but to say that the law itself is essentially neutral—that it is mere process without purpose—is another. Judge Bork's position can be well summarized by saying that he rejects, root and branch, the following resolution of the Republican party Platform of 1860, upon which Abraham Lincoln was elected president of the United States.

> Resolved, That the maintenance of the principles promulgated in the Declaration of Independence and embodied in the Federal Constitution, "That all men are created equal; that they are endowed by their Creator with certain unalienable rights; that among these are life, liberty and the pursuit of happiness; that, to secure these rights, governments are instituted among men, deriving their just powers from the consent of the governed," is essential to the preservation of our Republican institutions . . .

Judge Bork's book begins with a discussion of the 1798 case of *Calder v. Bull*, in which Justice Samuel Chase, in a concurring opinion, had appealed to "the great first principles of the social compact" (which meant the principles of the Declaration of Independence), as possible grounds for judicial limitation of legislative power. According to Bork, here was the first time that a justice of the Supreme Court would "cast covetous glances at the apple that would eventually cause the fall."

But what Chase had to say about the "social compact" was not different from what James Madison said on countless occasions. It was not different from what Chief Justice Marshall would say in 1819, in the case of *Ogden v. Saunders*. Commenting upon Article I, Section 10 of the Constitution, which declares that no state shall "pass any law impairing the obligation of contracts," Marshall said that

> These words seem to us to import that the obligation is intrinsic, that it is created by the contract itself, not that it is dependent on the laws made to enforce it. When we advert to the course of reading generally pursued by American statesmen in early life, we must suppose that the framers of our Constitution were intimately acquainted with the writings of those wise and learned men, whose treatises on the laws of nature and nations have guided

public opinion on the subjects of obligation and contract. If we turn to those treatises, we find them to concur in the declaration that contracts possess an original intrinsic obligation, derived from the acts of free agents and not given by government.

Later, in the same opinion, Marshall spoke of how the excesses of the state legislatures, before the adoption of the Constitution, had caused

mischief . . . so great [and] so alarming, as not only to impair commercial intercourse . . . but to sap the morals of the people and destroy the sanctity of private faith.

A major purpose of the Constitution, said Marshall, was "to guard against the continuance of [this] evil . . ." It would do this by imposing "restraints on state legislation." And Marshall left no room for doubt that it was a proper function of the courts to impose such restraints.

It cannot be emphasized too strongly, not only that Marshall (unlike Bork) believed in "an original intrinsic obligation . . . not given by government" as the ground of some of the most important provisions of the Constitution, but that he believed that this belief informed the understanding of the Framers and of the public opinion that ratified their work. A jurisprudence of original intent would then of necessity have been—in decisive respects—a jurisprudence of natural law or natural right. Judge Bork is of course perfectly free to reject natural law and natural right—as he does—but he cannot consistently call his rejection of original intent, original intent. He cannot have it both ways.

Judge Bork did not always think about original intent as he does now. In "The Supreme Court Needs A New Philosophy," published in *Fortune* December 1968, he wrote:

A desire for some legitimate form of judicial activism is inherent in a tradition that runs strong and deep in our culture, a tradition that can be called "Madisonian." We continue to believe there are some things no majority should be allowed to do to us, no matter how democratically it may decide to do them. A Madisonian system assumes that in wide areas of life a legislative majority is entitled to rule for no better reason than that it is a majority. But it also assumes there are some aspects of life a majority should not control, that coercion in such matters is tyranny, a violation of the individual's natural rights. Clearly the definition of natural rights cannot be left to either the majority or the minority. In the popular understanding upon which the power of the Supreme Court rests, it is precisely the function of the Court to resolve this dilemma by giving content to the concept of natural rights in case-by-case interpretation of the Constitution.

Bork's notion of a "Madisonian system" here is less than perfect since, according to Madison, there is never an area of life in which "a legislative majority is entitled to rule for no better reason than that it is a majority." No aphorism is more characteristically Madisonian than that "all power in just and free government is derived from compact." And, as Madison wrote in his famous essay on "Sovereignty," a majority may do only those things "that could be *rightfully* done by the unanimous concurrence of the members." The word "rightfully," underscored by Madison himself, emphasizes the fact that a natural moral law underlies and undergirds all the constitutionalism of original intent. According to Madison, in the same essay,

> the reserved rights of individuals (of conscience, for example) in becoming parties to the original compact [are] beyond the reach of sovereignty, wherever vested or however viewed.

This means—in flat opposition to the Bork of today—that the free exercise of religion is a constitutional right, whether or not it is written into the Constitution. In the "Madisonian system" (as in that of John Marshall) the understanding of the nature of "the original compact" is the key to all constitutional interpretation. However imperfect Bork's understanding of "the Madisonian system" in 1968, we venture to say that, had he enunciated it at his hearings, he would almost certainly have been confirmed as a justice of the Supreme Court. I am the more persuaded of this because in the same article he wrote that

> Legitimate [judicial] activism requires, first of all, a warrant for the Court to move beyond the limited range of substantive rights that can be derived from traditional sources of constitutional law. The case for locating this warrant in the long-ignored Ninth Amendment was persuasively argued by Justice Arthur J. Goldberg in a concurring opinion in *Griswold v. Connecticut* . . .

In Judge Bork's new book, there is a chapter entitled "The Madisonian Dilemma and the Need for Constitutional Theory." The "Madisonian system" of 1968 now dissolves into the "Madisonian Dilemma." And the "concept of natural rights" disappears altogether. In short, the "system" became a "dilemma" when natural rights—that is to say, genuine original intent—disappeared. The dilemma, however, is Bork's, not Madison's.

*     *     *

The Bork of 1990 no longer recognizes the possibility of a "legitimate form of judicial activism." All judicial activism is now seen as the fruit of original sin. The principal vehicle for such activism, according to Bork, has been "the concept of 'substantive due process.' " And, says Bork, substantive due process was introduced into constitutional jurisprudence by Chief Justice Taney in his opinion for the Court in the case of *Dred Scott* (1857). Bork's accusation against Taney for gratuitously inventing the doctrine of substantive due process is the linchpin of the entire argument of his book.

Dred Scott had sued for his freedom in the slave state of Missouri, where he had returned, after having been taken by his master to live in Minnesota Territory, in which slavery had been prohibited by the Missouri Compromise legislation of 1820. Scott claimed his freedom on the ground that he had been taken by his master to reside (he was not a runaway), and had resided, in a federal Territory in which slavery had been prohibited by federal law. But Taney's opinion declared that the 1820 legislation had been unconstitutional, because Congress had no lawful power to deprive a slaveowner of his property, merely because he had exercised his constitutional right to migrate to a United States Territory. To do so would violate the Fifth Amendment's prohibition against depriving a person of his property "without due process of law." Congress had no power over slavery in the Territories, said Taney, other than "the power coupled with the duty of guarding and protecting the owner in his rights." According to Bork, however,

> The definition of what is, or is not property would seem, at least as an original matter, a question for legislatures. How then [Bork asks] can there be a constitutional right to own slaves where a statute forbids it?

According to Bork, Taney's "transformation of the due process clause of the Fifth Amendment

> was an obvious sham, it was a momentous sham, for this was the first appearance in American constitutional law of the concept of "substantive due process," and that concept has been used countless times since by judges who want to write their personal beliefs into a document that, most inconveniently, does not contain those beliefs.

Bork says that "Taney was determined to prove that the right of property in slaves was guaranteed by the Constitution." He quotes Taney saying that no one would presume that Congress could make any law in a Territory—for example, establishing a religion—that it is forbidden to make by the First Amendment. "All well and good," Bork comments, adding however that

> there is no similar constitutional provision that can be read with any semblance of plausibility to confer a right to own slaves. It may well have been the case that the federal government could not then have freed slaves in states where the laws allowed slavery without committing a taking of property for which the fifth amendment to the Constitution would require compensation.

Among Bork's innumerable errors in dealing with this case (and it would take at least fifty pages to explain them all) is the foregoing reference to the federal government freeing slaves and then compensating their owners. Under the antebellum Constitution, the federal government had no power whatever either to free slaves in the slave states or to compensate their owners. The same Republican platform that resolved that the principles of the Declaration of Independence were the principles of the Constitution also resolved

> That the maintenance inviolate of the rights of the States, and especially the right of each State to order and control its own domestic institutions according to its own judgment exclusively, is essential to that balance of powers on which the perfection and endurance of our political fabric depends . . .

This was common ground to the free soil movement and to the most ardent advocates of slavery. In 1862—in the very midst of the Civil War—Lincoln attempted to provide for compensation for loyal slave owners, who were losing their slaves by the mere attrition of the war. He did so by recommending a series of constitutional amendments, authorizing the federal government to make payments to states that undertook programs of compensated emancipation. It never even occurred to Lincoln that the "takings" clause of the Fifth Amendment might authorize the federal government itself to buy and free slaves, or even to pay for slaves that had run away.

We return, however, to Bork's amazing assertion that there is nothing in the Constitution that can be said "with any semblance of plausibility to confer a right to own slaves." He repeats this even more emphatically when he asks,

> How did Taney know that slave ownership was a constitutional right? Such a right is nowhere to be found in the Constitution. He knew it because he was passionately convinced that it *must* be in the Constitution. (Emphasis is Bork's.)

Well, the answer is that, although the Constitution does not "confer" a right to own slaves, it most assuredly recognizes such a right. Moreover, it recognizes that right as arising, not from the action of judges, but of legislatures. Here is the text of Article IV, Section 2, para. 3.

> No person held to service of labor in one State, under the laws thereof, escaping into another, shall, in consequence of any law or regulation therein, be discharged from such service or labor, but shall be delivered up on claim of the party to whom such service or labor may be due.

This is the fugitive slave clause. The original Constitution never uses the words "slave" or "slavery," preferring euphemisms in their place. Article I speaks of "adding to the whole number of free persons . . . three-fifth of all other persons." Can it be doubted that the "other persons" are unfree, that is, slaves? Or that their slavery is regarded by the Constitution as lawful? But the Constitution, in Article IV, not only recognizes the lawfulness of the right to own slaves—a lawfulness arising from the actions of the legislatures of the slave States—but it pledges the full power of the federal government to making that right secure, whenever the slave shall escape from his master into a jurisdiction where slavery is forbidden. The phrase "shall be delivered up" is categorical, and implies an obligation on Congress to pass enabling legislation, if such should be necessary. So far as I know, no one, in two hundred years, has ever made the fantastic assertion that Bork makes, that the right to slave ownership "is nowhere to be found in the [original] Constitution."

In short, it was not Taney who read the right to slave ownership *into* the Constitution; it is Judge Bork who has read it *out* of the Constitution. Judge Bork was so passionately convinced that Taney's opinion represented a reading of his personal beliefs into a Constitution that did not contain such beliefs that he was blind to the extent to which the Constitution actually did embody those beliefs.

It is clear moreover—from Article IV—that Taney did not form his opinion in *Dred Scott* on the basis of the due process clause of the Fifth Amendment alone. The substantive element also rested in part on Article I, Section 9, in which it is said that

> The migration or importation of such persons as any of the States now existing shall think fit to admit, shall not be prohibited by the Congress prior to the year one thousand eight hundred and eight . . .

This clause is an exception made to the power granted to Congress in Section 8, "to regulate commerce with foreign nations," as well as that "to establish a uniform rule of naturalization. . . ." No one has ever doubted that, however ponderous the euphemism, Congress was prohibited thereby from interfering—for twenty years—with the buying of slaves on the west coast of Africa, where they could be obtained much more cheaply than in any of the States. Taney held—not unreasonably—that this concession to business profit was evidence of a "right to traffic" in slave property as "an ordinary article of merchandise and property." Taney could more plausibly have referred to it as extraordinary rather than ordinary. If, however, one puts together—as Taney did—the substantive and substantial consideration given by the Constitution in these several places to the profit and security of slave property and the slave trade, it was not unreasonable for him to conclude that it was unconstitutional to deprive a person of such valuable considerations merely because he took them with him into a United States Territory. Or, to be more precise, it was not unreasonable for him to conclude as he did, if one draws one's inferences concerning the intent of the Constitution, from the text of the Constitution alone, in the manner commended by Judge Bork. In any event, it is certainly the case that Judge Bork makes his case against Taney only by the most shameless expurgating and bowdlerizing of the Constitution's text.

What then was wrong with Taney's opinion in *Dred Scott*? Let us recall that in all the places in the Constitution in which slaves are referred to euphemistically, they are called "persons." And we must recall that in the Fifth Amendment the Constitution says that

> No person shall . . . be deprived of life, liberty, or property, without due process of law. . .

Now, the persons held to service or labor in Article IV (like those imported under Article I, section 9) were so held (or imported) not as persons but as chattels. But a person, qua person, is possessed of a rational will. And a chattel, qua chattel, is a piece of movable property without a rational will. Under the law of slavery slaves were always regarded as human persons for some purposes—e.g., by being held responsible for their actions under the criminal law—while at the same time they were regarded as chattels, mere extensions of their master's will, like a horse or a dog or an ox. Hence they could not make contracts, for which reason there was no legal marriage among them. That the law of slavery at once regarded the slaves as persons and as chattels—notwithstanding that, in reason and in nature, a person cannot be a chattel, and a chattel cannot be a person—was what made slavery indeed a "peculiar institution." In the slave States themselves, the character of a chattel always took precedence of the person in the slave. But what happened when he was taken to a Territory? Why should the positive law of slavery follow him? Looking within the four quarters of the text of the Constitution, Taney inferred that Negroes (whether free or slave) were regarded by the Framers as

> beings of an inferior order . . . and so far inferior, that they had no rights which white men were bound to respect; and that the Negro might justly and lawfully be reduced to slavery for his benefit. . .

These are the decisive words in Taney's opinion—ignored by Bork. They justified Taney, in his own mind, in deciding that when the master took his slave into a Territory, the master was the "person" who could not be lawfully deprived of his property. But Lincoln and the Republican party, looking to the words of the Declaration of Independence, said that the slave was equally a human person with the master. Under "the laws of nature and of nature's God" the right to liberty took precedence of the right to property. This was because, underlying the positive law of property, was the natural right—the natural liberty—of every human being to own himself. This was also the ground of the right of contract, referred to by John Marshall. The positive law of slavery might overrule the law of nature in the slave states, but it could not extend beyond their boundaries, except for the reclaiming of fugitives.

The case of *Dred Scott* can only be understood if one realizes that in it the chatteldom of slavery and the personhood of the slave have come into uncompromising contradiction. That contradiction can be resolved only by recourse to the principles of natural right and natural law, as embodied in the Declaration of Independence. For this purpose, Judge Bork's conception of "original intent" is perfectly useless. But if it is useless here, it is useless everywhere: for the reason that in this case the distinction between the compromises of the Constitution and the principles of the Constitution is brought into sharper focus than anywhere else. It is because the Civil War amendments (to which one might add the Nineteenth Amendment) have eliminated the most evident contradictions between the Constitution and its principles, that the question of what those principles are, has become more obscure. Yet, as I believe it can be proved, the meaning of the Fourteenth Amendment, and in particular the meaning of its "due process" and "equal protection" clauses, depends in the highest degree upon the correct understanding of where Taney went wrong in *Dred Scott*. And of that Judge Bork has not an inkling.

# The Closing of the Conservative Mind

1. Judge Bork's analogy between natural law and the forbidden fruit of the Garden of Eden is not however original. Consider the following:

> I do not propose to argue questions of natural rights and inherent powers; I plant my reliance upon the Constitution ... When the tempter entered the garden of Eden and induced our common mother to offend against the law which God had given her through Adam, he was the first teacher of that "higher law" which sets the individual above the solemn rule which he is bound, as a part of every community, to observe ... Why then shall we talk about natural rights? Who is to define them? Where is the judge that is to sit over the court to try natural rights? ... I say then I come not to argue the questions outside of or above the Constitution, but to plead the cause of right of law and order under the Constitution ...

Jefferson Davis, in the Senate, May 8, 1860. *Jefferson Davis, Constitutionalist: His Letter, Papers, and Speeches,* ed. Dunbar Rowland, Vol. IV, pp. 253, 254.

# Seven Answers for Professor Anastaplo

### HARRY V. JAFFA

The first of Professor Anastaplo's seven questions is: "What more should be said on behalf of Attorney General Meese with respect to the matters touched upon by Mr. Jaffa?" In addressing this question, I am reminded irresistibly of a scene in *Duck Soup*. The revolution in Freedonia is at its climax, and the four Marx brothers are manning the guns. Shells fly overhead and crash behind them. Mrs. Teasdale (Margaret Dumont) enters stage right and asks, "What's going on here?" To which Groucho replies, "We're defending your honor, which is more than you ever did."

Professor Anastaplo is attempting more on behalf of the former attorney general than either he, or anyone in the Justice Department, or in any of the official or semiofficial conservative think tanks, has ever done. The short answer—indeed the sufficient answer—to this question is "Nothing."[1] It is Professor Anastaplo—not Mr. Meese, who couldn't care less—who takes issue with my assertion that no one, either on or off the Court, has ever expounded the theory of original intent with greater eloquence or conviction than Chief Justice Taney in the case of *Dred Scott*.

Professor Anastaplo finds it difficult to credit with either eloquence or conviction "an argument that is patently false." But surely, an argument need not be true to be eloquently expressed. Consider Antony's speech—of unsurpassed eloquence and equally unsurpassed hypocrisy—over the dead body of Caesar, in Shakespeare's *Julius Caesar*. Antony was utterly cynical about the truth of his speech. But there is no reason—known to me—to think that Taney was saying what he did not believe to be true. Professor Anastaplo finds (as do I) the critical defect in Taney's opinion to be his assertion that "Negroes of the African race" were, at the time of Revolution and at the time of the adoption of the Constitution, believed to be "so far inferior that they had no rights which the white man was bound to respect." For this reason, Taney maintained, they could not have been

303

included in the humanity referred to in the Declaration's proposition "that all men are created equal." Anastaplo points to Blackstone for evidence of the opinion of most Americans in 1776 as to the humanity of blacks and their natural rights. He could have supplemented this with countless contemporary quotations of Americans in America at this time to prove the truth of this contention. None of this, however, has any bearing on whether Taney was sincere in his mistaken belief.

Taney conceded that the words of the Declaration in themselves seem to have included black men no less than white. But, he said, the state of public opinion at the time was such that these words could not have meant what they said. It was inconsistent with the character of the men who signed the Declaration, Taney said, to have included Negroes in the proposition that all men are created equal, and then to have failed to abolish slavery. Taney certainly seems to have assumed—apparently unconsciously, and certainly without any argument—that the ground of morality is something like Kant's categorical imperative. "Original intent" as Taney understood it would be an inference, not so much from what the documents of the revolutionary period said, as from the maxims upon which the statesmen of the period were supposed to have acted. It is proper to point out that this assumption of Taney's is not intrinsically unreasonable, and it does not imply an internally inconsistent interpretation of the Founding. It is mistaken nonetheless in that it does not understand the Founding Fathers as they understood themselves. More important, it does not recognize that prudence and a prudential morality—and not anything like the categorical imperative—was the ground of statesmanship as they understood it. There was in fact nothing inconsistent with recognizing the moral wrongness of slavery, while recognizing at the same time that this was only the first step in a long process, leading to the "ultimate extinction" of slavery.

Professor Anastaplo finds it difficult to credit Taney with sincerity. But why? Taney's opinion about the Founding is almost universal among the "intellectuals" of the academy—his colleagues and mine—today. I recall an evening at St. John's College, Annapolis, not many years ago. I had given a lecture on "How to Think About the American Revolution." After the lecture, the discussion began, and it lasted until one o'clock in the morning. There was only one topic for the entire four (or more) hours. It was, "Why did the Founding Fathers not abolish slavery, if they were sincere in asserting that all men are created equal?" As far as I recall, I made virtually no headway in persuading the members of the St. John's College community that the failure of the Founding Fathers to abolish slavery did not detract from the sincerity of their conviction that slavery was morally wrong. I pointed out to them what Lincoln had pointed out, in his speech on *Dred Scott*, namely, that it never was in the power of the statesmen of the Revolution to abolish slavery, no matter how much they may have wished to do so. I pointed out that it was not at all wonderful that a nation of slaveholders—and all thirteen states were slave states in 1776—had not abolished slavery. What was wonderful was that a nation of slaveholders had declared that all men are created equal, and thereby had made the ultimate abolition of slavery a moral necessity. I also pointed out that the fourscore and seven years required to accomplish this abolition was a very short period in human history, particularly since slavery was perhaps the oldest institution of human civilization next to the family.

Although the St. John's students and faculty who participated in the discussion were, for the most part, experienced exegetes of the *Nicomachean Ethics*, they seemed uninterested in applying Aristotle's conception of prudential wisdom to the historical (and moral) reality of the American Founding. Despite the reference to the dictates of prudence in the Declaration of Independence itself, they took it for granted—as did Taney—that the morality of the Founding Fathers could only be vindicated on Kantian grounds. Although few of them knew who Taney was—before the evening began—their view of the Founding was dogmatically Taneyite.

The near universality of Taney's opinion today is seen in its appeal equally to the radical Left and the radical Right. One distinguished scholar (and federal appeals court judge)—who belongs to the Black Power wing of contemporary American historiography—has written that, had the authors of the Declaration written that "all white men" or "all white men who own property" are created equal, they would more accurately have conveyed their meaning.[2] This happens also to be the Marxist interpretation of the Founding, although I do not think that Judge Higginbotham is a Marxist. But the old line state's rights conservatives (whose views predominated in the Meese Justice Department) are very far from disagreeing with Judge Higginbotham or the Marxists. State's rights conservatives tend to fluctuate between the Calhounites, who think that the Declaration did include Negroes and therefore was irrelevant, and the Taneyites, who think the Declaration was relevant, but only because did not include Negroes. For the latter, the equality of the Declaration is a collective equality, as it is in the proletariat of Karl Marx.

Consider these remarks from "The Constitution from a Conservative Perspective," a lecture at the Heritage Foundation, March 10, 1988, by James McClellan, president of the Center for Judicial Studies (known to the cognoscenti as the Headquarters of the Army of Northern Virginia).

Whereas the original Constitution and the Bill of Rights (as originally understood) have enjoyed the universal acclaim of thoughtful conservatives, a number of amendments, particularly the 14th, have proved to be anathema . . .

That the Constitution *with slavery* has enjoyed "the universal acclaim of thoughtful conservatives" implies of course the acceptance of Taney's (or, alternatively, Calhoun's) constitutionalism. This is reinforced by the vigorous assertion that the amendments abolishing slavery, and attempting to guarantee the equal protection of the laws to all persons, are "anathema." Left and Right, each for its own reasons, agrees with Taney's (or, alternatively, Calhoun's) opinion.

Professor Anastaplo writes that

Mr. Meese is correct in sensing that Chief Justice Taney did not believe in "original intent," else he would have approached the slavery question quite differently . . . One can see in Taney, as in Calhoun, how reason can be subverted by passion.

I do not see how Mr. Meese could have sensed anything about Taney's belief in "original intent," because as far as I know he did not know that it existed. Following Rehnquist, Meese found the evil of *Dred Scott* only in the Court's alleged usurpation of the powers of Congress. Neither Meese nor Rehnquist found the dehumanization of the Negro to be an objectionable feature of Taney's opinion. Rehnquist, we know, would not have done so in any case, since he does not believe in anything that might be called an "idea of natural justice," such as is implied in the idea of dehumanization. For Rehnquist—an uncompromising legal positivist—the Declaration of Independence has no more status in constitutional interpretation than it had for Calhoun. It is all very well for Professor Anastaplo to say that one can see how, in Taney and Calhoun, reason can be subverted by passion. But he must recognize that it has been subverted in exactly the same way in the great majority of our contemporaries, including the luminaries of present-day jurisprudence.

Professor Anastaplo writes that one should not

accept as readily as Mr. Jaffa seems to do the Taney proposition that the Constitution is friendly to slavery. Rather, the Constitution of 1787 can be read as reflecting a grudging accommodation to slavery . . .

The operative expression in the foregoing is "can be read." Indeed, the Constitution can be read as reflecting the aforesaid accommodation. That is how I and Professor Anastaplo—and some few of our contemporaries—read it. But it can be so read only if one makes the principles of the Declaration the touchstone of the Constitution, as those principles were interpreted by Abraham Lincoln. Without this touchstone, the Constitution "can be read"—indeed it can hardly be read otherwise—than as a proslavery document. Attorney General Meese did on one occasion—in his Dickinson College speech of September 17, 1985—read it in the Lincolnian way, and I congratulated him for having done so. But his record from that day forward is one of apparently complete amnesia of what he said on that occasion. Let me here record my conviction that the Dickinson speech was—perhaps accidentally—written under the influence of the Lincolnian understanding. But the reaction of the Confederate constitutionalists in the Department of Justice (many of them recruited from the Center for Judicial Studies) was so sharp and strong that the experiment was never repeated. I am confident that Mr. Meese himself was blissfully unaware of this reenactment of the Civil War—a reenactment in which the Confederacy triumphs—within his own public persona.

Professor Anastaplo writes that there are

> Two other features of the Taney opinion in *Dred Scott* which Mr. Jaffa seems to acquiesce in . . . One is that Congress could not act to restrict slavery in the Territories if slaves were regarded as merely property. But due process should not be taken to mean that particular kinds of property cannot be singled out for special legislative treatment (and even complete suppression) in various circumstances. It is hardly likely that the state legislatures that abolished property in slaves from 1776 on violated the due process clauses in their constitutions.

There was no question, before the Civil War, that states had a sovereign right, either to include, or to exclude slavery, from among their domestic institutions. There is no proper analogy therefore between the bearing of "due process" upon the right of states, on the one hand, and of Congress or a territorial legislature, on the other hand, to abolish property in slaves in federal Territories. Taney's opinion, moreover, did not regard slaves *merely* as property. From the premise (however erroneous) that the right to property in slaves was "expressly affirmed" in the Constitution, Taney held with perfect consistency that slave property was indeed "singled out" for protection by the due process clause of the Fifth Amendment.

The second "dubious feature" in Taney's opinion, in which I seem to acquiesce, according to Professor Anastaplo, is

> the assumption that what the Court said in defining the powers of Congress with respect to the Territories was binding upon the Congress . . .

Anastaplo "doubts the propriety of judicial review" in such matters, and thinks that Lincoln, although perhaps exercising a prudent reserve, doubted it too.

Happily, this is one of the most discussed issues in the Lincoln-Douglas debates, and if Lincoln exercised any reserve about it I have not been able to detect it. The person who doubted the effective power of the Court to bind the Congress was not Lincoln but Douglas. It was Douglas who repeated, over and over again, that the power of the Court either to authorize or to forbid slavery in the Territories was merely "abstract." According to Douglas, the practical or effective power, either to protect slavery, or to exclude slavery, rested neither with the Court nor with the Congress, but with the people of the Territories. Only they could pass the local police regulations upon which the actual existence of slavery depended. If they denied slave owners that protection, slavery would by that fact be excluded. If they provided such protection, then slave property could be held safely and enjoyed. That was what Douglas meant by popular sovereignty.

Lincoln ridiculed this doctrine as saying that a thing (slavery) could lawfully be driven from a place (in the Territories) where the Supreme Court had said that it had a lawful right to be. As we have seen, Taney had held (and Douglas would not dispute it) that the right to hold slaves in any United States Territory was a right "expressly affirmed" in the Constitution. To say that such a right might be barren and worthless, because of the failure of either a territorial legislature or of the United States Congress to enact the laws necessary to make it valuable, was entirely inadmissible, according to Lincoln. "Why, there is not such an abolitionist in the nation as Douglas after all," are Lincoln's last words in the joint debates. Here is the argument leading up to that conclusion.

> I suppose that most of us . . . believe that the people of the Southern states are entitled to a congressional fugitive slave law—that it is a right fixed in the Constitution. But it cannot be made available to them without congressional

legislation. In the judge's language, it is a "barren right" which needs legislation before it can become efficient and valuable to the person to whom it is
guaranteed. And as the right is constitutional I agree that the legislation shall
be granted to it—and that not that we like the institution of slavery . . . Why
then do I yield support to a fugitive slave law? Because I do not understand
that the Constitution, which guarantees that right, can be supported without
it. And if I believed that the right to hold a slave in a Territory was equally
fixed in the Constitution with the right to reclaim fugitives, I should be bound
to give it the legislation necessary to support it. I say that no man can deny his
obligation to give the necessary legislation to support slavery in a Territory
who believes it is a constitutional right to have it there. No man can, who does
not give the Abolitionist an argument to deny an obligation enjoined by the
Constitution to enact a fugitive slave law . . . I say if that Dred Scott decision is
correct then the right to hold slaves in a Territory is equally a constitutional
right with the right of a slaveholder to have his runaway returned . . . I defy
any man to make an argument that will justify unfriendly legislation to deprive
a slaveholder of his right to hold his slave in a Territory, that will not equally, in
all its length, breadth, and thickness furnish an argument for nullifying the
fugitive slave law.[3]

Lincoln's words here, it must be noted, gave a great impetus to the
movement of events towards secession and civil war. The deep South
believed sincerely that Taney's opinion in *Dred Scott* was correct—and that
the only power granted by the Constitution to Congress over slave property in the Territories was "the power coupled with the duty of guarding
and protecting the owner in his rights." The phrase "coupled with the
duty" embodied concisely what Lincoln said at the end of his debates with
Douglas. From Lincoln's perspective, the Southerners were justified when,
in the Democratic National Convention in Charleston in May 1860, they
insisted that a federal slave code for the Territories be included in the
platform. It was the refusal of the Douglas Democrats to accede to this
demand that led to the secession of the deep South from the national party.
This was the true beginning and sufficient cause of the secession of the
same States from the Union after Lincoln's election. The question for
Lincoln was not primarily whether the opinion of the Court could bind the
Congress, but whether the Court understood the Constitution. If the
Court had been correct in holding what it did hold in *Dred Scott*, concerning the constitutional power and duty of Congress in the Territory, then
there was no question in Lincoln's mind but that that opinion would have
been binding. The Lincoln-Douglas debates leave no room for doubt on
this point.

In concluding this point, I would remind my readers of what is said in "Who Killed Cock Robin?" concerning a hypothetical "reverse" *Dred Scott* decision. There is no question but that Abraham Lincoln would have considered binding a Supreme Court decision holding that the constitutional power of Congress in the Territories was the power, coupled with the duty, of assuring the exclusion of slavery. At the time of the Wilmot Proviso, Lincoln held that—by the laws of nature—freedom followed the flag, and that any and all territory acquired by the United States was *a priori* free territory. Only positive law could make slavery lawful. In its absence, the condition of any United States Territory was freedom. Congressional legislation was necessary, he thought, to make this exclusion unambiguous and effective. Lincoln's position resembled that of Madison on the Bill of Rights. In 1787 Madison had held the position (maintained in the *Federalist*) that a bill of rights would be superfluous because the United States had no constitutional power to do those things that the Bill of Rights would forbid it to do. Nevertheless, he led the way in the first Congress in drafting and adopting the first ten amendments. He did so, not because he thought his previous views were mistaken, but because he had come to believe that what was merely implicit had to become explicit, if the public mind was to rest secure in its belief in these limitations upon federal power.

## II

Professor Anastaplo asks,

> Does Mr. Jaffa recognize sufficiently the shortcomings of the equality which he so eloquently extols?

Among those alleged shortcomings are

> an emphasis upon self-centredness and upon private right—and these in turn can promote relativism, if not even nihilism, and hence another kind of tyranny . . . In any event, is it not "freedom," even more than "equality" which appeals to mankind's noblest opposition to slavery?

Abraham Lincoln would have been puzzled, if not astounded, at the thought that the equality he so eloquently extolled could be set in opposition to the freedom (or liberty) he extolled with equal eloquence. After all, his opposition to slavery—the denial of liberty—was grounded in the principle of equality. In the language of the Revolution, freedom and equality had been largely synonymous. If they differed at all, it was as complementary, but never as opposing or contrary terms. Consider Virginia's Declaration of Rights (June 12, 1776), "That all men are by nature equally free and independent . . ."; and that of Massachusetts (1780), that "All men are born free and equal . . ." It is in Tocqueville's *Democracy in America* that equality and liberty are set against each other. But Tocqueville ignored the Declaration of Independence, and the theory it embodied, in his analysis. For Tocqueville equality meant primarily and essentially an equality of condition. The liberty to which he opposed it was the liberty of men to cultivate their talents and pursue their ambitions in such a way as to produce inequality of condition. He saw egalitarianism— as does Professor Anastaplo—as a leveling force, using the power of the majority to discourage, or even punish, those who excel by their talents and achievements. Certainly, in our time we have seen the spurious appeal to equality as a force for redistributing wealth, not as a charitable aid to the deserving poor, but to punish enterprise and industry. Its most powerful motive is envy. Perhaps the most lucid expression of this kind of egalitarianism is Marx's classic formula for distributive justice in a communist society: "From each according to his abilities, to each according to his needs." This divorce of the idea of work from the idea of reward for work is not merely utopian, it is against nature, and hence against the idea of natural rights and natural justice embodied in the Declaration of Independence. By abandoning the connection between justice and nature it does indeed lead both to the nihilism and the tyranny that Professor Anastaplo so justly fears.

In a celebrated passage of the celebrated tenth *Federalist* Madison speaks of "the protection of different and unequal faculties of acquiring property" as "the first object of government." It would be perfectly correct to emend this passage to say that it is the *equal* protection of *unequal* faculties which is intended. As such, this is in perfect harmony with the principle of equality, *rightly* understood. We must remember that this is said in the context of the Madisonian solution for the problem of faction—above all of the problem of majority faction. The entire number ten is devoted to showing how a republican regime can be made to serve the principles of natural justice, over against a naked majoritarianism based upon a false notion of equality.

The passage in the *Federalist* about protecting "different and unequal faculties" is usually interpreted to mean that the rights of property shall be protected from appropriation or expropriation by a merely numerical majority. This interpretation is correct, but insufficient. It also means that the poor or the weak shall not be unjustly deprived of their equal right to their own property. In facing the terrible prejudice against Negroes, Lincoln would concede that in some respects they were not his equals. (The only respect in which he actually ever made this concession was color. Of course, to say that black is not equal to white, means no more than that black is not white.) Of the black woman, he once declared, "In some respects she certainly is not my equal; but in her natural right to eat the bread she earns with her own hands without the leave of anyone else, she is my equal, and the equal of all others." Of course, a natural right to eat the bread one earns implies a natural liberty to earn that bread, and to earn it in a free market. And a *free* market is one to which all breadwinners have *equal* access. No one may arbitrarily be excluded from the free competition of the market place, or compelled to labor at an occupation inferior (i.e., unequal) to one to which the principle of freedom of contract might entitle him or her. And freedom of contract, one should remember, is a necessary implication of the natural right to ownership of one's own person, with respect to which all men are created equal.

Concerning the envy of the rich by the poor, animated by a false idea of equality, and leading to class warfare, Lincoln wrote as follows.

> Nor should this [the rights of labor] lead to a war upon property. Property is the fruit of labor—property is desirable—is a positive good in the world. That some should be rich, shows that others may become rich, and hence is just encouragement to industry and enterprise. Let not him who is houseless pull down the house of another; but let him labor diligently and build one for himself, thus by example assuring that his own shall be safe from violence when built.[4]

I do not think that the essential harmony of liberty and equality—rightly understood—can be better or more eloquently expressed than this.

## III.

Professor Anastaplo asks,

> Does Mr. Jaffa mean to leave the impression that theory alone determines political practice?

To this he adds,

> Not enough seems to be made by Mr. Jaffa of nature (or personal temperament) and of circumstances in everyday political life. If he did make more of these, he would not be as apt as he is to subject political men to the most exacting philosophical scrutiny.

Let me reply, first of all, by saying that I was convinced long ago, as I believe Professor Anastaplo was, both by Aristotle and by Leo Strauss, that the best possible regime is one ruled not by philosophers but by gentlemen. The gentleman, qua gentleman, does not need reasons for being moral. Indeed, the true gentleman tends to regard the giving of such reasons as demeaning. In this lies both his strength and his weakness. But Leo Strauss—more than Aristotle—persuaded me that the philosophy that Socrates called down from the heavens was a necessary adjunct to the regime of gentlemen. This was because gentlemen qua gentlemen are nearly defenseless against false gods and false theories. Such theories might—and frequently do—destroy the ground of virtue in the souls of the nongentlemen, and sometimes even in the souls of the gentlemen. Gentlemanship means the activity of the moral virtues guided by practical wisdom. Gentlemanship implies a harmony between the moral virtues, and the regime in which the gentlemen predominate. Gentlemanship requires that the gods of the city—and I here use classical terminology—look with favor upon these virtues, and those who practice them. The rule of gentleman is *a priori* possible only within the cities that look to such gods. Philosophy, insofar as it renders doubtful the belief in such gods, or any gods, may justly be regarded as a doubtful blessing, if not a curse. (This is of course *a fortiori* true of the poetry by which philosophic teachings are transmitted to the young, and thereby to future citizens.) Where the gods of the cities are hostile to the virtues—where they elevate bad faith, cruelty, or selfishness, over morality—it may be necessary for Socratic philosophy to turn the city towards a purer religion. Consider the quest of the King of the Khazars for a better religion, in Judah Halevi's *The Kuzari*.[5] It may also happen that non-Socratic philosophy—or the influence of such philosophy—may elevate bad faith, cruelty, and selfishness over morality. We see that, above all, in Machiavelli, and the Machiavellians who—with notable exceptions—have dominated the theoretical landscape (and the poetry that has accompanied it) for over four hundred years. We can see the pernicious possibilities of philosophy, more than a millennium before Machiavelli, in the comic (but serious) debate between the just and the unjust speech in Aristophanes' *Clouds*. From that debate we may infer that a new Socrates—different from the one presented in the play—will, and indeed must, come to the aid of the just speech, as he does in the encounter with Thrasymachus in the first book of the *Republic*. For the refutation of the thesis that justice is the interest of the stronger must be seen as the reversal of the result of the contest in the *Clouds*. That encounter between Socrates and Thrasymachus is reproduced, in its essentials, in Lincoln's debates with Douglas in 1858. The Gettysburg Address—as the last word in the Lincoln-Douglas debates—is Socratic poetry in the service of gentlemanship and morality.

The political life of the West was transformed by the establishment of Christianity within the Roman Empire. That establishment was anticipated a century before by the extension of citizenship from Rome to the provinces. In principle, and in its own self-consciousness, the city of Rome became the world. Since there was now, in principle, but one city, there could now, in principle, be but one God. This marked the end of the ancient city, and of the possibility of a natural harmony between gentlemanship and the gods of the city. Christian monotheism was not the religion of one particular people—as was the monotheism of ancient Israel. In claiming the authority of truth with respect to the human soul qua human soul, it broke the bonds that had hitherto connected the laws of each particular city with a particular God or gods. There was no such thing as an "establishment of religion" in any ancient city. The idea of establishment implied an act by a preestablished political order. In the ancient city, however, the city arose from a preexisting religion. The God of Israel freed the Israelites from bondage, led them out of Egypt, gave them their laws, and by these acts made them into a polity. The Christian God comes to sight as the savior of each individual human soul. He may break the bondage of Original Sin, but not the shackles of those compelled to "make bricks without straw." He is not the lawgiver of a particular polity.

The establishment of Christianity, in banning the ancient gods, broke the bond between God or the gods and the law that had characterized ancient Israel, ancient Rome, and every other ancient city. From the tension that now arose between the merely human and particular cause of law, and the universal and divine character of the justification of law, resulted the millennial struggle for supremacy between the secular and the sacred, between popes and emperors within the Holy Roman Empire. This struggle continued in different forms throughout the Reformation.

The ancient legislating gods required primarily obedience, but the One

God of a universal empire required primarily faith, or belief. The political establishment of a universal religion elevated "theory" over "practice" in a way unknown in the ancient world, creating a problem unknown to Aristotle's *Politics*. Political life henceforth was dominated, not by the requirements of laws directing human actions as such, but by the requirements of faith directing men's souls toward eternity. If men's dearest interests were in another world, if the interests which they shared with aliens and enemies were in some sense dearer than those they shared with friends and fellow-citizens, then citizenship became problematic in a way unknown to the ancient city. Coercion in matters of faith, coercion unrelated to morality or to disobedience to any laws prescriptive of justice or the common good, was virtually unknown in the ancient city. It was incompatible with the idea of gentlemanship. Now it became central to the political process. Henceforth, Western man was faced, not with the political problem properly so called, but with the political-theological problem. One might in this connection consider the differences between the laws against atheism in Plato's *Laws* with the laws against heresy and infidelity in the Holy Roman Empire or in any of the Christian states of the Reformation. These differences illuminate and indeed explain why the status of gentlemanship—and of untheoretical politics—became so problematic in the post-classical world.

Suffice it for the present, that the foregoing problem remained unsolved for nearly fifteen hundred years. Its solution is to be found in the principles of political obligation, set forth in the Declaration of Independence, and in the principles of religious liberty, set forth in the Virginia Statute of Religious Liberty, both of them the work of Thomas Jefferson. Of course, Jefferson's practical statesmanship was an outgrowth of the work of the philosophical statesmanship of Spinoza and of John Locke. (Jefferson himself acknowledged Locke, but rejected Spinoza. We, however, cannot ignore Locke's debt to Spinoza.) But it would be a mistake to see Jefferson as nothing more than the epigone of his teachers. The American Founding represents such a harmonization (not synthesis) of the claims of reason and of revelation as to make possible, perhaps for the first time, the rule of Christian gentlemen.

The true theory of civil liberty may be found in Lincoln's "abstract truth, applicable to all men and all times." That all men are created equal, that there is no such distance between man and man—as there is between man and beast, or between man and God—implies that no man has any right to govern another without that other's consent. This is the ground of the rule of law, of ruling and being ruled in turn. A universal ground of political obligation is found in the particular act of each consenting individual. Without any church or intervening religious authority, the sanction of monotheistic religion is preserved, nonetheless, in the idea that the rights authorizing the consent of the governed are rights with which we have been endowed by our Creator. Respect for the rights of man becomes a part of our duty to God.

Religious liberty is grounded in the metaphysical freedom of the mind. Because of it, coercion in matters of faith is destructive of all merit in professions of faith. Therefore, a man's civil rights can have no more dependence upon his religious opinions than upon his opinions in physics or geometry. These wise theories of civil and religious liberty are necessary conditions of gentlemanship in the modern world, not substitutes for it. But gentlemanship—the qualities necessary for the deserved supremacy of the untheoretical moral virtues within the political community—is possible only within the framework of these theories. In this sense, the emancipation of practice from theory must be a work of theory.

Professor Anastaplo writes that

It is imprudent to regard as radically flawed human beings those political men who hold dubious theoretical opinions.

Such an attitude, he adds,

can be discerned to have been critical to the intolerance both of the Inquisition and of Stalin.

To which I reply, exactly so. But the decency of the gentleman was virtually helpless against the Inquisition. This is illuminated by the scene in Dostoevski's *Brothers Karamazov*, when Jesus—a gentleman—is silent before the Grand Inquisitor's theoretical arguments in behalf of tyranny. Moreover, since gentlemen are ordinarily pious, their Christian piety was often at war with their decency. It took the principle of separation of church and state, as set forth in the Virginia Statute, to reunite their piety and their decency, and thereby to liberate both their religious faith and their gentlemanship.

Professor Anastaplo reminds us of the intolerance of Stalin's regime— and he might have mentioned Hitler's as well. He reminds us thereby of how a universal Science has replaced God as the highest authority for modern man. He reminds us, therefore, that the authority of Science has been utilized to undermine morality—and thereby gentlemanship and human decency—as completely as theological intolerance ever did. Moreover, the arguments vindicating the absolute authority of the party, as advanced in the confession of Rubachev (Bukharin) at the Moscow show trials of 1936, as portrayed in Koestler's *Darkness at Noon*, are virtually the same as those vindicating the Inquisition, as portrayed by Dostoevski.

We must remember that two of the greatest minds of the twentieth century were in the service of the two greatest tyrants of all time— Heidegger for Hitler, and Alexander Kojeve for Stalin. Gentlemanship is powerless to deal with such a phenomenon. Only a Leo Strauss could make the case against both Heidegger and Kojeve. For it was the self-destruction of reason in modern philosophy which was the necessary condition for the nihilistic loyalties generated in the regimes of Stalin and Hitler. Only by Strauss's destruction of this destruction has it been possible to restore the intelligibility of the political horizon of gentlemen.

Strauss made possible not only the restoration of gentlemanship, but of that highest form of gentlemanship which is statesmanship. It was Strauss who directed his students both to Lincoln and Churchill, who not only were great gentlemen, and skilled in the political arts, but who understood—as mere gentlemen could not—the evil wrought in the practical and political world by false theories. Apart from Strauss's destruction of historicism, apart from his restoration of the idea of understanding the great books as their authors understood them, the attempt to recapture the meaning of the statesman's art, by understanding Lincoln and Churchill as they understood themselves, would never have been possible.

### According to Professor Anastaplo

Too much of an emphasis upon the theoretical may even be seen in Mr. Jaffa's insistence upon the natural-right tradition of the Declaration of Independence to the virtual exclusion of the prescriptive rights of the English-speaking peoples. This is to ignore the central place given in the Declaration to the grievances grounded in the British Constitution.

In documents I have cited in " 'Original Intentions' of the Framers" it is clear that the elements of right in the British constitution to which the colonists appealed in the Revolution were regarded by them as being at one and the same time prescriptive and natural—" . . .it is an essential, unalterable right, in nature, ingrafted into the British Constitution, as a fundamental law . . . ." is a typical expression of this. (Letter of the Massachusetts General Court of 1768, cited above.) Prescriptive right was authoritative only when it was in accordance with natural right, or at least not contrary to natural right. I believe that every one of the grievances mentioned in the Declaration were regarded as violations of rights in nature. They may also have represented violations of British constitutionalism, but that in itself is merely incidental. Prescription, in and by itself, could furnish no ground of right, once the die had been cast for independence. In 1776 nothing lay closer to the historical and prescriptive heart of the British Constitution than the establishment of the Church of England with an hereditary Protestant monarch at its head. But nothing was more anathema to Americans, after independence. Prescription could no more make religious establishment or hereditary monarchy acceptable, than it could those "twin relics of barbarism, polygamy and slavery."

## IV.

Professor Anastaplo asks,

> Is there not an inevitable tension, because of the very nature of things, between philosophy and the city?

I believe I have already given the substance of my answer to this question in the foregoing. Let me observe that the relationship between philosophy and the city is equally one of tension and of mutual dependence. Philosophy cannot subsist without the city. But the health of the city depends, not upon philosophy, but upon morality. The natural representative of morality is not the philosopher, but the gentleman. But the gentleman cannot survive except with the assistance—not of philosophy *per se*, such as we see in the *Clouds*—but of political philosophy, such as we see in the *Republic* (and in the Lincoln-Douglas debates).

Professor Anastaplo thinks it is unfair of me to hold political men like Messrs. Meese, Rehnquist, and Brennan, to standards of theoretical scrutiny which, he concedes, are proper in the case of a "professional philosopher" like Leszek Kolakowski. But the former are essentially gentlemen gone astray (like the legendary Whiffenpoofs), while the latter is merely pretentious.

Let us consider for a moment the phenomenon of "professional philosophy." A philosopher is by definition a lover—a lover of wisdom. Another name for a professional lover, however, is prostitute. How a whole profession came to pin the tail of the donkey on itself (to mix my metaphor somewhat), in humorless unconsciousness of what it was doing, is a matter of some curiosity. Philosophy became a profession, however, not when those called philosophers accepted pay, but when they became only one specialized discipline within the many disciplines of the modern university. Each of these disciplines certified the competency of its practitioners by a degree called doctor of philosophy. The original premodern meaning of philosophy was that it was the attempt to replace opinions about the whole universe by knowledge of that whole. The recollection of this meaning is preserved in the word university, as characterizing the institutional home of philosophy. It is also preserved by the fact that each of the disciplines called its peculiar, but very partial and limited (and hence unphilosophic) knowledge "philosophy." Now, however, a doctorate of philosophy *in philosophy* was only one of many doctorates *of philosophy*. In more ways than one, as Leo Strauss often said, the discipline now called philosophy is only the rump of the original animal. Modern science, he said, represents the successful branches of modern philosophy, and what is still called by the name of philosophy represents only its residual elements.

I quoted from Professor Kolakowski's Jefferson lecture of 1986 at the beginning of Appendix B of ' "Original Intentions' of the Framers." The self-evident truths of the Declaration of Independence were, he said, in the light of the philosophic tradition "either patently false, meaningless, or superstitious . . ." It is needless to repeat what I have already said about this assertion. The Declaration of Independence expresses an opinion about man, God, and the universe, seen as a whole. This wholeness is simply beyond the range of Professor Kolakowski's comprehension. As a genuine "professional" he has no more notion of what the Declaration of Independence meant than if it had been inscribed on the Rosetta Stone. Truly, the rump does not know what the head once thought. Whatever their shortcomings, Messrs. Meese, Rehnquist, and Brennan are important people, because they hold—or have held—important offices. Most of their errors are what has been certified to them as truth by professional philosophers. This was notably evident in Rehnquist's casual and unquestioning acceptance of the fact/value distinction. This distinction, which underlies all of his jurisprudence, is one he accepted on authority, apparently without the least acquaintance with the proofs, real or alleged, upon which it rests. I agree with Professor Anastaplo that we should address the professional philosophers on their own turf—and he and I have both done so. But we cannot wait to instruct the jurists (and political men generally) until we have transformed the academic study of philosophy. Political men are victims of false doctrines given currency by the academy, and authority by the name of science. As members of the polity, we are all victimized by them together. In our free society, resting as it does upon opinion, we can be emancipated from untrue opinion only by true opinion, opinion resting upon hard reasoning, reasoning for which there is no substitute.

## V.

Professor Anastaplo asks,

> Does Mr. Jaffa mean to leave the impression that "the consent of the governed" is for the Declaration of Independence, as well as for himself, a necessary basis for legitimate government in all circumstances?

Professor Anastaplo knows my answer to this so well that I can only assume he is asking it on behalf of others! I have remarked, time and again, that the consent referred to in the second paragraph of the Declaration, must be understood to mean *enlightened* consent. In a memorable passage I often quote, George Washington declared that

> The foundation of our empire was not laid in the gloomy age of ignorance and superstition, but at an epoch when the rights of mankind were better understood and more clearly defined than at any former period . . .[6]

The Declaration itself refers to both "barbarous ages" and "merciless savages." One must assume that the consent that gives rise to the just powers of government is neither barbarous nor savage, but rather grounded in that understanding of the rights of man of which Washington wrote. It may certainly be the case that, in ages—and places—of ignorance and superstition, despotism in some form or other may become legitimate, because necessary. Certainly the existence in human societies of cannibalism, human sacrifice, slavery, polygamy, suttee, or untouchability, may require and therefore justify government that does not rest upon the consent of the barbarians or savages themselves. In fact, the Civil War amendments to the United States Constitution, although nominally grounded in consent, were actually imposed upon the defeated South by the victorious Union armies, and with entire justification. Having fought for the principle that some men might govern other men without their consent, the former Confederates could not reasonably complain of this compulsion in behalf of consent. However paradoxical the event, it was only by accepting the principles embodied in those amendments that the erstwhile rebels could be readmitted to a government grounded in their consent. Barbarism, however, must not be equated with primitivism—as it cannot be in the case of those antebellum Americans who fought for slavery, not as a necessary evil, but as a positive good. There is scientific barbarism as well, represented in our time by both Nazis and Communists. The failure of the Weimar Republic to outlaw these parties became the death sentence of much more than the Weimar Republic itself. The adherents of these murderous regimes had no more right than cannibals to participate in a free government. The right of revolution proclaimed in the Declaration of Independence—the right to alter or abolish governments—is a natural right to be exercised only when governments become "destructive of these ends." The ends are "to secure these rights," viz., the equal natural rights to life, liberty, and the pursuit of happiness. To destroy or to enslave other human beings, whose rights are equal to their own, is not a permissible end of the right of revolution. Nazis who followed Hitler, or Communists who followed Stalin, had no right to anything but an emancipation from their dangerous delusions. How this right might prudently be implemented is another question. But the principle is clear.

Professor Anastaplo says that "the consent of the governed" in the Declaration of Independence

> can be translated into terms used by Plato and Aristotle, but not without significant distortion. Certainly, Plato and Aristotle, as well as the Bible, recognize the possibility of just regimes without benefit of the consent of the governed. Mr. Jaffa, in his stance here, seem more in the spirit of Rousseau . . .

As I have argued above (and elsewhere), the problem of political obligation became a moral and political problem only with the establishment of monotheism as the predominant form of the religion of the West. For Plato, Aristotle, and the Bible, the source of political obligation was in the divine lawgivers of the city. This is as clear in Plato's *Laws* as it is in the *Torah*. It is one of the attributes of a gentleman that he needs no argument as to why he should be law-abiding. The *Nicomachean Ethics* is addressed only to those who are already disposed towards virtue and are in need only of instruction in how to become virtuous. But for the generality of the citizens, it is clear that for Aristotle as for Socrates, Xenophon, and Plato, the gods of the city remain the ground of the obligation of law. I have not distorted the relationship between the teaching of the Declaration and the teaching of the classics, because I have never identified the two in the sense implied by Professor Anastaplo. The classical political solutions are strictly speaking only for the ancient city. The Declaration addressed a problem peculiarly that of the Christian West, arising from the conflicting claims of reason and of revelation. The idea of human equality, independent of sectarian identity, led to the idea of the enlightened consent of the governed as the ground of law. It enfranchised Aristotle's idea of law as "reason unaffected by desire" by removing from the jurisdiction of theology and theologians the judgment of rationality. It was no less pious for doing so, because it incorporated into the idea of enlightened consent respect for the rights with which all mankind had been endowed by their Creator. Thus— as I have maintained—it made obedience to law, based upon consent, among our duties to God. In the Declaration—and more generally in the American Founding—we find a principled ground for law that we cannot find in Aristotle. What we do find, however, is fully in accordance with Aristotle's intention, within a framework consistent with biblical religion.

I believe my argument must be distinguished radically from Rousseau's since it both admits and requires for its foundation such an understanding of morality as one finds in the *Nicomachean Ethics*. The consent arising from the general will is a formal substitute for moral rationality, not a means of implementing it. The moral rationality of the *Nicomachean Ethics* and of the *Politics*, like that of the Declaration of Independence, is grounded in the objectivity of the distinctions between man, beast, and God. These distinctions in turn imply that "great chain of being" which is the metaphysical ground of the universe, and the object of philosophical speculation. For Rousseau, if I understand him, these distinctions have lost their evidence, and both philosophy and politics have thereby lost their respective sovereignties.

## VI.

Professor Anastaplo asks,

> Does Mr. Jaffa recognize sufficiently the merits of that freedom which he routinely subordinates to equality?

In Question II (with which this is paired) Professor Anastaplo had challenged me to recognize the shortcomings of equality, and now he repeats the same question by calling my attention to the merits of freedom! But as he well knows, I deny the premise of both forms of the question, and in particular deny that I—any more than Abraham Lincoln—have ever subordinated freedom to equality. I do not believe it is possible to do so, because the subordination of the one to the other would imply the misunderstanding of both. The fact that black human beings and white human beings are equally human beings is the ground of their equal right to freedom. To deny the one can only lead to the denial of the other. To affirm the one is also to affirm the other. As Alice learned in Wonderland, words can be made to mean whatever one wants them to mean. But in the vocabulary of the Declaration of Independence, and in Lincoln's vocabulary, no such distinction between freedom and equality as that suggested by Professor Anastaplo is tenable. The Gettysburg Address moves from the proposition of human equality, to the "new birth of freedom," and hence to the preservation of popular government. That these three are surely one was as surely Lincoln's faith as was his faith in the oneness of God.

For Lincoln, the essence of *liberty* was to give to all an *equal* chance. A fair start in the race of life is precisely the ground upon which the recognition of excellence depends. In removing the shackles of class, of race, of religion, of ethnic origin, the principle of equality provides the rewards of liberty hitherto denied to talent and virtue.

Professor Anastaplo observes that "freedom can deteriorate into simply living as one likes," that is to say, into license. To which we add that the principle of equal rights can deteriorate into what Leo Strauss called "permissive egalitarianism." It is easy to see that in their corruptions, freedom or liberty and equality are one. But equality uncorrupted rests upon the recognition of the inequality of man and beast, and of man and God. It implies an objective order of being, upon which is founded a prescriptive moral order. Liberty can deteriorate into license only as one forgets or ignores that one's liberty arises from one's nature, and can never be a liberty to reject or defy "the laws of nature and of nature's God." Our equality with other human beings is an equality within the boundaries of those same laws. It is an equality which arises from our rational nature, and which obligates us to know and obey the laws of that nature. It is an equality not only in one's rights, but in the duties arising from those rights. There is no ground here for mere permissiveness.

## VII.

Professor Anastaplo asks further,

What more should be said on behalf of Chief Justice Rehnquist and Associate Justice Brennan with respect to the matters touched upon by Mr. Jaffa?

He thus ends as he began, now entering pleas in behalf of the two justices—one conservative and the other liberal—as he did with respect to the former attorney general. Professor Anastaplo takes heart in the fact that

> Justice Brennan could say, upon the recent elevation of Justice Rehnquist, "He's going to be a splendid chief justice."

From this he concludes that

> Decent conservatives and decent liberals do have much in common.

But I would remind Professor Anastaplo that I ended " 'Original Intentions' of the Framers" with the observation—based, I believe, upon compelling evidence—that

> modern liberalism and modern conservatism . . . stand upon common ground. They are mirror images of each other. They differ only as to where Right and Left are located in the images.

Although I have no doubt that Brennan and Rehnquist are decent men, it is not their decency that is so conspicuous among the things they hold in common. It is their denial of the idea of natural justice, of "the laws of nature and of nature's God" that animated the generation of the American Founding. I am certain that Chief Justice Taney was every bit as decent a human being as Justices Brennan and Rehnquist. He was a man of strong moral and religious convictions, who was personally opposed to slavery and who freed his own slaves. Had he lived his life in a private station, that life might have been noted only for its purity and blamelessness. But as Aristotle says, "rule shows the man." As chief justice, and author of the opinion of the Court in the case of Dred Scott, he was one of history's greatest disasters. Justice Brennan, albeit a decent man, concurred in the Court's decision in *Roe v. Wade*, which many competent judges both of law and of decency regard as a disaster equaling if not surpassing *Dred Scott*. In that case Justice Rehnquist dissented on the ground that the Court, in ruling unconstitutional the abortion laws of fifty states, was usurping the legislative authority of the people of those states. This opinion was, I believe, perfectly correct. I find no fault with Justice Rehnquist for carefully avoiding any moral arguments with respect to abortion. In the circumstances of this case, that was the right thing for him to do. I only observe that, as far as it went, his dissent in *Roe v Wade* was entirely consistent with his legal positivism. It is difficult to imagine an exercise of state—or federal—legislative power that Justice Rehnquist would not uphold.

Professor Anastaplo has good things to say about Mr. Justice Rehnquist's opinions with respect to the free speech guarantee of the First Amendment. He finds it

> difficult to see what practical differences there are likely to be, in terms of how cases should be decided, between Mr. Jaffa and the chief justice, whatever theoretical shortcomings Mr. Jaffa may discern in the chief justice.

But Rehnquist's patronage of free speech is less an attachment to the cause of free speech, seen as a necessary ingredient of free government, than it is a manifestation of his inability to find any rational standard by which to distinguish free speech from any perversion or corruption of speech. What follows is a critique of the chief justice's opinion for the Court in the case of *Falwell v. Flynt.*

Our conservative Chief Justice Says Its All Right
To Call Your Mother an Incestuous Whore

The Supreme Court of the United States, in a unanimous (8 to 0) decision, has reversed a lower court ruling, which had upheld a jury's award of $200,000 to the Reverend Jerry Falwell in his suit against Larry Flynt, publisher of *Hustler* magazine. Flynt had published a fake advertisement for Campari liqueur, in which Falwell was portrayed as a drunk whose first sexual experience had been with his mother in an outhouse. The jury held that since this "satire" had been labeled (in small print, to be sure) as fiction, Falwell had not, strictly speaking, been libeled. But they awarded him the damages for his pain and mental suffering. The jury clearly felt that the image conjured up in the minds of many thousands of people of the young Falwell and his mother in the outhouse—whether or not they had paid any attention to the disclaimer—was so degrading and debasing, that Flynt should be punished, and Falwell indemnified. But the Supreme Court of the United States has decided that the jury was wrong, and that the representation of Falwell as having had sex with his mother in an outhouse is speech protected by the First Amendment.

> Debate on public issues will not be uninhibited if the speaker must run the risk that it will be proved in court that he spoke out of hatred; even if he did speak out of hatred, utterances honestly believed to contribute to the free interchange of ideas and the ascertainment of truth.

Thus spoke the Court in *Garrison v. Louisiana* (1964), in a passage cited to justify the present decision. But can the Court honestly believe that such a representation of the Reverend Falwell and his mother contributes to "the free interchange of ideas and the ascertainment of truth"? Larry Flynt, the publisher of *Hustler*, is a declared enemy of all traditional morality— indeed of all human decency—whether that of the Bible, or of unassisted human reason. Whether it is fornication, adultery, incest, or sodomy, Flynt wishes to destroy the dignity of moral restraint by mocking and ultimately destroying our sense of shame with respect to such things. His intent was not so much to make Falwell ridiculous, as to make the horror of incest— and the dignity of the human family—ridiculous. I for one would not deny Flynt full freedom of speech to argue—if he wishes—that all moral precepts such as that embodied in the prohibition of incest are primitive superstitions. But Flynt has no interest whatever in the "free interchange of ideas." And he has about as much interest in promoting "the ascertainment of truth" as he has in promoting chastity. I do not think that public exhibitions of shamelessness—or of pornographic exhibitionism—have anything to do with promoting the ends of free speech.

The opinion of the Court was written by Chief Justice Rehnquist, who placed the case in the context of political cartooning as a feature of "public and political debate" in a free society. He gave a number of examples of such cartoons, beginning with one of George Washington riding a donkey, with the caption underneath asking, "Which one is the ass?" Yet even Mr. Rehnquist sensed that it strained credulity to imply that "the caricature of respondent and his mother in *Hustler*" belonged to this genre. It was, he admitted, "at best a distant cousin" of even the most acerbic and hostile of the political cartoons he had described, "and a rather poor relation at that." In fact, the chief justice admitted (half-heartedly, to be sure) that Hustler's portrayal of Falwell and his mother did not really deserve First Amendment protection at all, but he thought that other (genuine) political cartoons and satires would be endangered, unless it received such protection.

> If it were possible by laying down a principled standard to separate one (viz., the *Hustler* genre) from the other (viz., the traditional political cartoon or satire), public discourse would probably suffer little or no harm. But we doubt that there is any such standard, and we are quite sure that the pejorative description "outrageous" does not supply one.

One might paraphrase the chief justice's argument at this point by saying that if we do not permit George Washington's mother to be called an incestuous whore, we might prevent someone from calling George Washington an ass!

Chief Justice Rehnquist did not deny that, however broad the protections afforded speech by the First Amendment's principles they

> like other principles, are subject to limitations. We recognized in *Pacifica Foundation*, that speech that is " 'vulgar,' 'offensive,' and 'shocking' " is "not entitled to absolute constitutional protection under all circumstances." In *Chaplinsky v. New Hampshire* (1942) we held that a state could lawfully punish an individual for the use of insulting or " 'fighting' words—those which by their very utterance inflict injury or tend to incite an immediate breach of the peace."

But, the chief justice concluded,

> the sort of expression involved in this case does not seem to us to be governed by any exception of the general First Amendment principles . . .

It is difficult for us to imagine what expressions are exceptions, and not deserving First Amendment protection, if calling a man's mother an incestuous whore is insufficiently "vulgar, offensive, and shocking." What insults are there that are so much more insulting as to constitute the "fighting words" of *Chaplinsky*? Mr. Justice Rehnquist thinks that

> outrageousness in the area of political and social discourse has an inherent subjectiveness about it which would allow a jury to impose liability on the basis of the jurors' tastes or views, or perhaps on the basis of their dislike of a particular expression.

But why is "outrageousness" subjective, while "vulgar," "offensive," and "shocking" are not? How do "outrageous" words differ from "fighting" words, in respect to their subjectivity? I would wager the eminent justices, that in any poll of adult American males, over 90 percent would say that calling a man's mother an incestuous whore is ample justification for punching someone in the nose. And I am confident that they would be supported by more than 90 percent of American womanhood. The public will be amazed, I think, to learn that the insult to Reverend Falwell, and to the memory of his mother, was merely subjective, and that the jury's reaction to "whore" or "incest" was merely a matter of taste, or that it merely reflected their subjective dislike of particular expressions. And what happened to the chief justice's famed jurisprudence of "original intent"? There is not even a whisper of it. Here if ever would have been an occasion to have asked what the Framers and Ratifiers of the First Amendment had in mind in distinguishing the speech that deserved, and that which did not deserve, constitutional protection. Are we not led to suspect that "original intent" is invoked only when it supports the chief justice's own subjective "value judgments"?

Larry Flynt is confined to a wheel chair (having been shot as a consequence of a previous outrage), and Reverend Falwell is a minister of the Gospel. Hence there was no question here of any recourse to physical chastisement for redress. Apparently there can be no question now of legal redress either. We may be sure, therefore, that this decision will go a long way towards promoting physical violence in cases in which one party is not a minister, and the other is not a cripple. This is a setback—not a victory—for the cause of free speech. This decision will have a chilling effect upon many who might enter public life, but are unwilling to accept such abuse—particularly when it is directed, not against themselves, but against their wives, mothers, or daughters.

Let us conclude our formal reply to Professor Anastaplo's "seventh query" by reminding him of the legal positivism grounded upon moral relativism, which constitutes the heart of Justice Rehnquist's jurisprudence. Justice Rehnquist holds that all moral judgments are "value judgments," and as such equally indemonstrable, equally immune to rational discrimination. All constitutional rights, e.g., to life, liberty, property, freedom of religion, speech, press, association, etc., are grounded in moral preferences or "values." Justice Rehnquist's opposition to "judicial activism" consists in holding that, in a democracy, the preferences of the people (i.e., the *demos*) expressed through their elected representatives—and not nonelected judges—ought to decide what these "values" mean and how they are to be implemented. As we have already pointed out, however, this is a non sequitur. If all values are equally subjective there is no reason to prefer one to another. There is nothing in a "preference" for democracy which requires one to prefer the legislature's value judgments to the judiciary's. Rehnquist's preference for legislative over judicial interpretation of the Constitution is itself—on Rehnquist's own premises—no more than a "value judgment." What if the people themselves *want* the Supreme Court to be the arbiter of the relationship between majority rule and minority rights? If that is what the people want, why is it not democratic? That was the thesis of Judge Bork's 1968 *Fortune* article. It is precisely at this point that Justice Brennan, and his followers, have the better of the argument. But, as Bork observed in the same article, the argument for the

Court as arbiter of the relationship between majority rule and minority rights is grounded in what Bork called the Madisonian system of natural rights. But this system—to use Bork's phraseology—assumes that constitutional rights are derived, not from subjective "values"—but from objective reality. According to Madison (and all the Founding Fathers) nature (and not value judgments) is the unchanging ground of our changing experience of the moral phenomena. Principles derived from nature do not evolve, as Justice Brennan supposes. Their application, however, should be guided by prudence, which always reflects an awareness, not of changing principles, but of changing circumstances.

While commending Mr. Rehnquist, Professor Anastaplo also warns him, when he writes:

> It is to be hoped that the chief justice will not so forget himself and his high calling as to subvert the teaching function of his office by proclaiming from the Bench what one of his predecessors did (in order to justify packing some Communist party leaders off to jail in 1951) . . .

What Professor Anastaplo found so offensive, was the following passage from Chief Justice Vinson's opinion for the Court in *Dennis v United States.*

> Nothing is more certain in modern society than the principle that there are no absolutes, that a name, a phrase, a standard has meaning only when associated with the considerations which gave birth to the nomenclature . . . To those who would paralyze our government in the face of impending threat by encasing it in a semantic strait jacket, we must reply that all concepts are relative.

Professor Anastaplo and I are agreed that "the teaching function" of the office of chief justice (and indeed of the Supreme Court as a whole) is not surpassed in importance by any of its other functions. That is why I find Mr. Justice Rehnquist's moral relativism and legal positivism so harmful, even though they do not always or necessarily lead to opinions or decisions with which I disagree.

I am quite confident, however, that Mr. Justice Rehnquist, had he been sitting on the high Court in 1951—Professor Anastaplo to the contrary notwithstanding—would have voted with the majority in upholding the Smith Act and in packing those Communist party leaders off to jail. The same reasons which led him to vote against the majority in *Roe v. Wade* (that the Court should not usurp the legislative powers of the states) would have led him to vote not to usurp the legislative power of Congress to decide upon the means to prevent the success of a conspiracy to overthrow the government of the United States by force and violence. And I must confess that I think he would have been as right in the one case as in the other. This does not mean that it is impossible that president and Congress might not in fact be engaged in a conspiracy against the constitutional rights of unpopular minorities. (In the House Divided speech of 1858, Lincoln charged two presidents, a chief justice, and a United States senator with just such a conspiracy.) As we shall see, Chief Justice Vinson conceded that the Court has a role to review the action of Congress to make sure that this does not happen. He held, however, that there is a strong presumption in favor of the political branches of the government when it comes to political judgments as to the political dangers that the country may be facing. Justices Black and Douglas, in dissenting in the *Dennis* case, believed that Congress in passing the Smith Act, and the executive in prosecuting Communist party leaders under it, were simply bending to a popular hysteria, and not to real danger. I believe that these dissenting justices, and those who, like Professor Anastaplo, agreed with them, were wrong.

Let me at this point enter my own dissent to Professor Anastaplo's assumption that the Court's opinion in the *Dennis* case rested upon moral relativism. The "relativistic" passage which he cites is preceded by the following.

> The basis of the First Amendment is the hypothesis that speech can rebut speech, propaganda will answer propaganda, free debate of ideas will result in the wisest governmental policies. It is for this reason that this Court has recognized the inherent value of free discourse . . .

What Chief Justice Vinson calls the "inherent value of free discourse" is not what Rehnquist means by a "political value judgment." Vinson implies that the benefits of free speech are intrinsic to the speech itself. Moreover, Chief Justice Vinson is not a relativist when he declares that

> Speech is not an absolute, above and beyond control of the legislature when its judgment, subject to review here, is that certain kinds of speech are so undesirable as to warrant criminal sanction.

This is a mere truism, and one which we saw Chief Justice Rehnquist repeat in the case of *Falwell v Flynt*. All speech is not free speech. Free speech has never been understood to include the right falsely to shout "Fire!" in a crowded theater, and there are many other such exceptions, such as libel, slander, obscenity, fighting words, speech aimed at conspiracies in restraint of trade, the speech of employers to their workers to dissuade them from joining unions, incitement to crime, etc. Among the kinds of speech inciting to crime that Congress has a right to prevent are speeches inciting to acts to overthrow the government by force and violence. It has generally been recognized that the speeches may be criminal only in relationship to some proximity of probability that the criminal acts might actually occur. (Falsely shouting "Fire" in an empty, rather than a crowded theater might be judged no crime at all. Or the "false" shout of "Fire" might be part of the play that the audience in the crowded theater is watching.) Of course, as already noted, Congress (or the president) may not strike at someone's freedom of speech on the pretext that a danger exists when there is none (e.g., by pretending the theater was full when it was empty), and the Court has a duty to consider whether such may not be the case. To repeat: that the danger from the Communist party was merely a pretext engendered by hysteria was the hypothesis of Justices Black and Douglas's dissents. That there was reasonable ground for regarding the danger as real was the hypothesis of Chief Justice Vinson's opinion for the Court. Who was right?

Constitutional cases are not decided in a vacuum. For good or for ill, all law is a by-product of politics. Politics is the fundamental reality, of which constitutional law is an epiphenomenon. No answer to the foregoing question can have any validity, unless we are aware of the circumstances in which the Smith Act was passed, and of the events that intervened between its passing and the prosecutions under it that culminated in the *Dennis* case.

The act was passed in 1940, at a time when the two bloodiest tyrants of all time—Hitler and Stalin—were allies. Nothing—not even the Moscow trials of 1936—revealed the character of the American Communist party, and the international organization of which it was a part, more completely than the reversals of the party line, first on August 23, 1939, and then on June 22, 1941. Prior to the first of these two dates, American Communists were supporting a "popular front," with the fanatical zeal and rhetorical extravagance with which they pursued all their enterprises. This meant an alliance of the Western "bourgeois" democracies—together with the Soviet Union—against "fascism," meaning primarily the regime of Adolf

Hitler. With the signing of the Molotov-Ribbentrop—that is, Hitler-Stalin—Pact, all talk of such a "front" ceased. From the moment that France and Britain declared war on Germany, shortly after the Nazi invasion of Poland on September 1, 1939, the American Communist party declared that the war was one between capitalist powers in whose outcome the peoples of the world had no stake.

Stalin's invasion and annexation of the eastern half of Poland—all of which Hitler had agreed to in their pact—drew no criticism whatever. Nor did the American Communist party recognize Stalin's murder of the entire Polish officer corps. The Polish army in 1939 had surrendered to the Soviets as they retreated from the Nazis. Some fifteen thousand commissioned officers were interned separately from about 300,000 noncoms and enlisted men. After the Nazi invasion of the USSR some twenty-two months later, the Polish army—minus its officers, who were never again seen alive—was released from internment and formed into units of the Red Army to fight against the Wehrmacht, which they did very effectively. The bodies of somewhat fewer than half the missing officers were discovered by the Nazis in July 1941 in shallow graves in the Katyn Forest—in what had been Soviet-occupied Poland. That they had been dead long before the Nazi invasion was confirmed at the time by the International Red Cross. Of course, Stalin's propaganda machine denied the allegations and called it all a Nazi plot. But the Poles—and Western intelligence—knew that what the Red Cross confirmed was true.[7]

After the fall of France in June 1940, with all of Western Europe subjugated, Hitler stood at the very summit of his fortunes—and on the very edge of complete victory. If the Nazi occupation of Eastern and Western Europe was any threat to the future of human freedom, the American Communist party did not recognize it. If there was any danger to the United States from what appeared to be the imminent conquest of Churchill's Britain, the American Communist party did not appear to notice it. All this changed overnight, however, when on June 21, 1941, the Wehrmacht crossed the Soviet border. Then and then only did Hitler once again become the threat to freedom which the American Communists had recognized before August 23, 1939.

Since the end of the Second World War, Communists, and their dupes and apologists, have insisted that Stalin's agreement with Hitler in August 1939 was intended only to buy time to prepare for the assault that he knew was coming. The real guilt, they say, was that of the Western appeasers—for example, the famous Cliveden set in England—who at Munich had deliberately turned Hitler to the East, in the expectation that if he was given a free hand to build his empire there, he would leave the West alone. (Churchill called this feeding the crocodile, in the hope that he would eat you last.) As a rejection of the policy of appeasement, taken by itself, this was and is perfectly correct. Everything in Hitler's propaganda, about Slavs, Jews, and Bolsheviks, suggested that the *Drang nach Osten* was what he cared about most. As a justification of Stalin's deal with Hitler, unleashing the assault upon Poland, and initiating the Second World War, it is one of history's damnedest lies. It implies that Stalin anticipated Hitler's attack and was preparing for it. In fact, Stalin stubbornly refused to believe that that attack was imminent, even up to the minute before it began. The movement of German troops, tanks, artillery, and supplies, from west to east up to the Soviet borders, was so enormous, that there could scarcely have been anyone in Europe who was not aware of it. Both Roosevelt and Churchill sent warnings to Stalin, but they were ignored. After all, they were capitalists, and Hitler was a brother socialist! History does not record a more paranoid assassin than Josef Stalin: before the war he had murdered almost all of his old Bolshevik comrades and had wiped out virtually the entire officer corps of the Red Army, upon suspicions that no one else believed—or dared to challenge. Yet Stalin for one time only in his life put his trust in someone. And that someone was Adolf Hitler!

The evidence of that trust is in the circumstances that cost the Red Army, in the early weeks of the war, several millions of men, most of them taken prisoner. (Some 2 million Russian POWs died in captivity.) Not only were the Soviet divisions not in a state of readiness, but whole army groups were deployed in positions near the frontiers, where they were exposed to the same blitzkrieg tactics that had destroyed the French army only a year before. Not a schoolchild in Russia did not know that Russian strategy in dealing with Napoleon consisted in allowing the invader to dissipate his forces over the great distances—and bad roads and bad winters—of Russia, and then counterattacking. In the end, this is how the Russians did defeat the Wehrmacht. But they must have taken twice the casualties that they would have taken had Stalin not been such an incompetent dupe. Hitler's attack employed hardly any deception. And yet he achieved complete tactical surprise. The facts refute any idea that Stalin had been warily preparing for the assault he knew was coming.

It is, moreover, impossible to reconcile the claim that Stalin was buying time in order to prepare for Hitler's attack with his aid to Hitler's war machine during the period of their collaboration. His pact with Hitler went far beyond nonaggression. Pursuant to his agreement with Hitler, he had greedily annexed the eastern half of Poland, together with Lithuania,

Latvia, Estonia, parts of Finland, Eastern Galicia, and Bessarabia (eastern Rumania). But pursuant to secret elements in that same agreement, he had supplied the German war machine with huge supplies of all kinds, but principally of oil and grain. Indeed, at the very moment the Wehrmacht crossed the Soviet frontiers, there were hundreds of loaded Russian freight cars moving supplies towards German destinations.

We should remember that the British blockade brought Germany to its knees in World War One. When Germany surrendered in 1918, its armies were still in France and were unconquered in the field. But the home front behind them had collapsed, because of food and material shortages. Stalin's pact with Hitler—if Hitler had kept his part of the bargain—would have assured Germany that this would not happen again.

Stalin must have seen that Hitler's true policy after the fall of France was the defeat of Britain. We have Liddell Hart's assurance that Hitler could almost certainly have accomplished this defeat had he concentrated his resources upon the Battle of the Atlantic. Churchill virtually concedes as much in his history of the Second World War. Stalin must have known—as President Roosevelt knew—that if Britain fell, an overwhelming maritime supremacy would have fallen to the Axis. Had Hitler controlled the British fleet, together with the German, French, and Italian fleets he would, together with Japan, have so surpassed the United States in naval power (and the resources of naval power) as to leave the American coasts indefensible. The United States would have had no option but to accommodate itself to Hitler's new world order. From every rational point of view, it was Britain, not Russia, that stood between Hitler and his dreams of a Thousand Year Reich. With victory over Britain, the Third Reich—in some sort of partnership with Italy and Japan—would have inherited the British, French, Dutch, Portuguese, and Belgian colonial empires. All this was within Hitler's reach, if only he retained Stalin as his partner. Stalin never expected him to jeopardize such sure success by making Napoleon's mistakes all over again. Yet this is what Hitler did. But let us make no mistake about it: the policy supported by the American Communist party was one which envisaged the end of American freedom in a world dominated by Hitler and his allies, among them the USSR. The junior partnership in the Thousand Year Reich, which Churchill rejected with such scorn when it was offered after the fall of France, was eagerly sought by Stalin and his followers.

The American Communists were not the isolated band of crackpot revolutionaries Justices Douglas and Black supposed them to be in their dissenting opinions in the *Dennis* case. However ineffectual they might have appeared to others, every one of them carried his marshal's baton in his knapsack. Their purpose was not merely to hold academic seminars on Marxism-Leninism. The American Communist party was no more "theoretical" than the powerless radicals who surrounded Lenin in Zurich. "To the Finland Station" was inscribed on their banners, as it was on the banners of all the members of the Comintern. The "seminars," such as they were (again, like those of Lenin in Zurich), were designed to create the morale that would enable them to serve as Fifth Columns, and as the core of future governments, just as much as the Nazi organizations in Norway (and elsewhere) had done, and as the Bunds in the United States and much of Latin America were prepared to do—and as the Communist parties in Eastern Europe were already doing. The Communist party, U.S.A., during the period of the Nazi-Soviet Pact—at the time the Smith Act was passed—expected to be in the vanguard of a new totalitarian world order, in which democracy and civil liberties would be wiped from the face of the earth.

Six months after the Wehrmacht invaded the USSR, the United States was attacked by Japan, and shortly thereafter Hitler declared war on the United States. The U.S.A. and the USSR became allies. The United States had begun providing lend-lease aid to the USSR even before Pearl Harbor. It continued to do so in ever- increasing amounts, up until the final victory in Europe—for which generosity it never received the least thanks. Thereafter it supplied food, fuel, and medical supplies to the Russian people, as it did to war-ravaged peoples everywhere. From the moment the United States entered the war on the side of the USSR the American Communist party gave full support to the American war effort. Communists enlisted and served with distinction in all theaters, many attaining high rank as officers. But the party never deviated from regarding Stalin's interests, as he understood them, as paramount. This was evident when the clamor arose in 1942 for a "second front now." An attempted invasion of Europe by Anglo-American forces in that year would have been disastrous. Only Churchill's influence prevented it. There were many lesser episodes of this kind, nearly all of them exploiting ancient American prejudices against British "imperialism," with the effect of steadily lessening Churchill's influence in the strategic planning of the combined chiefs. As Leo Strauss was wont to say, the American conception of an empire—encouraged then by the Communist party—was one of a regime whose dominions were separated by water.

When the war ended, the admiration, and even affection, of the American people and their government towards the Red Army, the Soviet peoples, and "Uncle Joe," was boundless. There was no largess that would have been denied to the Soviets in helping them repair the devastation of war and rebuild their economy. The Soviet Union—and all of Europe—was invited to participate in the Marshall Plan. In the Baruch Plan of 1946 the U.S. offered to place its nuclear weapons program under international control, in a partnership, with the USSR, which had not then detonated its first nuclear device. All these overtures Stalin refused. The Iron Curtin descended. Communist parties under Stalin's absolute control, backed by the Red Army and the Secret Police, imposed on all of Eastern Europe a despotism every bit as ruthless as the one from which they had so recently been liberated. Stalin's pledges, made at Yalta, to provide free elections in Poland (or anywhere else) were ruthlessly thrust aside. The Cold War had begun. Once again, the American Communist party showed unmistakably where its unquestioned loyalties lay. It blindly endorsed Stalin's tyranny in everything it did, and worked tirelessly to obstruct and oppose every effort to resist and contain the spread of the new Soviet Empire. But the Communist party, U.S.A., had important allies in its crusade, because the pre-Pearl Harbor isolationists were nearly as vigorous in opposing resistance to Stalin as they once had been with respect to Hitler.

In the politics of those years, the myth that the Communist party was just an American political party, and not part of an international conspiracy, was an essential feature of Stalinist propaganda. Because it coopted the rhetoric of liberal democracy and of liberal internationalism, communism was in certain respects a greater danger than national socialism had been. In the name of communism, Stalin claimed to speak for the whole human race, where Hitler had spoken only of Aryan supremacy. In denying credibility to this Stalinist myth, the prosecutions under the Smith Act—like the prosecution of Alger Hiss, and the loyalty and security programs initiated by the Truman administration—performed a necessary and invaluable political service. Together with the Un-American Activities Committee of the House and the Internal Security Committee of the Senate, they voiced those fears of the American people that enabled them to come to grips with their new international responsibilities—in preserving from Stalin the freedom which they had just saved from Hitler and the Axis.

In the years following the war Stalin came very close to succeeding where Hitler had failed. In 1946, in the words of Winston Churchill, nothing stood between the Red Army and the English Channel but the American monopoly of the atom bomb. Churchill's Iron Curtain speech sounded the tocsin of Western resistance and led eventually to the formation of NATO. The advice which he had given a decade earlier, and which had gone unheeded, now fell on more receptive ears. The disintegration of the Stalinist empire, of which we may see the beginning four decades later, was what Churchill prophesied would happen if the West stayed the course against it. As he said in the Iron Curtain speech, the Russian Communists did not want war, they wanted only the fruits of war.[8]

Professor Anastaplo and I do not, I think, differ on the essential nature of the free speech guarantees of the First Amendment. We differ concerning the *Dennis* case, because we differ as to the facts concerning the nature of the Communist conspiracy, both at the time of the passage of the Smith Act, and at the time of the prosecutions of the Communist party members in 1950. In *The Constitutionalist*, Anastaplo quotes the following from Justice Black's dissent in *Dennis*:

> These petitioners were not charged with an attempt to overthrow the Government. They were not charged with overt acts of any kind . . . They were not even charged with saying anything or writing anything designed to overthrow the Government. The charge was that they agreed to assemble and to talk and publish certain ideas at a later date: The indictment is that they conspired to organize the Communist party and to use speech or newspapers and other publications in the future to teach and advocate the forcible overthrow of the Government . . .[9]

The political naivete of this passage is remarkable considering that when it was written the United States (under the aegis of the United Nations) was engaged in a very large war against Communist North Korea, a war supported and supplied by Stalin. Needless to say, the American Communist party took the communist, not the American, view of this conflict. It was also widely believed at the time—correctly in my opinion—that Stalin's goals in this conflict were not only to dominate Japan (and therewith the Far East altogether), but so to tie down American military power in the Far East as to cause it to disengage from Europe.

In the same footnote—and on the same page—of *The Constitutionalist*, Professor Anastaplo reproduces passages from a letter of Earl Browder, published in the *New York Times* of January 8, 1954. Browder writes that he had given sworn testimony before a Senate Committee

> that the Communist party under my leadership from 1930 to 1945 was not a conspiracy for the overthrow of the existing Government of the United States, that it did not engage in espionage for Russia, that it did not accept orders from Moscow, and did not wish to subordinate America to Russia . . .

It is not clear whether Professor Anastaplo expects us to take this assertion seriously. No one who accepted the evidence upon which Alger Hiss's conviction in 1948 was based could doubt that members of the American Communist party engaged in espionage. Concerning the denial by Browder that the party was engaged in a conspiracy to overthrow the government of the United States, I submit the following from an interview by Roy Howard with Stalin, published in the *New York World-Telegram* of March 4, 1936.[10] At one point in the discussion Howard called to Stalin's attention

> Mr. Litvinov's letter of November 16, 1933, to President Roosevelt, containing the famous paragraph 4, reading "not to permit the formation or residence on its territory of any organization or group . . . which has as an aim the overthrow *or the preparation for the overthrow of*. . .the political or social order . . . of the United States . . ." [Italics added.]

Howard then asked Stalin,

> Did not Browder and Darcy, American Communists, appearing before the seventh congress of the Communist International in Moscow last summer, appeal for the overthrow by force of the American government?

Stalin replied

> I don't recall what Browder and Darcy said. Maybe they said something of that nature, but the Soviet people did not found the American Communist party.
> The American Communist party was created by Americans. Its existence in the United States is legal . . . What Browder and Darcy may have said in Moscow probably will be said a hundred times in stronger terms on American soil. It would be unfair to hold the Soviet government responsible for the activities of American Communists.

No Muscovite since Stalin would doubt Stalin's disingenuousness in pretending not to remember what Browder and Darcy said. There were no speeches at the seventh congress that had not been approved beforehand by the Kremlin—if not actually written under its direction. In any case, we have Roy Howard's word for it that Browder and Darcy had in fact called for the overthrow of the American government. In remarking that what Browder and Darcy "may have said" in Moscow would be said "a hundred times stronger on American soil," Stalin shows that Browder was lying in the 1954 letter to the *New York Times*.

Roy Howard then pressed Stalin, asking

> is it not a fact that their activities [viz., those of the American Communist party at the seventh congress] occurred on Soviet soil contrary to the terms of paragraph 4?

This was Stalin's reply.

> You mention the activity of American Communists on Soviet soil; what does activity of the Communist party mean? Organization meetings, sometimes strikes, demonstrations, etc. They couldn't possibly organize them on Soviet soil. We have no American workers in the USSR.

If, as Stalin implies, the functions of the American Communist party were directed to organizing American workers, why were Browder and Darcy in Moscow at all? Above all, why were they, as an American political party ["represented by ballot even in national elections," Stalin noted] calling in Moscow for "the overthrow by force of the American government"? Is it not plain that they were doing so as members of the Communist International, and that this was no mere academic exercise in Marxism-Leninism? Their intent, at every level of their activity, was to act with other communist parties—and to as great an extent as possible with communist governments—to bring about a condition in which the overthrow of the government of the United States would become possible. This was precisely what they were charged with doing under the Smith Act.

From all of the foregoing we conclude that the decision in the *Dennis* case—and the opinion of the Court (whatever its technical legal merits or demerits)—was fundamentally sound.

A word needs to be said about the political sentiment of anticommunism—sometimes called "McCarthyism"—in the period following World War II. Professor Anastaplo was to some extent a victim of this sentiment when in 1950 he was asked by the character committee of the Illinois bar the wholly improper question, as to whether he had ever been a member of that unpleasant band of enemies of human freedom. I say the question was improper, since there was no ground for supposing that

Anastaplo, any more than the man asking the question—or any other living human being—had countenanced the aims of the Communist party. It was also irrational because, as the case of Alger Hiss proved, had he been a secret Communist he would not have hesitated for a moment to deny his connection with that party. It was apparent from the outset that Anastaplo refused to answer the question because the very idea that he might have been a Communist impugned his integrity, and he believed that in defending that integrity he was defending the integrity of the American Constitution and the principles upon which it was based—the principles of the Declaration of Independence.

I think it important to recognize that there was no difference between Professor Anastaplo and his inquisitors as to the tyrannical nature of communism. They failed to realize that the very reason for his refusing to answer their questions was what made him an indomitable enemy of tyranny. He, on the other hand, failed to realize the importance of the political exigencies under which they were laboring because of the treachery of Stalin and his American allies.

The political chances that had led to the replacement of Henry Wallace with Harry Truman, as Roosevelt's vice-president in 1945, measure how close Stalin might have come to complete success in the years immediately following Roosevelt's death. Nothing could have prevented Stalin's complete victory over freedom had the president of the United States been his witting, or unwitting, accomplice. And Wallace's behavior in the years following 1946 provide ample reason for believing he would have been just that. For Wallace belonged to the ranks of those who saw in Truman's Churchillian antagonism to Stalin a betrayal of the legacy of Franklin D. Roosevelt. For these people, British imperialism, symbolized by Churchill—and not communism—was the real enemy. It was Truman who invited Churchill to Westminster, Missouri, and who sat on the platform as he delivered the Iron Curtain speech. Truman soon became— along with Churchill—an arch demon of the Cold War. It was Truman's supreme political achievement, however, at one and the same time, to persuade the Republicans—in the person of Senator Vandenberg—to abandon isolationism, while persuading the Democratic party to abandon Roosevelt's fatuous illusions about Stalin. Truman's expulsion of Wallace from his cabinet, and his expulsion of Wallace's followers from the government, were a necessary foundation for the anticommunist foreign policy he followed from late 1946 onwards.

The loyalty-security programs of the Truman years were the heart of what later was known—incorrectly, I believe—as "McCarthyism." The driving out of the government of the Communist and proto-Communist followers of Wallace by Truman was an absolutely necessary condition for his policy of containment. Because of it Wallace broke with the regular Democrat party and formed the Progressive party in the 1948 presidential election. By it, he hoped to split the Democrat vote and defeat Truman. But it was precisely the rallying behind Wallace of the Communists and their fellow-travelers that proved Truman's anticommunist credentials to the American people, and led to his stunning upset victory. All this is brilliantly explained and documented in Samuel Lubell's *The Future of American Politics*—the definitive work on the 1948 presidential election. It would have been more than one could reasonably have expected of human nature to think that the politics that had carried Truman to victory in 1948 would have been abandoned in 1950. But in a popular government such as ours, it would have been impossible to carry on a bipartisan foreign policy which represented a break with strong traditions in both parties without the strongest popular support.

I would conclude by reminding my readers that, before the publication in 1959 of *Crisis of the House Divided*, American historical scholarship was nearly unanimous in condemning Lincoln for fanning the flames of the slavery controversy in the House Divided speech and in the Lincoln-Douglas debates. It was said that he exploited an emotion-laden issue for the sake of his own political ambition. That same scholarship saw the Civil War as an unnecessary war, because the question that divided North and South was a moral question, which could not be resolved by compromise, whereas true statesmanship (it was thought) would have worked for a practical solution that ignored the moral differences.

Lincoln's policy was one of containing slavery, preventing its spread, although leaving it untouched (ultimately to wither and die) in the States in which it already existed. What Lincoln saw as fundamental to that policy was recognition of the moral wrong of slavery. Without recognizing that, the people would not be prepared to make the sacrifices that might be required to oppose the spread of slavery. All the practical compromises that ignored the moral question would sooner or later break down, Lincoln thought, because it would always be in someone's interest to enslave other human beings. It seems to me that Churchill and Truman's (and, I might add, Leo Strauss's) policy with respect to communism directly parallels Lincoln's with respect to slavery. Like Lincoln's policy, if it was to succeed it required first and foremost a moral condemnation of communism in the popular mind—a hatred of communism, like slavery, as something intrinsically evil. Such moral condemnations cannot be expressed always with the equivocations and reservations of philosophic casuistry. The hunt for copperheads during the Civil War was not always as humane or restrained as Lincoln himself might have wished. What was supremely important was that the Union was preserved, slavery was destroyed, and the rule of law as an expression of human equality was vindicated. If—as I pray we do—we see communism today beginning to reveal itself to be "in the course of ultimate extinction," it is because—like slavery in 1860—it was resisted at the crest of its power, at a moment when it might easily have triumphed.

# Seven Answers for Professor Anastaplo

1. See, however, the "Afterword: Four Letters to Edwin Meese III."
2. Leon Higginbotham, *In the Matter of Color: Race and the American Legal Process, The Colonial Period*, Oxford, 1978.
3. *The Collected Works of Abraham Lincoln*, Roy P. Basler, ed., Rutgers University Press, 1953, Vol. 3, pp. 317–18. (Henceforth, *CW*.)
4. *CW*, Vol. 7, pp. 259–60.
5. This eleventh-century work is available in an English translation. Schocken Paperback Edition, Schocken Books, New York, 1964.
6. *George Washington: A Collection*, W. B. Allen, ed., Liberty Classics, 1988, pp. 240–241.
7. For an authoritative account by a member of the Polish underground, see J. K. Zawodny, *Death in the Forest*, University of Notre Dame Press, 1962. More recently, Zawodny's account has been confirmed from sources within the former Soviet Union itself.
8. These words were written in the summer of 1989, before the fall of the Berlin Wall, and the subsequent dissolution, first of the Soviet Empire in Eastern Europe, and then of the USSR itself.
9. George Anastaplo, *The Constitutionalist: Notes on the First Amendment*, Southern Methodist University Press, Dallas, Texas, 1971, p. 620, note 46.
10. Stalin's interview with Roy Howard was brought to my attention by Dr. John West.

HARRY V. JAFFA

A.

# The Founders of Our Founders: Jerusalem, Athens, and the American Constitution

To his seven questions Professor Anastaplo has added three appendices. These are lectures which were given at different times, not in their origin directed specifically to me. Nonetheless, they have the most profound relevance to the ground, not only of American constitutionalism, but of all constitutionalism, as seen in the light of the work of Leo Strauss. The title of the first of these lectures is at the head of this paragraph. The lifework of Strauss can perhaps be best summarized as the attempt to comprehend the meaning of that civilization constituted in its center and at its peaks by Jerusalem and Athens. It was also, of course, an attempt to preserve the idea of such a civilization from the self-destruction of reason, and the destruction of faith, in modern philosophy. Professor Anastaplo's lifework and my own can perhaps be best understood in the light of the relationship of Jerusalem and Athens to the American Constitution or, alternatively, of the relationship of the American Constitution to Jerusalem and Athens. Our work also is devoted, of course, to preserving the dignity of the American Founding from the corrosive effects of that relativism, dissolving into nihilism, against which Strauss had warned.

Professor Anastaplo has in fact raised for my consideration this question: Is not the American Constitution—as an expression of the principles of the

Declaration of Independence—an expression of the attempt by modern philosophy to solve the problem of political life by lowering its goals? Is it, that is, an attempt to remove from political concern and contention differences concerning what is the human good, the good of the human soul—the central concern of both classical philosophy and of the Bible—and replace it with concern for the good of the body? Professor Anastaplo has, I believe, indicated his own position with respect to this question by declaring "the Founders of Our Founders" to be Jerusalem and Athens. However, Professor Anastaplo wishes me to address this question because there are among the "Straussians" those who maintain that the true philosophic progenitor of the American Constitution (whether in his own person, or disguised as John Locke!) is the radically modern Thomas Hobbes.

Hobbes replaced the *summum bonum* with the *summum malum*—fear of violent death—as the central concern of political philosophy. Hobbes was able to do this by insisting that the only ultimate reality was body and its motions, that the only good of a body possessed of sensation was pleasure, and that the idea of an immaterial soul (or an immaterial God or good) was a delusion. According to this school the Founders believed with Hobbes (secretly, to be sure, while maintaining outward piety) that mankind might enjoy an immortal peace once it had been persuaded to accept materialism, hedonism, and atheism, as the ground of political life. From this perspective, the true albeit clandestine intention of the Founders was a regime that might sing of the Star Spangled Banner, while being in truth "the land of the fearful and the home of the coward." There would then be little ultimate difference between a regime built upon the principles of the Declaration of Independence, and one built upon the principles of the Communist Manifesto. Marx is seen as the latter-day version of Hobbes (in fact, Hobbes modified by Rousseau, so that modern natural right is transformed into History). If the difference between capitalism and communism becomes one of means, and not of ends, an intelligent Communist might be persuaded that a free market and not centrally directed collectivism is the true road to peace and prosperity. But we may be confident that "the God that failed" communism would in the end also fail a liberal democracy that had no higher view of man and his destiny than that of Hobbes or Marx. That the free market can prevent the dehumanization of man is no part of the argument of free market economics. I think—as I believe Professor Anastaplo does—that a mankind dehumanized by Hobbes's or Marx's (or their nihilist successors') conception of the soul might seek its fulfillment as well in war and genocide (or cannibalism) as in peacefully grazing in the meadows of modern consumption.

However plausible the view of the American Founding as radically modern (Hobbesian, crypto-Marxist, or neonihilist) might sometimes appear, it is radically mistaken, because it ignores the way in which the Founding Fathers (and Abraham Lincoln, their greatest interpreter) understood themselves. The view is plausible, I might add, because of the successful sophistry with which materialism, atheism, and hedonism have for over four centuries presented themselves as alone consistent with the ground of modern Science. Science has been visibly and tangibly successful in providing through technology the goods of the body, both by increasing the supply of goods for consumption, and by conquering so many of the diseases to which the body—by the uncontrolled efficient causes in nature—is heir. And these are the very things—health and wealth—for which most people through most of human history have prayed. Certainly, what is called religion today often (whether consciously or not) replaces God with Science, even as it prays to God. (People pray that Science will find a cure for cancer, or a cure for AIDS!) One might even say that the consummation of contemporary religion, from its own point of view, would come in that day when Science had answered all its prayers, for health, wealth, peace, and freedom—so that there would be nothing left to pray for, and God might be conveniently forgotten. This is what Hobbes and Marx expected to happen. The withering away of the state and the withering away of revealed religion (not to mention philosophy) are part of the same process.

The virtues of Science are not to be gainsaid. The question with which we are faced is not whether the goods of Science are real—nor whether the free market and democratic institutions are not more apt than communist institutions to produce such goods and deliver them with reasonable fairness. That the needs of the body should be satisfied decently is not to deny that they should be satisfied. The question is whether the Founding Fathers believed, any more than the representatives of Athens and Jerusalem, that the goods of the body are the only, or the most important, of human goods. Did they not believe—as I think Professor Anastaplo and I believe—that the goods of the body are conducive to genuine happiness only when they are in the service of the immaterial goods of the soul? Aristotle in the *Nicomachean Ethics* says that men wish for and pray for the external goods. But, he says, what they should pray for is that these goods be good *for them*. The men who pledged to each other their lives, fortunes, and sacred honor, meant to found a regime in which life, liberty, and property would be more secure than in any which had preceded it. But they were keenly aware that concern with a long and prosperous life could be either honorable or dishonorable. Only an honorable concern would have been consistent with their intentions as Founders. They could not therefore have been disciples of someone (e.g., Thomas Hobbes) who taught that courage was not a virtue and that honor was not a good.

Leo Strauss, writing of Aristotle's *Politics*, observes that

> The moral virtues cannot be understood as being for the sake of the city since the city must be understood as being for the sake of the practice of moral virtue.[1]

To this he added that

> Aristotle is the founder of political science because he is the discoverer of moral virtue.[2]

Aristotle's understanding of the relationship of morality and the city—as stated (and I believe endorsed) by Strauss—is precisely the one we attribute to the American Founding Fathers. To say on the contrary that morality is for the sake of the city implies that the nonmoral ends of the city determine the content and character of morality. This would be the Machiavellian reversal of Aristotle, which the Founding Fathers rejected. I believe that this—or something very much like it—is what Strauss had in mind when he wrote, in *Thoughts on Machiavelli*, that

> The United States of America may be said to be the only country in the world which was founded in explicit opposition to Machiavellian principles.[3]

Be it remembered that the United States justified itself—that is to say, maintained that it was acting justly—by invoking "the laws of nature and of nature's God." Clearly these laws were understood to be moral laws, as is confirmed by the fact that the signers of the Declaration appealed to "the Supreme Judge of the world for the rectitude of [their] intentions." But it is equally clear that these laws were understood to be antecedent to and independent of the will of those who were founding a new regime. The American Founding Fathers cannot then be understood as Machiavellian princes.

That the American Founding lowered the goals of political life is presumed shown by its supposed rejection of both the best regime of classical political philosophy and the truths of divine revelation as the guiding theme of its politics. These are supposed, by those who see the American Founding as Hobbesian, to have been replaced by comfortable self-preservation. But the American Founding—the *novus ordo seclorum*—understood itself to be the best regime of Western civilization—not the best regime of Plato or Aristotle, and not the best regime according to the Bible. It understood itself in this novel way precisely because it addressed itself to a peaceful and civilized resolution of the conflict of these two different conceptions of what was the best regime. These conflicting roots of the civilization they found in their own souls might now flourish in this new kind of polity. "Free argument and debate" would replace the demand for orthodoxy and the punishment of heresy as attributes of good government. Thus the Founding Fathers believed that it was possible to have the grandeur without the misery of the equal presence within the regime of Jerusalem and Athens. The American doctrine of separation of church and state transformed their theoretical dissonance into a practical harmony.

Professor Anastaplo writes that "thoughtful men have worked out responsible accommodations between these contending approaches," viz., between Jerusalem and Athens. To this he adds that however smooth and enduring an accommodation may be, it cannot help but regard one or the other of the two approaches as ultimately authoritative. I do not, however, regard the resolution in the American Founding merely in the light of an accommodation, however smooth and enduring. It was indeed an accommodation, but one grounded upon principle. As I have argued above, the end of the ancient world, marked by the extension of Roman citizenship to the provinces and followed by the establishment of Christianity, created a problem unprecedented in human history. All law, in the ancient city, was, directly or indirectly, divine law. By breaking the link between God and law, the Roman Empire—having become "holy" according to its own understanding of itself—understood political obligation as devolving from pope or emperor (or some combination of both) downwards to the lower ranks of polities and of persons. This, however, gave little ground either for individual freedom or for political independence. Western man's allegiance was moreover divided between the City of God and the City of Man. After some 1,500 years of *stasis*, the American Declaration of Independence resolved the contradictions inherent in the *ancien régime* by pronouncing the authority of law to be derived from the social contract by the enlightened consent of the governed. And the authority of that consent was itself said to be derived from the rights with which all men had been equally endowed by their Creator, under "the laws of nature and of nature's

God." Thus was forged the chain which linked the municipal authority of legitimate human government with the divine government of the universe while restoring moral autonomy to political life.


Professor Anastaplo quotes a professor of church history who contrasts the "infallible and divine truth" taught by Jesus with "the uncertain philosophical conclusions" of "limited and finite minds," even minds such as those of Socrates, Plato, and Aristotle. But if we ask what was Jesus's moral teaching, we will find nothing more fundamental than the golden rule, the injunction that "whatsoever you would that men should do unto you, do you unto them." Let us ask, however, who is the "you" to whom this admonition is addressed? Is it not all human beings everywhere? Does not Jesus presuppose that with respect to their possession of rights, and their corresponding obligation to respect the rights of others, "all men are created equal"? In short, the doctrine of the Declaration is already implied in Judaeo-Christian ethics. In a sense it is the ground of that ethics. Certainly Lincoln had nothing less in mind when he spoke of the great proposition as "an abstract truth applicable to all men and all times." And this truth is itself a truth no less of unassisted human reason than of divine revelation.

As the epigraph of his Appendix A, Professor Anastaplo has given us *Deuteronomy* 4:5-6, a passage famously cited by Leo Strauss in his autobiographical preface. In it Moses tells the children of Israel to keep the statutes and judgments that the Lord God had commanded. For this, he says,

> is your wisdom and your understanding in the sight of the nations, which shall hear these statutes, and say, Surely this great nation is a wise and understanding people.

But surely if Moses—and God—expected the nations of the world to recognize the wisdom and understanding of Israel, then recognition of that wisdom and understanding must somehow be a human potentiality. As such it must belong to what we call human nature, whether or not we believe that nature itself is God's creation. If the recognition of wisdom and understanding is possible in those to whom revelation has not been vouchsafed, then that recognition cannot depend wholly or simply upon divine revelation. Let us recall Meno's dilemma: how can one recognize something of which one is altogether ignorant? St. Paul, in the Letter to the Romans, says that

> When the Gentiles, who have not the law, do by nature what the law requires, they are a law to themselves. They show that what the law requires is written on their hearts . . . (*Romans* 2, 14-15.)

From this it would appear that the concept of "the laws of nature and of nature's God" by which the good people of the colonies justified their independence before all the nations had ample foundation in both the Old and New Testaments.

No one has expressed more powerfully than Leo Strauss the nature and the unsolvability of the disagreement between Jerusalem and Athens— between revelation and reason. "Yet," he has written, "this very disagreement presupposes some agreement."[4] In disagreeing, they must at least agree on the importance of what they are disagreeing about. "Negatively," says Strauss, ". . . there is perfect agreement between the Bible and Greek philosophy in opposition to those elements of modernity" in which morality is depreciated as a merely human contrivance, having no ground in either God or nature, and no obligation beyond whatever utility it may be judged at any moment to have. Moreover, says Strauss,

> One can say, and it is not misleading to say, that the Bible and Greek philosophy agree in regard to what we may call, and we do call in fact, morality.[5]

Let us repeat that, according to Leo Strauss, Jerusalem and Athens are agreed negatively in their opposition to the moral relativism (dissolving into nihilism) of modern philosophy. They are also agreed affirmatively— for all practical purposes—as to what that morality is that civil society ought to protect and promote. There is no reason then, from Strauss's perspective—no reason grounded either in modern philosophy or modern science— why one should not understand that "the city [whether ancient or modern] must be understood as being for the sake of the practice of moral virtue." At any rate this, I am convinced, is what the American Founding Fathers understood, when they expressed such sentiments as that in the Northwest Ordinance,

> Religion, morality, and knowledge, being necessary to good government and the happiness of mankind, schools and the means of education, shall forever be encouraged.

I am in agreement with Professor Anastaplo—as both of us are in agreement with Leo Strauss—that there is no final resolution that we can now imagine between the ultimate differences of Jerusalem and Athens. According to Strauss, however, the "unresolved conflict" between the two "is the secret of the vitality of Western civilization." Indeed, "The very life of Western civilization" is the "fundamental tension" of these "two conflicting roots." But the genius of the American Founding consists above all in freely permitting this tension and this conflict to be *the* transcendent end of political life, the end which the activity of moral virtue ultimately serves. In this way, the very differences of Jerusalem and Athens become the highest ground of harmony and peace. There never was any intrinsic reason why the theoretical conflict of Jerusalem and Athens—any more than the theoretical conflicts within philosophy and biblical religion—should have racked Western civilization with sectarian political struggle. Unresolved theoretical questions call only for continuing—perhaps eternal—discussion. They ought not to make enemies of those who, on moral grounds alone, are friends. On the contrary, such discussions, according to Aristotle, are the ground of the highest form of friendship. In such discussions, unlike those of politics which call for decision and action, truth alone is the goal, and friendship itself requires that the friends do not defer to each other's opinions for the sake of any good extrinsic to the discussion itself. True theory ought therefore always to strengthen friendship, and therewith morality and good citizenship. Whatever undermines the moral consensus, however, undermines the possibility of true theory, of genuine philosophy and genuine religion.

# B.

# The Ambiguity of Justice in Plato's *Republic*

Professor Anastaplo's discussion of the theme announced in the foregoing title is acute. To address each of the difficulties that he raises would require little less than a full commentary on the *Republic* itself. The relevance of these difficulties to the American Founding lies, however, in the following consideration. The *Republic*—*the* dialogue on justice—cannot answer the question, What is Justice? except by resort to myths, or noble lies. The nonmythical truth about justice would seem to be as obscure at the end of the dialogue as at the beginning. Yet the American Founding boldly and confidently asserts that there are self-evident or rational truths, which are the basis of the just powers of government.

In taking up this difficulty, we turn to part of that lengthy passage in Leo Strauss's *The City and Man* quoted by Anastaplo.

> One cannot help contrasting the *Republic* with the other dialogues which raise the question of what a given virtue is; those other dialogues do not answer the question with which they deal; they are aporetic dialogues. The *Republic* appears to be a dialogue in which the truth is declared, a dogmatic dialogue. But since the truth is set forth on the basis of strikingly deficient evidence, one is compelled to say that the *Republic* is in fact as aporetic as the so-called aporetic dialogues. (Pp. 105, 106.)

A Socratic dialogue originates in the premise that we know only that we know nothing. But knowledge of ignorance is not essentially ignorance, it is essentially knowledge. We cannot know *that* we do not know, without in some sense knowing *what* we do not know. By inquiring into what we do not know we learn more about our ignorance, and thereby we may make progress in wisdom. In the *Republic* we learn more and more of the enigmas that lie at the heart of the problem of justice. As we learn more about the problem of justice we become more just, even without knowing in any final sense what justice is. Progress in wisdom always enlarges our awareness of our ignorance as our inquiries reveal more and more of what it is that we do not know. The wisest man in the world—for example, Socrates—is wisest precisely because he knows better than anyone else what it is that he does not know. Starting from Socratic premises, there is no real expectation that philosophy—love of wisdom—will ever transform itself into wisdom proper. As we learn from the Plato's *Apology of Socrates*, eternal felicity, as imagined by Socrates, is not final contemplation of the eternal truth (which is supposed to be the activity of Aristotle's God), but rather eternal questioning of those presumed wise to unmask their unwisdom.

But philosophic activity, thus understood, is in tension with moral and political life. As Strauss puts it a little later in the passage from which we (following Anastaplo) have already quoted,

> The theme of the *Republic* is political in more than one sense, and the political questions of great urgency do not permit delay: the question of justice must be answered by all means even if the evidence needed for an adequate answer is not yet in . . .

To put the matter bluntly, we cannot wait until we have an adequate answer to such questions as "What is courage?" (and the *Laches*, an entirely aporetic dialogue, gives us none) before we train an army for war. Our enemy (and there is always an enemy) does not wait upon the outcome of our seminars before attacking. The motivation of a Platonic dialogue is not contingent upon its utility for any political or non-philosophic purpose. Just as for the orthodox Jew, the reward for the fulfillment of the Torah's commandment is the commandment, in a Socratic conversation the reward for the dialogue is the dialogue. The *aporia* of the dialogue, which reveals hitherto undisclosed knowledge of ignorance, is its own end. Yet there is a political purpose in this self-contained human activity. It demonstrates that end-in-itself which the city is intended to serve, that end which alone among human activities can make the city good and thereby just.

It is also true, moreover, that each time Socrates exposes the ignorance of someone else, he displays his superiority. The accusation against Socrates, that he seeks victory rather than truth, has a certain plausibility. Socrates's dialectical victories demonstrate what it is that can ultimately justify the sacrifices that the city must ask of its citizens when it sends them into battle. That Socrates's art is the perfectly political art is shown by the fact that in the *Gorgias*—apparently contradicting what he says in the *Apology*—Socrates declares that he alone among the Athenians practices the art of the statesman. Although Book I of the *Republic* is aporetic with respect to the definition of justice, it is not aporetic with respect to the superiority of Socrates to Thrasymachus. In proving himself "stronger" in the decisive respect, Socrates establishes his right to rule on Thrasymachus's own premises. Philosophy is stronger than sophistry, and sophistry can become strong only by becoming the handmaiden of philosophy. In the end, it is by sophistic myths that Socrates confirms his rule—or the rule of philosophy—in the *Republic* taken as a whole. Still, it is clear that the philosophers in the *Republic* are not ruled by the myths. For them, as for Socrates, progress in wisdom, understood as progress in knowledge of ignorance, is sufficient to justify their way of life. That way of life is objectively best, and the morality that serves it is the objectively true morality.

Let us conclude here by observing that the theme of the *Republic*, the objective superiority of philosophy among all the arts which direct human life, itself suffers none of the defects which may be found in the definitions of justice. The ambiguity to which Professor Anastaplo points does not undermine, but rather supports, this conclusion. The superiority of philosophy—of purely theoretical activity having no end beyond itself—mirrors the self-contained activity of God in the universe, which the polity can at best only imperfectly reflect.

The idea of "the laws of nature and of nature's God" is derived from classical political philosophy. Like Socrates in the *Republic* and in the *Gorgias* the Declaration of Independence identifies despotism as the quintessence of injustice with reference to these laws. It does not define justice, but speaks rather of "the just powers of government." Those powers, derived from the consent of the governed, rest upon the mutual recognition by the governed of their humanity. The consent of the governed must be enlightened, because it clearly does not authorize the government either of barbarians or savages. Barbarians and savages are those who do not understand the essential meaning of what it is to be a human being: that there is no such difference between man and man as there is between man and beast, or between man and God, that intrinsically justifies despotic government.

The government whose powers are just will not only be nonarbitrary (that is to say a rule of law) but a limited government: only a limited government can reconcile majority rule with minority rights. But the ultimate—the highest—reason why government should be limited is that human wisdom is limited. Unassisted human reason cannot solve the problem of the ambiguity of justice. Reason cannot rule upon the claims of faith, nor faith upon the claims of unassisted reason. Only if philosophy could be transformed into wisdom proper—the ultimate aim of modern philosophy, particularly evident in the contentions of Hegel and Marx—could the case be made that government might be at once beneficent and despotic. (This was the contention of Kojeve, and the ground of his Stalinism, vigorously refuted by Strauss, in their famous confrontation in *On Tyranny*.)[6]

The essentially aporetic character of the Socratic dialogue is supreme testimony to the proposition that philosophy cannot be transformed into wisdom, and that moderation ought therefore to govern human affairs. Moderation thus conceived is not moral indifference, rather is it the extreme opposite of such indifference. It is the virtue that lies at the heart of the rule of law and of that moderate constitutionalism which is taught by the Declaration of Independence.

# C.

# Private Rights and Public Law:
# The Founders' Perspective

Professor Anastaplo's third lecture is as always acute and profound in its treatment of its topic. I think, however, that I have already met the challenge it presents to my argument. The case for private rights in public law rests essentially upon the case for limited government. Limited government presupposes the distinction between state and society, which is itself derivative from the distinction between church and state. These are distinctions unknown to the ancient city, but indispensably necessary to good government in the postclassical world, for reasons we have amply given.

Above all, however, the rule of law and limited government, despite the different means for their achievement in the ancient city and the modern state, depend upon the Socratic insight which transcends the distinction of ancient and modern politics. This is the insight into the limits of human wisdom. Every Socratic dialogue, and especially the *Republic* is a lesson in the limits of human wisdom, and therewith a lesson in the need for moderation. Intrinsic to that moderation, as an element of what we call Western civilization, is the recognition of the possibility that divine revelation may cast light where Socratic inquiry can uncover only knowledge of ignorance. But the light of divine revelation can be truly enlightening—rather than blinding—only when it enters the soul without the adventitious intervention of worldly rewards or punishments. The American doctrine of separation of church and state, Jefferson's doctrine of religious liberty, is therefore the heart of all private rights, of all minority rights beyond the control of the majority.

# An Epilogue to Seven Answers

1. Leo Strauss, *The City and Man* Rand McNally, Chicago, 1964, p. 27.
2. Ibid.
3. *Thoughts on Machiavelli* (1958), Midway Reprint, University of Chicago Press, p. 13.
4. "Progress or Return," in *The Rebirth of Classical Political Rationalism*, Thomas Pangle, ed., Chicago: University of Chicago Press, 1989, p. 246.
5. "Progress or Return," op. cit., p. 270.
6. Now available in a "revised and expanded edition," including the Strauss-Kojeve correspondence, edited by Victor Gourevitch and Michael S. Roth, the Free Press, 1991.

# Professor Jaffa and That Old-Time Religion

## GEORGE ANASTAPLO

*[James] Burnham is in favour of suppressing the American Communist Party, and of doing the job thoroughly, which would probably mean using the same methods as the Communists, when in power, use against their opponents. Now, there are times when it is justifiable to suppress a political party. If you are fighting for your life, and if there is some organisation which is plainly acting on behalf of the enemy, and is strong enough to do harm, then you have got to crush it. But to suppress the [American] Communist Party now, or at any time when it did not unmistakably endanger national survival, would be calamitous. One has only to think of the people who would approve!*

—GEORGE ORWELL (1947)

## I.

I put seven questions to Harry V. Jaffa in the Spring 1987 issue of the *University of Puget Sound Law Review*. Professor Jaffa provided seven answers in the Winter 1990 issue of the same law review. These characteristically Jaffaian and hence instructive answers also served as his contribution to the remarkably generous *Law and Philosophy* volumes kindly published in my honor by the Ohio University Press in 1992.

There is no need for me to speak again to most of the questions I first put to Mr. Jaffa in 1987. Various arguments I made in connection with those questions have been developed further in my 1992 *American Moralist* volume. Additional arguments may be located by consulting my bibliography in the second volume of *Law and Philosophy*.

Mr. Jaffa, even when he is mistaken in the theoretician's (to be distinguished from the ideologue's) emphasis that he evidently cannot help but place upon practical arguments, continues to challenge his readers. A critical difference between him and me has to do, it seems, with the status of that moderation which prudence both depends upon and promotes. Perhaps an even more critical difference between us, which I can do no more than touch upon here, is implicit in my opinion that however sensible it is to approach moral and political decisions in a thoughtful manner, the highest activity of the human mind is not ultimately devoted either to the moral virtues or to statesmanship (vital though they may be to a good life) but rather to philosophy and perhaps to theology.

## II.

Mr. Jaffa's most extended comment in his 1990 reply to me takes off from the familiar reservations I had repeated in 1987 about the way that the American Communist party had been dealt with in the United States during the Cold War. That which was done again and again to American Communists was good neither for them nor for the United States. Also, it was so unbecoming as to be a disturbing affront to anyone truly dedicated to republican proprieties, especially to anyone who subscribed to the noble assurance of the 1785 Virginia Statute of Religious Liberty "that it is time enough, for the rightful purposes of civil government, for its officers to interfere when principles break out into overt acts against peace and good order."

Before Mr. Jaffa settles down to his 1990 comment on the Communist party, however, he takes Chief Justice Rehnquist to task for his 1988 opinion in *Hustler Magazine* v. *Falwell*. Mr. Jaffa does not seem to appreciate the strategy of the chief justice in conceding as much as he did in *Falwell* to libertarian impulses. Was he not concerned, at least in part, that judicial reactions against an excessive jury verdict might contribute to an even broader ruling by the Court (in favor of all forms of expression) than the one he offered his colleagues? Nor does Mr. Jaffa seem to appreciate why it is that the disposition of the *Falwell* case did not elicit any dissents in the often-divided United States Supreme Court. Even conservative justices are obviously reluctant these days to permit unpopular speakers to be officially penalized either for the ugly mode in which they express themselves or for the questionable moral doctrines they espouse. Perhaps they remember how the repressiveness among us during the Cold War got out of hand, crippling the country at large. Among the risks that dedicated republicans must now run, therefore, is that their freedom will produce, or at least will permit, some nasty (if not even monstrous) things along with many desirable effects. It remains to be seen whether we can, in our troubled circumstances, have effective political discourse without also licensing, if not even rewarding, public shamelessness.

Mr. Jaffa's discussion of the Communist party issue takes up almost as much space in his 1990 reply to me as the rest of his "Seven Answers." Since that Communist party discussion is, in effect, a provocative restatement by him of his Cold War positions, I am encouraged to consider how that long struggle looks now, especially with the collapse we have at last witnessed of the Soviet Union.

# III.

Our treatment of the American Communist party since the Second World War affected, among other things, how we dealt in this country with those who questioned the dominant Cold War doctrines among us, doctrines which long diverted us from our truly serious moral and social problems as a people. I have indicated from time to time (as in the 1966 review, reprinted in my *Human Being and Citizen* volume, of Mr. Jaffa's *Equality & Liberty* book) my reservations about Mr. Jaffa's positions in these matters.

Consider, also, the remarks I made, as chairman of a panel on Leninists and Straussians, during the 1983 American Political Science Convention in Chicago. That panel had been prompted by the insistence of some political scientists that neither Leninists nor Straussians could be trusted, as intellectual imperialists, to respect the academic freedom of scholars. I opened our lively session with these observations:

> Some of you may wonder, as do I, why I should have been selected as chairman on this occasion. Perhaps a sufficient reason can be traced to someone's kindness in wanting to assure me a seat in this room. The attendance here today, as at the other related panels about Leo Strauss [1899–1973] at this Convention, surely testifies to Mr. Strauss's enduring appeal and to the Claremont Institute's skills in organization (for which, no doubt, Harry Jaffa should be able to take considerable credit).
>
> Another reason I can think of for my chairing this meeting bears on our immediate subject, "Neither Leninists nor Straussians: The Political Intention of Leo Strauss." After all, I am on record as having advocated, for some years now, that both Communists and Straussians, if otherwise qualified,

should not be precluded, because they *are* either Communists or Straussians, from serving on college and university faculties in *this* country.

Indeed, one can argue, any sizable American faculty that does not have decent and articulate representatives of both of these critical persuasions among its members today is depriving students of instruction vital for sensible political discourse in the twenty-first century. If we should ever be tempted to forget how important sensible discourse is for a fully humane life, we should reflect upon the implications of such things as the remarkably stupid, and recklessly callous if not even simply wicked, action yesterday over the Sea of Japan, at the news of which we have all been properly appalled.

The reference here was to the shooting down the day before (September 1, 1983) of a Korean Air Line passenger plane that had violated Soviet air space. In the course of the panel discussion that followed I interjected these comments:

> I consider myself obliged to say, in response to the objection we have heard that I referred in my introductory remarks only to "one select group of heinous crimes," those of Communists, while ignoring those of Fascists—I am obliged to say that I personally own the distinction, the deserved distinction, of having been the only American to have been declared *persona non grata* by the Greek colonels, a neo-Fascist regime.
>
> It did not seem to me relevant to our immediate concerns here today to say anything about the subject of Fascism in my introductory [as distinguished from my concluding] remarks. Anyone who is interested in what I have had to say about the Greek regime between 1967 and 1974 may consult various articles of mine placed in the *Congressional Record* during that period.

I was declared *persona non grata* by the Greek colonels' government in 1970 and again in 1971. A decade earlier I had been declared *persona non grata* by the Soviet Union, leading to my expulsion from that country in July 1960. Even so, I was there long enough to see how inept the Russians could be and how fragile as well as oppressive their way of life was. I was also able to see, during our six-month, sixteen-thousand-mile family camping trip across Europe in 1960, the much, much greater human and industrial resources of Western Europe compared to those of our official nemesis, the Soviet Union. (My expulsions from the Soviet Union and Greece are described in the first essay in my *Human Being and Citizen*.)

My concluding remarks at the 1983 American Political Science Association panel included these observations:

> Among the things to be learned from our exchange today, which it is well for the students of Leo Strauss present to keep in mind, is a lesson which I have many times urged upon them: it is prudent to remember and to insist, when

appropriate, that Mr. Strauss hated Fascism deeply—and that he had good reasons for doing so and, perhaps even more important, he had good reasons *in* doing so, that is, in explaining what is wrong with Fascism.

It should be useful for Leo Strauss's students to reflect upon what intelligent scholars of good faith do manage to find objectionable in the Straussian persuasion and *why*—and what, if anything, can be done about this and how. It could be, of course, that there may not be much to be done about this—but it is well to face up to that, too.

I continue to believe that Straussians are sorely needed on university campuses in this country. Also needed, but not to the same extent, are learned apologists for the Fascism of our time, such as Martin Heidegger and Antonio de Oliveira Salazar, and learned apologists for the Communism of our time, such as Georg Lukacs, Alexandre Kojeve, and Mikhail Gorbachev. Academicians also need opportunities to confront intelligent racists from whom they can hear sophisticated versions of the heretical opinions that are so influential in the community at large.

My most extensive comment on Mr. Strauss thus far has been in the 1974 eulogy of him reprinted in my book, *The Artist as Thinker*. It can be instructive to figure out why both that generally well-received eulogy and my useful 1988 review of Allan Bloom's wrongheaded *Closing* book have been cold-shouldered by an influential minority of highly partisan Straussians. Their perverse compliment has deprived me and others, and perhaps also themselves, of what might have been salutary corrections: it can be sobering, especially for the self-indulgent, to try to defend in public their private recriminations. But, then, Mr. Jaffa himself (who is at least as "conservative" as his bitterest critics) has never been given by them the full measure of recognition that is his due as perhaps the best-informed student today of the American political heritage. In short, the occasional displays of an unfortunate clannishness by some of my gifted schoolmates can help one begin to see "what intelligent scholars of good faith do manage to find objectionable in the Straussian persuasion."

## IV.

The key question for us throughout the Cold War, *as it bore upon how we conducted ourselves in this country*, was not the question of how evil Josef Stalin and his cohorts were. That was apparent enough to informed observers, just as it has been to observers of those latter-day Stalinists, the ruthless Maoists in China, and the insane Khmer Rouge in Cambodia.

Rather, the key practical question for us depended on a proper assessment of what the strengths and prospects of the Soviet Union were. This assessment influenced how we should conduct ourselves, what we should do with our spiritual as well as our material resources, and what kind of people we should be.

Consider what I said, in my 1980 introduction of Mr. Jaffa at Rosary College (set forth in my 1987 *Puget Sound* article), about my seeing the Russians "as much more vulnerable (both politically and militarily)" than did Mr. Jaffa. What would have been in our best interest to do then, and probably in the Russians' interest as well? It should be generally apparent now, as it was to a few of us here and there then, that the massive military expenditures of the Reagan administration, with their unfortunate effects on our own and perhaps the world economy, should never have been resorted to.

Western Europeans were much less exercised about the Soviet threat in the 1980s, as well as before, even though they were far less armed and far more exposed than we were. They were also much more cautious than we were about allowing themselves to be either politically corrupted or economically debilitated by unreasonable fears of the Russians, and not only because the United States was willing to go to the extremes it did.

In short, we simply were not sensible about how we conducted ourselves as Cold Warriors during the past quarter-century. One consequence of our miscalculation was that we did not do what we could have done to contribute to a peaceful transition in Eastern Europe to a more reliable political and economic order. Another consequence was that we made far more at home of dangers to be avoided than of a way of life to be cherished, a way of life that is celebrated in the two volumes of constitutional commentary I have prepared for the Johns Hopkins University Press.

## V.

The dramatic confirmations we now have about the chronic weaknesses of the Soviet Union should move the more vigorous Cold Warriors among us to reconsider their diagnoses and prescriptions of recent decades. Both undue fearfulness and unseemly vindictiveness marred the American responses to the grossly exaggerated Communist party threats within the United States.

I was known to be dubious about the Communist party conspiracy and related espionage prosecutions in this country throughout the Cold War period. I found those measures, as I have indicated, both self-destructive and unbecoming. (See, for example, my discussions of the *Dennis, Hiss,* and *Rosenberg* cases in my 1971 book, *The Constitutionalist: Notes on the First Amendment.*) But then, I had reservations also about the impeachment campaign mounted against President Nixon in the 1970s. (See, for example, my *Human Being and Citizen* volume.) My general approach to such matters is reflected in the letter I sent to a number of newspaper editors on December 18, 1992:

> The Weinberger perjury case that is challenging President Bush as his term of office draws to an end in 1993 brings to mind the Rosenberg espionage case that challenged President Truman as his own term of office was ending in 1953. I am one of those who continue to believe that Mr. Truman should have, before his departure, commuted the Rosenbergs' death sentences to life imprisonment. Instead, he left that traumatic matter for his politically inexperienced successor to handle, with the result that Julius and Ethel Rosenberg were dead within six months. Those senseless executions are not accomplishments that our country can recall with pride.
>
> It is generally recognized that Caspar Weinberger vigorously opposed the Reagan administration proposal to swap arms for hostages. Unless there should be much more involved here than has already been revealed, it seems both unfair and wasteful to insist at this late date upon subjecting Mr. Weinberger to a trial on the charge of having misled congressional investigators about the ill-fated Iran/Contra usurpation. Such a trial, whatever its outcome, would be an undeserved ordeal for someone as high-minded as Mr. Weinberger. The arguments properly made from time to time against some of his policies never questioned his patriotism.
>
> Should not Governor Clinton be urged, especially by those of us who supported his disciplined candidacy this year, to recommend publicly (as well as privately) to the president that Mr. Weinberger be pardoned before his trial date in early January? Such a nonpartisan appeal to Mr. Bush by the president-elect would contribute to a generous spirit of reconciliation and common purpose in the decade immediately ahead for our troubled country. Surely an ailing Caspar Weinberger, in the twilight of an illustrious career as a dedicated public servant, deserves better from his fellow citizens than the peculiarly traumatic indignity of a senseless criminal prosecution.

Mr. Jaffa approved the recommendation that Mr. Weinberger be pardoned, just as he had approved much earlier what I had said against the Nixon-impeachment campaign.

My general approach to such matters is quite different in spirit from those who still like to believe of Cold-War American Communists that "every one of them carried his marshal's baton in his knapsack." This is indeed the old-time religion, and not without its own ever-wily Satan and enterprising witches to treasure and contend with. It is this kind of approach to such matters that contributed to the systemic confusion, if not even national paranoia, that found grim expression in the unnecessary American sacrifices in Vietnam. It contributed also to the widespread loss of confidence in the statesmanship and war-making power of the United States. It certainly does not help, in any event, to invest every challenge we happen to confront with the magnitude of our Civil War crisis.

Echoes of a healthier, pre-Cold War state of affairs may be heard in the dedication to my *American Moralist* volume: "To the sacred memory of seven very young men we grew up with in Carterville, Illinois, and who went off to war with us a half-century ago but who never returned." That volume includes my 1966 talk in Chicago against our involvement in the Vietnam War. It also includes my 1984 talk at the Max Planck Institute in Heidelberg about, among other things, the need to plan properly for a sensible transition from the Cold War. I suggest, in a February 1993 memorandum on the murderous revival of ancient feuds in the Balkans, that "among those most benefitted when just and decent actions are insisted upon are the unfortunate men and women who might otherwise disgrace themselves and endanger their descendants by indulging in shameful atrocities." This too, it seems to me, is a healthier approach than what we now see all around us.

## VI.

Differences will no doubt continue between Mr. Jaffa and me not only about what the Cold War was about but also about how we Americans should have responded to it. Certainly, we need to keep in check that corrosive spiritedness which so often enslaves us. Leo Strauss's advice should be helpful here: "Indignation is a bad counselor. Our indignation proves at best that we are well meaning. It does not prove that we are right." (*Natural Right and History*, p. 6)

Organized spiritedness on a grand scale may be seen in the appalling devastation that we were responsible for during the misconceived 1991 Gulf War. Unorganized spiritedness, also on a grand scale, may be seen in the mounting violence among us to which we have become accustomed. We do seem to take for granted an explosive way of life that depends as much as ours evidently does on private ownership of the most devastating weapons, on casual murders and legal executions, and on massive prison populations—and all on a scale that makes us the uncontested "leaders" of the Free World.

Thus, differences between Mr. Jaffa and myself do remain. They extend, for example, to how affirmative action should be used by us (the issue here, it still seems to me, is prudential, not constitutional) and to how homosexuals should be both talked about and treated in this country. I believe it both fair and humane to insist that the typical homosexual in this country today, just like the typical American Communist party member since the First World War, probably wants truly good things for himself, for his friends and family, and for his country. (See my essay, "Subversion, Then and Now," in my collection, "Freedom of Speech and the First Amendment: Explorations.")

## VII.

I have, for years now, been venturing to offer my fellow citizens controversial arguments about issues of the day. Those arguments, so far as I can tell, do not seem to have made much if any practical difference. Such arguments have not been limited to Cold War matters. It should be no surprise, for example, that my 1974 advocacy of the abolition in this country of broadcast television, a major source for us of both waste and shamelessness, has gotten nowhere so far. (That advocacy may be seen in *The American Moralist*, a manual of sorts prepared by Don Quixote for the Lone Ranger. I was, as a United States Army Air Corps navigator during the Second World War, much more successful in having the sometimes demanding courses I laid down followed by my fellow officers.)

The record both of the public-policy debates of the Cold War and the consequences of what was done then by the United States at home and abroad may eventually contribute to a sound understanding of the opinions upon which our overall approach to the issues of that day was based. The arguments made by various Cold War dissenters in recent decades may yet be more instructive for our successors than they evidently were for our contemporaries.

However serious the political difference I have had with Professor Jaffa may have been on occasion, they have been almost inconsequential when compared to the standards and aspirations that we have shared, beginning of course with what we learned in our youth from Leo Strauss, as well as from the Bible, Aristotle, Plato, Shakespeare, and Lincoln. Among the other things Harry Jaffa and I somehow share are, first, my grateful recognition that I have yet a lot to learn from him and, second, his generous recognition that there is a lot he still needs to teach me.

# "Our Ancient Faith"
## A Reply to Professor Anastaplo

HARRY V. JAFFA

Professor Anastaplo writes that a critical difference between us "has to do, it seems, with the status of that moderation which prudence both depends upon and promotes." He also writes that "an even more critical difference between us, which I can do no more than touch upon here, is implicit in my opinion that . . . the highest activity of the human mind is not ultimately devoted either to the moral virtues or to statesmanship (vital though they may be to a good life) but rather to philosophy and perhaps to theology."

I can reassure my old friend that the "more critical difference between us" does not exist in my mind. I would remind him that when Socrates "called philosophy down from the heaven and forced it to make inquiries about life and manners and good and bad things" he was said thereby to have become the founder of political philosophy.[1] But as the founder of political philosophy, Socrates was also the founder of a new way of looking at the whole, that is to say, he became a refounder of philosophy. The achievement of Leo Strauss closely parallels that of Socrates, even as modern philosophy closely parallels pre-Socratic philosophy, in its inability to say anything humanly important about the human things.[2] If human beings are part of the universe, then whatever enables us to understand human beings must thereby enable us better to understand the universe of which they are a part. In what it asserts about man, the Declaration of Independence itself embodies propositions about God and the universe, propositions that are metaphysical, no less than moral and political.[3]

I have therefore believed for a long time that the separation of concern with the moral virtues (or statesmanship) and philosophy, is dialectical rather than substantial. Concerning this I have written elsewhere as follows:

The sharp separation between theory and practice, as it exists formally in Aristotle's text (but not in Plato's) fits his (i.e., Aristotle's) own apparent understanding of the qualitative physical differences between heaven and earth, as well as the eternity of the visible universe, differences and distinctions no longer tenable in the form in which we find them in his works. I think Strauss's preoccupation with the problem of Socrates in his later years reflects the conviction that the reconstruction of classical political philosophy requires a reliance upon the moral distinctions as the key to the metaphysical distinctions. Political philosophy—meaning thereby first of all moral philosophy— must become the key to philosophy itself. We have access to theoretical wisdom only by taking the moral distinctions with full seriousness.

I noted Strauss's "marvelous eulogy of Churchill,"[4] which flashed on the screen of our memories a moment in time—1940. But that moment in time reflected an eternal presence—that of good and evil—in the human condition.

The tyrant stood at the pinnacle of his power. The contrast between the indomitable and magnanimous statesman and the insane tyrant—this spectacle in its clear simplicity was one of the greatest lessons which men can learn, at any time.

Later, Strauss urged that

We have no higher duty, and no more pressing duty, than to remind ourselves and our students, of political greatness, human greatness, of the peaks of human excellence. For we are supposed to train ourselves and others in seeing things as they are, and this means above all in seeing their greatness and their misery, their excellence and their vileness . . .

From this I concluded that

"Seeing things as they are" refers to the being of things, their metaphysical reality. Yet that being is seen as goodness.[5] The spectacle of "political greatness, human greatness"—together with its evil opposite—becomes then a ground of philosophy itself, because the philosopher himself looks to this spectacle to contemplate the being of things which becomes manifest in the spectacle. The great statesman thus brings to light the distinctions which are the ground of theoretical as well as of practical philosophy. In Strauss, the moral distinctions become the heart of philosophy. And statesmanship thus itself becomes part of philosophic activity, seen in its wholeness.

In the Bible, one's duties to God (theory) are certainly of a higher order than one's duties towards one's fellow human beings (practice). But there is no disjunction between the two. One cannot honor the Creator by depreciating the image of God in His creation. Indeed, one's access to God is by means of that image. In that, the Bible and the Declaration of Independence are in full agreement.

Mr. Anastaplo says that there is a critical difference between us concerning the status of moderation, especially in its relationship to prudence. Taken in the abstract, I doubt that there is any such difference. How we apply our principles is a separate question from what they are. Churchill is best remembered for his warnings against Hitler in the 1930s. Churchill's great leadership in the war against Hitler would never have come to pass had those warnings been heeded, and had the democracies' resistance not foundered in a nearly suicidal pacifism. Churchill is less well remembered today for his warnings against Stalin, and is hardly remembered with honor by Mr. Anastaplo.[6] Yet his warnings against Stalin were heeded, they were the initiating force behind the policy of containment, and led to a victory over Communism far less costly than that over Nazism. Mr. Anastaplo agrees—I think—that Churchill was prudent and moderate in his condemnation of the Munich agreement, but implies that he was imprudent and immoderate in his warnings against Stalinism. I cannot see any distinction in principle between the threats represented, first by Hitler, and then by Stalin. They are the two greatest mass murderers of all time. And Stalin—no doubt because of his longevity—murdered at least twice as many as did Hitler. Both represented versions of the same late nineteenth-century social Darwinism that saw higher forms of life emerging out of lower forms, with the higher forms having the right to enslave or exterminate those they deemed either counter-evolutionary or counter-revolutionary. Both made unlimited claims to hegemony, although the Marxist-Leninist doctrine of world revolution was more unequivocal in its declared aggressiveness than Hitler's. I do not understand that Chamberlain's refusal to take the danger of Hitler with the seriousness it deserved constituted a claim to moderation or prudence. Nor do I see that the would-be appeasers of Stalinism differed in this from the Chamberlainites.

Professor Anastaplo makes much of the fact that

> The Western Europeans were much less exercised about the Soviet threat in the 1980s, as well as before, even though they were far less armed and far more exposed than we were.

So were they "less exercised" by the threat of Hitler in the 1930s! The difference in the outcomes of the threats of the 1930s and 1980s is that the United States exercised a leadership in the containment of communism that it did not exercise—until after Pearl Harbor—in the containment of Hitlerism, and then at much higher cost.

Mr. Anastaplo thinks that the aforesaid Europeans were

> much more cautious than we were about allowing themselves to be either politically corrupted or economically debilitated by unreasonable fears of the Russians . . .

I deny that we were either "politically corrupted or economically debilitated" by the policy of containment of communism. Our isolationism after World War I contributed mightily both to the Great Depression and to World War II. The prosperity both of Europe and Asia today—outside the communist, or former communist world—surpasses anything in the past. Anastaplo echoes President Jimmy Carter's warning in his speech at Notre Dame University against the "inordinate fear of communism." Not long after Carter delivered this warning, however, the Soviets invaded Afghanistan. Seeing this as the first step of a flanking movement toward the Persian Gulf—and possibly toward the "soft underbelly" of NATO—the president issued the Carter Doctrine, placing the entire Persian Gulf region under American protection. At the same time he—unlike Mr. Anastaplo—admitted he had been wrong about what he had said about the fear of communism.

In the decade following the invasion of Afghanistan more than a million Afghans are believed to have perished. Among the Soviet techniques of conquest was the wholesale dropping of tiny fragmentation bombs, concealed in toys. When the Afghan children tried to play with them, their fingers, and sometimes their hands, were blown off. Then the parents would leave the villages, and flee to Pakistan for medical help—which was what their would-be conquerors wanted them to do! It was largely American arms—notably Stinger missiles—to the Afghan resistance that in the end convinced the Soviets to abandon that enterprise.

Mr. Anastaplo refuses to draw the only prudent conclusion that I believe anyone can draw, from the fact that the USSR and the Warsaw Pact assembled the greatest aggregation of military power, both in absolute and relative terms, that the world had ever seen. No one could imagine that the armaments that lay behind the central front in Germany were merely defensive. Indeed, the well-advertised—and often rehearsed—military doctrine of the Warsaw Pact forces was that of the blitzkrieg. Moreover, the nuclear superiority that the USSR achieved by the end of the 1970s nullified the nuclear shield that the U.S. had extended over Europe hitherto. Yet as Churchill had said in 1946, the USSR wished to have the fruits of war without war. It aimed at "finlandization" rather than direct conquest, although not necessarily as its ultimate goal. It was because the spirit of appeasement—expressed in the slogan, "better Red than dead"—played so large a part in the public opinion of the European Left, that those elements pretended indifference to the danger of Soviet conquest. But let us not forget those who laughed at the occupation of the Rhineland in 1936: "Ha, ha," they said, "so the Germans are invading Germany!" Nor the Frenchmen who said, "Better Hitler than Blum." Only from such perspectives as these could it be said that some Western Europeans were more "moderate" than American policymakers during the Cold War.

Right through its last decade, the Soviet Union's economic deficiencies in the civilian sector never impaired its military power, any more than it had done in World War II. What broke the back of the USSR was not economic weakness, but the realization that Europe would not be "finlandized," and that it could not secure the fruits of war without going to war. The ever-growing contrast between the prosperity on one side of the Iron Curtain, and the poverty on the other, steadily undermined the confidence even of the Soviet rulers themselves, in the doctrines of Marxism-Leninism. When in 1959 Khrushchev said "We will bury you"—explaining that he meant in consumer goods—it was still possible for a Soviet ruler, as well as for Western intellectuals, to believe this. By the time Gorbachev took over, only Western intellectuals could believe it.

The measures pursued by Ronald Reagan were decisive in bringing this to bear upon the Soviet government. He pursued a threefold policy that represented statesmanship of Churchillian stature. First, he undertook a complete rebuilding of the American military strength that had deteriorated badly in the wake of the Vietnam War and the Carter presidency. Next, in 1983 he deployed the Pershings and the cruise missiles in Western Europe, targeting the USSR with intermediate range nuclear warheads. Third, and perhaps most important of all, he initiated a program of research and development of a ballistic missile defense (SDI). This, if it were deployed, threatened to cancel the effectiveness of the strategic first strike threat that the USSR—over a period of fifteen or more years—had acquired by enormous effort and economic sacrifice. Although the feasibility of SDI was derided by many at home, it never seems to have been doubted by Mr. Gorbachev, who used every weapon in his political arsenal to persuade President Reagan to abandon it. When he failed to do so, the Soviet policy of intimidation ceased to hold out any believable hope of succeeding. With the failure of that hope, the USSR was on the road to extinction, although Mr. Gorbachev never intended it to be so.

Mr. Anastaplo thinks that we were politically corrupted by the Cold War, and that we failed to cherish the way of life celebrated in his own constitutional commentaries. But there is never a time when one's way of life is more cherished than when it is most threatened. This was true of the American Civil War, it was true of Britain's finest hour, and it was no less true of the rallying of the free world against communism in Harry Truman's presidency. According to David McCullough's splendid biography, on one of their last meetings, when both the old warriors were retired from office, Churchill told Truman, "You, sir, saved Western civilization."

I think that is the glorious verdict—by the most competent of all judges—not only upon Truman, but upon the people of the United States, whom he represented in 1950, as Churchill had represented the people of Great Britain in 1940. Nor should it be forgotten that in helping its defeated enemies of World War II in this period—Germany, Japan, and Italy—the United States displayed a magnanimity absolutely unprecedented in the history of nations.

As to the persecution of dissidents—communist or otherwise—in the course of the Cold War, my memory is very different from that of Mr. Anastaplo. His version is indeed assiduously promoted by the opinion makers within the universities and within the media. But I do not believe it corresponds to reality. I began teaching in 1945, and received my first tenure track appointment in 1951 at Ohio State University—then the largest campus in the country, in the heart of middle America. I never knew personally anyone there who ever suffered persecution or discrimination because of the allegation of communist sympathies.[7] Anyone who actually had such sympathies was invariably shielded by his liberal colleagues—who were the controlling majority within all the liberal arts departments. On the other hand, no one who had ever expressed the least sympathy with "McCarthyism" (however defined) would have had any chance for appointment, promotion, or tenure.[8]

Mr. Anastaplo reminds us of the notorious assertion by a member of Yale's political science department, that neither Leninists nor Straussians should ever be granted tenure. The reality, however, was that Leninists (or at least Marxists) have fared far better in our universities than Straussians. And with the end of the Cold War, our faculties have moved abruptly to the left, to the greater advantage of Leninists, and the greater disadvantage of Straussians.

Mr. Anastaplo's own experiences from 1950 to 1961—recorded in *The Constitutionalist: Notes on the First Amendment*—constitute an important and illuminating episode in the Cold War. But they constitute as well an episode in American constitutional history and American constitutional law that transcends the Cold War. His defense of the right of revolution—announced in the Declaration of Independence—as an essential element in American constitutionalism, puts him in the company of Frederick Douglass and Martin Luther King, Jr. The lesson I would draw from his experience has however less to do with the atmosphere of the Cold War, than with the consequences of the ruling relativism in the universities and in the bar. It is this relativism and the denial that first principles have any foundation in reason, that has denied as well the place of the principles of the Declaration of Independence in constitutional jurisprudence.

Because he refused to answer certain questions put to him by the Committee on Character and Fitness of the Illinois bar, Mr. Anastaplo was refused admission to the bar. The questions were, had he ever been a member of the Communist party, and did he believe in the right to advocate the overthrow of the government of the United States by force and violence. On the ground of his rights under the First Amendment, he refused to answer the first question. As to the second question he insisted that the right to advocate the overthrow of any government that had become tyrannical—the right appealed to by the American people in their act of separation from Great Britain in 1776—was the foundation not only of American independence but of the constitutions that followed upon that independence. It was therefore always the right of an American citizen to ask whether the government of the United States had become such a government. In this he was unquestionably right.

He appealed the decision against him of the Illinois bar through the state courts of Illinois to the Supreme Court of the United States, acting—with indomitable persistence and perspicacity—as his own attorney every step of the way. The case of *In re Anastaplo* ended in 1961 with the Court deciding against his appeal, by a vote of 5 to 4. The majority opinion had nothing to do with the merits of Mr. Anastaplo's answers, or refusals to answer the committee of the Illinois bar. In fact, the majority opinion paid an extraordinary tribute to his character, and to the sincerity of his patriotism in defending—according to his own lights—the Constitution. Any suspicion that he had ever had any sympathy with communism—or any other form of tyranny—was, as Lincoln might have put it, "as thin as the homeopathic soup boiled from the shadow of a pigeon that had died of starvation."

The majority decided only that the State of Illinois, acting through the Committee, had not exceeded the latitude allowed it by the Constitution, in deciding upon the qualifications for admission to its bar. The ringing dissent in his favor, by Mr. Justice Black, was less an analysis of the issues in the case, or an endorsement of Anastaplo's argument with respect to the principles of the Declaration, than a ceremony of induction into the Hall of Fame of American Civil Liberties. Among the ironies of the case is that Black—as we have seen above[9]—was a resolute opponent of bringing natural law doctrines to bear upon constitutional interpretation. Yet what was principled in Anastaplo's stand was precisely that it did bring to bear upon the Constitution standards derived from "the laws of nature and of nature's God." Yet Black's one reservation in his praise of Anastaplo was instructive. He said that Anastaplo might be faulted, if at all, only for taking too much upon himself, in his defense of the liberties of us all. Black's remark certainly invites us to ask whether the stand Anastaplo took was strictly required by the virtues of moderation and prudence. After all, the committee that interrogated him knew that there was nothing in the record to justify their questions, as they bore on Anastaplo himself. But they felt that public policy, formed through representative institutions, had a right to exclude Communists, or communist sympathizers, from the bar. And they believed—rightly or wrongly—that it would have appeared arbitrary on their part, and unfair to others, if in the questioning of candidates one rule was not applied equally to all. I think it was this view— that it would have been unfair to refrain from asking him questions that they put to others—that decided the case against him, even in the minds of many whose personal sympathies were very strongly in his favor. Indeed, it might be said that Anastaplo forced such persons to decide between what they—with a sincerity equal to his own—felt was their duty to the country and justice to himself. Viewed in this light, the conflict might be said to have been tragic, in the sense that there was hubris on both sides.[10]

As it turned out, however, Anastaplo played the role of Antigone, or

Socrates, or Thomas More, only up to a point. Although a brilliant law student—perhaps the most exceptional the University of Chicago has ever seen—he never became a member of the bar. However, his contributions to the law, in particular constitutional law, as a professor of political science and as a professor of law—and as both teacher and writer—have I think exceeded those of any member of the bar (including his classmate Robert Bork) over the last forty years. I might even add that I do not think that Anastaplo's career as a member of the bar—although it would certainly have been far more prosperous in worldly goods—could ever have equaled the one that resulted from his exclusion from it. I mention this not so much as a tribute to Anastaplo, but to the essential good nature of the American regime which—the alleged mistreatment of Communists to the contrary notwithstanding—does not often persecute its "martyrs."

In 1951 George Anastaplo was not so learned or sophisticated as he later became. In reviewing *In re Anastaplo*, however, I was struck by how much stronger his case was than he had made it out to be. What the committee that interrogated him, and the public at large, could not understand, was how a right of revolution might be invoked against a government that was freely elected, that might be freely criticized, and that might be turned out in the next election. The right of revolution invoked by the thirteen colonies in 1776 was directed against the authority of a king they had not elected, and a Parliament in which they were not represented. However, in protesting the Alien and Sedition Acts of 1798, in the Kentucky Resolutions of that same year, Jefferson appealed to the same right of resistance in the Declaration against a Congress and president that had been freely and constitutionally elected. He charged elected officials with the exercise of powers not delegated to them by the Constitution, and inconsistent with the principles of republican government. In so doing, they were said to have acted as tyrannically, in principle, as the king and Parliament of Great Britain! Jefferson challenged his fellow citizens to

> say what the government is if it be not a tyranny, which the men of our choice have conferred on the President, and the President of our choice has assented to . . .

Such measures, Jefferson said,

> may tend to drive these States into blood and revolution . . .

According to Jefferson, "blood and revolution" are the ultimate recourse of any people against tyranny, whether the government be elected or not. And Abraham Lincoln, in 1861, while denying any justification for the Southern States to resist the elected government of the Union, was mindful nonetheless of Jefferson's teaching, when he conceded that

> If by a mere force of numbers a majority should deprive a minority of any clearly written constitutional right, it might, in a moral point of view, justify revolution . . .

It was an essential principle of the Founding that the tyranny of a majority may be as obnoxious as that of any minority. Constitutional government is designed to prevent both kinds of tyranny, and the right of revolution is the ultimate recourse against either. Anastaplo performed a signal service in reminding his interlocutors of this.

It must always be borne in mind, however, that the right of revolution is a *natural* right. As such, it has to be viewed within the larger context of the political philosophy of natural rights, of which it formed a part. Governments might be altered or abolished by the people, the Declaration of Independence says, not for any purposes whatever, but only when they become "destructive of these ends," viz., of the security of the unalienable rights with which all human beings have been endowed by their Creator. And, to repeat, Jefferson himself is witness to the conviction that this can happen under an elected, as under a nonelected government. It should however be remarked that neither Jefferson nor any of his party—the Republican party—ever actually advocated the use of force or violence. In reminding the people of the *right* of revolution, they sought to inform public opinion of the nature and seriousness of the violations of the Constitution that they alleged. This in fact proved to be their electoral strategy, and led to the Republican victory in the elections of 1800, and the control of both the Congress and the presidency. Recourse—in speech, not in deed—to the right of revolution was an appeal to the principles of the Revolution, to remind their fellow citizens that the Constitution existed to implement principles antecedent to itself, and that it was not merely a document of positive law. Jefferson's appeal helped to assure that ballots, not bullets, would henceforth preserve the people's rights under the Constitution. It seems to me that in this Anastaplo was following Jefferson's example.

Among the rights that the Constitution is designed to "protect, preserve, and defend," none looms larger than the right of property. In the

American Revolution—whose slogan was "taxation without representation is tyranny"—it was practically and politically perhaps the most important of all. At the end of the *Summary View of the Rights of British America* (1774) Jefferson penned these immortal words:

> The God who gave us life, gave us liberty at the same time: the hand of force may destroy, but cannot disjoin them.

The liberty in question was the liberty to have our own properties taxed or regulated only by our own government. So intimately related were the rights of liberty and property. Against nothing, therefore, might the right of revolution more properly be exercised than against any government that placed the rights of property in jeopardy. No communist government, no government dedicated to abolishing private property, could ever be legitimate, from this perspective.[11] It seems to me that the conflict in 1951 between Anastaplo and the Committee of the Illinois bar could have been resolved, if the indissoluble bond between the right of revolution and the right of private property had been seen for what it truly was. And while even a free election is not of necessity a sufficient condition of legitimacy, a society in which the bearing of the right of revolution in preserving the Constitution is understood, is best able to avoid the occasions of revolution itself.[12] Certainly the committee should have been instructed that the government of the United States was, in its Founding, buttressed by the right of revolution, not undermined by it. And it should have been instructed that even if—against all probability—a communist government should come to power by a free election, there would be an indefeasible right to overthrow it by force and violence. The right of revolution, rightly understood, is above all conservative.

Mr. Anastaplo takes issue with my critique of Chief Justice Rehnquist's opinion in *Flynt v Falwell.* He thinks that I did not appreciate "the strategy of the chief justice in conceding as much as he did . . . to libertarian impulses." Perhaps he is correct about this. Perhaps the Court saw the jury award of damages to the Reverend Falwell as constituting an abuse of tort law. My objections, however, were to Rehnquist's stated arguments. He said he could not find any "principled standard" to separate the Hustler genre—i.e., characterizing Falwell's mother as an incestuous whore—from genuine political cartoons or satires. He did not think that the word "outrageous" supplied one. It seemed to me that underlying Rehnquist's inability to find the principle in question was his commitment to the view that all moral judgments are "value judgments." My main point was that moral reasoning might have supplied him with the principled standard he said he lacked, if he had not started *a priori* from the premise that such moral reasoning is not possible.

Finally, I come to Mr. Anastaplo's belief that

> It is both fair and humane to insist that the typical homosexual in this country today, just like the typical American Communist party member since the First World War, probably wants truly good things for himself, for his friends and family, and for his country.

I don't know whether I—or Professor Anastaplo—knows what a "typical" Communist, or "typical" homosexual is. That there were simple-minded Communists, and simple-minded Nazis (i.e., useful idiots), who joined their respective parties for the same reason that others have joined the Boy Scouts or Girls Scouts, is entirely possible. The Communists I have had in mind were apologists for the genocidal Stalin, just as the Nazis I have had in mind were apologists for the genocidal Hitler. In neither case can I see any reason to think that the things that they wanted were good things.[13]

I would remind Professor Anastaplo that the homosexual behavior to which, I think, offense can be rightly taken, is called sodomy. It is condemned equally by the laws of Moses and the laws of Plato. It is condemned in the New Testament as well as the Old. It is condemned in Jefferson's revised criminal code for Virginia of 1791, as well as in the Common Law. Sodomy has been peculiarly a vice of aristocratic classes throughout the ages. But it has always, until now, been considered a vice, and a sign of decadence in those societies in which it has been prevalent. Those who commit murder, theft, adultery, or rape do not as a rule say that these things are not wrong. Unless they plead guilty—when charged with crime—they defend themselves by saying that they did not do it.

Today sodomites are not merely practitioners of an ancient vice. They are a political movement, and one of utmost virulence, determined to convert society to their view of morality. It is not enough for them to do what they do in the privacy of their bedrooms. Now young men march in giant parades, fondling and kissing each other for the edification of hundreds of thousands of spectators. They demand legislation to protect them from "discrimination," and define discrimination in such a way that anyone who does not accept their "lifestyle" as worthy of admiration and emulation becomes a bigot. In their demand that society pour unlimited resources into finding a cure for AIDS is the assumption that society has no right to ask them to change their behavior even if that behavior is the cause of the disease. They demand legal status for homosexual "marriages." Not only are they to be accepted on equal terms in the military, but in any vocations—such as teaching or leading Boy Scout troops—in which they may advertise themselves as role models. A determined attempt is being made to introduce sodomite propaganda into the public school curriculum, beginning with the first grade. Six year olds are now being given such books as *Heather Has Two Mommies*, and *Daddy's Roommate*, so that they will grow up emancipated from the moral prejudices bound up with the traditional family.

In the good old days, liberals like Mr. Anastaplo would defend the right of Communists to hold teaching posts, provided that they did not use the classroom as a vehicle for communist propaganda. The sodomite movement, however, is uncompromising in its insistence upon using the schools to convert children to their way of thinking about sex, marriage, and the family. And they are aided in their cause by a more widespread movement—of which they are essentially a part—that holds that sexual promiscuity of any kind is a form of human liberation, and to be desired as such. In this they belong to that utopianism—of which Marxism is so notable an example—which believes that mankind's destiny is to return to the Garden of Eden, with no forbidden fruit. Morality as a restraint upon desire, is seen as the greatest enemy of human freedom. Although in practice, communist movements have been almost puritanical in their attitudes towards sex, it should be remembered that the abolition of the family was announced as a goal in the Communist Manifesto of 1848.

Mr. Anastaplo should see that in their repudiation of the very idea of nature as the ground of the moral order homosexuals even more than Communists are enemies of every good thing we associate with the Declaration of Independence. To anyone who doubts this I ask, Why are slavery and genocide wrong? What *reason* is there to distinguish the subjection of a Negro slave to his master in the antebellum South, from the subjection of any horse to its human rider? What *reason* is there to distinguish the slaughter of cattle in the Kansas City stockyards from the slaughter of Jews in Nazi death camps? Are we to be told that these are merely "value judgments" and that there literally is no reason at all to make such distinctions? Is there not an authentic *reason* in the objective fact that Negroes and Jews are human beings of the same nature as those who would enslave or slaughter them? Is there not a mutual relationship of rights and duties among all human beings, arising from the existence of a nature common to them all?

I would remind those who think that we should be "free to choose" whatever it pleases us to do, that we did not choose to be born human beings and not animals of another species—although most of us would think it our good fortune. We did not choose to be born at all, yet we are obligated to our fathers and mothers (especially if they are good fathers and good mothers). Men and women, whether married or not, may or may not wish to have children, but if the children come, their duties towards them are determined by their human nature. While nature does not determine how we act—so that we are free to become good human beings or bad human beings—it does determine, within broad boundaries, what is a good human being and what is a bad one.

It is fashionable today to assume that in matters of sexual conduct whatever is done by consenting adults is morally justified. To anyone making this assumption I would ask, Does consent legitimate incest? Was the suicide of the nine hundred members of the Jonestown community (including several hundred children) morally acceptable because it had been agreed upon in advance? If one man persuades another that he is so far superior that the other is lucky to be his slave, has no third party a right to interfere? In general, are consenting relationships based upon fraud no less binding than those that are not? Should Shylock have had his pound of flesh? A man and a woman may enter upon marriage agreed that each of them shall be free to commit adultery whenever it pleases them. While in such a case this may make future reproaches awkward, it does not make adultery less offensive in itself, or less damaging to their children or to society.

In traditional moral philosophy and theology consent cannot legitimize any relationship that is intrinsically wrong. According to the Declaration of Independence, governments derive "their just powers from the consent of the governed." Not *any* powers, only *just* powers. As we have seen in Jefferson's Kentucky Resolutions, any act—even by the most perfectly representative of elected governments—that infringes upon the natural rights of mankind, may nonetheless be wrong.

If then slavery and genocide are wrong, it is because the relationship among human beings must needs be regulated by the mutual recognition of those rights and duties which are necessary for the peaceful, friendly, and mutually beneficial relationship of human beings in society. Jesus digested the need for this recognition into the smallest compass, when he said that we should do unto others as we would have others do unto us. It is a tacit premise of the golden rule, that it is addressed not to Jesus's disciples alone, nor to Greeks or to Jews, but to all human beings everywhere and at all times. With respect to the rights and duties within which human well-being is comprehended, "all men are created equal."

Man is a social animal, and no one can secure what is desirable for himself except in partnership with others. According to Aristotle, if a man had all the health, wealth, freedom, and power that he desired, but lacked friends, he would not wish even to live. But the root of all friendships, as it is the ground of the existence of the species, is that of a man and a woman. As nature is the ground of morality, the distinction of the sexes is the ground of nature. Nature—which forbids us to eat or enslave our own kind—is that which has within itself the principle of coming-into-being. Mankind as a whole is recognized by its generations, like a river which is one and the same while the ever-renewed cycles of birth and death flow on. But the generations are constituted—and can only be constituted—by the acts of generation arising from the conjunction of male and female. The root of all human relationships, the root of all morality, is nature, which itself is grounded in the generative distinction of male and female.

For the same reason that the God of the Bible is a jealous God, sexual friendship is by its nature jealous. The family, which is the primary institution of society, upon whose health the health of society as a whole depends, is constituted by the sexual friendship of husband and wife. That friendship, in its right ordering, is an exclusive one. The prohibition equally of incest and adultery are intrinsic to the friendships, not only of husband and wife, but of parents and children, and of brothers and sisters. The most intense love may exist, and should exist, within families, and among friends outside of families. If they are not to disrupt the family, however, they may not be sexual friendships. Wives do not expect to be in sexual competition with other women—or other men—for their husband's affection. And husbands do not expect to be in sexual competition with other men—or other women—for their wives' affection. Sodomy strikes at the ground in nature of the structure of the family, and of the moral commands and prohibitions that make the family a viable institution.

Abraham Lincoln once said that if slavery is not unjust, then nothing is unjust. With equal reason, it can be said that if sodomy is not unnatural, nothing is unnatural. And if nothing is unnatural, then nothing—including slavery and genocide—is unjust.

# "Our Ancient Faith"
# A Reply to Professor Anastaplo

1. Leo Strauss, *Natural Right and History*, p. 120.
2. One should compare and contrast Strauss's "Epilogue" on the scientific study of politics with Socrates' account (in Plato's *Phaedo*) of why he rejected the teaching of Anaxagoras. (Cf. "An Epilogue" in *Liberalism Ancient and Modern*, Basic Books 1968).
3. It was Professor Anastaplo himself who first pointed out to me—and the world—that God appears in the Declaration as legislator, judge, and executive. See his essay, "The Declaration of Independence," *St. Louis University Law Journal* 9 (1965), p. 390.
4. Quoted in full as the Epigraph of *Statesmanship: Essays in Honor of Sir Winston Spencer Churchill*, edited by H.V.J., Carolina Academic Press, 1981. It is taken from the transcript of Strauss's class at the University of Chicago, January 25, 1965, the day after Churchill's death.
5. The ending of *Thoughts in Machiavelli* is as follows:

   It would seem as if the notion of the beneficence of nature, or of the primacy of the Good must be restored by being rethought through a return to the fundamental experiences [that is to say, the human experiences of good and evil] from which it is derived. For while "philosophy must beware of wishing to be edifying," it is of necessity edifying.

   I understand this to mean that one cannot transcend the moral-political dimension of human life by turning away from it, but only by taking it with full seriousness. It is for this reason, I believe, that philosophy is said to be of necessity edifying.
6. Of course, the wisdom and virtue of Churchill's resistance to Hitler, no less

than that of his resistance to Stalin, has not gone unchallenged. Beginning with A.J.P. Taylor's *The Origins of the Second World War* in 1961, there has been a recurrent reassertion of the 1930's pacifism and socialism (as represented by George Lansbury, rather than Clement Attlee and Ernest Bevin) against Churchill. There has also been a recurrent strain of neo-fascism (of the kind represented by Lady Astor and the Cliveden set) which denies that Hitler was ever Britain's enemy. David Irving has I think been their representative. A new book—which I have not yet seen—by John Charmley (*Churchill: The End of Glory*, Hodder and Stoughton, 1993) is said to denounce Churchill with renewed vigor.

Among those who challenge the wisdom of Churchill's resistance to tyrants are those who deny the authenticity of the distinction between freedom and tyranny enshrined in the Declaration of Independence. They are heirs of Thomas Hobbes, when he said that tyranny was merely monarchy misliked. Or of William Rehnquist, when he called the choice of a constitution that safeguarded individual liberty a value judgment, that had no intrinsic rational justification. I believe that Churchill's reply to all such critics would be that it was precisely so that books like theirs could be published, that it was necessary to resist Hitler and Stalin.

7. I believe one member of the faculty (someone I did not know)—a physics professor who refused to answer questions put to him by a committee of the Ohio legislature—was dismissed. My recollection is that there was evidence that he was, in fact, a member of the American Communist party.

8. The reality of the political atmosphere within the academy as I experienced it is brilliantly represented by Mary McCarthy (no relative of the Senator from Wisconsin) in her 1952 novel, *The Groves of Academe*. It is the story of how an entire faculty falls into line behind an instructor who had once belonged to the Communist party. He is a loathsome character, who in the normal course of events would not have had his appointment renewed, for reasons having nothing to do with politics. He exploits his colleagues anti-anticommunism however, to compel them to back him for tenure. In the ensuing conflict, the president of the college is broken by the faculty for opposing the reappointment.

9. See page 56.

10. One is reminded that in the trial of Socrates, the vote for the death sentence was larger than the vote for his conviction. In short, some voted for the death sentence who believed him to be innocent! But Socrates had provoked the court by insisting that the crime of which he had been found guilty, was in fact the greatest good anyone had done the city, and that he should be rewarded for it like an Olympic victor. Anastaplo's belief—whether expressed or implied—that he was a better citizen than the members of the committee, is not without Socratic precedent.

11. But consider also Aristotle, *Politics*, 1281 a 15–18:

. . . if the poor take advantage of their greater numbers to divide up the property of the rich, is not this unjust? No, by Zeus, for it was passed by the highest authority [viz., the people] in just form. But if this is not unjust, what can the extreme of injustice be?

12. It is significant that the seceding States of the South, in 1861, did not appeal to the right of revolution. They appealed—however speciously—to the right of secession as a constitutional right. They went to great lengths to avoid appealing to a right whose exercise would obviously apply far more to their slaves than to themselves.

13. Professor Anastaplo refers to his book *The American Moralist* as "a manual of sorts prepared by Don Quixote for the Lone Ranger." It seems to me, however, that in the case of Communists and sodomites, he reverses roles with the Don, who saw giants and armed men where there were only windmills and sheep. Professor Anastaplo sees windmills and sheep where there was in fact mortal danger.

   AIDS is a venereal disease of the utmost deadliness, whose origin in the United States is entirely a result of sodomite activity. Every single case of AIDS is either the direct or indirect result of sodomy. See my pamphlet "Homosexuality and the Natural Law" (The Claremont Institute, 1990).

# PART V

# Afterword

# Four Letters to Edwin Meese III

The following letters were written, in part, in pursuance of a further answer to Professor Anastaplo's query, "What more should be said on behalf of Attorney General Meese?"

I had already replied "Nothing" to Professor Anastaplo when, in August of 1991, I had an occasion, described in Letter I, to pursue the matter further. In Letter II, I refer to a very cordial meeting of Mr. Meese and myself, at which I was able to hand-deliver a copy of my first letter, which he said he had never received. In Letter III, I comment on the fact that there had not yet been any response such as he had promised.

In April of 1992, Mr. Meese visited Claremont where he delivered an evening public lecture on "original intent" jurisprudence to a large audience. Pi Sigma Alpha, the political science honorary society, had, however, arranged a private afternoon reception for him in Denison Library of Scripps College. When we met, he followed his usual cordial greeting by saying that he was still trying to find time to reply to my first letter. I responded that there was no time like the present, and launched into my critique of the Meese-Rehnquist-Bork interpretation of the case of *Dred Scott*. After a few minutes he countered, "This is a reception." When a chorus of voices arose, "No, no, we want to hear you and Professor Jaffa," he replied, "I came here to drink apple juice." End of dialogue. Letter IV was written shortly thereafter. Needless to say, it has elicited no more reponse than its predecessors.

# I.

August 24, 1991

Hon. Edwin Meese III
c/o The Young America's Foundation
110 Elden Street
Herndon, Virginia 22070

Dear Mr. Meese:

I just received a flyer from the Young America's Foundation announcing the Henry Salvatori Distinguished Lecture Series featuring yourself as lecturer.

I write in part because I believe we have so much in common that we ought to have even more. I start from the fact that for eighteen years I was Henry Salvatori Research Professor of Political Philosophy at Claremont McKenna College and Claremont Graduate School. I might add that before that I was a speech writer for Barry Goldwater, and composed the draft of the speech that he gave to the Republican Convention in 1964, including the famous lines about "extremism in defense of liberty . . . " I might also add that I voted for Ronald Reagan every time his name was on the ballot, whether in the primary or in the general election, and whether for governor or for president!

During my tenure of the Salvatori professorship (of which I am now emeritus) I published *The Conditions of Freedom* (1975), *How to Think About the American Revolution* (1978), *Statesmanship: Essays in Honor of Sir Winston Churchill* (Editor and Contributing Author: 1981), *American Conservatism and the American Founding* (1984), as well as perhaps a hundred articles, both political and scholarly.

In 1987 in the *University of Puget Sound Law Review* I published a monograph entitled "What Were the 'Original Intentions' of the Framers of the Constitution of the United States?" It was preceded by a Foreword by Lewis E. Lehrman, calling me

> one of the most persuasive advocates of what Professor Edward S. Corwin called the "higher law" doctrine of the Constitution: namely, that the first principles of the American regime, according to which the positive law of the Constitution must be interpreted in ambiguous cases, are codified in the natural law doctrine of the Declaration of Independence.

Mr. Lehrman then pointed out that mine was a minority view, the consensus in the legal profession being represented by Benno Schmidt, former dean of Columbia Law School and now president of Yale, when he said that

American constitutional law is positive law, and the Declaration of Independence has no standing in constitutional interpretation whatsoever.

Notwithstanding this consensus, Mr. Lehrman pointed out—as I do in my monograph—that

> Attorney General Meese, in his Dickinson College speech . . . agrees with Jaffa (not to mention Jefferson, Madison, Marshall, and Lincoln) that "there exists in the nature of things a natural standard for judging whether governments are legitimate or not."

However, Chief Justice Rehnquist, in his lecture on "The Notion of a Living Constitution," gives voice to legal positivism in its most uncompromising form, when he says that

> If a society adopts a constitution . . . that . . . safeguards individual liberty, these safeguards do indeed take on a generalized moral rightness or goodness. They assume a general social acceptance neither because of any intrinsic worth nor because of any unique origins in someone's idea of natural justice but instead simply because they have been incorporated in a constitution by a people.

No statements in the history of jurisprudence are more contradictory than yours at Dickinson College and the Chief Justice's in the lecture cited. Your subsequent identification of "original intent" jurisprudence with the positivism of Rehnquist and Bork (inter alia) led you down a pathway to ultimate incoherence on this subject, as I believe I have shown in my "Appendix A: Attorney General Meese, the Declaration, and the Constitution." Because you followed Rehnquist you utterly misinterpreted the significance of the *Dred Scott* decision, as I believe I have shown beyond a reasonable doubt (or beyond a possible doubt by a reasonable person!).

I am a firm believer in "original intent" jurisprudence. As Lincoln said, however, calling a tail a leg does not make it a leg. And calling something "original intent" does not make it such.

The amazing and uncompromising assertion of an equal natural right of all peoples to freedom, from behind what was once the Iron Curtain, is as much a denial of Rehnquist's denial of that right, as it is of Lenin's and Stalin's. And the nomination of Judge Clarence Thomas—a firm believer in that same natural right—has brought this question to the fore again, in jurisprudence no less than in politics. I would hope that in these stirring times we might be brought to an agreement that would make you once again the witness to the truth that you were at Dickinson College.

Sincerely,
Harry V. Jaffa

# II.

October 28, 1991

Hon. Edwin Meese III
c/o The Heritage Foundation
214 Massachusetts Avenue, N.E.
Washington, D.C. 20002

Dear Mr. Meese:

It was good seeing you, and having even a brief discussion at the recent meeting of the Philadelphia Society. I was glad to be able to put into your hand the letter I had written to you last August 24th, and which you evidently never received.

With that letter I had also enclosed my July 9th, 1990, article in *National Review*, entitled "The Closing of the Conservative Mind," another copy of which I now send as well.

In Bork's book, *The Tempting of America*, he has chapters on what he calls liberal and conservative revisionism. None of the authors he discusses ever addressed his arguments directly, as I have done, in two law journal articles and in two *National Review* articles. To paraphrase Abraham Lincoln, in his reference to Judge Douglas and himself in 1858, "Judge Bork is a great man, and I am only a little one." Nevertheless, Judge Bork will not have the better of the argument on original intent because, from his lofty eminence, he continues to ignore what I have written. This is all the more true, I think, because the differences between Judge Bork and myself parallel very closely those that divided Lincoln and Douglas.

Could you not therefore use your great influence, both with Judge Bork and the Heritage Foundation, to arrange a "Lincoln-Douglas" debate between us on this paramount issue as to the "original intent" of the Constitution of the United States?

With best wishes,
Sincerely,
Harry V. Jaffa

# III.

December 30, 1991

Hon. Edwin Meese III
c/o The Heritage Foundation
214 Massachusetts Avenue, N.E.
Washington, D.C. 20002

Dear Mr. Meese:

After our meeting at the Philadelphia Society conference last October, I wrote a second letter to you, a copy of which I enclose. Since I have had no reply, I wonder whether (like the first letter) you never received it. In any event, I try again!

May I, from the perspective of a half century of the study of history—and of one who has participated himself in the process by which "the judgments of history" are rendered—make this suggestion? That is, that your tenure of office as attorney general will be remembered chiefly because you challenged the reigning schools of jurisprudence by raising (in a public manner) the question of the "original intent" of the Constitution of the United States. How you will be remembered, however, will depend upon how you left this question after having raised it.

That the legal positivism of both Judge Bork and Chief Justice Rehnquist is utterly inconsistent with a jurisprudence of original intent I take to be proved beyond argument (although I am ready to renew the argument if anyone wishes to do so). For this reason, your purpose in raising the question of original intent remains unclear, if not plainly self-contradictory. Most commentators think that what you meant by it is nothing more than result-oriented (or whose ox is being gored) conservative decision-making, with no better foundation in principle than the liberal decision-making on the other side. As things stand now, that, I fear, is what the judgment of history is likely to be.

With all good wishes,
Sincerely,
Harry V. Jaffa

## IV.

April 9, 1992

Hon. Edwin Meese III
c/o The Heritage Foundation
214 Massachusetts Avenue, N.E.
Washington, D.C. 20002

Dear Mr. Meese:

Thank you for coming to Claremont. Perhaps you might return some time in the near future, when we might formally arrange a seminar on the question of "What Were the 'Original Intentions' of the Framers of the Constitution of the United States?"

I am sorry that you thought it inappropriate to continue our discussion of the *Dred Scott* case because it seemed incompatible with the social imperatives of a wine and cheese reception. I fear that, in my little world, there is *no* occasion on which social imperatives stand in the way of serious discussion of *Dred Scott* or (which is the same thing) of Abraham Lincoln.

While a wine and cheese reception may have been an imperfect venue for our discussion, it was the only one that had ever presented itself to me since I published my monograph on original intent in the spring 1987 issue of the *University of Puget Sound Law Review*. That monograph has rigorous critiques of yourself, Bork, and Rehnquist. These critiques were supplemented in three subsequent articles in the same law review, as well as by two widely read articles in *National Review*. To the best of my knowledge, there has never been a breath of recognition of these writings from yourself or any of your associates. A lecture of mine on this topic at Heritage in the spring of 1988 was never published, and a second lecture was canceled when it was known I would address the same topic.

My letter to you, inviting your discussion of our differing understanding of "original intent," was sent more than eight months ago. When we met last October, you promised to get back to me about it. You never did. Last week you said you were still trying to find time to answer me. You will certainly pardon my feeling that such a time was not likely to occur in the foreseeable future. Yet I think it is very short-sighted of you to disregard what I have to say about original intent, since (at the very least) it postpones the time when what you say on the subject can be taken seriously by serious scholars of the subject.

I believe I am the only critic of your views who believes as you do in the proposition that the principles of the Declaration of Independence are the principles of the Constitution. Russell Kirk, the guru of the paleocons, completely rejects this opinion, never loses any opportunity to depreciate the

Declaration, and calls it, "not particularly American," and "French philosophy." Irving Kristol, the wizard of the neocons, recently declared that he was
not aware that the Founding Fathers

> ever wrote anything worth reading on religion, especially Jefferson, who
> wrote nothing worth reading on religion or almost anything else. (*The
> Spirit of the Constitution*, AEI Press, 1990.)

So much for the author of the Declaration—and of the Statute of Virginia for
Religious Liberty! So much indeed for the Founding generation altogether,
and hence for original intent jurisprudence. The late Martin Diamond, while
praising the Declaration of Independence, had adopted the view (earlier made
famous by John C. Calhoun) that the Declaration offered "no guidance"
either in the drafting, or for the construing, of the Constitution. His views
have become canonical at AEI (they are also shared by the Center for Judicial
Studies), and I am regarded as the blackest of heretics. If they could burn me
at the stake, they would do it!

The truth is that Bork and Rehnquist fall right within the parameters of Kirk
and Kristol and Diamond; and—since all the liberals are against you—I am
probably the only living soul who has written on original intent who agrees
with your central thesis. Your statement of this thesis is lacking in the historical
and philosophical depth that it needs to be taken with the seriousness it
deserves.

It might amuse you, as a historical curiosity, to know how the Lincoln-
Douglas debates of 1858 came to be held. Douglas was the vastly better
known man. He had been a central figure in the struggle
that ended in the Compromise of 1850. It was he that engineered Clay's
compromise proposals through the Congress. He would in all probability
have been the Democratic nominee for president, either in 1852 or 1856, had
it not been for the ill fame in the North of the fugitive slave law (which
Lincoln had also supported, and which had been part of the Compromise). In
the spring of 1858, however, Douglas had gained recognition as the leader in
the Congress of the fight against the Lecompton (or proslavery) Constitution
for Kansas, and hence had repaired his fences with the free soil movement.
The Eastern leaders of the Republican party even wanted Lincoln to withdraw
from the Senate race in his favor.

In the spring and summer of 1858 Lincoln was out to destroy Douglas's
credentials as a free soil leader. He would frequently attend Douglas's
speeches and rallies. At the end of one of Douglas's speeches, Lincoln would
stand up in the audience and tell the crowd that if they wanted to hear the
other side, they should return (usually in three hours) to hear him. In those
days, when there was no radio, television, movies, or spectator sports, that was
like being given a free ticket to the world series!

Douglas was of course outraged that Lincoln would use his (Douglas's) popularity to gain an audience for himself. The joint debates were then arranged, on Lincoln's promise—but only on Lincoln's promise—that he would attend no more of Douglas's own meetings. But without Lincoln's breach of all recognized decorum in addressing Douglas's own meetings, the joint debates would never have happened. So I trust you will indulge me in having followed, even into such pathways, the great example that is always before my eyes.

Perhaps you think I was too aggressive in pursuing the question of *Dred Scott*. You, however, had agreed with Bork and Rehnquist that the great error of Taney in his opinion for the Court consisted in declaring unconstitutional the Missouri law of 1820, thereby usurping powers belonging to the Congress. But the issues in *Dred Scott* went far deeper than a question of jurisdiction. Constitutional questions and political questions have been intertwined since the first days of George Washington's presidency. After *Marbury v Madison* it was inevitable that, sooner or later, the Supreme Court would declare an act of Congress unconstitutional. I do not think that either you or I (or Abraham Lincoln) would have objected, if the Taney Court had been antislavery and had declared a federal law unconstitutional because it *extended* slavery to virgin territories. According to Lincoln, the moral question involved in the slavery question was more fundamental than the legal or constitutional question, because in the decisive respect it determined how one would understand the legal or constitutional question.

Taney's error lay not (as Bork would have it) in an erroneous attempt to guarantee substantive due process to Scott's owner. It was rather in his denial that Negroes were entitled to any constitutional guarantees because (according to Taney) they were not included in the proposition "that all men are created equal." For this reason, he held, they were, by the original intent of the Constitution, "so far inferior that they had no rights which the white man was bound to respect." They had no natural rights which the government was instituted to secure.

In your article in *Policy Review* ("The Battle for the Constitution," Winter 1986) you wrote that

In the 1850s the Supreme Court under Chief Justice Roger B. Taney read blacks out of the Constitution in order to invalidate Congress' attempt to limit the spread of slavery . . . There is a lesson in such history. There is danger in seeing the Constitution as an empty vessel into which each generation may pour its passion and prejudice.

It is astonishing that in writing as you did you were, whether you knew it or not, echoing Taney himself. For it was none other than Taney who, in *Dred Scott*, first enunciated in classic style the doctrine of original intent or original understanding as the basis of constitutional jurisprudence. The Constitution, he said,

> speaks not only in the same words, but with the same meaning and intent with which it spoke when it came from the hands of its Framers, and was voted on and adopted by the people of the United States. Any other rule of construction would abrogate the judicial character of this Court, and make it *the mere reflex of the popular opinion or passion of the day.* (Italics added.)

As I pointed out in the *UPS Law Review*, this proves nothing so much as that urging a jurisprudence of original intent is no guarantee that one will have one. In the decisive respect, Bork and Rehnquist are as far from the real thing as Taney himself.

You wished to draw a lesson from history. But that assumes that you know the history from which you would draw the lesson! You were right in saying that Taney "read blacks out of the Constitution." But you were mistaken about Congress's attempt to limit the spread of slavery. In the 1850s, prior to *Dred Scott*, Congress was very far from attempting such a thing. Its proceedings were in exactly the opposite direction. The Kansas-Nebraska Act of 1854 had repealed the Missouri Compromise law of 1820, which had banned slavery in the remaining Louisiana Territory north of 36 30. This act of Congress opened a vast new domain to the incursion of slavery. Different members of Congress gave different reasons for the removal of the slavery restriction. The Calhounites had always maintained that it was unconstitutional because it violated the constitutional equality of the States by discriminating against the property of citizens of slave States. Now Senator Stephen A. Douglas joined them by saying that it violated the constitutional principle of popular sovereignty, which required that the presence or absence of slavery in the Territories be decided by the inhabitants therein. Whatever explanation one accepts (or rejects), the record provided the Court with ample reasons for believing it was following Congress, not usurping its powers, in holding the Missouri law unconstitutional.

Before 1854, however, Congress, in the territorial laws of 1850 for Utah and New Mexico (which concerned land taken from Mexico), had declared that the States formed therefrom might come in, either as slave States or as free States, as their constitutions might prescribe. That neutrality between freedom and slavery (the initial departure from the precedent of the Missouri law of 1820) was bad enough. But worse still was the provision that, during the period before the formation of a State constitution, questions as to the legality of slavery might be appealed directly from a territorial court to the Supreme Court of the United States. Thus the *Congress* wrote into law the premise that a question that *Congress* could not itself resolve—the legal status of slavery in a United States Territory—might best be resolved by turning it over to the Supreme Court.

In the spring of 1857, both Pierce, the outgoing president, and Buchanan, the incoming president, exhorted the country to accept the forthcoming decision of the Court as a final settlement of the slavery question. If the Court usurped the powers of the elected branches of the government, then it must also be said that the elected branches seduced them into doing so! If passion and prejudice went into the making of the *Dred Scott* decision, it was the passion and prejudice of all branches of the government, and not only that of the Supreme Court.

Bork and Rehnquist both misread the issue in *Dred Scott*, because they did not see, and did not want to see, the bearing of natural law and natural rights upon constitutional interpretation. Taney did not, as Bork thinks, invent "a right [to slave ownership that] is nowhere to be found in the Constitution . . ." (*The Tempting of America*, p. 31.) The right to slave ownership is plainly recognized in (but not only in) the fugitive slave clause of the Constitution (Article IV, Section 2, para. 3).

But the right to slave ownership so recognized is inherently ambiguous because of the ambiguity of the fact that the "persons . . . held to service or labor" under the laws of the slave States are, by the laws of those same States, also regarded as chattels. Indeed, it was as chattels, and not as persons, that the persons in question were "held to [the] service or labor" from which, according to the Constitution, they were not to be allowed to escape.

But a chattel is by definition a piece of movable property without a rational will; while a person, also by definition, is possessed of a rational will. The legal paradox of slavery is well expressed by James Madison in the fifty-fourth *Federalist*. The slaves, he says,

> are considered by our laws, in some respects, as persons, and in other respects, as property. In being compelled to labor not for himself, but for a master; in being vendible by one master to another master; and in being subject at all times to being restrained in his liberty, and chastised in his body, by the capricious will of another, the slave may appear to be degraded from the human rank, and classed with those irrational animals, which fall under the denomination of property. In being protected on the other hand, in his life and in his limbs against the violence of all others, even the master of his labor and his liberty; and in being punishable himself for all violence committed against others, the slave is no less evidently regarded by the law as a member of the society, not as a part of the irrational creation; as a moral person, not as a mere article of property.

Madison, like Lincoln after him, accept the authority of the positive laws of slavery in the slave States, notwithstanding the fact that it was (in Madison's own words) only by a "pretext" that "the laws have transformed the Negroes into subjects of property." And, he adds,

> it is admitted that if the laws were to restore the rights which have been taken away, the Negroes could no longer be refused an equal share of representation with the other inhabitants.

But what are "the rights which have been taken away"? Obviously, they cannot be rights which the slaves previously enjoyed under positive law. They can only be natural rights, to which they are entitled under "the laws of nature and of nature's God." In the dispute over Dred Scott, it was Lincoln's thesis (and that of the free-soil movement generally) that in the absence of a positive law of slavery, the natural law of freedom prevailed. Hence the natural condition of the territories was freedom. A positive congressional enactment of freedom was necessary, only because the slave State representatives—like Bork and Rehnquist today—denied the existence of any natural law of freedom. *What Lincoln and the free-soil movement generally demanded, in opposition to the opinion of the Court in Dred Scot, was recognition of the natural law of freedom, as the ground of the constitutional law of the territories.*

Rehnquist, in his celebrated dissertation on the "Living Constitution," says that if a society

> adopts a constitution and incorporates in that constitution safeguards for individual liberty these safeguards do indeed take on a generalized moral rightness or goodness. They assume general social acceptance neither because of any intrinsic worth nor because of any unique origins in someone's idea of natural justice but instead simply because they have been incorporated in a constitution by a people.

According to Rehnquist there is no *intrinsic worth* or *natural justice* which guides a people in preferring a free constitution to a slave constitution. Moreover, according to Rehnquist, the judgment that discriminates between freedom and slavery cannot be guided by reason.

> There is no conceivable way in which I can logically demonstrate to you that the judgments of my conscience are superior to the judgments of your conscience, and vice versa.

Hence Rehnquist flatly denies what is axiomatic for James Madison (and all the other Framers and Ratifiers of the Constitution): that there is a natural right to freedom, possessed by all human beings, a right whose enjoyment may depend upon the positive law, but whose existence is entirely independent of the positive law. According to Madison, Negroes are naturally and intrinsically moral persons and not property, because they are naturally and intrinsically human beings. If Mr. Rehnquist is not blind to intrinsic reality, Madison could demonstrate to him—and I am prepared to act as his surrogate—that slavery, however expedient it may seem to some, being against nature, is for that reason morally wrong. This moral judgment—the heart of the Declaration of Independence, the heart of everything that Abraham Lincoln ever stood for—is inseparable from a jurisprudence of original intent.

Without coming to grips with this argument, it is impossible for you or anyone else to gain credit for the thesis that the principles of the Declaration of Independence are indeed the principles of the Constitution.

Sincerely,
Harry V. Jaffa

# Index